FREE
To Be
ME

Bach Flower Remedies, and natural insights
to help you unravel your mind
and transform your life naturally

DAWN CHRYSTAL

Take time out to work on you
♡
Dawn

BALBOA.PRESS
A DIVISION OF HAY HOUSE

Copyright © 2021 Dawn Chrystal.

All rights reserved. No part of this book may be used or reproduced by any means, graphic, electronic, or mechanical, including photocopying, recording, taping or by any information storage retrieval system without the written permission of the author except in the case of brief quotations embodied in critical articles and reviews.

Balboa Press books may be ordered through booksellers or by contacting:

Balboa Press
A Division of Hay House
1663 Liberty Drive
Bloomington, IN 47403
www.balboapress.com
844-682-1282

Because of the dynamic nature of the Internet, any web addresses or links contained in this book may have changed since publication and may no longer be valid. The views expressed in this work are solely those of the author and do not necessarily reflect the views of the publisher, and the publisher hereby disclaims any responsibility for them.

The author of this book does not dispense medical advice or prescribe the use of any technique as a form of treatment for physical, emotional, or medical problems without the advice of a physician, either directly or indirectly. The intent of the author is only to offer information of a general nature to help you in your quest for emotional and spiritual well-being. In the event you use any of the information in this book for yourself, which is your constitutional right, the author and the publisher assume no responsibility for your actions.

Any people depicted in stock imagery provided by Getty Images are models, and such images are being used for illustrative purposes only.
Certain stock imagery © Getty Images.

Print information available on the last page.

ISBN: 978-1-9822-6047-7 (sc)
ISBN: 978-1-9822-6048-4 (e)

Balboa Press rev. date: 02/25/2021

You are the result of your thoughts

You can become the total result of what other
people have thought about you

Are you happy with what has been produced for you?

Step up and become the author of your own life

'All through my earlier life, I felt a constant sense of
injustice about the way things had been in my life.
The Remedy VERVAIN helped me to recognise that everything
happened as it was meant to, for my soul's growth and purpose.
When I was in a calmer state of mind I put my
efforts into resolving my underlying issues.
Instead of getting uptight and angry about what happened, I now
put that passion into making changes in other people's lives.
I have a great passion for guiding and inspiring others, and
helping them recognise how they can turn their life around.
I feel so much lighter, and every day I celebrate
being able to make a difference.'- Dawn

CONTENTS

Foreword xi

PART 1: HELPING YOU TO HELP YOURSELF

Chapter 1: Simplify your life, one step at a time 1
Chapter 2: Do not wait to be perfect 12
Chapter 3: Your healing journal becomes your new friend 24
Chapter 4: Finding joy is your purpose today 33
Chapter 5: The start of a natural healing journey for you 40
Chapter 6: How do the Bach Flower Remedy essences work? 44
Chapter 7: Breathe 49
Chapter 8: Simple signposts 58
Chapter 9: How can you produce the feel-good
            chemicals for yourself? 87
Chapter 10: Connecting your left and right brain 93
Chapter 11: Bach Flower Remedies for extreme mental
            and emotional pain 102
Chapter 12: Are you grounded? 107
Chapter 13: Healing hands 118
Chapter 14: Are you fearful for others? 131
Chapter 15: Raise up your vibrations with
            chanting and singing 150

Chapter 16: Healing your inner-child 155
Chapter 17: Are you anxious about something coming
             up in the future? 163
Chapter 18: Create your new life with affirmations 175
Chapter 19: Bach Flower Remedy healing cards 191
Chapter 20: Not every day will be a good day 197
Chapter 21: Simple meditation 199
Chapter 22: How you can lift up your spirits naturally 207
Chapter 23: Visualising your future 213
Chapter 24: Finding joy is your purpose 220

PART 2: HOW THE PAST HAS IMPACTED ON YOU

Chapter 25: Exploring a new way of understanding you 235
Chapter 26: Your neurological levels 237
Chapter 27: Anger can make you feel sick 241
Chapter 28: The Conscious-Competence learning ladder 247
Chapter 29: Freud's theory 251
Chapter 30: Are you a spiral of negative emotions? 261
Chapter 31: The pre-frontal cortex:
             Do you really have control? 267
Chapter 32: What is your state of mind? 277
Chapter 33: Do not quit 286
Chapter 34: How do these techniques work alongside
             the Bach Flower Remedies? 292
Chapter 35: Forgiveness 295
Chapter 36: A meditation technique to aid forgiveness
             of others, and heal your soul 345
Chapter 37: Psychic attack 353
Chapter 38: What you believe is true for you 362

PART 3: ALL ABOUT THE BACH FLOWER REMEDIES

Chapter 39: The Bach Flower Remedies.. 367
Chapter 40: You may need medication with your
 natural techniques and Remedies 372
Chapter 41: Who discovered the Bach Flower Remedies? 378
Chapter 42: How to make, and take your Bach
 Flower Remedies 384
Chapter 43: Rescue Remedy 386
Chapter 44: What can you expect when taking the Remedies? ... 392
Chapter 45: Why use the Bach Flower Remedies? 399
Chapter 46: Different Personality Types 403
Chapter 47: Other states of mind 408
Chapter 48: Working with a pendulum to choose your
 Bach Flower Remedies 411

PART 4: WHERE TO FIND YOUR BACH FLOWER REMEDIES

Chapter 49: The emotional groups of
 the Bach Flower Remedies 416

PART 5: WHY I CHOOSE TO WRITE THIS BOOK

Chapter 50: Why this book?.. 527
Chapter 51: Every cloud has a silver lining 541
Chapter 52: I bring you this message today. There is so
 much more to you 548
Chapter 53: Training in Bach Flower Remedy therapies 555

Acknowledgements...557
Dawn's Healing Journey..561

FOREWORD

I have been working with the Bach Flower Remedies for over twenty-five years. I am truly passionate about the Remedies, and amazed at the wonderful natural healing gift they bring, to enable people to turn their lives around at any stage of life.

Whichever direction I have taken on my journey, and whatever challenges life has presented to me, I have always been led back to the wonderful Bach Flower Remedies. I had spent the majority of my life feeling detached from the reality of my life, and who I was. It is through these wonderful, gentle Flower Remedies that I have been able to discover the truth of who I am, and what my purpose on this earth can be.

The Remedies brought me an inner confidence, self-belief and a whole new sense of well-being I had never experienced before. It wasn't long before I started to get more clarity about the way I had lost myself. The sense of peace which came to me with this understanding was priceless, and I gained a whole new perspective on my life, and my sense of purpose.

The Remedies' natural healing powers have always helped me come back to a place of harmony and balance. The strength and courage I have found through the Remedies, have made me passionate and eager to share them with everyone who comes my way.

I am still fascinated, at how such a small, dilute amount of Bach Remedies can create such an impact. I am proud, and privileged, to be able to work with these beautiful healing Remedies created for us all by Dr Bach. It is often beyond the realms of my expectations, to see the amazing shift and speed of recovery within people who choose to use them.

I have created a whole section in *'Free to be Me'* later in your book about the Bach Flower Remedies.

Take some to read about the Bach Flower Remedies, to discover how these wonderful Remedies can help you to naturally heal your life.

Throughout this book, I also share with you some simple techniques you can use each day, to enable you to get a greater insight into yourself. You can also explore how the past may be holding you back, how you can learn to live in the moment, and how you can create your new future. All the techniques are easy to access, they are natural, and they work. Every technique will be enhanced by the Remedies. They will support you, and ease you through the challenges and changes you are going through.

Every simple technique will gently enhance your feelings of well-being, and your life.

Every step will bring you closer to a state of peace and harmony.

From today, every new choice you make will start to empower you, and bring you a greater insight into who you are destined to be.

Every choice you make will make a difference to the quality of your life.

This is your day to restart your life.

And every day, from this day forward, will be a new opportunity to reset your life back on track.

Whatever is holding you back, let me show you some ways you can turn it around. As you learn to leave the past behind, and heal yourself, you will feel ready to move on. Your future can be changed right now. You can create whatever you believe is possible.

I may not have all of the answers you need, but as you start to tap into your inner potential, you will find all the answers you seek. You have everything you need within you. You can turn your life around.

From this day, I encourage you to listen more to your higher self, your inner wisdom, and know that you will be guided to take the right steps. The more you listen to this inner wisdom, your own inner guidance, the closer you will become to finding the truth of who you really are. The more you listen to, and follow your inner wisdom the closer you will come to your ideal life.

Every day, remind yourself that you are being guided, you have inner wisdom, and you are working towards your ideal life.

To be able to share my insights and the Bach Flower Remedies with you in this book is truly an amazing gift. Distance is never a problem. Wherever you are, I can find a way to help you.

My mission, is to help and encourage you to empower yourself, so you too can gently create the life you desire, and the life you deserve.

Dawn Chrystal

CHAPTER 1

SIMPLIFY YOUR LIFE, ONE STEP AT A TIME

THE WHOLE CONCEPT OF *'FREE to be me'* is to help you simplify your life, and find deep inner peace. Use *'Free to be Me'* as a working manual. Each day take out ideas you feel drawn to, and start to include these in your day.

Each and every person reading this book will need something different. There is no wrong way to work through your healing journey. Experiment with each of the breathing exercises, the affirmations, and the other simple techniques, and you will find your deep inner peace.

As you start to peel away anything which no longer serves you, you will feel ready to take the next step. The more you take responsibility, and become accountable for your well-being, the more uplifted you will feel. Remember, this is your journey, and there is a right way for you. Keep it simple, and do what feels right for you each day.

Start right now

Before you go any further, bring your attention to your breath. As you breathe in, slowly say to yourself, 'I have deep inner peace'. Feel the vibration of deep inner peace flowing into every cell of your body. Release your breath.

Keep repeating this simple breathing exercise as you flow through your day. Always be fully present in whatever your choice is today.

Set a goal a day

It takes time to adapt to changes. Be patient, and be gentle on yourself as you start to create changes in your life. Every day, set one simple goal that you feel you can stick to, and then set the intention to follow through on that goal every day. When you achieve this goal you are starting to empower yourself to take back your own personal power.

Start gently repeating to yourself throughout the day, 'I am feeling calm now, I have the power to create my ideal life. I can do this'. Be very proud of yourself, and enjoy each step of your journey. As your journey progresses, you can start to increase the amount of goals you set for each day. Always keep it realistic so you do not overwhelm yourself with the changes.

Throughout 'Free to be Me' I will offer you a list of choices for each day. Make the changes which feel right for you each day, and then keep revisiting the lists as you feel more empowered. Be gentle, yet firm with yourself, and always be proud of the steps that you take. You are working towards creating your ideal life, and this will take time and patience. Praise and encourage yourself every day.

I woke up

What happens, when you wake up one day, and realise you do not like what you see in your life?

The person next to you seems like a stranger, and what you believe to be true, no longer is.

I was struggling, with a re-occurring chest infection and sore throat, and I felt like I just wanted to sleep the rest of my life away. I had this strange clicking noise in my ears, and an almost whining noise with every breath I took. I kept getting this strong feeling of grief flushing through my body. I had constant stomach cramps and had this constant urge to lash out. I had no idea why I felt so sad, or what I was grieving for.

I felt desperate to break this cycle of recurring unwellness and constant stress. I had no energy, and yet a good night's sleep was eluding me. I had been for a Kinesiology and Optimum health balance with a wonderful lady called Susanne Lakin. During the balance procedure she mentioned some things my body was holding on to, like old rigid patterns and grief. At the time I could not totally connect with what she was finding. I went to her to get some relief and understanding about my imbalance of shifting from constant energy bursts to feeling unwell. She said I needed to work more on my boundaries.

I woke up the next morning at 3.42 am, and suddenly had this awareness that I did not know who I was. I didn't like the way I was feeling about myself, and my physical body was a mess.

Although this sudden awareness was a shock to my whole system, I suddenly felt this overwhelming sense of knowing I had to change this. In a split moment, all the self-help books I had been reading had started to make sense. I had a surge of thoughts and inspirations flooding through my mind. I was going through a period of transition, and my body was reflecting how I was feeling. I was going through a period of letting go of the old, to prepare for the new. This feeling of grief was my soul wanting to let go, and move beyond the pain I was feeling.

Dr Bach's famous philosophy, kept running around and around in my mind. He said, 'When there is a void between your true self and your thinking, is when dis-ease sets in'. Suddenly I could see the sense in what he was saying. I had lost my way. I had lost myself.

I jumped out of bed and read up on the angel number 342, the time I woke up, in Doreen Virtue's Angel Number book. With every number there is an important message. The message said, 'Your prayers have increased your faith and your connection with the angels. All these factors will help you in every area of your life'.

I felt a sense of inner strength and gratitude starting to rise up inside me. And then I started to read through my symptoms in the book 'You can heal your life, by Louise L. Hay'. It was a light-bulb moment.

All of my physical symptoms in my body were parts of me which were crying out to be heard. I had been on a constant see-saw of emotions, torn between trying to rationalise what I was feeling, sometimes feeling cross or agitated, and not wanting to put blame on myself or others. I was confused and disoriented. I had lost my way, and myself. The fog had lifted. I felt like I was alive again. I wanted to, and was ready, to start to change my life.

At the beginning of my journey I went through some real emotional roller coaster moments, followed by flashes of insights and clarity. You too may go through some times of confusion and lack of understanding. With persistence, tenacity, and the support of the Bach Flower Remedies and other natural techniques and therapies, you will start to regain your composure and find more harmony.

The Remedies will help to lift the heavy veils of mental and emotional confusion, to bring you new insights and clarity. With the support of the Remedies you will shift into a stronger place, where you will feel enabled to make new choices and see which steps you need to take to help you move forward.

The whole concept of *'Free to be me'* is to keep it simple. Some of the techniques will seem too simple, but they will make a difference to the quality of your life. Sometimes it may seem like I am repeating the same thing over and over, but it needs to be heard, over and over again. Scientists have said it takes sixty-six days to create a new pattern in your mind. Start today, and imagine what you could create in sixty-six days.

Every day set the intention to nurture and encourage yourself. Be patient, yet persistent with yourself and the steps you take, and every moment of every day praise yourself for the progress you are making.

Every emotional event, and every trauma you have been through, has had an impact on how you feel and behave today. Gently peel away the layers of what no longer serves you, and allow your mind and your soul to gently heal itself.

As you nurture yourself, and simplify your life, you will be able to rise above whatever is holding you back, and you will blossom into the person you were born to be.

My intention for you

Throughout this book I take you through the gentlest natural steps to help you discover ways to help yourself. Each day along this journey, you will gain a greater understanding of what is causing your confusion. We will go through a profound healing journey together to help you gain a greater understanding of yourself. And through this understanding you will find your inner peace, contentment and happiness.

Through simple techniques you will be able to identify what is holding you back, and how you can take gentle steps through a journey of transformation and self-discovery.

You will be able to heal the relationship you have with yourself, and discover the real you. You will uncover the person you were born to be.

When you embrace this new relationship with yourself, you will get a better relationship with other people and every situation in your life.

Age is not a barrier to changing your life. Wherever you are, and at whatever age you start, today is the perfect day for you to reinvent yourself.

Remember, when you can understand yourself, you can change your life.

The Bach Flower Remedies and the other natural techniques I share with you will help you to peel away the layers to help you discover the cause of any disharmony you may be feeling.

Continue to take this gentle journey each day through *'Free to be me'*, and you can discover the person you were born to be.

If this is not for you

I know this book is not for everybody. Many of you may have everything you need, and are very content with the life you have. Maybe you picked up this book because you have recognised someone around you needs to address some issues they are uncomfortable with.

Perhaps you know someone who has lost their way, is lacking in confidence, has low self-esteem, is anxious, depressed or is suffering mentally or emotionally? Maybe you have been drawn to this book because you know someone who is struggling with their relationship, with themselves, or with others?

If you recognise this book is not for you, please pass it on to someone who would like some direction and support, or better still, read this book and use the techniques to reach out to that person today.

My intention is that this book finds its way into every school, place of education, doctors' surgery, and any place where people go looking for guidance, understanding of themselves, and emotional support. If you have found it helpful please guide your family, friends or local support networks towards this book.

There are far too many people wandering around under a cloud of self-doubt and confusion.

Take time to process what you are learning

At the beginning, when you start to study yourself and your feelings, you may feel overwhelmed by the changes you are choosing to make.

The Bach Flower Remedy ELM helps when you are feeling mentally, emotionally or physically overwhelmed. It will bring you the ability to cope, one step at a time. You can start taking, and using the Remedy ELM to help you work through the things you need to change, one step at a time. You cannot overdose on the Remedies. If you feel overwhelmed at any stage of your journey ELM is the Remedy to support you, and WALNUT will help you to adjust to the changes you are making.

CERATO will bring your renewed belief in yourself, and LARCH will bring you renewed confidence.

WALNUT will help you to gently adjust to the changes you are making, and CHESTNUT BUD will help you to create and maintain new patterns of thinking and behaviour.

ROCK WATER will encourage you to be gentle on yourself, and IMPATIENS will bring you patience and an understanding of synchronicity.

Praise and thank yourself for every step you take.

Be gentle on yourself

Alongside using the Remedies, bring the exercises I introduce to you into your daily life, and give your body time to adjust. It will take time for you to process and adjust to any changes, and that is okay.

Be gentle on yourself, and be patient with yourself as you create your new way of life.

Read about the Bach Flower Remedies, but do not try to remember every Remedy. Start to become familiar with the Remedies which you can recognise you need at this time. This is a simple but effective way to learn. We tend to remember more when the subject is relevant to us personally.

Take some time to read through the first few pages of the Bach Flower Remedy section which explains why Remedies work alongside medication, and how important it is to work alongside your doctor for the best results for your well-being.

Hopefully, you have started a healing journal to use alongside your book. This will help you keep a record of your progress, and anything which is important to you in one place.

Remember your healing journal is also a place where you can keep a record of your achievements and important milestones on your journey.

The more you do things for yourself, and nurture yourself the more empowered you will feel.

I must say at this stage, if you cannot access the Bach Flower Remedies at the moment, all the other exercises within the book will still be very effective. The Remedies would complement everything you are doing for yourself, and help you move more gently through the transformations you are about to create. You can start to use them at any stage of your healing journey.

If you do not have the Remedies, or are unsure where to start with them, you can contact me and I will make you a personalised bottle tailored to your needs. Please feel welcome to book a guided Remedy session with me via email. My email address is dawnchrystal62@gmail.com. The first two sessions will be half price, plus postage and packing, when you mention you are reading 'Free to be me'.

Consistency brings results

When you are familiar with the simple daily exercises, pick up your book each day, and open it up on one page, and see what you are being encouraged to do for yourself today. Or flick through, and see which part attracts your attention each time you open your book.

This will encourage you to work more with your intuition, your higher self. It will help you trust in your intuitive self, and reassure you that you are listening to your higher self. It will help you feel more in control of your life and recognise that you have the freedom to choose.

Again, some of the exercises within each chapter are repetitive, and I do not apologise for this. The only way to get good at something, is to keep repeating the process over and over again, until it becomes natural. This will help you to overcome any natural resistance you may have to creating the changes you need to make, and to enable you to maintain those changes.

It will also help you recognise, acknowledge and gently ease through your negative emotions, enabling you to make a space to create a new pattern, which will ultimately lead you to the place that you would like to be in your life.

It is far more effective to consistently do any new exercise for ten minutes every day, rather than one five-hour session each week.

This gentle consistency will help your mind and your body to adapt more readily and easily to the new patterns you are creating.

Scientists say it takes sixty-six days to create a new pattern, and for it to become a natural pattern of thinking and behaviour. Start today and imagine what you can create in sixty-six days.

Thank your mind for the new patterns it is creating and thank yourself for the wonderful steps you are taking.

Remember every step you take, however small, will make a difference. Every step will bring you new blessings.

Investing in you

At the beginning you may be very aware of some of your moods and emotions. Take some time to read through the Remedy section, and start to identify which of the Bach Flower Remedies would be most appropriate to support you. Pick the Remedies you can relate to the most when in your negative state of mind. Look at the positive states too, because that is your true potential, and how the Remedies will help you to feel.

You could start to buy these single Remedies to support you at this time, and as you start to recognise other states of mind coming up for you, you can buy those Remedies. Most people start off collecting the Remedies a few at a time.

The Remedies are available as a set of 38 Remedies on-line, or in some health food stores. If you are working with a budget, it is better to gradually invest a small amount in you for the moment. Start by buying the Remedies you recognise will help you at this time. You don't need to wait to buy every Remedy to get the benefits of using them.

Every Remedy you choose today will bring you great benefits, and help move you to a place of stronger self-belief, inner strength and clarity. They will help your mind to rise above the situation which is holding you back.

Always think of buying things to support you as an investment in yourself. The more you invest, the more value you are putting on yourself. As you start to value yourself, the rest of your world will start to fall into place. Please always be fully present in every choice, and every action you choose to make each day. The more at peace you are with your choices, the more you will value who you are.

If you are unsure where to start, please contact me through my email dawnchrystal62@gmail.com and I will do your first two consultations for half price, plus postage and packing.

Your consultations will include a bottle or Bach Flower Remedies made up specially for you, and it should be with you within 7 days.

Please listen to me

A little voice inside my head was always screaming out to be heard. The questions it continually asked were:

'What about me? Who am I? What's wrong with me?'

You might recognise these questions yourself, or you might have other questions which torment you.

When I began to realise I had choices, I wrote a list of things I wanted to change, then I turned them into positive affirmations. I used the affirmations to re-affirm what I was working on accomplishing.

I put these affirmations all around the house, to remind me of my new-found way of life. Every time I saw my affirmation I would repeat it to myself, alongside using my affirmation every time I took my Remedies. I would encourage you to do the same. The more you do for yourself, the more empowered you will feel.

To get you started, this was my list of affirmations:

I am not on call to everyone all of the time.

I have needs of my own, which may not be the same as my family, colleagues or friends.

I honour my own needs. I do not have to agree to every request from others.

I don't have to carry on doing something, just because I have always done it.

Time relaxing is time well spent.

I will remember there is no such thing as the perfect wife, husband, mother, father, child, teacher, carer. I will be the best I can be.

Time spent feeling guilty could be spent doing more enjoyable things.

I will not always do things for others, if they are capable of doing them for themselves. If will allow myself to recognise this,

I will remember, at all times, especially in the face of criticism, difficulties and anxiety, that I am doing the best I can!

I will not allow someone else's opinion of me, or my beliefs to become my reality, and I will not allow my opinion to be influenced by others.

I am willing to take control of my life. I know it is okay to be true to myself. I know it is okay to put myself first, and say no! I am enough.

Although the Bach Flower Remedies are extremely efficient when taken by themselves, using affirmations can help you work through your recovery, and create a new mind-set to support you.

Choose an affirmation each day, and repeat it to yourself frequently throughout the day. Not only do affirmations really work, but they can speed up, and support the Bach Flower Remedies' healing process.

I have created some Remedy balance cards to help you, with affirmations for each state of mind you may be struggling with. Choose the affirmation which best suits you at the moment, and add an emotion to the affirmation. You could choose from emotions such as lovingly, peacefully, allowing, compassionately, joyously, calmly, proudly, serenely, pleasantly, proudly, affectionately, confidently, enthusiastically.

An example of your chosen affirmation could be 'I calmly confront them', or 'I am happily releasing these feelings and allowing in new uplifting feelings'. Try different affirmations to help yourself make those changes. Choose one which flows well for you, and fits in with your circumstances. Every situation, and every person, will need their own supporting affirmation.

Take it a stage further, by acknowledging the thing which is holding you back within your affirmation. Maybe, 'Although I am tired, I lovingly assert myself', or 'Although I am nervous, I am feeling confident in myself, and my abilities'. The Bach Flower Remedy cards will support you on your healing journey. Each Remedy card contains a brief description to help you understand how you are feeling now, what to expect from using the Remedy, and a choice of affirmations to repeat to yourself throughout your healing process. The cards are available through me directly on my website www.dawnchrystal.com.

A glimmer of hope

Twenty-seven years ago I was walking around in a state of confusion. Like many others, I couldn't identify why I didn't feel right – I simply knew I felt really unhappy, and constantly felt exhausted. I felt devoid of emotion, and constantly on the verge of a crisis, unwellness or a breakdown.

But I was one of the lucky ones, because a total stranger recognised my distress, and offered me a glimmer of hope, in the form of a bottle of Rescue Remedy. The lady who gave it to me, said it might help me and my daughter, who was also in a really fearful place. My perspective of myself, and my life, was about to change.

Within two weeks of starting to take the Rescue Remedy, I was feeling a lot calmer, and my daughter began to sleep through the night for the first time in three years. It felt like a miracle. The Rescue Remedy had brought me a great sense of relief. I didn't understand how it worked, but it made a huge difference. It felt like the answer to my prayers.

CHAPTER 2

DO NOT WAIT TO BE PERFECT

I AM VERY AWARE, THAT throughout this book, there are aspects of my grammar which may not be 'proper English', or grammatically correct. I am also very aware, that I do repeat myself many times, but this is just me. This is my way of helping you to work through, and process what I am explaining to you. I spent much of my life focusing on all my mistakes, and beating myself up about what I couldn't do, and that led me deeper and deeper into a hole of depression and anxiety.

This book is based on the years of therapy sessions, and self-help workshops I run. In those workshops and therapy sessions, I have become very aware that we only take on board about ten per cent of what we hear in any session. Imagine each page is a new workshop. At each workshop, each page you will get what you need from this session.

Take what you need from each page, and bring the guidance into your day. The exercises are repeated on future pages, and I know you will feel ready to embrace the steps you need to take, at the right time for you. You are unique, with your own past experiences, and your own beliefs and ways of learning. Each person reading this book will learn in their own way. Do not berate yourself for the bits you do not do. I will take you through those steps time and time again, until they naturally become a part of your life. We all need to process, learn and progress at our own speed, to get the most out of our learning.

I say again, take what you need from each page, and bring what feels right to you into your day, and then bring in the next step, and the next. This is an exciting new journey for you, and it will unfold for you as it is meant to. Nurture and encourage yourself as you go, and you will blossom each day.

What was wrong with me!

My younger years were very confusing, because I did not understand about my learning difficulties. Nowadays my ways of learning would be described as ADHD learning. On top of this, I have a short term memory loss, and sequential learning challenges. All of this had a significant impact of my lack of learning, and the way I perceived myself.

I spent the majority of my younger years thinking there was something wrong with me, but that started to change when I started to learn more about myself, and the challenges I had been through. I started to get a greater understanding of myself, and of my own unique ways of learning. Through the techniques I am going to share with you, and the support of the Bach Flower Remedies, I started to gradually peel away the layers of false thoughts and beliefs I had held about myself.

It took some time, and lots of effort, but the more layers I peeled away, the more I started to understand myself, and the more compassion I gained for me. As my compassion and insights grew, I started to like and appreciate the experiences I had been through, and the person I had become, with all my flaws and imperfections. I started to have this burning passion to want to share my journey, and my teachings with others, especially children.

I could never have imagined how passionate I would become to want to stand up and talk to others. Before my journey of discovery I couldn't even talk to myself, let alone anyone else. I was introverted, and spent the majority of my life feeling isolated and alone. But that was about to change. As my confidence grew, I gained a real passion for writing and sharing my experiences. I had a choice to make. I could wait until I learnt better grammar, or I could put this book out there now.

I am presenting this book to you just as it is. If you notice grammatical errors, please look beyond those, and see the message within these words. Each word is filled with love, and with a passion to want to help you if you feel weighed down by the thoughts which are spinning around in your mind. If you can acknowledge that something in your life is out of balance today, this is the right place to be.

- If I can touch one person today, and encourage them to turn their life around, my mission will be complete, and everything I have experienced will be worth it. I sincerely hope you are that special person. Start to embrace and celebrate who you are today.

Each and every person reading this will be unique. Your uniqueness should be celebrated every day. As you read and explore the pages ahead, start to peel away your layers of labels and inhibiting thoughts, to reveal your hidden strengths and wonderful qualities. Step up just as you are today, and start to get in touch with who you were born to be.

There really is so much more to you

Do you ever stop to consider why you are the way you are?

Are there some heavy aspects of you which just seem to override your joyful days? Do you find yourself wondering why you react the way you do to situations, when you know deep down inside that it was not the best way to deal with the situation in hand?

We all have this inner knowing of what is right, and what is wrong, and yet we can constantly create patterns of behaviour which seem contrary to what we want to be.

How many times have you felt stressed, or over-reacted, and then thought, 'Why did I do that?' How often do you react with anger, when there is something deep inside you which says, 'This does not feel right. This is not who I am'? How many times during the day do you consciously, or unconsciously berate or compare, or even condemn yourself?

All of these contradictory thoughts constantly whirling around inside your mind are what can cause, and can compound, your feelings of discontent, stress or even create feelings of anxiety and depression.

Always remember, every emotional event, and every trauma you have been through, has had an impact on how you feel and behave today. Gently peel away the layers of what no longer serves you, and allow your mind and your soul to gently heal itself. You can change how you feel about yourself when you start to release the thoughts and the feelings which have been holding you back. When you learn to become proactive in your life, instead of reactive to everything that happens, you will become the master of your own life.

Listen to yourself

From today, please stop and pay more attention to how you are feeling. Do not berate yourself for what you have been doing, or are doing. Do not have regrets about the thoughts you have been having, or the things you have been through. Everything has happened for a reason.

What if I said, that everything that has happened to you in your life, was part of your bigger plan to help you to find yourself?

This thought may make you feel uncomfortable, but please keep returning to this thought.

You are who you are today, because of everything you have been through. Your past has given you your character, your strengths and your weaknesses. You only see how you are as a problem, when you do not fully understand the whole picture. When you are in a state of disharmony with yourself you have a tendency to focus on what you believe is wrong, rather than what has gone right for you.

If you believe that what has happened to you is wrong, you will always be in the victim mode, and your brain will respond by keeping you in your primitive state of survival, which then brings in more and more tension, and ultimately stress and more disharmony. You are who you are meant to be right now. When you start to get a greater understanding of yourself, and why you are the way you are, everything else will start to fall into place.

From this day, start to value yourself, and improve your feelings of self-worth. Start to have greater respect for yourself and all that you are. When you value yourself you feel more empowered, and from this place you can build yourself up to the person you were born to be.

When you stop to pay attention to you, and how you can and need to help yourself, you can start to turn your life around. We all need someone to stop and listen to what is happening to us. Stop waiting around for others to acknowledge you, or to tell you how well you are doing. You need to acknowledge you, and how well you have done.

From today become your own best cheerleader. Praise, respect, encourage, nurture, thank, acknowledge, and love yourself every moment of every day, (PRENTAL). When you become your own best friend your world will take on a whole new meaning. From today, take the time to listen to yourself, and what you can do for you. When you start to treat yourself as someone special you will change your life and everything that is happening, within you and around you.

This world can seem like a lonely place, and you will have times of feeling alone. As you recognise these moments, of feeling alone, start to go to an inner place of healing, a place of contentment, and inner peace and quiet. Within this place, you can start to talk to and nurture yourself, and your soul. Within this bliss-filled place of peace, you will receive the greater understanding of what you need to do, and how you can help yourself.

Take yourself to a place of gratitude whenever you feel lost, confused or disoriented. Say thank you to yourself for this time for reflection and introspection. Take as much time as you need, to learn to be more still in your mind. And from this blissful place, you will find all the answers you need.

Listen to what is happening. Acknowledge where you need help, and become your own best friend. Any disharmony you are feeling today, is your soul calling out to you, to make some changes. Your soul is saying I am ready to move beyond this situation now.

When you listen to your own needs, and make gentle adjustments each day, you will start to feel more empowered. You will feel enabled to see solutions, and insights into ways you can lift up your spirits. The more you lift up your spirits, the more your feelings of well-being will increase. These wonderful new feelings will carry you forward. As you respect yourself and grow, you will attract towards you the right people, and they too will respect you, listen to you and support you. It follows the universal law of attraction, what you think about, you will attract towards you.

As you increase your feelings of self-worth, and the value you put on yourself, you will attract to you people who will value you for who you are. This is your day to start to create the life you desire. This is going to be the best day of your life, and from this moment on, every day will become the best day of your life. From this moment in time, start to treat yourself as your own best friend. Start to praise, respect, encourage, nurture, acknowledge, and love the beautiful person you have grown to be today. As you nurture yourself, the rest of your life will start to fall gently into place.

Are you ready to take a chance on you?

'Opportunities are everywhere for us all. Why then do you struggle so much with lack of opportunities?

Quite often, your mind is so preoccupied with all the trivialities of life, you are not prepared, or open to receive the chances which are being shown to you.

'Trivia?' you may ask, 'These problems, this stuff, is real to me. It is weighing heavily on my mind.'

And yes, we agree with you. The burdens you carry are indeed heavy. You have much to deal with. What if you could find some peace within this chaos? What if we could help you, to separate yourself emotionally from the chaos?'

You may have been floundering around, trying to make the best of your life, and the situations you find yourself in, but somewhere deep within you, there is a yearning for something different, to be something or someone different. You may have had a strong sense of knowing that something is wrong, or out of order, but you cannot put a finger on what it is.

Each of you has a very powerful mind, a mind which can manifest anything you perceive as possible. What if you could turn your life around? Just take a moment to make a new decision. You could choose to take twenty minutes from each day to recharge your batteries, to lift yourself up above the stress and anxiety you are living with. Will you take that chance?

What if it was possible to achieve anything you perceive as possible? Would you take a chance?

Each of us has the ability to make new choices, but more often than not, we continue on a treadmill of stress, which keeps us in the turmoil.

Take twenty minutes each day, to start to transform your life. Take a moment to open one page of this book right now, and see what it is calling you to adjust. The Bach Flower Remedies, and the simple techniques I introduce you to, will help to lift the heavy veils of mental and emotional confusion, to bring you new insights and clarity. You will shift into a stronger place, where you will feel enabled to make new choices, and see which steps you need to take to help you move forward.

The whole concept of 'Free to be Me' is to keep it simple. Some of the techniques will seem too simple, but they will make a difference to the quality of your life. Sometimes, it may seem like I am repeating the same thing over and over, but it needs to be heard, over and over again. Scientists have said it takes sixty-six days to create a new pattern in your mind. Start today, and imagine what you could create in sixty-six days.

Every day, set the intention to nurture and encourage yourself. Be patient, yet persistent, with yourself and the steps you take, and every moment of every day praise yourself for the progress you are making. Every emotional event, and every trauma you have been through, has had an impact on how you feel and behave today. Gently peel away the layers of what no longer serves you, and allow your mind and your soul to gently heal itself.

As you nurture yourself, and simplify your life, you will be able to rise above whatever is holding you back, and you will be able to get clarity around whatever is happening in your life.

Every step you take will make a difference. It takes sixty-six days to create new patterns in your mind. Start today, and imagine what you could create in sixty-six days. As you unravel and quiet your mind, you will simplify your life, and you will blossom into the person you were born to be.

What has drawn you to this book today?

Do you get a feeling that something needs to change? Do you sometimes feel hypocritical? Like you are acting in a way which is contrary to what you know is right? Then you are in the right place today to start to create some changes. Let your mind be open, to explore simple ways in which you can transform your life. Most of what I am going to share with you is not rocket science. Somewhere in your mind, you already know you should be doing these things for yourself, but do you do them? Do you correct things as you go, or do you go deeper and deeper into a state of denial, disharmony, or even apathy?

I am going to take you on a gentle journey, to help you unravel your mind, and your life, to help you get back to a place where you can be free to be yourself. Some of what I am going to say on your journey with '*Free to be Me*' may seem hypocritical, or in contradiction to a previous step you have taken.

One minute, I am saying love yourself for who you are, you are enough, and the next, change the way you are. You may feel like you are having split standards and conflicting thoughts, and that is okay. This is the place you are meant to be right now. I am just reflecting back to you the way your mind is working at the moment, and helping you look at ways you can adjust this.

Can you relate to this inner conflict? Does this relate to the way you work within your own mind? How many contradictory thoughts do you have each day? Take a moment to stop and reflect on how you talk to yourself each day. What do you say about you? What do you say about your life? Is what you are thinking about true, or have you convinced yourself it is true? Is the way you perceive yourself really the truth?

If you recognise you are having conflicting thoughts about yourself and your life, and your thoughts have become uncomfortable for you, it means this is the perfect time for you. This is the time when you are ready to step up, and adjust anything that has become out of balance. The inner conflict is your soul talking to you, to get your attention. This is your soul saying, 'You have lived too long in this place of inner conflict and confusion'.

When you are having contradictory thoughts, you are keeping your mind in a state of confusion. It does not know which way to tell you to go.

As you start to be more aware, and specific about the thoughts you choose to use, you will start to have more clarity.

Your thoughts are your driving force, and you need to be giving yourself the best opportunity every day.

As you change your thoughts, you will change your life.

The steps I take you through are all stepping stones, to help you to unravel what is going on within you and your mind. And then each step will help you realise just how much more potential you have, what your inner strengths are, and what a wonderful person you really are.

Each step will start to bring you an awareness of how you may have gone off track, and help you discover how you may have become confused or disillusioned. Then together, we can explore simple ways to gently help you to take back your personal power. Take some time out to consider what is going on in your life.

What is getting you down? Has illness or stress got on top of you?

Do you feel like you are not coping with something, or not coping with your life?

Do you feel lost, or unsure of who you are?

Take out a notebook, and start to write down anything you think is out of order. Put today's date on this page. This is the beginning of your healing journey, and your healing journal is the place where you will be able to map out your life, and create a whole new way of living. You are not looking at why you feel like this yet. You are just offloading, and emptying your mind. Keep writing until you run out of thoughts. An empty mind becomes a more open, and receptive mind.

Stop to consider this thought. Sometimes the onset of illness, or pain in your precious body, has been given to you to save your life. Is this really your soul saying, 'I am in pain. I am feeling disharmony. Please listen to me'.

It is often not until you have pain or illness, that you stop to adjust the way you treat yourself, and your body. So many of us constantly live under a constant veil of stress, not knowing or comprehending the impact it is having on our mind and body.

Is this you? Are there some things you would like to adjust? Are you feeling ready to make some changes?

Today is the day you could step up and create a gentler and more appropriate way of life for yourself. Today is the day you can start to turn your life around. It is not about striving to be perfect. It is about feeling, and being enabled to move beyond any confusion you are experiencing right now, to become the best version of you. It is about discovering the truth of who you are, and who you are meant to be.

Gentle steps

At every step, stop to take time to nurture yourself, and appreciate who you are at this moment in your life, and if you recognise elements of you which you don't like, or you feel uncomfortable with, then step up and make those changes, one step at a time. Do not try to rush this process. It will take as long as it needs to take. You are starting on a new journey of discovering who you really are. It will take time, and it will take tenacity. But every step will make a difference.

Scientists say it takes sixty-six days to create a new pattern, so I was tempted to make this book into a daily sixty-six day workbook, to help you work through the process of change, and help you keep on track. But I realise each and every person reading this will grow at their own pace. Become accountable for yourself, your progress, and your life, and step up to make the changes you need. Start today, and you will find renewed peace and your inner happiness.

Keep a record of the journey you take, and remember every small step you take will make a difference. It does not matter how many times you need to start again. Persistence will pay off. You will never go back to the old place where you started if you have the tenacity to keep working on you. Some of the exercises are very similar, and may seem repetitive, but the more consistently you use them, the more easily your brain will adapt to the new patterns you are creating.

Although scientists say it takes sixty-six days to create a new pattern, I believe that becoming passionate about making changes, and loving yourself enough to make those changes will keep you on track, and every day you will get uplifting results from the steps you take. You are truly worth it. It will take as long as it needs to take. You are not in a race; you are on a gentle journey of discovery and healing.

Choose to find a friend or someone you trust to talk to about your healing journey and how you feel. Every day praise, encourage and nurture yourself. Set your own daily goals, and then weekly goals. The more you become accountable to yourself, and your progress, the greater your rewards will be. Be gentle on yourself if things do not go to plan, or you go off track sometimes. Today is the best day to start again, every day.

Whilst you are holding feelings of discontent towards yourself, you will never feel like you are enough. Start to appreciate, respect, like, and even love, yourself. This is the day to turn your life around. Take some time each day to respect just how far you have come, and how well you have done to get this far. It really does not matter if you think you have messed up, you have still managed to get to this day in your life. Even setbacks are steps forward. You can often learn more from the setbacks, than you do from the pieces which run smoothly. Every day you are growing. Thank yourself for the journey you have taken, and the challenges you have overcome. Step up and become accountable, and you will transform your life.

Which way will you go today?

Today you are enough. Today is about finding the balance for you. The balance between striving to move forward and learning to be still, contented, and at peace. Bring the balance of inner peace and harmony into your life. It does not matter how big, or how small, those changes are that you need to make. At every step, stop to appreciate who you are. The best place to begin to heal is by respecting yourself and the journey you have taken.

Be happy with who you are today. Be happy with all that you have accomplished. When you are happy and contented you can achieve so much more. So much more happiness, joy, contentment and peace, within every aspect of who you are. When you work in harmony with yourself, you can truly appreciate who you are, and true happiness will come from within you.

Self-praise, appreciation and self-recognition is imperative, but so is honesty and integrity. If you have any patterns of behaviour which seem to be making you feel disheartened, or disillusioned about who you are, step up, and start to gently adjust what you would like to change.

PRENTAL you throughout every day

Praise, respect, encourage, nurture, thank, acknowledge, and love yourself every moment of every day. When you become your own best friend, your world will take on a whole new meaning. This is your new action plan for each day.

Praise *yourself, and every action you take*
Respect *yourself, and every emotion you feel*
Encourage *yourself, and every step you take*
Nurture *yourself, every moment of each day*
Thank *yourself, for everything you overcome and achieve, and for every blessing in your life*
Acknowledge *yourself, for all your good work*
Love *yourself unconditionally, regardless of what you are going through*

Let you be the centre of your universe, and you will find the key to your inner happiness and peace of mind. When you start to treat yourself as someone special, you can overcome, and work through any situation you meet, and through loving yourself, you will find your true self. When you step into your truth, you can create a whole new world around you, and you then become the catalyst for helping every person you meet.

CHAPTER 3

YOUR HEALING JOURNAL BECOMES YOUR NEW FRIEND

CONSISTENTLY TAKE YOUR THOUGHTS OUT of your mind and offload them into a healing journal. Write down anything which pops into your mind that is causing you to feel out of sorts or confused. Or maybe there is just something you would like to change. Writing down your thoughts, and acknowledging them, is a massive step towards healing yourself.

Never underestimate the power of offloading your thoughts and your feelings into your healing journal. As you empty your mind, you are lightening your load, and creating a space in your mind where you can start to heal your life. Keep it simple, and write down everything that you feel is distressing you, and is troubling your mind. When you start to listen to you the rest will start to fall into place.

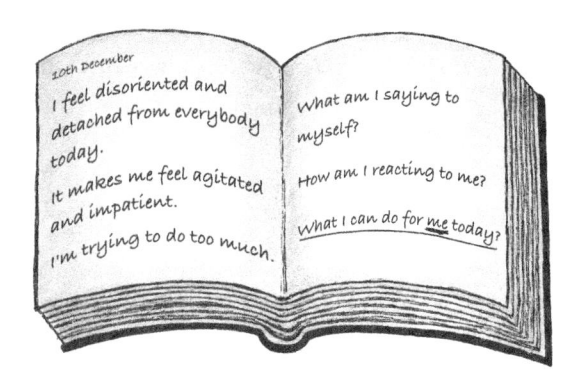

> 10th December
> I feel disoriented and detached from everybody today.
> It makes me feel agitated and impatient.
> I'm trying to do too much.
>
> What am I saying to myself?
> How am I reacting to me?
> What I can do for me today?

FREE TO BE ME

For some people, making changes may seem daunting, or overwhelming. If this is how you feel about change, start to change things in your life in small steps. Each day, set the intention to make one change your priority, and work with that for today. Then the next day, add a new intention to the one you worked with yesterday.

The Bach Flower Remedy, for helping you to work through times of change and transition is WALNUT.

ELM is the remedy for if you feel overwhelmed by the changes you need to make. ELM will bring you renewed confidence and the ability to cope with things, one step at a time.

Every person reading this will have different needs, and their own unique way of dealing with changes in their life. Take what you need from each page, and work with that choice today. Take the next step when you feel ready. Your journey will be as unique as you are, and you will get your desired outcome at the perfect time for you.

Every day, and at every step, take some time to appreciate, and praise yourself for the things you have overcome, and accomplished. Frequently throughout the day, take a few moments to count your blessings, to increase your feelings of gratitude. Keep a record of the blessings you have in your life, so you can refer to these during times when you feel like you have lost your way. And once again, thank yourself for the important steps you have taken today. Start with healing today, and in time your past experiences will start to make more sense, and take on more meaning.

Day One. Start each day with a gratitude plan

As you wake up, say, 'Thank you' to yourself, and take some time to remind yourself of five things you appreciate, and for which you feel truly grateful. Smile to yourself.

Take some deep slow breaths into your body, and say, 'Thank you' for every breath you take, and, 'Thank you' to your body for the blessings it brings to you. Say to yourself, 'Deep inner peace' as you take six slow deep breaths.

Think of something you would like to achieve today.

Take five minutes to visualise, encourage, praise and thank yourself for the steps you are going to take. It may be something very small today, and it could be something slightly bigger tomorrow. Keep it realistic and choose something you know you can accomplish, like I will drink more water, or I will smile at everyone I meet today.

Set the intention to do random acts of kindness every day, for yourself, and for other people. The kinder you are, the more your mind releases the chemical oxytocin, and the more contented and compassionate you feel. As you get these wonderful healing chemicals flowing through your body, your feelings of self-worth will increase, and the more in touch you will feel with who you are meant to be.

The very essence of who you are is love, and the more love and kindness you give out, the more the loving feelings will flow. Every choice you make from today will make a difference.

Talk to those around you about your loving intention, and set yourself a goal to follow this through throughout the day. Praise and thank yourself every time you accomplish your goal.

At the end of your day, take some time before you go to sleep to write down how well you have done. Praise yourself, and thank yourself, and then make a record of the goal, or goals you achieved today. Before you drift off to sleep take a few minutes to recollect five things you have accomplished today. Praise yourself for the steps you have taken. Going to sleep with an attitude of gratitude and self-praise, will help to lift up your feelings of self-worth, and encourage your mind to feel more at peace as you drift off to sleep.

Continue to do more random acts of kindness throughout each day, and notice how your life starts to feel so much better. The random acts of kindness do not take anything from your day. Keep the acts simple at the beginning, like smiling at everyone you meet today, opening a door for someone, or complimenting them on the way they look. Making a point of sincerely saying, 'Thank you' to others is a great way of connecting, building bridges, and lifting up the way you feel about each other.

When you start to go with the flow of these loving feelings, you are starting to move to a place where each person can start to raise up their own vibrations, which then enables everyone to start believing and empowering themselves. As your self-worth goes up, you are lifting others too.

Are your patterns of thinking real, or are they merely ingrained patterns you have adopted? More often than not, your thoughts, and your beliefs about yourself, are far from the truth of who you really are. The more you use these false ingrained thought patterns, whether they are appropriate for you or not, the deeper impact they can have on you. It is when these patterns of thoughts have become so ingrained, that you are living them as your reality, that feelings of disharmony start to creep into your mind.

In time, you may experience a deep feeling that you have lost your way, that you have strayed away from the peaceful person you wish you could be, but you cannot put your finger on what you are experiencing, or how you can adjust these feelings of disharmony. This can create an even deeper feeling of inner conflict within your mind. I believe this is often the deeper underlying cause of feelings of dis-ease within your body.

You will be able to recognise many of these negative states of mind in the despondency and despair group of Bach Flower Remedies in this book. These feelings of despondency and despair are usually a result of false negative thought patterns and feelings which have been going on, and left unaddressed or corrected, for a long time. Take some time out to flick forward in your book, and read about the Bach Flower Remedies in the Despondency and Despair group, page 418. Can you recognise some of the ways you are feeling today in the negative states of mind of each Remedy?

Be gentle, and nurture yourself as you go

Please do not see these feelings as bad, or berate yourself for the feelings you are experiencing. Simply acknowledge this is how you feel right now, and start to reset and refocus your mind, by looking at the positive potential each Remedy can bring you. This would be a good time to start to invest in you by buying the Bach Flower Remedies you recognise will help you.

What are you saying about you? Take a few moments to write down how you feel about you right now. Are you content and at peace with who you are? How do your thoughts make you feel? Your feelings of discontent can show themselves as feelings of heaviness, sadness, extreme tiredness, anger or frustration. You may be feeling nervous or stressed, disillusioned or anxious, or even depressed and mentally confused. Some feelings can even result in a manifestation of physical pain or dis-ease. You may recognise the dis-ease within your body as discomfort, or if unchecked it can literally become the underlying cause of disease.

My understanding is, whether you look at pain in your body as disease or disease, these can manifest as a result of long-term disharmony between your true self and your state of mind.

Through years of research and observations of people, I have come to an understanding that many forms of anxiety, stress and depression have come about as a result of suppression of your true self. In this state you undermine your own self-worth, and undervalue yourself. It can seem impossible to see the good within yourself, and this can lead to deeper turmoil of low self-esteem, feeling suppressed, or even depression. Suppressing your true self can lead to feelings of deeper confusion and even loss of hope and joy.

This confusion all starts with the way you are thinking about, and seeing yourself. The words you use, your thoughts, and your perception have become out of balance. When your true self has been suppressed by your thoughts for too long, your physical mind is not living in the reality of who you could be. Take some time to consider how your thoughts and your feelings may have become out of balance.

Start writing your thoughts in your healing journal. Take some time to write down your thoughts, and how they make you feel. How do you feel about these thoughts now you are looking at them again? Are they helping you? Or are they detrimental to you, and the way you feel about yourself and your world?

Take some time to stop and reflect. Maybe sleep on these thoughts, or go for a walk to process what you are experiencing. As you walk away from your journal, take a few moments to praise yourself for the steps you have taken. Thank yourself, and feel grateful for the important progress you are making today. Come back to your healing journal when you feel ready to work on changing these thoughts. I am very aware that some of the mental or physical imbalances you may be experiencing could be genetic, or caused through chemical imbalances or illness, but even if this is the case, how you think about yourself can still be influencing the way you feel about yourself.

If you do start to recognise you are not in a good emotional or mental place in your mind this could be a good time to reach out for help from a good friend or a professional person. And always remember, sometimes you may need medical support as well. Every aspect of you and your healing journey should be approached from every angle. The more support you have the more smoothly your healing journey will unfold.

As you start to recognise any feelings which are out of balance, find a good friend or professional person to confide in. Do not keep pushing those thoughts and feelings back down. Maybe you could dedicate one hour of each day to talking about your feelings. It really does make a difference if you share your thoughts. It helps your mind to process what you are experiencing, and can be a great healing time for you.

Your higher self is wanting to help you

Having an awareness that things have become out of perspective is the optimum time to step up, and make a choice to start again. Acknowledging you feel disharmony, or any discontent, is a sign that this is your soul's time to start to make changes. This is your higher self working with you. Your higher self is stepping in and starting to lead you. When you start listening to your higher self, your soul, this is the time you can get in touch with you, and who you are meant to be. You will now be ready to start to discover what you can really achieve. This is the time you can really find out who you are meant to be.

Awareness brings clarity

You are acknowledging you are ready to start to make significant changes. When your higher self is stepping in, and trying to help you to correct the way you have become, it is simply because you have lost your way. You have strayed from the person you were born to be. It is not a time to berate yourself for what has gone wrong, but to celebrate you have a new choice.

These feelings of discontent may have been coming to the surface for a while, to allow you to recognise where you need to make changes, and how you may have lost your way. These feelings will start to heal as soon as you start to work with you, instead of against you. This is a time to celebrate that you acknowledge there is more to you, and this is the day you are going within yourself to discover your real you.

How you think about you, influences the way you feel about yourself.

If you recognise you have become unhappy with the way you feel about you, this is a turning point. This is the perfect time to step up and make changes.

Can you really change how you feel?

Often these patterns have become so ingrained, that you do not even stop to consider that the way you have become is far from the truth of who you really are. Often you cannot comprehend that these false patterns are the underlying cause of your discontent. From today, start to acknowledge that you have the ability within you to be able to tap into your patterns of thoughts and behaviour. You can correct them. And you will be able to understand, and rectify the way you feel about you.

Take some to read about the following Bach Flower Remedies in the **Bach Flower Remedy section page.** *The Remedies can be taken straight from the stock bottles you buy in the shops, or they can also be diluted in water for a more gentle and subtle release of your emotions.*

When you first start taking the Flower Remedies they can bring your emotions to a more intense state as the healing starts to happen.

This is a natural part of the healing process, and the more intense feelings will soon subside as your body releases the old feelings.

If your emotions do feel too intense, put your chosen Bach Remedies in water, and sip the water throughout the day, until the calmness comes.

If you find yourself in a place of discontent, and you feel like you have a dark cloud over your head, use the Bach Flower Remedy MUSTARD for a few days. It will help to lift you back to a place of cheerfulness and clarity.

If you find yourself thinking your situation is hopeless, or you feel helpless to turn things around, the Remedy GORSE will bring you renewed hope.

If you are feeling like you are apathetic, and have lost the motivation or drive to make change use WILD ROSE to bring you renewed inner drive and motivation.

If you feel consumed by emotional anguish use AGRIMONY and SWEET CHESTNUT to help you release the anguish, and see a way forward.

If you recognise the underlying cause of your discontent is anger use HOLLY to release the anger.

If you feel frustrated, and can see no sense of purpose to your life use WILD OAT to help you acknowledge, and feel more at peace with your situation.

If you have lost the sense of who you really are, CERATO will help you to start trusting in yourself again, and bring back your sense of identity.

Taking back your own personal power

Starting to acknowledge how you feel, and how you can help yourself, will help you to feel more empowered and motivated. Write down the Remedies you can relate to, so you can start to keep a record of what you are using to help yourself. This would be a good time to start to invest in the Remedies you recognise will help you. All of the Remedies can be taken individually, or you could make a combination bottle of Remedies. Keep consistently taking the Remedies until you feel a sense of relief from your heavy feelings, and then you can introduce other Remedies you feel drawn to.

There are so many underlying causes which can affect you, and often they are so deep that it may seem hard to believe you can tap into them. The thought and behaviour patterns you are living in this moment are often a result of so many influences, shocks, traumas and inputs that have happened to you in this lifetime. Some of the patterns may even be from past lives. They may seem so ingrained it can seem beyond your powers of perception that you can modify them. The Remedies will help to lift you out of these heavy feelings you have been experiencing.

Today I ask you to step up, and firstly acknowledge that who you are today, is exactly who you are meant to be right now. This is the person you have chosen to be today, at this moment on your journey. From this day, start to become your own best friend. Start to honour the beautiful person you are deep down inside, and all the different aspects of who you have become. You are a truly wonderful creation. Never ever, berate or give up on yourself. You are an amazing person.

The ultimate aim of *'Free to be Me'* is to help you find deep inner peace, and find the person you were born to be.

Before you go any further, bring your attention to your breath.

As you breathe in, slowly say to yourself, 'deep inner peace'. Hold your breath for a few seconds. Feel the vibration of deep inner peace flowing into every cell of your body.

Slowly release your breath, and keep repeating this simple breathing exercise as you flow through your day.

Be gentle on yourself. When you take away the pressure of 'I have to change this', and go with the flow of 'I am lovingly choosing to change this', everything will start to fall into place.

Whatever you are experiencing right now, you can turn it around.

Sing, sing, sing

Next time you start to feel anxious, start to sing to yourself, and recognise how you start to feel after singing for a few minutes.

Every aspect of you is important. It is what makes you the unique and beautiful person you are.

CHAPTER 4

FINDING JOY IS YOUR PURPOSE TODAY

CHOOSE TO FIND JOY WITHIN each moment of your day. Choose to do things which are bringing you joy and happiness. It may be walking in nature, spending time alone, or with someone special. It may be watching a favourite movie, reading, doing nothing, learning something new, listening to music, singing, painting, writing, baking, or mending a pair of socks. Whatever you choose to do, be more grateful for the choices you have, and really start to appreciate how blessed you are to have these gifts, and the more uplifted and filled with gratitude you will feel.

However small your blessings may seem, your attitude of gratitude will lift up your spirits and bring you more feelings of well-being and harmony. The more you appreciate your blessings, the more blessings you will attract towards you. Whatever makes you feel joyful will lift up your spirits. Lifting up your spirits with joy helps you to rise above things which are keeping you feeling stuck. Whether it is stuck in your thoughts, or stuck in a situation that is going on around you, finding something to do which brings you joy will help you to raise up your vibrations. Feeling joy brings you more feelings of love and compassion, and is the highest vibration of all.

It is almost impossible for your body to feel joy when it is stressed and tense. When you are worried, tense or stressed your brain produces the chemical cortisol to help you deal with the stress you are experiencing. But when you are joyful your brain produces soft healing chemicals to lift up your spirits.

Sing, sing, sing

Next time you start to feel stressed or anxious, start to sing to yourself, and recognise how you start to feel after singing for a few minutes.

When you are producing the cortisol, it can seem really hard to see the joy, or the good within anything in your life because your mind assumes you are in a stressful situation, and so it needs to stay alert. When you are in this state for long periods you can become more hard-hearted. In this state your heart centre is more closed down and everything feels more intense. It can be hard to get yourself to that place of joy and peace within your mind and your heart. It can feel like everything and everybody is against you.

If you find yourself in this state of mind right now read about the Bach Flower Remedies HOLLY and WILLOW. Can you relate to the negative state of mind of each of these Remedies? Now take some time to read the positive states of mind. The positive states are your true potential. When life has been hard or challenging, and you feel like you have no control over what has happened it is natural to go into the negative state of mind.

The Bach Flower Remedies will help you to release any harsh thoughts and feelings you have been holding, and shift you gently into your true potential. Your real potential is to be feeling and living with unconditional love and joy, and to be able to take back responsibility for yourself. Your greater purpose on this earth is to be able to find joy and unconditional love within your precious body. The more love you feel, the happier you will feel. Your joy and happiness will bring peace to your soul. As your energy vibrations rise up, you will encourage others to find that joy within themselves. You will become the shining light for others to follow.

Wheel of gratitude

There may be times when you are struggling to connect with any feelings of love or joy. Many years ago, when I was in a really bad emotional place, I was given a piece of paper with a circle on it. The circle was divided into 16 pieces, and in each section I was encouraged to write something that I was grateful for. At first, I really struggled to think of things that I was grateful for. My mind kept flicking back to all the things I believed were wrong.

I started with those more obvious things, which I must confess I had, up until this moment in time, probably overlooked and not really appreciated. When your mind is so consumed by stress and anxiety, it can seem hard to see the good within anything in your life.

My gratitude wheel started off with my children, and then my dog, and then my bed, my bed covers, my friends, my...........It took me some time, to start to connect with things for which I was truly grateful, but the deeper I looked the more things I found.

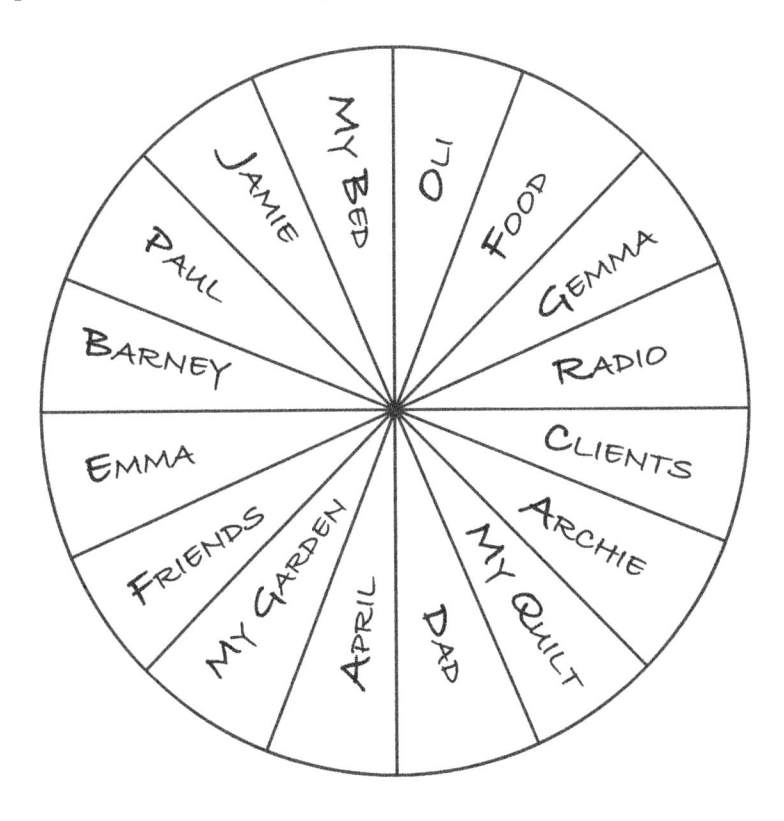

As I said earlier, it can be hard to recognise the good things in life, when you are so consumed by thoughts which are full of discontent, but the more I started to recognise the blessings I did have in my life, the better I started to feel. I cannot explain exactly how I felt, but I had this unusual warm feeling start to flow through my body, and I remember that at some stage of filling in my wheel of gratitude, I even started to feel quite emotional, and overwhelmed by this new experience of seeing the good within my life.

It was some time afterwards, that I learnt that when you start to support yourself, and connect with things which make you feel grateful, you trigger a chemical and neurological response in your body. When you think of things which you are grateful for, you are becoming proactive in your own natural healing, and are enhancing your own feelings of well-being. This is your body's own natural emotional response, which you should be connected to at all times, but you can lose touch with when you are stressed or disorientated.

Your turn to create your wheel of gratitude

Give your mind a break from the worrying or negative thoughts which are consuming you. Take a piece of paper, and draw a big circle on it. Divide the circle into 16 pieces, and then write something in each section that you are grateful for. At the beginning, you may struggle to think of 16 things, but keep looking for things which you can include, and add them at a later time.

It does not matter if they are very small things, or large things. Remember to add people and opportunities you have in your life too. Every time you use your wheel of gratitude, you are giving your mind a new focus.

Create other wheels of gratitude and scatter them around your home. Every time you mind sees the gratitude wheel, it triggers the feel-good chemicals in your brain. The more you start to recognise the good and the blessings within your life, the stronger and more grateful you will start to feel.

You could do this exercise frequently, and keep adding new things you feel grateful for. Put the diagram up on the fridge or on your wall so that every time you see it you are reminded of how many blessings you have in your life.

When you have more time you could add pictures or photographs which represent the things you are grateful for. The more visually attractive it is, the more readily your mind can respond to the wonderful feelings you are connecting with. When your eyes see the pictures, it triggers your mind to reconnect with the good memories and happy feelings, which then triggers your brain to produce the feel-good chemicals, and brings you a neurological response of well-being. Everything feels better when you are focusing on the things for which you are grateful.

Take it a stage further, and do a circle of happiness. Write down 16 things which make you feel happy. And then, when you feel ready, you could create a wheel of love, and add 16 things which make you feel loved, or that you love. Anything you do which is creative, and with the intention of seeing the love, gratitude and happiness within your life, will help you to start to move into the flow of natural all-encompassing love. Your brain will support you by producing feel-good chemicals, and your feelings of well-being will start to flourish. The more love you feel, the more you will blossom.

As I am writing this message to you, the song 'All You Need Is Love', by The Beatles, popped into my mind. When you start to work with your creative mind, and go with the flow of love, anything is possible. Singing is a wonderful and natural way to lift up your spirits. Maybe this could be your song for today. Sing along, and notice how quickly you start to feel uplifted.

Whenever you recognise you are starting to feel unhappy within your mind, or you feel confused, weary or bogged down with anything, take a few minutes to give your mind a gentle nudge to focus on the good things that are happening in your life. We all need a little reminder sometimes to refocus our minds. Take some time out to refocus your mind before you go any further.

Sometimes you may need a distraction. One of my favourite pastimes is watching musicals, and uplifting movies. Some of my favourite inspirational movies are Sister Act, The Greatest Showman, Evan Almighty-Acts of Random Kindness, The Shift by Dr Wayne Dwyer and The Celestine Prophecy. Each one is uplifting and carries a really powerful message. They are movies you could watch time and time again, and each time you will feel uplifted and inspired.

It is important to give your mind a break from needing to process things, whether it is work or family commitments, or learning something new. Your mind needs a break. When you return to the tasks in hand you will feel more refreshed and ready to take the next step forward. Which movies could you watch to lift up your spirits and give your mind some much needed time out? Have some on hand for days when you do not know what else to do, or you need a little relaxation time or a boost.

So blessed

As I was coming to the end of finishing this manuscript, I was feeling very blessed, and within this wondrous feeling I was attracting more and more wonderful people into my life. I had completely forgotten about this wheel of happiness, when I was introduced to another like-minded soul called Ben Hunter. Within our conversation he reminded me of this simple, yet amazing technique for increasing our feelings of joy and happiness, so thank you Ben for coming into my life at the perfect time. This is such a simple method of increasing our feel-good feelings, yet I overlooked it.

Don't wait for everything to be in place in your life before you start to make changes. Keep it simple, and start right where you are today. Start with the things you have right now, and the rest will come naturally to you when you are ready. When you start going with the new loving flow of your life, you too will get exactly what you need at the perfect time.

Joy is your trigger

When you are thinking about, or doing, something that makes you feel joyful, you are fulfilling your purpose for yourself. Finding joy and happiness is the greatest gift you can give to yourself, to those around you, and to the world. Joy brings you the greatest relationship you could have with yourself.

Choose to follow the path of joy, and you will achieve your desired outcome. Your life's purpose is supported by the joy and passion you feel when you are working towards your purpose. Joy will bring you more harmony and passion, within every relationship and within every challenge and every task you do.

This passion will keep you motivated, and give you more energy. It helps you to see the good within what you are experiencing. It will give you the tenacity and the patience to keep moving forwards, even when it may seem unclear how things will turn out, or where you are going.

Joy has the power to remove obstacles on your path, and attracts to you what you really need. It also helps you to rise above suffering, and recognise you do not need to suffer. Let feeling joy be your purpose each day.

Living with joy in your heart, and within your body is the most precious gift you can give yourself. As you start to live in the feelings of joy you will attract towards you more and more opportunities to experience joy and love.

If you are struggling to find something which helps you to feel joy, call on Lord Maitraya, the Laughing Buddha. He will help you to find things which allow you to feel joyful. He will help you to feel joy within your precious body.

When you start to live a life filled with joy, the feelings of love and harmony will naturally start to flow for you. You will feel a new sense of lightness, and you will feel a new sense of freedom.

CHAPTER 5

THE START OF A NATURAL HEALING JOURNEY FOR YOU

IT IS HARD TO SEE the good in people around you, or in the situations you are in, when you are not happy with who you are. Your mind is like a compass, it can only take you in one direction at a time. Where are your thoughts leading you?

Your mind can only focus on one thing at a time. When you are not happy with one aspect of your life, it is hard to be totally content in any area of your life.

Your mind cannot separate whether what you are thinking about is happening in the past, present, or the future. Your mind cannot tell if you are actually in the situation now, or if you are just thinking about it. Your discontented mind cannot tell if what you are thinking about, is about you, or someone else. It just acts on the information you are focusing on.

Your mind cannot differentiate between what is the truth, or what has just become a pattern of thinking. The more you focus on something the more realistic it seems to you, whether it is good, bad, true or untrue, real or your imagination, in the past, present, or the future. Your mind does not know if you are talking about yourself, or about someone else.

What you are thinking about, and constantly giving attention to, will send your mind off on a journey of trying to process what you are thinking. Your mind will react by giving you a thought process, and your brain starts to create neurological responses to help you to deal with whatever you are focusing on. Is it any wonder it is hard to feel content, when the majority of what you are thinking about all day long is not even relevant to this moment in time.

This constant confused thinking is what can create and compound your feelings of tension, distress and anxiety. Throughout *Free to be Me*, I will take you on a gentle journey, to explore, firstly how you can start to correct your way of thinking to bring you an optimum state of mind, and quality of life. And then take you on a journey of self-discovery, to help you understand how your mind and your life has become so confusing. This will help you get a greater understanding of how your mind has been influenced and moulded.

I will also introduce you to the wonderful Bach Flower Remedies, because to me they are the greatest gift I have ever been given. The Remedies were the catalyst to helping me to start to change my life. The Remedies will help you to correct any emotions which are out of balance, and discover, and maintain a new uplifting perception of yourself, and of your life.

Healing you helps to heal your relationships

It is hard to have a contented relationship with other people, when you do not have a good relationship with yourself. By correcting, and healing the relationship you have with yourself, you will get a better quality of life in all of your personal and working relationships.

From this day, imagine your mind as a games console. You cannot play two games at the same time. You need to be able to delete one game, to allow the next one to start playing. To be able to step into the next step of your journey, you need to start to release your old way of thinking, to allow the new uplifting programme to start working for you. Throughout *Free to be Me*, I take you through gentle and natural ways to help you release the old programming in your mind which no longer serves you, to allow you to experience the new ways of thinking. As your thinking changes, you will start to flourish.

With your new ways of thinking, you can create a whole new way of life for yourself. When you can release the past and start to understand yourself, you can change your life. Take this gentle journey through '*Free to be me*', and discover the person you were born to be. You are going to go through a great time of transformation. Go with the flow and gently transform your life.

Keeping it simple really worked for me

Before I first started to use the Bach Flower Remedies I had never heard of them. I had no understanding of how they worked, and limited understanding of what each combination of Remedies would do for me. Carol Richardson, the beautiful lady who gave them to me, kept it really simple. She would say something like, 'This bottle of Remedies will give you more confidence,' or, 'This will help you to be more assertive.'

My life and my mind were so confused, that simplicity was as much as I could understand. The fact that this gentle lady wanted to help me, and had confidence in the healing power of the Remedies, was enough to lift me out of the hopeless place I was in. It wasn't long before I started to get my first spark of inspiration and an insight to how my life had become so confusing.

The healing process which followed over the next months was nothing short of a miracle. I was able to get more clarity about myself, and renewed hope and motivation. As my confidence grew I set about changing my life. My new perspective helped me to recognise that just because you have been put down does not mean you have to stay down. You can change anything when you are ready and willing to do so.

I am so very grateful to Carol Richardson for introducing me to the Remedies, and to Dr Bach for the amazing healing gift he has given us. My passion for the amazing Bach Flower Remedies never fades. Every day people are sent towards me for help and support, and the Remedies' healing qualities are infinite.

I have worked with countless people over the years, from young babies to those at the end of their lives, and it never ceases to amaze me how the Remedies can help anyone in so many profound ways. I have worked with individuals, in schools, colleges, healing centres and hospitals, and helped people of every age recognise how they can empower themselves, and get back on track if they have lost their way. Showing people how the Remedies can help them find renewed confidence, opens a new door, which allows them to see their true potential. It is through watching the amazing healing potential of the Remedies over the years, that I have felt inspired to write my version of a Bach Flower Remedy book, a guide to natural healing and joy.

I hope this book can reach people all around the world. People who I would never have the opportunity to meet. People from all walks of life who are ready to change their lives. This book can help each person reading it recognise how their life has become out of balance, and that they too have a choice, to make a decision to change any aspect of their life if they are not happy with it.

My wish would be that everyone should have an opportunity to bring their life into a natural state of harmony and peace. I believe everyone should have a choice to find out about the wonderful healing properties of the Bach Flower Remedies, and be able to choose to bring them into their lives. The quality of life they can bring you is priceless.

With so much confusion in the world, so much stress, depression and anxiety, and a massive increase in mental unwellness, conflict, and disease, more people are looking for natural alternative and complementary ways to help themselves. We are going through times of great changes and transformations, and it is more important than ever that we find a way to stay centred and feel empowered.

The simplicity of the Bach Flower Remedies is their natural appeal to so many nowadays. They don't cover up the problems. They gently help you to move from a place of mental confusion and emotional discomfort, to a place of greater understanding about yourself and your life. They enable you to feel empowered in every situation you meet.

CHAPTER 6

HOW DO THE BACH FLOWER REMEDY ESSENCES WORK?

THE FLOWER ESSENCES ARE MOST effective when they are ingested. When they are ingested they settle between the circulatory system and the nervous system. This creates an electro-magnetic current, which in turn sets in motion a sympathetic resonance to subtly correct disharmonious states of being.

There are other Flower essences which can also help with emotional states of mind, and states of dis-ease within the mind and body, such as the Australian Bush Remedies and the Essiac essences created by Rene Caisse. These are also both readily available through the internet.

For many years native cultures throughout the world have been using parts of herbs, plants, flowers and trees as Remedies to treat dis-ease. The Swiss doctor Paracelus (1493 to 1541) conducted experiments researching the properties of the early morning dew from plants to treat many dis-eased states.

Four hundred years later, Dr Edward Bach, a highly respected Harley Street doctor, created his range of 38 essences. Dr. Bach's 38 Flower essences were the first to be generally accepted, and are still widely available today for anyone to use. You can purchase them from many high street chemists, supermarkets, health food stores and through the internet. You can also have personal combinations of Bach Flower Remedies made for you by a Bach Flower Remedy practitioner.

How the essences of the Remedies are made

The stock bottles of the Bach Flower Remedy essences are created in two ways. Most of the more delicate Flowers are prepared using the 'sun method'. This involves floating the Flower heads in pure water for three hours, in direct sunlight. This transfers the energy vibrations of the Flowers into the water. This method is often referred to as potentisation. Woodier plants, and those that bloom when the sun is weak, are generally prepared by the 'boiling method'. The flowering parts of the plant are boiled for half an hour in pure water.

In both cases, once heat has transferred the energy in the flowers to the water, the energised water is mixed with an equal quantity of brandy. This mix is the called the 'Mother tincture'. The Mother tincture is further diluted into brandy (at a ratio of two drops of mother tincture to 30 ml of brandy) to make the stock bottles that you can purchase in the shops.

You can use the Remedies directly from the stock bottles, but apart from in extreme emotional states, it is recommended that the stock bottles are further diluted in a 30 ml sterile bottle, with a mix of ¾ mineral water to ¼ brandy or glycerine to preserve the mixture. The Remedies can be further diluted in water when you take them, or they are taken directly on the tongue.

Using Hahnemann's homeopathic principle, the more dilute the essence is, the stronger the potency becomes. So when you have your own bottles of essences you can dilute them even further to increase their healing efficiency.

What is a Flower essence?

It is a liquid plant, or gem preparation which carries a distinct imprint or pattern of a specific plant or Flower.

It is a vibrational method of treating a disharmonious emotional state, which is often the precursor to, or the potential for, dis-ease.

It is a completely natural and safe form of therapy.

How do the Flower Remedy essences work for you?

They help you to realise and utilise your own unique potential.
They work on a subtle level, making them very gentle in their action.
They help you to help yourself, but they cannot change those things you have no wish to change.

How is the best way to use them?

Before sleeping, and when waking up, are two most beneficial times to take your chosen Remedies, and the following doses some time during the day.
They can be taken on the tongue, or in water.
If circumstances permit, they are best taken on their own, or diluted in water.
They can also be added to other drinks and with meals, if this is more appropriate.
You cannot overdose on the Flower Remedy essences.
When choosing a Flower Remedy essence for you, trust your intuition. It is usually right.
The Bach Flower Remedy essences are not a replacement for any medical advice, treatment or medication you may need. You should always ask for some advice from your doctor when making any changes.

What are the benefits of taking the Bach Flower Remedies?

They allow you to look at, and acknowledge states of emotional disharmony and dis-ease with love and compassion, allowing the harmful dis-ease to fragment and melt away.
They gently release the need for control, and allow you to acknowledge and recognise all is as it is meant to be.
Encourage a more holistic approach to dealing with any dis-eased state.
They allow you to reconnect and rebuild anything which has become distorted or confused.
Help to transform your dis-eased state to harmony, and strengthen your potential for wellness.
They help to restore your faith in yourself, and in life.

They help to clear the way to re-connection with your true self, and all that is meant to be.

The essences help you to re-establish your vital life-force energy and motivation for life.

They allow you to refocus, and restore your sense of rhythm, and allow you to freely develop and manifest your future.

Before you move on with your journey of discovery

It is not negative or selfish to love yourself and put yourself at the top of your priority list. The more prepared you are to start respecting yourself, the easier it is to start going with the flow of changing your life. The more you start to love and appreciate yourself for who you are right now, the more prepared and ready you will be to move forward. As you love, nurture and respect yourself, others will start to adapt to love and respect you, too. It is as simple and profound as the rising and falling of the sea. One simply follows the other.

If people around you do not value or respect you, maybe this is the best time to start to make some changes. Start to talk more about how they make you feel. If you do not feel ready to talk write down your feelings in your journal. Maybe you can write a letter as if you are talking to them. Freeing up your mind of pent-up feelings can free you up to start healing your emotions.

Thank yourself for anything you recognise you need to change today, and then keep encouraging and praising yourself for the steps you take throughout the day. Always start and finish your day by counting your blessings, to encourage your mind to start living within a flow of gratitude and compassion.

Be gentle on you

Do not complicate life by the harsh thoughts and feelings you have about yourself. The harsher you are, the more hurt you feel, and the more confused you become.

The kinder and more loving you are, the more loved and valued you feel, and the more easily you will flow through life. It is the natural flow of nature. Choose to become a force of nature.

Bring the Bach Flower Remedies into your life. Let their natural healing bring you into the flow of love. Allow them to gently move you into the natural flow of your life.

How do you want to change your life?

Each day is a chance for you to be helping yourself to start again.
Each day count your blessings, take small steps forward, and encourage yourself with praise and gratitude.
This is your chance to shine.

CHAPTER 7

BREATHE

TODAY WE ARE GOING TO start with studying a simple change, which will almost instantly bring you a calmer mind, and a better quality of life. Are you breathing? Of course you are, or you would not be reading this. Let me re-phrase the question. Are you breathing properly?

Your body starts to become more relaxed when you gently change and adjust your breathing patterns. When you are stressed you have a tendency to take shallow rapid breaths. Shallow breathing when you are stressed can keep you in a constant state of stress, worrying, and even heightened anxiety.

Deeper gentle breaths can replenish and revitalise your whole body, and bring a calmer mind. There is one thing in life you cannot manage without. Your breath. But are you getting the most out of your breathing?

The majority of us breathe every day without giving a second thought to how valuable and precious this aspect of us is. We take our breath for granted, and give it the minimum of attention. Although our breathing happens naturally, we do not always breathe adequately. If you are breathing correctly, how deep your breathing is will usually depend on the activities you are doing. As a general guideline the more energy you are using, the more deeply you need to breathe. Taking slower, deeper breaths when you are doing strenuous work is more effective and beneficial for your body.

You may be familiar with a problem that can occur when you are exerting your body, using a lot of energy, and are still shallow breathing.

If you are shallow breathing and exerting your body, the oxygen which is carried by the red blood cells flows faster between the heart and the brain, and this can cause feelings of light-headedness and dizziness.

If you are tense and uptight, you should automatically start taking deeper, slow breaths, in and out. This would be more beneficial too when doing more strenuous exercises, or doing something which needs more concentration. But you don't always naturally do so.

Instead, you continue to take rapid, shallow breaths, which further create feelings of dizziness and light-headedness. The more stressed you become, the more rapidly the oxygen will flow, and the more disoriented you can feel. Your heart is beating faster, and you start to feel anxious. One of the feelings which can come from this is feeling anxious or panicky, often referred to as panic attacks.

Slow it down

Taking deeper, slower breaths can help you maintain, or regain your composure. It can help you to maintain calm, regardless of what you are doing, and it can also revitalise your energy whenever you are feeling tired, and your body is weary.

When you are stressed, your brain produces cortisol and adrenaline, which keeps your body and mind in a state of high alert, which then increases the tension in your body and adds to your feelings of being stressed. It can often seem hard to break out of this stressful cycle.

When you are caught up in this cycle of tension, parts of the brain are starved of energy flow, and can shut down. So then it becomes even harder to make the right decisions, which can then add to your frustration. Inappropriately, at the very time we need more breath and more calm, we naturally tend to hold our breath, or limit the amount of air we inhale by shallow breathing.

Unfortunately, nowadays, with more stressful situations being loaded onto us every day, many of us naturally breathe with increasingly shallow breaths. We spend a lot of our life shallow breathing into our upper part of the lungs, which can be adequate at times when we are quietly sitting reading a book or watching television, but totally insufficient when we are stressed.

As with exercising, when you are stressed, and taking shallow breaths, the heart pumps faster, and the blood flows more quickly from the heart to the brain. Again, this can cause feelings of light-headedness and dizziness. This, in turn, can make you feel even more stressed, and can even cause anxiety and panic attacks.

When in a constant state of stress we often do not take time to stop to readdress our shallow breathing, and so it gets progressively shallower. When another stressful situation occurs, it creates even more of a problem, with more stress and more tension, and even more rapid breathing. It can become a vicious cycle.

Start making the simplest and most effective change today. Slow down, and deepen your breathing to give you the best possible chance to deal with whatever shall come your way.

Take it a stage further, by thanking your breath as it flows. Then thank your lungs for the precious work they do for you. Follow this through, by saying, 'Thank you' to other parts of your body your attention is brought to.

Go with the flow of gratitude, and do not try to process, or think too much about where your attention is drawn to in your body. Your body will show you where it needs attention. The more you thank your breath and your body, the more uplifted you will feel.

My understanding is, that every cell in your body has a consciousness, and responds to how you treat it. If you disregard your body, and take it for granted, it will feel dejected and unloved. Start to make radical changes for yourself today, by acknowledging the precious gifts your breath and your body bring you, and you will be going with the flow of love and gratitude. The more you get into this gratitude flow, the more your self-worth and feelings of well-being will flourish.

Activating your energy flow

Whenever you feel tired, take a few moments to gently tap on your thymus gland. Your thymus gland is just above your heart, and below your throat.

Tap on this point for a few moments. This releases an energy flow into your arms and your heart. The more you tap on this point, the more the energy then flows into the rest of your body.

If you have aches or pains in other parts of your body, gently tap in the area where there is discomfort. This can help to gently release stagnant energy, increase your circulation, and help bring you some pain relief. It can also help you to feel more energised.

If you have chronic pain, gently tap on the area around where the pain is, to start your circulation moving. If it hurts too much, gently place your hand on the point of the pain, and do gentle circular movements with the palm of your hand. Being gentle on yourself can be far more effective, as your body responds to the kindness you are giving it. Anything you do to release some of your pain, will increase your feelings of well-being.

THE REMEDIES BRING RELIEF

The Bach Flower Remedies can also help you create, and maintain new ways of dealing with stress.

You can get relief from any symptoms of stress with the support of the Remedies. The more you use them, the more relief you will get. The Remedies will not only help you to heal your feelings, they will help you maintain new more uplifting thoughts and feelings. As your emotions start to feel less intense your mind is more able to see solutions.

This is where my real healing journey began

One of the most common results of feeling stressed, and not being able to see a way through, is suffering with panic attacks. Panic attacks often come about because you are in a constant state of stress and anxiety, and often consumed by worrying and fears.

Feeling anxious and panicky had felt like a major part of my life for many years. I found it hard to separate the feelings of panic from who I really was. At some stage, I almost felt resigned to the fact this was just the way it would always be, and I just had to learn to manage these frightening experiences with medication, until I started to take back control of my breathing and my mind.

When you are panicking, the heart starts to beat faster to help you deal with the stress you are going through. The blood rushes up to your head, and causes you to feel light-headed. As your heart pumps faster and your head feels dizzy, it brings an even deeper feeling of fear and distress. There is too much oxygen flowing too quickly from the heart to the brain.

When you are in a state of stress, a part of your brain shuts down, and you can find it impossible to make any rational decisions. Your stomach can feel cramped, and the palpitations in your heart are fuelled by the surge of adrenaline and cortisol flowing through you.

The gentlest way to start to calm down any stress, anxiety or a panic attack is to take your attention to your breathing, and start slowing down your breathing with deep shallow breaths.

You could place your hands cupped gently over your mouth and nose, to reduce the intake of oxygen. Breathe slowly into your hands, and very slowly breathe in again. Keep the very deep, slow breaths flowing until you feel the calm resume.

I used the Bach Flower Remedies alongside my new breathing techniques, and within a few weeks I was able to start feeling more in control of what was happening to me and my body each day.

Every day I would say thank you to my Remedies as I took them, and throughout the day I would think about, or say how grateful I was to have my bottle of Remedies. Throughout the day I would say 'Thank you' to my Remedies for the support and help they were giving me. The Remedies were truly my saviour. They gave me something to believe in, and helped me to start believing in myself again. The stronger this insight became, the more my feelings of self-worth would grow.

Through this self-belief I started to get glimpses of who I really was, and the more I used them, the more I started to like and even love myself. Through this new insight, anything seemed possible.

Take a moment to say 'Thank you' to your Remedies as you take them, and notice how much more uplifted you start to feel when you trigger this feeling of gratitude. If you take your Remedies in water, say thank you to the water as well. The more feelings of gratitude you experience the more uplifted you will feel and the more you will be supporting yourself.

Please stop right now

Take a deep, slow breath, right down into your tummy. Hold it for 4 seconds, and then, very slowly, release your breath to a count of 4.

Very slowly, breathe in again to a count of 4, hold it to a count of 4, and slowly release to a count of 4. Thank your breath as it flows.

Repeat this for about six breaths, or until you feel calmness flowing through your mind and your body. This helps you to release stress and anxiety.

You could place your hands on your tummy, and feel your hands rising and falling with each breath.

Giving your mind something to focus on distracts you from the stressful situation you were experiencing.

You do not have to feel stressed to feel the benefit of doing this exercise.

The more you practise this, the more prepared your body will be to deal with anything stressful which comes along. Thank your body for the calmness it is bringing you.

Encourage yourself to take deeper and slower breaths frequently throughout the day, and then thank yourself for doing so.

Rescue Remedy can help with extreme stress, tension, anxiety and panic attacks. It is often the first effective combination of Remedies to use, to bring calm, and a release from the stress and traumatic feelings you are experiencing. You may need other Remedies to complement the Rescue Remedy, but using the Rescue Remedy is a good place to start for most people. It can help to bring calm and courage to most situations. It can be used as a preventative too, before an impending situation you are worrying about.

Breathe to control your stress

Do not wait until you feel stressed or panicky. Start practising taking deeper shallow breaths throughout your day. You need to slowly breathe, deep down into the lower part of the lungs, which then expands the diaphragm and stomach muscles. As you breathe in, push your breath out in to the back of your lungs too.

The oxygen can then flow more easily and gently to the other parts of your body. Breathing deeper, and more slowly will help alleviate the sudden rush of oxygen to the brain, which occurs when you are shallow breathing and suddenly become more stressed.

If you do start to feel stressed, practise breathing more slowly and deeply, and start to notice and acknowledge how your deeper slow breathing helps you to deal with your stress.

Slow deep breaths will help bring you back to a place of calmness. The slower and deeper your breaths are, the less stressed you will feel, and the quicker calm will come to you.

Rapid breathing creates more stress, whereas calmer, slow deep breathing creates a calmer state of mind, and brings a less stressful way of being.

Your body is not designed to breathe deeply all of the time, but when you start to practise deeper breathing, it will help you whenever you start to feel anxious or stressed. It will help you to start to create a safety technique which will support you whenever you feel a stressful sensation coming into your body.

You are exploring new, more beneficial ways of working through your life. You are creating new patterns for your mind to work with, and creating new muscle memories within your body. The more you practise these new habits, the more efficiently your body will automatically respond to anything stressful in your life.

Consciously start to be aware of your breathing throughout the day, and start to alternate slow shallow breaths with deep slower breaths. Thank yourself and thank your body each time your awareness is brought to your breathing and its need for change. Your body will often get your attention by showing you pain and discomfort.

Do not wait until you are stressed to start changing the way you breathe. Start now. Praise yourself for the changes you are making. Through your breath you are creating a new pattern of improved self-esteem and self-worth. The more you acknowledge and work with this, the easier it will be to go with a more natural flow of healing yourself.

Start taking slower, deep breaths frequently throughout the day, just so you can get the sensation of how much more relaxed your body can feel. Start to notice when you are holding your breath, when you are tired, when you feel out of breath, when you are stressed. One of the signs of being stressed is holding your jaw rigid. Notice if you are doing this, and bring your attention to your breaths to alleviate this tension in your jaw.

Randomly, throughout the day, take a few deep breaths in and out, to see what a difference it can make. Notice how it can calm your mind and revitalise you. The more you practise deeper, slow breaths as a way of relaxing your body and mind, the more naturally it will start to happen when you meet a stressful situation.

Use your healing journal to record any situations where you notice you start to feel stressed. Make a note of how your new breathing patterns soothed and calmed you. How many breaths did it take before calm resumed? Make a note of the date you started to work with each situation which creates stress for you. Praise yourself for the way you have helped and supported yourself today.

If you feel your body tensing up, take a few slow deep breaths into your stomach. Recognise how many breaths you need, to find, and feel the calmness again. Taking your attention to your breathing also distracts your mind from the stressful situation you are dealing with.

Use an affirmation which reassures your mind, and starts to create a calmer way of thinking about your situation. You could start with something as simple as, 'I am embracing feeling calm' as you breathe in, and 'I am feeling safer', as you slowly breathe out.

If you practise this throughout the day, your mind will start to recognise this as a comfortable and more natural way to deal with stress. Remember you are overriding old patterns, and the more you practise, the more easily your mind will start to adapt to these new ways of coping.

Combine your deep breaths with a grounding exercise. Stamp your feet on the ground, and start to feel the tingling sensations in your feet and legs. There is a grounding exercise coming up for you. Thank your body for this new way of feeling more relaxed and centred.

Remember, the slower your breaths are, the more quickly calm will resume. You could carry grounding crystals such as citrine, rose quartz, smoky quartz, tourmaline and black obsidian to ground yourself too. The crystals resonate with your energies and help you to maintain your feelings of being supported, safe and grounded.

Drink more water

Drink more water to help you re-energise your body. Stress can seriously dehydrate your body and limit your ability to think clearly and rationally. Drinking some water can help your body deal with the stress. Drinking water helps to energise your whole system, including your nervous and your skeletal system. Often when you are tired, it could be that your body is dehydrated. Drinking more water can energise you on so many levels, and it helps you to have more clarity and maintain concentration. When your body or your mind feels tired, take a drink of water to bring yourself back to a more receptive and productive state.

Breathe slowly when you think

Practise breathing more slowly and deeply when you are thinking. This will allow your mind time to process your thoughts as you think. Your thoughts will flow more fluently and calmly. You will be able to maintain a sense of calm, regardless of what you are thinking about or addressing. From this calmer place your mind will start to bring you solutions. It is often hard to see solutions when your mind is so consumed by stress.

When you feel stressed or anxious, distract your thoughts by thinking of something which brings you happiness, and then gently tap on the centre point on your forehead, just above your eyebrows. Keep thinking of your happy thoughts. Continue tapping and breathing until calmness comes.

Take this a stage further. Practise breathing more slowly and deeply when you are talking. This will allow your mind time to process your thoughts as you talk. Take a breath between thoughts, to allow you time to process what you are talking about, and the recipient time to process your words too. Your words will come across more fluently and calmly. You will maintain a sense of calm, regardless of what you are speaking about or addressing.

You will have more fluent and productive conversations. You will be perceived by others as being calmer and more assertive. When you speak calmly and boldly, other people will take what you have to say more seriously, because you are presenting your thoughts with composure, and so the message comes across with a greater impact. You will feel more empowered because you have maintained calm, and got your message across in a more constructive way.

We will use your breath as a tool throughout this book- it's a tried and trusted, long established technique to manage your mind and your body. Remember to compliment yourself as you go.

CHAPTER 8

SIMPLE SIGNPOSTS

THERE MAY BE TIMES WHEN you struggle to find joy in your day, or are unable to see a way forward. Take some time to create a simple technique to give you a starting point each day. We all sometimes need some direction on which way to go. The simpler you keep your journey, the easier it will be to take the necessary steps forward.

Take a piece of paper or card. Cut it up into smaller rectangles. On each rectangle write an inspirational word or thought for today. These are your new inspirational cards, and a good starting point for each day. Anytime during the day when you need some inspirational guidance pick one of your cards as a guideline.

Each day, pick one of the cards to use as a starting point in your day. What does your card say to you? What do you need to focus on today? Keep the card near you throughout the day to remind you where you need to prioritise and focus your thoughts and actions.

Here are a few ideas to get you started. I am choosing peace, I am choosing joy, I am relaxing, I am joyfully listening, I joyfully let it go, I gently take deeper breaths, I am proud of myself, I am feeling confident. What other thoughts could you write on your inspirational cards?

> *Every day in every way I am getting stronger.*

> *Today I . . . . .*
> *Stay focussed*

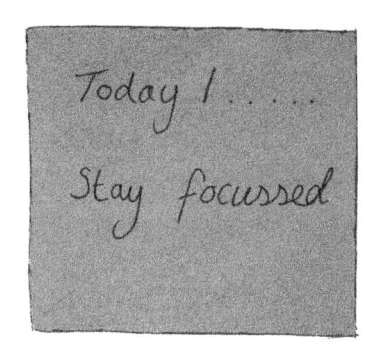

Choose words which you can relate to. Add the thoughts which you know you need to work on. Keep adding to your list of inspirational words as other thoughts pop into your mind. As you read through this book, other thoughts and affirmations may come into your mind. Allow your pack of cards to grow as you grow.

If ever you feel like you are unsure of yourself, your feelings, or what you are experiencing, intuitively choose another card to bring you a new focus for the day. Continue to use your cards to bring you more clarity and a renewed perspective. The more you work with your cards, the more you will start to trust in the power of your own ability to help yourself. You are working on trusting your intuition to guide you, and giving your mind a positive focus to start working with. You are creating a new way of supporting yourself.

Keep praising yourself for the steps you have taken. Thank yourself, and take a few moments to count your blessings before you move on. Remember, the more you appreciate yourself and the actions you take, the more you will increase your feelings of self-worth and self-belief.

When you have more time, you could decorate your cards with a simple picture, or a colour. Doing something creative helps to expand the creative part of your mind, which helps you to start seeing new possibilities and solutions, instead of just the challenges and problems. Being creative can help you to relax your mind, and from this more relaxed space you can tap into your inspirational ideas and insights.

Remember, when you give your mind a direction to follow, it starts to work with you, to take you towards what you are thinking about.

Set your desires in action. Tell the universe what you desire. It all starts with the thoughts you choose.

Do you thrive with stress?

Some of you may be experiencing the stress of dealing with one, or many emotional imbalances in your life. For every emotional imbalance that is not addressed, it can create a small amount, or a great deal of stress, constantly throughout your day. If there is any stress, whether it is minor or major stress, your brain produces cortisol and adrenaline, which enables you to keep functioning through your daily life. Whilst this can be fine for short spells, after a while your body can feel more constantly or frequently under attack from the continuous flow of adrenaline and cortisol.

Some people, some personalities, may thrive on stress, but the majority of people under constant stress end up tired, tense and even anxious or depressed. It is when your body is under constant tension and stress that you can lose your body's natural ability to fix itself. It is often when we ignore the initial signs that our mind or body is suffering, that stress can manifest as something bigger like a panic attack, meltdown or illness.

Even if you have reached that point of saturation, there is still so much you can do to help yourself right now. Start with changing your breathing patterns, and follow the gentle steps I will take you through. Even learning something new can seem stressful at first. Drink plenty of water to help your mind function more effectively, and walk away from your book for a while if you need to. It is better to learn small steps at a time and put them into practise.

Did you know that the average mind can only process and digest twenty minutes of learning at any one time before it needs a break? Thank yourself for recognising when your mind is feeling tired, and give yourself a break. Choose to do something which feels good to you. Every small steady step will bring you great results.

Yawn, stretch, shake it out. (YSSiO)

Yawning can help you release tension and de-stress your brain and your body. Whenever you feel any tension in your body take a moment to take a deep breath, stretch out your body, and then shake the tension out of your body. This is a natural way to increase your circulation and release tension.

Sometimes you may feel an urge to yawn. Yawning is your body's natural way of expanding air deep into your lungs to increase the amount of oxygen flowing through your body. After yawning take a moment to shake out your body, and release any stress, out through your fingertips and through your feet.

When you stretch open your jaw to yawn, it improves the circulation to your brain, which in turn lowers its temperature. When you are stressed the temperature in your brain increases, so yawning helps to reduce the temperature. It is your body's natural way to cool you down during times of stress and pressure.

If you find yourself yawning excessively, it could be a sign that you need to breathe deeper, and more slowly, to cool down and de-stress your brain, and increase the flow of oxygen to your body. Yawning often happens when you are feeling bored, under stimulated, tense, stressed or even too hot. You may even feel a need to yawn when you are trying to concentrate. Allow it to happen, and your brain will do its own natural healing process of regenerating your mind and your body. Yawning can be a great way of releasing tension and keeping you alert.

If you do notice yourself yawning excessively, and it feels like it is happening far too often, take some time to seek some medical advice. It could be a sign that something needs to be addressed.

Releasing trapped energy

Yawning can be your body's natural way of calming your body from stress. If you feel anxious, panicky, or you feel like you just cannot pull yourself together, it is usually because you are all up in your head, and thinking far too much.

Try this simple exercise. It will calm your nervous system, and can help to reverse problems. This can help with headaches, lowering blood pressure, tension, stress, skin conditions, and insomnia.

Put one finger in your navel, and another finger just above your eyebrow line, your third eye, and then push in, and pull them both upwards. Hold this position for a few moments, as you take deep breaths in, and out.

You may feel sensations of warmth or tingling flowing through your body, and this is natural. Your body is gently releasing the stress and tension. This will help you increase the flow of energy through your nervous system.

Do this exercise each morning, before you get out of bed, to set up your body for the day. Repeat this again throughout the day, and always do it before you go to sleep at night. Each time you do this exercise, swiftly follow it through with thinking of a happy thought. Think of something which makes you feel happy.

As you hold this thought, gently tap on your third eye, the point just above your eyebrow line, and breathe. This increases your flow of happy feelings through your body. When your body is flowing with happy emotions, there is no room for stress and unhappiness.

Throughout Free to be Me, I have included many different exercises which will have a similar healing effect. Try out each of the exercises, and bring the ones which feel most effective to you, into your daily life. They will all be effective, but each person may have a preference to which ones they prefer to use. As your journey progresses, you can incorporate more of the exercises into each day. Remember you always have a choice. What may not seem right for you today, may be more beneficial at a later date.

The more you recognise what is right for you, the more you are acknowledging your needs, and the more in tune you are becoming with you. Take a few moments to start your day saying how well you are doing, and how great you look. Praise yourself for every step you take and nurture yourself through every challenge you meet.

Continue to compliment yourself each day, and throughout your day. You can change your day with your compliments. Do not wait around for others to compliment you, or to recognise how good you look today, or how well you are doing.

Start this day with a compliment, and allow the wonderful warm nurturing feelings to start to flow through your body. Every kind word you say to yourself will make a difference. You can change your world with the words you choose to use today.

You could take it a stage further, by thanking yourself for recognising your true beauty. We all need compliments to lift us up and warm our soul. Become your own best cheerleader from today.

Mirror talk

The next time you look in the mirror, look towards your feet first, and then run your eyes up your body, towards your head. This helps to increase the energy flows up through the meridians in your body.

You could increase this flow, by placing your hands down by your side, and then sweeping your hands up in front of you, towards your head. The more you practise this, the more you will lift up your energies, and your feelings of well-being.

You can enhance your happiness feelings, by saying an uplifting compliment to yourself as you look at your reflection in the mirror. This will help to increase your feelings of self-worth. Combine this with an affirmation which will carry you through the day.

Are you feeling fearful, anxious or stressed?

When you feel stressed, anxious, or fearful about something, it is hard to focus on anything else. A simple technique, to help you work through your fears and stressful times, is to gently rub your eyes. This helps to release chemicals which will help to alleviate your fears.

Gently rub your eyes with the back of your fingers. Do this very gently for a few seconds, or for a few minutes, depending on how fearful or anxious you have been feeling.

At the same time, breathe slowly into your tummy, as you say to yourself, 'I feel safe'.

You can repeat this as often as you feel it is necessary.

Do you sometimes feel like you want to shut the world out?

It is a natural response, to want to shut yourself away from the world when you feel anxious.

As soon as you start to realise your fear or anxiety levels are rising, take some time to cup your hands over your eyes for a few minutes.

Place your fingertips together on the centre of your forehead. As you cover your eyes, take deep, slow breaths into your tummy. Hold your breathe, and slowly release.

Think of a colour, and breathe that colour into your breaths. Feel the tension and fears start to gently subside.

You can repeat this simple exercise many times through the day, to help support your mind and your body through fearful or worrying times.

You can choose to do these two exercises together, or at separate times during the day, whenever you feel the need to close down your mind for a few minutes. As you do either of these exercises, your anxiety, stress and tension will gently start to calm down. The more you practise this, the easier it will be to alleviate your fears and anxieties.

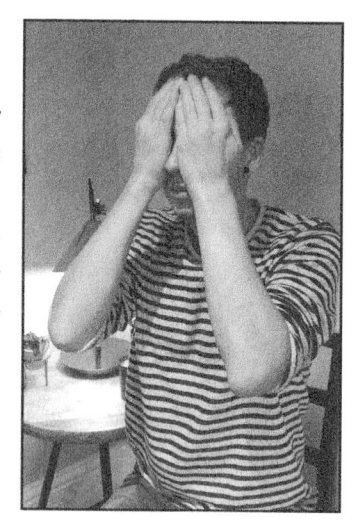

When your mind and your body are free from anxiety, you will feel calmer, and be able to get more clarity and renewed confidence in yourself. All of the techniques within your book *Free to be Me,* are this simple. Take yourself through a gentle journey of discovery. Gently peel away the patterns of thinking, and behaviour which no longer serve you, to reveal the person you are destined to be.

Take yourself to a safe place

Think of something for which you are truly grateful. Something which makes you smile. It could be a person, a pet, a memory, or a favourite place. Take a moment, to notice those warm fuzzy feelings you have inside your mind, and inside your tummy. These are your feelings of inner peace and contentment. Your body is starting to create feelings of peace and happiness through your thoughts.

Take yourself through gentle steps, and natural techniques, to help you find your inner contentment and happiness each day. When you can peel away the layers of false beliefs, and the stress and tension you carry in your precious body, you can get in touch with your natural inner contentment and happiness, and discover the person you were born to be.

Would you like to peel away the layers of false illusions, make new choices each day, and reveal who you are meant to be?

When you have just a few minutes to spare in your day, randomly open this book at any page, and see what your higher self is calling you to work on today. This will help you to work on trusting your intuition, your higher self.

Start to listen to, and work more closely with your higher self, and you will soon start to get back in touch with your true self.

Never too late to help yourself

If illness or disability has overtaken your body, do not despair. You can still follow the natural steps, and you can still achieve a better quality of life for yourself.

We all come to moments in our lives, where suddenly things do not make any sense. What we believed to be true until now, does not feel comfortable any more. More often than not we disregard these signs, and carry on struggling through life, trying to make the best of it. It is often through critical moments in our life, that we have a real wake up call, and reality fully sets in. Unfortunately, it is often only through illness, accidents or other radical changes like loss of a job or a loved one, that we stop to reassess what is really happening in our lives.

I want to say, you always have a choice to make changes. It does not matter if you started to have this feeling of unrest a week ago, or years ago, you can start to make changes today.

Do you need to wait until you start to feel unrest within you? No. Start to make simple changes today, and you will become the creator of your own future. When you step up, and start to make some simple changes, you will feel more empowered and in control of your life. Your life becomes what you think about. Are you happy with the life you are creating? Is this the life you desire, or the life you have settled for?

Thank yourself for noticing where you need to make changes. Make a note in your healing journal of what you want to change. Every day, start your day with your gratitude plan, and your new goal for today. Every day is a new chance to reset your intentions. Anything you do for yourself will benefit your emotional and spiritual well-being. Many people I know have turned their mind-set and their life around, and expanded their life span, just because they decided they wanted a better quality of life, and made some simple changes.

Keep it simple. Acknowledge how you feel, breathe deeper, sing inside your mind, or out loud, and drift gently back into the flow of your day.

Often, a breakdown within your body can be turned into a breakthrough. You can turn your life around, one gentle step at a time. What, if we consider for a moment, that everything which has happened to you has been for a reason.

At the moment, you may see only obstacles which keep you from growing. If you are not happy within this place you find yourself, you can choose to go deeper into the hole of avoidance, and maybe even start to feel disillusioned, with yourself and with your life.

Or you can treat what has happened as a new opportunity. Start to see this moment of realisation, as an opportunity to start to evolve and grow, a new chance to turn your life around.

How do you see the experiences you have been through?

Today is your chance to turn your experiences, and your viewpoint around, to create the life you choose.

Use your healing journal to make a note of any changes you would like to make. Make a note of the date too, so you can monitor any observations you make, and your progress.

The Bach Flower Remedies ELM, GENTIAN, GORSE, and SWEET CHESTNUT will help you if you feel overwhelmed by the changes you need to make, and bring you more optimism, renewed hope and renewed inspiration and insight.

WILD ROSE will help lift you out of any feelings of apathy where you have lost the motivation to make changes. It will bring you inner drive and motivation.

We all need a little boost sometimes, and the Remedies will bring you an uplifting state of mind which will help you to move forward. ELM helps you to break down the changes you need to make, and brings you the renewed ability to cope, one step at a time.

My oldest client, Marjorie, was sixty-eight when she first came to meet me. She was lost, angry, confused and fit to burst. She had lost her way due to various significant traumas over a period of time, and her feelings had made her feel unwell. We talked through her situation and before long uncovered the feeling and events that she had previously tried to bury.

She recognised that she hadn't fully processed the events, and allowed herself time to heal. Without doing so, she couldn't break the cycle of anger, depression, stress, feeling guilty and less than worthy. When she started working with the Bach Flower Remedies, and incorporating the powerful techniques I am sharing with you, she created a whole new way of life for herself. The Remedies gave her the ability to grow and move forward by bringing her renewed clarity, motivation, and a whole new zest for life.

She learnt to adapt to a new way of understanding that we cannot go back in time to change our life, or the mistakes we have made. And that we cannot make others be happy. She was able to acknowledge that each person is responsible for their own spiritual well-being and happiness, and no other person can make that happen for them. This understanding gave her the freedom to choose her new way of life.

She moved all around the country, and did all the things she wanted to do before she departed from this earth. At the end of her life she went to the other side knowing she had done her best, accomplished what she wanted to, and knowing she would meet with her loved ones again. She was happy and more peaceful within herself, and had a greater understanding of what her life experiences had been about. That was a great place for her to be when her life on this earth ended.

Anything you do to heal yourself on this earth can enable your soul to be freer to move on. At whatever stage of life you are in when you start to make those changes, today is the perfect time to start.

We must all remember that the one thing you cannot do is turn back time. But you can choose to create a life that is more compatible with who you are now, and who you are destined to be in the future.

How stressed do you feel at this moment?

Would you like to bring back some peace and harmony into your mind, and your body?

Do you want to explore a way to bring some inner strength and self-belief back into your life?

Listen to your inner calling, and nurture and encourage yourself as you take this new journey today.

Remember to listen to yourself, to your body and its pains, and act now to improve your situation, one step at a time.

On a scale of 1 to 10, what is your level of stress at the moment? What is today's date? Make a note of this, and keep checking what your level of stress is throughout the day.

The more you work with your gentle breathing exercises, the more your stress levels will go down. The more you work on yourself, the more you increase your feelings of self-worth. As you increase your feelings of self-worth, your feelings of well-being will naturally follow.

Marjorie's Message

*No matter how much fame and fortune you create,
If you do not feel content with who you are inside your mind,
It will never be enough.*

*Never compare yourself with anyone else,
Or compromise your needs to please another.*

*The world is your oyster, when you can see the jewel in every experience.
The growth in your soul is beyond compare, and
the love that you feel is priceless.*

*When you can find the balance between striving for something new,
and being at one with yourself, you will have all the abundance you need.
When you find your passion for life, and love what you do,
you have found the joy of life, the fountain of love.*

*The true meaning of life is finding your happiness within.
Nothing can ever touch it, or take it away.
When you love who you have become,
and you love every step of the journey you take,
you have found your inner peace.*

This is your journey,
and only you can love yourself enough to make this life complete.

When you find your inner happiness, and your mind is at peace,
your heart will be full, and your soul will rejoice.

Your world will be complete, and you too will feel complete

Are you sitting at a crossroads?

Today, maybe you recognise you've been sitting at a crossroads for some time, and do not know which way to go. Maybe there's something stirring inside you, which says, 'I am not truly happy, I am not content any more.'

Have you lost your inner peace? Have you lost your sense of who you are?

Before we go ahead, please pat yourself on the back. Give yourself the recognition that you picked up this book today, and that you have chosen to look at a different insight into your life.

The insights and the solutions brought to you through the healing powers of the Bach Flower Remedies, and through a greater understanding of yourself, will help you to find your inner peace and happiness. You will start to recognise what no longer serves you, and be able to recognise and acknowledge where you have gone wrong. But let's not focus on where you have gone wrong; let's look at how you can help yourself today.

This is your new day

'*Free to be me*' will bring into your life the insights that you need. It will expand your thinking through your higher self, to help you recognise that today is the day when you can make a new choice. The choice to step up and to be yourself.

Please choose today, to take a deep breath in, followed by another and another, and recognise how precious and free flowing that breath is. And, just as naturally as your breath flows each day, you can choose to change the thoughts and feelings which flow through your precious body.

Thank your body for every breath it takes. Thank your breath for the gift of life it brings you. When you start to live with an attitude of acknowledgement and gratitude, you will automatically start to lift up your spirits. Being, and feeling grateful, is one of the quickest ways to lift up the energy vibrations in your body.

How much do you take for granted, that you can start to be grateful for today?

Saying 'Thank you', kick-starts your brain to begin producing the feel-good chemicals. It's a natural chain reaction to feeling grateful, and a wonderful way to kick-start every moment of every day. Even when it seems like there is nothing to be grateful for, or when a challenge presents itself, take a moment to say, 'Thank you for this challenge'. It may sound crazy, but when you say 'Thank you', you are starting to create a new muscle memory pattern within you, which then starts to lift up your spirits and comforts your body.

This feeling, then helps your mind to start rising above the situation you are dealing with, and enables you to start seeing solutions. Saying 'Thank you' for this lesson, helps your mind to start looking for the good within the situation, so you are further supporting your body by raising up your energy vibration.

Remember, when you are frustrated with a situation, you trigger off more stress chemicals, and your mind goes back into old similar patterns of thinking, and behaviour to help you deal with your current situation. When you say 'Thank you', you trigger off a release of softer, soothing and healing chemicals which starts to support your body, your mind and your soul.

Every positive step you take to help yourself, will increase your feelings of self-worth, and will also start to trigger more feelings of being empowered. As you feel more empowered, your self-worth raises up again, and your own self-belief and self-esteem will flourish.

Which thought pattern do you want to follow? Which one will help you to move forward today?

As I started to retrain my mind to look for the good within each opportunity, I didn't need to say 'Thank you for the challenge'. I started to say 'Thank you. That's interesting'.

Every day, when I was presented with a challenging situation, or I was about to react to something, I took a deep breath, and said to myself, 'Thank you. That's interesting'. This gave my mind a few moments to go to a calmer place, and show me a more appropriate way of dealing with what was happening. It did take me some time before I could discipline myself to not react, and many times I still did totally over-react, saying things, or doing things I totally regretted.

But by gently retraining myself to say, 'That's interesting', I was giving my mind, and myself some space to start to retrain my mind to start thinking in a more appropriate way. It took some time to re-learn a new way of being, but the more I practised this, the more uplifted I started to feel. The better I felt, the less I felt a need to react.

Start to make this simple change in your life today. When you are presented with a challenging situation, or when you sense you are going to react in an inappropriate way, take a moment to say to yourself, 'That's interesting'. This gives you a brief respite moment, for your mind to observe what is happening, reset itself, and respond in a more appropriate way.

Today, when you make each new choice, you can step beyond the chaos, into your inner peace and into a new way of life for yourself.

We are privileged that you are sharing and embracing the healing journey that you are taking. Dr Bach and I, and all the beautiful people that I've met on my journey have brought me to this place, where I recognise that the majority of us are all too hard on ourselves: we have great expectations, and are never satisfied with what we have achieved, and how far we have come. We are constantly striving to be somewhere, or to be something else, but never reaching a place where we are feeling totally satisfied. Lasting happiness seems to be an illusion which we cannot quite reach.

Today, I ask you to please embrace the beautiful person that you are, and how well you have done to get this far.

Start to respect you and your body

Which way will you go today? Recognise that this physical body you have been given, is a gift which carries your soul and your spirit. It carries you forward every day. More often than not, you criticise and take for granted this physical body. You disrespect, and disregard its need for calm, and peaceful love and nurturing.

'We give you a question: 'What if today you could change your life? What if today you could step up and be a brand new person?'

'We are not saying there is anything wrong with you. We are saying you may have gone off track, and this, my friend, is the uneasy feeling you have stirring deep inside you.'

'An uneasy feeling where you feel dissatisfied, you feel unrest, you feel unsettled within your heart, your body and your soul. You have an unsettled feeling that something is not quite right.'

'Maybe you feel that you have lost your way, or even lost yourself. Maybe you get a deep feeling there should be more to life'

Let me say, 'Today, you are enough'.

Today if you need to, and are ready and willing, you can change your life. Today, choose to step into your inner peace. Step in and listen, listen to your heartbeat, your breath, your body, your pain.

They are telling you something: they are telling you how you can help yourself. They are calling you to help you recognise where you need help, and to encourage you to come to a place where you can find more inner peace and contentment. Stop and listen.

Some of your pains may remain with you. They will bring you a greater compassion for yourself. Stop for a moment, and recognise that each cell of your body has a consciousness which needs nurturing and tenderness. When is the last time you had compassion for your body and its pain?

Do you criticise and condemn the way you are, and the actions you take? When is the last time you had compassion for yourself?

Please step up this day. This is the day when you can change your life. This is the day to start giving compassion to yourself.

Start to find within you, the love that you have been seeking from around you.

Can you feel love for yourself at this moment? Start giving yourself love, give yourself tenderness and respect, and give yourself the care and the nurturing that you seek from outside. And from this place, you will find your inner peace. You will find the beautiful person that you were born to be. Listen carefully, for your body is telling you where and how you can change.

This is the beginning of a brand new journey for you. Embrace not only the journey, but the crossroads you are sitting at.

9 simple things you can do for yourself each day, starting today.

Start each day with the intention of having a good day.

Take a few moments before you move out of your bed, to take some deeper gentle breaths, and to keep this flowing through your day. Breathe in 'deep inner peace' with every breath in, and then breathe out stress.

Use an uplifting joy-filled affirmation to start your day.

Acknowledge and give thanks for the blessings in your life, and smile as you think of those blessings.

Move gently out of your bed and stretch out your body. Thank your body as you move.

Drink some water, and make a choice to eat healthier food. Thank your water, and your food.

Recognise if you are using negative words through this day, and turn them around.

Empty your mind into your healing journal, and choose to talk to a friend if necessary.

Do 10 random acts of kindness today, for yourself, and for others.

When you start to acknowledge how important you are, and are ready to commit to helping yourself, you can turn your life around.

How can you simplify your life today?

Do you spend life in a constant whirl, of trying to fit as much as you can into a day? Do you stop to catch a breath, or appreciate just how stressed you are. What if you could slowly adjust life just a bit at a time, and achieve so much more?

Sometimes we need to stop and observe what is happening to us, to realise the impact of our actions. Maybe this is the time for you to stop and de-clutter your life. Where do you spend your time in your mind?

So, why have you picked up this book today? How do you want to make changes today? Are you ready to de-clutter your life?

The majority of us spend far too much time thinking about things which are keeping us in a place of discontent. This is such a waste of your time, of what could be valuable uplifting thinking and healing time in your life. If you start by changing your thoughts, and creating new thought patterns, your uplifting supporting actions will soon follow. Each day you can bring in a few simple changes and ideas, which will help you be far more productive and increase your feelings of well-being.

You could follow this through by valuing the time you have each day, and the way you use it. There may be things you could let go of, to give you some more quality time.

Become accountable

Take some time to write down which thoughts you can work on today in your healing journal. Are these thoughts holding you back?

Write down some new thoughts which could be more appropriate and uplifting. How could your thoughts help you to be more productive?

Take a few moments to think of something which brings you happiness, and then, using your finger tips, gently tap on the centre point on your forehead, just above your eyebrows. Keep thinking of your happy thoughts. Continue tapping and breathing until calmness comes.

Take it a stage further by gently tapping on your thymus point, the space between your heart and your throat, to increase your energy flow.

Did you know?

When you do something for yourself, your brain produces dopamine, which helps you to feel more contented, supported, and ready to move on. Then, as you take courageous steps, your brain produces motivational endorphins.

Transform your life, one step at a time

Congratulate yourself again for picking up this book today. Self-praise does make a difference. It does not matter if the praise is coming from around you, or from within you. You will feel supported by the choice of words you use.

What is happening in your life today, that has brought you to the place where you recognise you need to make some changes at the moment?

It can be the simplest things which can cause you to feel out of sorts. It often starts with a feeling deep inside, which says I do not feel happy with the way things are. It could be a feeling or sadness or disappointment, or everything I try doesn't seem to bring me a feeling of contentment.

It can feel like something is wrong, but you just cannot put your finger on what it is. It can feel like you are constantly reaching out and trying new things, but nothing brings you total satisfaction.

When something is feeling out of balance, life can seem very confusing, and sometimes it is hard to understand what you are really feeling.

Why are you feeling discontented today?

Let's break down what is happening to you. Start with today. What is causing you to struggle today?

It can often seem like the more you try, the more confusing life can feel. Let's start to focus on the cause of your feelings of dis-contentedness. First, read through the following list and consider which of these situations apply to you. Tick the ones you can relate to. This will help you to start to focus your mind on solutions. You need to acknowledge the problem to be able to readdress it.

You can also refer back to your list in the future to see how far you have progressed. Maybe there are other things going on which are causing you to feel out of sorts. Add anything to your list which is causing you to feel disharmony today.

Take out a notebook, and start to write down your thoughts.

What is niggling away at you?

Is it a lack of confidence, or are you feeling overwhelmed? Has life got on top of you, or got you down?

Are you struggling to get on top of things? Do you feel like the harder you try the more discontented you feel?

Are you struggling in school, at college, at work or in your relationship?

Do you find it hard to retain information, or stay focused on your tasks?

Do you get consumed by feelings of not being good enough? Are you lacking in confidence, or low self-esteem?

Does lasting happiness seem hard to reach? On a deeper level, do you feel lost, in pain, or are you feeling adrift in deep confusion?

Are you struggling to cope with the past, or an ongoing trauma? Are you desperately wanting to move past a painful event, but don't know how? Has life dealt you a sudden shock, or are you living in a constant state of trauma?

Do you feel that nothing brings you a feeling of complete satisfaction or inner peace? Are you successful at work, but never satisfied?

Are you in a potentially loving relationship, but feel disconnected, angry or empty inside? Do you find it hard to get in touch with those loving feelings?

Do you blame yourself for things which have happened? Do you berate yourself for things that have gone wrong?

Do you feel undervalued or unappreciated? Do you feel lonely, or that you don't belong? Do you have feelings of helplessness and frustration?

Have you lost sight of who you really are, or what you are meant to be doing with your life? Are you struggling to find peace in your mind today?

Be honest about how you feel right now. Write down the date against any observations you make about your life feeling out of balance. Leave some space so you can keep coming back to add anything else which is troubling you, and any observations and progress you make. Take some time to thank yourself for the things you notice are out of balance.

Only you can answer these questions today. Or can you?

Can you really identify what is causing you to feel uptight, stressed, anxious, frustrated or disillusioned?

Sometimes it is obvious what is causing your distress. But sometimes it is hard to identify what is causing you a problem, or an inner feeling of discontent. We become so ingrained in the patterns we have adopted we can lose sight of what is our reality.

My reason for creating this book, is because I have been through all of the above confusion. And through my own healing journey, the people close to me, and the clients and students I meet every day, I realised I wasn't the only one who was struggling with life. I want to share with you the experiences and the wisdom I have gathered, to help you explore how you too can turn your life around, especially if you feel you have lost your way.

Through my healing journey, I discovered something very powerful, which completely changed my perspective of myself, and the way I was seeing my life.

'Your mind is a very powerful piece of machinery, and it will repeatedly give you what you think about if you do not give it a new way of thinking'.

In the beginning, every workshop or natural healing therapy I tried, and every avenue, brought me back to the same message. I could change my life if I chose to change my thinking. Although I could hear what was being said to me, it took me a while before I really started to accept and work with this concept. There always seemed to be a reason to not work on myself. It seemed like anything and everything would get in my way.

It was during a very deep time of confusion, which led to yet another mental breakdown, that I was led down a path which was to change my life forever. I was introduced to the wonderful Bach Flower Remedies. The lady called Carol, who introduced me to these natural Remedies, said they would help me work through my confusion. She said I could take back control of my life by taking back control over my emotions. This felt like a life-line. Carol was saying similar things to all the other self-help books I had read, but this time I found that the significant, and crucial difference was, she was offering me something which could genuinely help and support me through the changes I needed to make.

She said the Remedies would help to soothe my emotional distress and turn my feelings around. I'm not sure if I really expected such a small dilute bottle of herbal Remedies to really help me. Nothing else had helped, but this seemed different. She genuinely believed in what she was offering me.

It was light-bulb moment, and suddenly I felt like there was a light at the end of a very dark tunnel. Carol said the Bach Flower Remedy SWEET CHESTNUT was the Remedy I needed to help lift me out of the dark emotional tunnel I felt trapped in. It wasn't just the situation I was struggling with, but the way I was thinking and feeling about it.

When I started to take the Remedies, and work with the idea I could heal my emotions, I now felt able to put into practise the other self-help techniques I had been learning. It seemed like the Remedies were the missing piece of my jigsaw. As the Remedies started to take effect, all the other self-help ideas seemed to be making more sense, and having a greater impact on the way I felt. The Remedies seemed to be soothing my emotions, and giving me a new space to see things more clearly.

I was gently, and very subtly led to understand how powerful simple natural Remedies can be, and the more I took my Bach Flower Remedy, and the more I did for myself, the better I started to feel on all levels.

The more I worked with this new discovery the more joy and self-belief I felt. I gained a greater understanding of how past events and my thinking were influencing me, and how such gentle techniques really could help me turn my life around.

My mission today, is to share with you the simplest way you can turn your life around, to help you to move forward as smoothly and as naturally as possible. Every day you work on you, you take yourself through a deeper healing journey that will help you acknowledge and identify more closely how you feel today, so you can have a greater understanding of yourself and discover who you are meant to be.

It's okay to feel grumpy

Before we go any further, please be realistic with yourself. It takes time to adjust to anything new, and there will be days when you do feel intense emotions. This is perfectly natural. Do not try to push these feelings down and try to pretend they are not happening. Go with the flow of your emotions, and try to understand what it is you are feeling, and why you are reacting the way you are.

Do not criticise or condemn yourself for the feelings you are having. Take a moment to say to yourself, 'That's interesting'. This gives you a brief moment for your mind to observe what is happening, reset itself and bring you to a deeper understanding of what is happening for you.

Thank yourself for noticing and acknowledging how you feel today. Count this new observation as one of your blessings today.

You may not always get an instant insight into why you feel like you do. It can take some time. Be gentle with yourself and the answers will come to you in time.

Keep in touch with your healing journal

Take some time to write down what you are experiencing, and any observations you have. Your healing journal is a place where you can offload your thoughts and your feelings, and have an on-going discussion with yourself to help you get more clarity.

Often intense emotions are a result of lots of accumulated feelings and habits. Start by breaking down your mood patterns to help you get a better understanding. As your journey unfolds and progresses you will start to become more aware of feelings you have buried. These could be fears and deep hurts which you may not have acknowledged in this moment, or they could be things which have happened long ago.

What feelings are you experiencing today? What are your thoughts? As your mind brings them to the surface they become an important part of your healing journey.

Acknowledge these feelings and write them down. They are potential milestones on your journey which need to be explored later.

At the beginning you do not need to work through how you can heal them, you are merely recording them. As your healing journey progresses, you will find techniques and methods to help you heal these insights and memories. Thank your mind for showing you what you can start to work on today. Count this as one of your blessings as you go to bed today.

Your healing journal is your new friend. It is a safe place where you can offload everything your mind, and your soul sees as important to you and your healing journey.

You are recording all the experiences, and milestones in your life which have had an impact on you and the way you feel about yourself. Your healing journal can store all this important information until you are ready to process it.

It may sound a bit strange, but take a moment to thank your healing journal for allowing you to offload and process your thoughts and feelings. The more grateful you become the better you will feel today. Remember to count your blessings before you drift off to sleep tonight.

Peeling away the layers

When you start to take more notice of your emotional state of mind, and you start to identify what you are feeling, you will start to get more clarity around the impact of your thoughts, and why you feel as you do today.

Take some time to think about what you say to yourself throughout today. Listen more carefully to the words you use. Those words are normally a reflection of what you are feeling. Your words create a neurological emotional response within your body, and as long as you keep using those words, you will keep having the same neurological responses. In this state of mind, your mind is creating behaviour patterns and muscle memories which will help you to deal with what you are thinking about.

Take some time to reflect. Are those thoughts and words helping you, or are they hindering or even harming you?

Throughout your healing journey, keep coming back to this question whenever your mind feels congested, or you become aware of your emotions feeling out of balance. This normally manifests as tiredness and tension, a dip in your energies, or mood swings. It can even manifest as physical pain.

Take the words out of your head, and put them on paper. Use your healing journal to keep all this information in a safe place. Write down each word, or thought pattern individually, and then choose one of those words to work with today. Thank yourself for what you are working on, and be grateful you have this choice.

Notice throughout the day, how many times you use your chosen word, or thought pattern. For example, if you are always saying 'I don't like technology', how do you think your mind will react? It will assume that you are not any good, and keep you in that state of belief because you are not giving your mind a chance to explore other options. Your mind has no choice. It is merely following your instructions.

I have used this example because anything technological has been one of my biggest obstacles. Until the day I got the opportunity to be a radio presenter. I became suddenly very aware of what I was saying to myself. I turned it around by starting to tell myself 'I am getting good at this. Every day this is getting easier. I am doing really well today. I can do it'. I created a string of uplifting positive affirmations to support my new learning, and after a few dozen hiccups I really did start to conquer the technology on the computer, and in the studio.

When you are choosing to encourage your mind to look for solutions and uplifting ways of moving forward, it will respond to your wishes. Take some time today to choose to look at what you say to yourself. Are you helping, hindering or even harming yourself and your progress, with the words you think and use every day?

On a deeper level of understanding.

You attract towards you what you think about. This simple understanding can be a real initiative to making some gentle, but very serious changes in the words you choose to use and think every day. The universal law of attraction is working with you every day. Do you like what you are attracting towards you?

Start to be more aware of the thoughts you are putting into your mind throughout this day, and if they are not supporting you, turn them around. Thank yourself for the new choices, and the understanding you are creating today.

I kept starting on making the changes I needed to adjust, and then I kept slipping back into my old patterns, and this is perfectly natural. When we first start to make changes our enthusiasm and motivation is high, but after a while we can lose that initial excitement and incentive. This is were the Bach Flower Remedies can be really helpful with defining and maintaining new patterns. They will help you to maintain your motivation and tenacity.

When you first start to work with the Bach Flower Remedies you will notice, and become aware of what your initial state of mind is. Choose the appropriate Remedies you need, and use them regularly as you make the necessary changes in your thinking patterns. Keep a record of the Remedies you choose, the date you start to use them, and how they help you.

Once you have worked through this initial state of mind, you will start to reveal other thought patterns and emotions which are underlying causes of what you are feeling.

The Remedies are gently peeling away the layers of emotions, to help you gently heal the deeper more ingrained patterns which have been impacting on you. Each time you have finished your combination of Remedies, an even deeper layer of thinking and emotions will be revealed to you.

Keep working through the layers as you do the other healing work on yourself. At each layer you will start to get an even deeper understanding of, not only the impact your thoughts have been having on you, but also the way your perception of yourself and your life has been created. Think of yourself as a beautiful Flower, and as you peel away the outer layers of petals you are revealing the deep and beautiful essence of your core. The deeper you go the more you will see your true beauty.

I am always fascinated by how such a small amount of Flower Remedies can have such an amazing healing impact on so many levels. It still amazes me today how they can gently, yet so powerfully move you from the negative states of our minds to the more uplifting states. The more consistently you use them the stronger you will become. The clarity and perception they bring is truly priceless.

The more you work with the Remedies, the more profound and rewarding the healing will be. The Remedies gently peel away the layers of what has become false, to allow you to blossom into the person you were born to be.

Simple things you can do for yourself each day

Simplicity brings you an uplifting feeling of well-being, and take you to a place where you can see solutions.

Start each day with the intention of having a good day.

Set yourself a new mini goal for today. Read your inspirational card to give you a focus for today. Start the day by giving yourself some time for you. Count your blessings before you move out of your bed.

Do random acts of kindness throughout the day. Be aware of your breathing patterns, and adjust them when necessary.

Recognise if you are using negative words, and turn them around. Use uplifting affirmations throughout your day to nurture and encourage yourself. Empty your mind into a healing journal.

Drink more water and eat healthier food. Start a gentle improved exercise routine, or do a virtual exercise routine.

Clear and ground your energies frequently. Start to wear brighter colours to uplift your energies. Praise and thank yourself for the great work you are doing.

Maybe you could create a check list for yourself and keep it nearby. Where could you pin up some copies around your home and workplace to help keep you on track. We all need a gentle reminder sometimes.

Add an affirmation to the top of your checklist to remind you to stay upbeat and on track.

Keep saying thank you throughout the day to lift up your spirits, and keep up your random acts of kindness.

De-stress as you go

It can take just a single moment to bring stress to your body, and take you into a spiral of tension and distress.

The good news is, that it can take just a moment to start to de-stress your body too.

Before you take another step, stop. Stop, and take a deep slow breath into your tummy, and as you breathe out, breathe out stress.

Slowly breathe in deep inner peace, and very slowly, breathe out stress.

Say thank you to your breath as it flows in and out.

Repeat this about six times, or until calm starts to flow through your body.

As you start to calm your breaths, tense up your shoulders, and then relax, and lower your shoulders.

Shake out your arms and your hands, and feel the tension releasing from your neck and your shoulders.

You carry a lot of tension in your shoulders, and it is hard to be relaxed or breathe properly when your shoulders are raised up and tense.

Gently swing your arms to release any tension in your chest and your arms.

Say thank you to your shoulders and your body as you release the tension.

Do a big yawn, and feel the way your mind and body starts to go to a calmer place. You may even feel a cool chill running through your body as your body relaxes. When you yawn you send cool air into your brain which helps to de-stress your brain. You are also moving energy within your body which may have become stagnant.

Any deep breathing, or gentle movement will help you to release any stagnant energy, which then allows the flow of oxygen to flow more smoothly. An increase in oxygen flow will help your concentration and you will feel more energised. As your breathing calms down, so will your mind.

As you continue to read through your book, frequently take a few moments to check if you are feeling tense. If you do feel tension, stretch out and relax your body with this simple breathing technique. Thank your body for showing you this tension. Stretch out, and breathe into any part of your body which feels tense.

Maybe take a few moments to run your fingers through your hair, lift up your hair, and gently massage your skull and the back of your neck to release any tension in your head. This will also improve your ability to concentrate and take on board the information you are processing. If you are feeling very tense stretch out your body, and maybe go for a gentle stroll before you carry on.

Do you need to drink some more water to replenish you? This may sound too obvious, but maybe you just need to go to the toilet before you do anything else. Anything you do for you, will encourage your mind and your body to support you and your progress.

When was the last time you gave yourself just a few moments to give yourself some nurturing? Remember the more you do for you, the more your feelings of self-worth will rise up. Your body and your soul feel appreciated, so you produce more of the feel-good chemicals to comfort and support you. Thank your feel-good chemicals as they flow through your body and bring you a sense of relief and well-being.

Make yourself and your well-being a priority. As you look after you, your feelings of self-worth will keep increasing and your inner happiness will flow. Look after you, and the rest will gently start to fall into place.

Useful Remedy tip

Throughout your journey you will find that the Bach Flower Remedies CHESTNUT BUD and CLEMATIS will help you with keeping your attention focused, and learning and retaining new information.

Create a simple plan for today

If you have come to a place where you recognise that you feel confused or discontented in some way, this is the best time to start to make some changes. It takes time to adjust to any new way of being, so please be patient with the process you are about to go through. The best way to create anything new is to do it repeatedly, and consistently.

At the risk of being repetitive, I will say again, 'It is far more productive to do something new every day for ten minutes, rather than one five-hour session once a week'.

It takes time, patience and persistence to create and maintain a new pattern.

Simplify your life. Just focus on today. Set yourself some short-term goals for this day. Put your plan in writing, and put a date on it.

Building your plan

A new simple plan for tomorrow could be.

Today, as I wake up, I will......

Smile, and take 6 deep slow breaths as soon as I wake up, and be grateful for the sleep I had.

Take a few moments to give thanks, and be grateful for the blessings and people I have in my life.

I will enjoy a big yawn and stretch out my body.

Give thanks for my breath, and for my body, and what it does for me.

Repeat my affirmation to myself 'Everything I joyfully set out to do today I can achieve'. 'Every day in every way I am getting stronger'. 'Everything is flowing smoothly for me now'.

Set a new reachable goal for today, and choose an affirmation which fits in with you and your day ahead.

On days when you have more time, work through your blessings and feelings of gratitude one by one, and say thank you. The more gratitude you feel the more uplifted you will feel.

Your affirmation will start the pattern of uplifting thoughts and feelings for your day ahead.

Move slowly out of your bed, sit on the side of your bed for a few seconds, stretch out your body, drink some water, and then move gently into your day.

Create a simple plan for today

Today, throughout my day I will...... Setting goals for yourself will help you to stay focused, and will help you feel like you are accomplishing something when you have achieved what you set out to do.

Recognise when I am tense, and choose to breathe more deeply and slowly.

Use more positive thoughts and words throughout my day, and repeat my affirmation to myself throughout the day. Take some slow deep breaths in and out if I start to feel stressed. I will take some time to meditate.

Take some time out, even if it is only a few moments, if I feel tired. I will listen to what my body is telling me, and make appropriate adjustments. Expect things to be better, and thank myself for the changes I make. I will empty my thoughts and feelings into a healing journal.

Choose to eat more healthily, and drink plenty of water. I will take some gentle exercise. Do frequent random acts of kindness, for myself and for others. I will smile at everyone I meet. I will seek out positive uplifting company. I will encourage, thank and praise myself as I go.

When you choose to do anything new for you, your brain will respond by starting to produce more feel-good chemicals to support the changes you are making. This then becomes a win-win situation, which further lifts up your energies, motivation and self-belief throughout the day.

Start your day with good intentions, and you will soon start to notice a difference. You can correct your patterns at any time during the day.

The more persistent you are, the more easily you will flow through the changes. Such a simple concept, and yet it will bring great rewards.

Start to praise yourself right now for the steps you are taking.

CHAPTER 9

HOW CAN YOU PRODUCE THE FEEL-GOOD CHEMICALS FOR YOURSELF?

WHEN YOU ARE SMILING, LISTENING to music, singing, or thinking of something that makes you smile your brain produces serotonin, which brings you happiness and joy.

Remembering, imagining, or thinking of a loving moment produces oxytocin, which brings you feelings of compassion.

Giving someone a twenty second hug, or receiving a hug produces the oxytocin too. You could even hug yourself to trigger the oxytocin release.

Reliving, or thinking about a success, or an achievement produces dopamine, which brings you feelings of success.

Thinking of a memory, or the intention of bravery and courage, produces endorphins, which brings you feelings of more confidence.

Resetting your flow of happiness

When you feel unhappy or stressed, your body feels tired and weary. Take a few minutes to acknowledge how you are feeling, and then use this gentle exercise to turn your day around. The next time you feel unhappy, or stressed, think of a happy memory, something which makes you smile or laugh. As you think of this memory, gently tap on the centre of your forehead, just above your eye brows. This is the point of your third eye, the place from which you can see things more clearly, and from a higher perspective. Tap on this place for a few minutes, as you smile, and breathe.

This will help to decrease your feelings of stress, and move you into your happy emotions. You can do this as frequently as you wish throughout the day. The more you use this simple exercise, the more effective it will be.

Set new intentions for each day

You need to reset your intentions for the day ahead. This will help you to stay on track and remain focused. Keeping it simple will help you remain on track and gently adjust. This is a new beginning. Keep resetting your intentions every day. You are giving your mind new patterns, new instructions to follow.

Have a 'not-to-do' list

Today....I will not wake up complaining. I will not criticise myself during this day. I will not get caught up in gossip. I will not complain or condemn anyone. I will not pick up my phone for the first hour of the day. I will not ignore my needs. I will not have negative thoughts. I will not put off what I know is important and necessary. I will not.............the choice is yours.

What would you like to stop doing today, so you can start to feel lighter and more uplifted from the time you wake up each day?

Have a 'priority to do' list each day

Select the priorities for your goals list each day. Be realistic and recognise you cannot change everything in one go. As you adjust one thing it can influence the way you feel about other situations in your life.

Today I make new choices

I will joyfully wake up and have an uplifting thought. I will take some deep breaths in and out, until I feel relaxed. I will breathe in deeper inner peace throughout the day. I will repeat my new affirmation to myself.

I will stretch and remind myself how blessed I am. I will say thank you to myself for the things I do for me. I will nurture myself throughout the day.

I will say thank you to others throughout the day.

I will listen to my body's needs. I will eat healthy foods. I will talk highly of myself. I will think, and talk positively about everyone, and everything. I will walk away from situations which bring me down.

I will meditate. I will take more exercise. I will listen to upbeat or relaxing music. I will do random acts of kindness throughout the day. I will..........

Modify your lists as you grow, and acknowledge just how well you are doing. Remember to add your changes to your list of blessings at the beginning, and at the end of each day.

Having an intention, a goal, to work towards gives you something to aim for, a sense of purpose. When you have accomplished your goal, it will bring you the feelings of achievement and satisfaction. Take a few moments to acknowledge what you have achieved, and praise yourself. The more you acknowledge your successes, the more your self-worth will go up. The more you raise up your self-worth, the more empowered you will feel. Keep your goals realistic and achievable.

What would you like to focus on today?

Choose things which seem achievable; simple changes which will make your life more upbeat and fulfilling. Add the word joyfully to each affirmation you choose, and start to notice how much more joyful you feel. Add the word 'gratefully' to your affirmations, and notice how much more grateful you start to feel about every experience in your life. Try working with different emotional words to see how your feelings respond. A few emotional words to use could be happily, peacefully, calmly, confidently, gratefully. Create your own list of emotionally supportive words so you have them ready for when you need them.

Everything you do for yourself, whether it is the things you stop doing, or new things you introduce, will help you to feel more organised, and help you to grow. Every step you take for yourself will bring you the wonderful feeling of self-gratification, and feeling more empowered. Your brain will respond appropriately by producing the gentle soothing chemicals which lift up your spirits, and bring you renewed energy, confidence and tenacity. With every change you make, you will start to feel more happiness and inner contentment.

Share your feeling of gratitude

From this day, make a more conscious effort to thank other people for the things they do for you. Take some time to praise them and encourage them throughout the day. When you thank, praise and nurture others you too will start to feel even more uplifted. Your brain is responding to these uplifting feelings you are sharing with others. It becomes a win-win situation for you and for all those around you. We all need to be more aware of lifting up each other's vibrations to allow each person to feel good about themselves.

Continue to do more random acts of kindness throughout the day and notice how your life starts to feel so much better. The random acts of kindness do not take anything from your day. Keep the acts simple at the beginning, like opening a door for someone or complimenting them on the way they look today. Making a point of sincerely saying thank you to others is a great way of building bridges and lifting up the way you feel about each other.

When you start to go with the flow of these loving feelings you are starting to move to a place where each person can start to raise up their own vibrations, which will then enable everyone to start believing and empowering themselves. As your self-worth goes up you are lifting others too.

I feel sure the reason we are all here on this earth is to help lift up each person's vibrations, to a place where they can be true to themselves and reach their real potential. Having an attitude of gratitude will turn your day around, and lift up every person you meet.

Every step in the right direction is a step up, and a step towards your new goal of a better quality of life. Every step takes you closer to the new person you are choosing to be.

Shake it off, scream it out

If you feel uptight, your mind feels overloaded, or you have an urge to scream out your tension, go for it. Thank your body for showing you it has this pent up tension and feelings.

Take a few moments to bring your attention to your voice. Take a deep breath in and then, as you breathe out give a big loud noisy sigh.

Repeat this a few times, until you start feeling a sense of relief flowing through your body.

Breathe in again, and this time, let your voice start to make whatever noise comes out. It could be a high pitched squeal, a scream, or a deep roar. Or anything in between.

Keep pushing the sound out until you run out of breath.

At the same time, shake your hands and your arms, and your shoulders. Let your whole body shake if you need to.

Keep repeating this, allowing whatever noise comes out, to flow. Do not try to control it. Let it flow.

Each time you do this exercise, the vocal noise, and the length of the noise you release, will vary. Through your voice you are allowing your body to release any trapped emotional, and often mental, energy you may have been carrying.

It does not matter how often you do this. Let your voice help you to release your tension and your stress. You may want to just shout or sing at the top of your voice. Whatever feels right for you today. Thank yourself and your body for the release which is happening. Thank those feelings for coming away from your body. Thank your voice for allowing this to happen. As you release the hurt and pain from your body you are creating a space for the healing to take place within you. A feeling of gratitude will replace all those old feelings you have let go of.

If you are angry about something, or with someone, shout it out. Get it out of your system, out of your precious body. You have been holding these feelings for long enough. Let them go now. The louder the noise, the better the release will be. When you have finished, you will be more able to get a clearer perspective on whatever was causing your distress.

When we are upset about something we often become too proud to admit it has impacted on us, or to ask for help to help us resolve the issue. We may not even realise the impact of how much we have been affected.

You can convince yourself that what you are thinking is the truth, so your perspective could become distorted, or maybe you convince yourself it doesn't really matter that much. Or, maybe you believe that nobody would understand you, so you bury the feelings deep down inside. It does not matter what your reason is, for not releasing these thoughts and feelings in the past, this is your time to let those thoughts and feelings go now.

A great time to do this releasing, is when you are in the car, or when you are out walking in nature, where no one can hear you. Let your feelings be released through your voice today.

A lot of the tension and stress you are carrying gets stuck in your body, around the heart and throat area. Releasing tension through your voice is a gentle yet profound way to help you release stress.

You will feel much more relaxed afterwards on many levels. You might even start to laugh, or cry. Your body is celebrating this new found power you are finding within you. Laughter and crying is a wonderful natural way to release stress, tension and trauma from your body and your mind. This will start allowing your body to heal. As you let these old feelings out, there is more room for the uplifting feelings and thoughts to start to flow.

Drink plenty of water to replenish your body throughout the day. Be gentle on yourself after any release, and always allow yourself time to adjust to the new feelings you are experiencing.

When you feel ready, reach out to someone you trust. Share your feelings with them to help you process and heal what you are feeling.

Maybe you could set aside one hour a day to talk about, and release your feelings. As you talk you are validating how you feel. It is amazing how much you can release in one hour, and how much better you will feel.

CHAPTER 10

CONNECTING YOUR LEFT AND RIGHT BRAIN

WHEN YOU STOP TRYING TO make things happen, and allow them to fall into place, you can manifest more easily what you need, and what is appropriate for you at this moment in time.

The more you stress over things and try to make them happen the more cortisol, the worry hormone, you produce. This keeps you in a state of stress and tension, and even fear, and it can seem impossible to get to any reasonable state of calm or clarity. Part of your brain switches off, and you cannot see or explore alternative ways to see what is happening. In this state of mind you cannot see solutions to what you believe to be true.

Your mind has no choice but to react to what you are thinking about. It is merely following through on the instructions you are thinking about, and helping you to deal with things in the most natural way possible. This is your primitive survival state kicking in to support you and your body. Even if this has become out of balance and inappropriate, your mind has no choice but to follow through on this process, until the time when you give it a new train of thought to follow.

As I have said earlier, your mind has no choice but to react to what you are thinking about. It cannot look for more appropriate solutions because you are not giving it permission, room to explore anything else.

This is where your affirmations and the Bach Flower Remedies can help you to adjust your thinking and maintain new, more uplifting and appropriate ways of thinking. You can use them alongside the following figure '8' exercise. Supportive Remedies could be CHERRY PLUM, ELM, OLIVE, SCLERANTHUS, WHITE CHESTNUT and VERVAIN. Or even GORSE, SWEET CHESTNUT or WILD ROSE. Take some time out to read about each of these Remedies, and choose to work with the ones which most relate to you and the way you feel right now. The Remedies will support you as you work through making any necessary changes you need to make.

Alongside today's date, make a note of the Remedies you can most relate to, and choose to work with those Remedies today. The Remedies will be working on your behalf whilst you make any necessary changes, and they will help you maintain the new patterns of thinking you correct. CHESTNUT BUD is a great Remedy to help you learn from the experiences you have been through, and any mistakes you may make. It helps you to create new patterns and maintain them, whilst learning from everything you experience. This then becomes your new wisdom, alongside a more uplifting way of thinking, which ultimately brings you new insight and clarity, and a whole new way of life.

CHESTNUT BUD helps you to tap into your teacher within. It brings out the best possible way of thinking about you, and whatever you are working through. It can also help with your memory retention, and learning new things. Pure magic.

Adjusting your thinking

Does it sometimes feel like your mind is too busy, or too cluttered to be able to get clarity or do anything sensibly? Do you find it hard to make decisions, or to keep your attention on what you are doing? Does it feels like your mind is going round and round in circles, and you cannot get any calm or peace in your head?

Working with the following simple figure '8' exercise is a gentle, yet very effective way to give your mind a new calmer more efficient way to reset itself. Over the years I have found it really helpful with children and with people who are very creative, and with people who have learning difficulties. It can also help to release stress and anxiety if you combine it with a slow deep breathing exercise. Try using this exercise if ever you are having inner-conflict in your mind. It brings your mind to a calmer more contented space where you can get more clarity and insight.

Take some time for you to create some calm and composure

Remember the underlying key to anything you do for you is to lift up your self-worth. The more you value you and do things for yourself, the better you will feel.

Take a few minutes to stop whatever you are doing, and bring your attention to your head. Imagine your brain is in two sections, the left side and the right side. The left side is your logical thinking side, and the right side is your creative inspirational side of your brain. Slow down your breaths as you do this exercise. The whole exercise needs to be done slowly and methodically.

Think of a figure '8' and imagine you are slowly drawing the '8' from left to right in your brain. Start in the centre of your brain.

Imagine slowly drawing the first half of the '8' around the left side of your brain, slowly drawing it upwards, down underneath, and then back to the centre of your brain.

Then complete the figure '8' by slowly drawing the second half of the '8' around the right side of your brain, over the top, down, and back to the centre.

Now take this a stage further. Slowly moving your most dominant hand, (usually the one you write with), draw the figure '8' in the air in front of you, going in the same direction as the image in your mind.

Continue doing this twenty times.

Then change the direction you draw the figure 8.

Circling the right side of your brain, slowly going underneath, slowly over the top, and back to the centre.

Then complete the figure '8' by slowly drawing the second half of the '8', under the left side, up over the top and back to the centre.

Now take this a stage further. Slowly moving your other hand, draw the

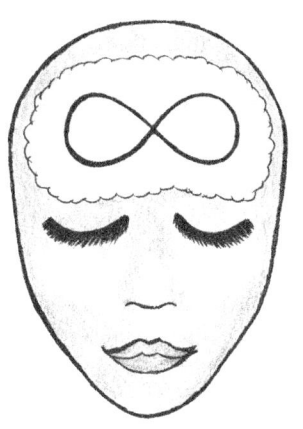

figure '8' in the air in front of you, going in the same direction as the image in your mind.

Continue doing this twenty times. This gentle slow exercise will help you connect your left and right brain. It can also help relax your mind when you feel overwhelmed, stressed, anxious, distressed, angry, or scattered in your thinking. It will help you to concentrate, stay more focused, bring a feeling of calm, well-being, and help you make better and more logical decisions.

Drawing '8's

Drawing the figure '8' on its side, on a piece of paper is a gentle way to start to retrain your mind to a calmer and more efficient way of thinking and working. It can help to still an over-active mind by slowing down and stopping the constant chatter in your head.

This is a great exercise to do within your school or work place, or when you cannot concentrate or get some clarity. It is highly effective when working with anyone, especially children who have been diagnosed with ADHD, or any learning difficulties. It can help them to refocus their attention.

When you are holding a pen or pencil in your hand to draw, it stimulates parts of your mind to help you retain information. Working with your sense of touch to stimulate your mind is called kinaesthetic learning. It helps parts of your brain to be more stimulated, enabling you to process what you are learning, whether you are reading it for yourself, or someone else is teaching you.

This exercise is one of the simple exercises I learnt, when I went to see a lady who does Brain Gym training. It can help you bring relief, from countless imbalances in your thinking and your emotions. The more you use the figure '8' exercise the more effective it will be. It is really simple, yet can make a big difference to the quality of your day.

Brain Gym helps anyone who is doing too much logical thinking, and anyone who is finding it hard to concentrate. It can help your mind function more efficiently, and is great for anyone who struggles with ADHD or has concentration and learning difficulties. It can help them maintain their focus for longer spells of time and process what they are learning. Bring it in as a simple drawing exercise to help them re-centre their mind.

Introduce different colours, and make it more fun by keep tracing over and over the 8, and creating patterns. Draw them left to right, and then right to left. And then up and down in both directions. It really does not matter which way they go. It will help you mentally, and it will make a difference to how your mind can focus, which will ultimately bring you a better learning experience and an improved quality of day. It can bring a calmer demeanour and help to bring emotional balance to many situations.

There is no age limit to using this exercise, and you can even use it when you feel under the weather, or if you are unable to physically move.

Calming and rebalancing your mind brings you healing on so many levels.

I find it particularly helpful when my mind is busy and I want to calm it down, especially at night time, or if I wake up in the night and my mind is restless. It can help you calm down your mind so you can drift up to sleep.

Use this exercise regularly when something is troubling you, and you can't see a solution, or when you have a project to complete and are finding it hard to maintain your concentration, or to stay focused. You can use it when you are in the middle of a project and cannot concentrate or see the next step. It can really help when you cannot seem to get an answer to something you are trying to think about, or you cannot get to a place where you start to take action. It can help you to still your mind to enable you to start taking action.

If you feel anxious or stressed, drawing the figure '8' can help to calm your mind to a state where you can start to see things more objectively, and your mind can then work with you in a more appropriate way, to bring in clarity to help you see the way forward. When your mind becomes calmer it will start to produce the serotonin and melatonin to help your mind and your body feel more relaxed and de-stressed. Remember, what you think about is real to you, whether it is true or not. When you work more with connecting your right side of your brain to your left side of your brain you can get more creative and constructive insight. If your thinking is not helping you, you can change it. Give your mind the best possible opportunities to help you.

Take it a stage further, and draw a figure '8' on several pieces of paper.

Place the pieces of paper around your home, especially beside your bed. Every time your mind sees the figure '8' it will start to trace the figure 8, and this naturally starts linking the left and right sides of your brain more effectively.

When you have a few moments to spare, take the time to mentally trace the figure '8' shape in your mind. The more you do this simple exercise, the more effective and supportive it will be for you and your mind. With practise it will only take a few moments to connect your left and right sides of your brain and reset your mind set. The more you do this exercise, the more naturally and effectively your brain will function.

All of the above exercises with the figure '8' will also help people who are too right-brained. In this state of mind people can often make irrational decisions, or are too hasty to make rational choices. If you are too right-brained, which many creative people can be, you often do not take time to think about an idea, or the consequences of what you are intending to do, before you jump in and taken action. This can often lead you to be too hasty, so can cause you to make mistakes, often big mistakes. When in a constant right-brain state you can keep constantly making the same mistakes, and even put yourself in inappropriate situations without fear of the consequences. You cannot, or do not see the dangers of the actions you are taking. You do not stop to think logically about what you are doing.

Unfortunately, in this state, you may even be incapable of making appropriate rational decisions and choices.

A good example of this would be a child who sees a friend on the other side of the busy road, and starts to walk across the road, without taking some time to evaluate the situation. They see their goal, their friend, but they cannot process the responsible actions they need to take. Because they are in their creative mind, they do not stop to go into their left brain to process the actions they need to take to stay safe.

It is not their fault. It is the way their brain is wired at that moment. They are in their childlike, 'anything is possible' state of mind. Within this 'right-brain' state of mind, they may not have the capacity to process what is happening, or what they need to do to act safely at that moment.

Some people stay in this mind-set. If you are very creative, and often find yourself feeling detached or day-dreamy, are unable to focus, or put your plans into action, you may be too much in your right-brained mind functioning. Using the figure '8' exercise can help you connect your right-brain and left-brain thinking so you can process things more effectively, be more productive, be more grounded and down to earth. This exercise can also help you if you keep having irrational thoughts or make wrong choices.

Children who have been diagnosed as ADHD, or who have short-term attention spans are often constantly working consistently within their right-brain. The figure '8' exercise can be a very effective way of helping them to be more focused, and to have longer spans of concentration. It can also help them to process what they are learning.

People who are very creative, or very spiritual can often be very right-brained, and find it hard to live in the real world. They can be constantly daydreaming and feel detached from reality. Doing all of these exercises can help them stay more realistic, and help them to feel more grounded.

If this sounds like you, try doing the figure '8' through your body. Imagine the figure '8' going from the top of your head, crossing down through your navel, and down to your feet. Keep repeating this until you feel more connected with your body.

Take it a stage further, by drawing the figure '8' in your mind when you cannot maintain your sense of living in the moment. You could enhance this by drawing the '8s' on paper.

When your mind feels disorientated or disorganised, or you feel stressed or anxious, take some time to play around with the figure '8'. Use it to doodle, and create patterns on a piece of paper. As you are drawing you are encouraging your brain to link the left and right sides more effectively. Introduce colours to enhance the experience. This is a really effective, and simple way to help children who may be struggling with their concentration span in school.

Other times when you can go into the extreme right-brained

functioning, is when you are in a highly stressed, anxious or traumatised state. You feel like you want to constantly escape from the situation you are in. You may frequently have ideas of wanting to get away, or run away from what you are experiencing. You may always be intending to take action but do not. The Remedy to help with this state of mind is CLEMATIS. It helps keep you in the present. You will feel more grounded, and feel more able to put into action what you have been thinking about and planning. CLEMATIS will help to keep you living in the present moment, so it helps you maintain your focus and concentration.

The figure '8' exercise can be a gentle way to help release someone who is suffering with PTSD, Post Traumatic Stress Disorder.

It can be a gentle way to help them reset their mind thinking, and help them to release the trauma and memories they have experienced.

This technique works on a similar level to the EMDR, Eye Movement Desensitisation and Reprocessing therapy. As your eyes move from left to right, it can help to desensitise your mind from the trauma you have been through, or are experiencing, and can help you to see alternative solutions.

You could combine your figure '8' exercise with your Bach Flower Remedies, your inner child healing and the self-forgiveness meditation. Read about each technique in your book, and choose which techniques feel right to you today.

Listen to the words someone uses when describing their experiences. Their words could be a clue to which Remedies they need. For example, if they say they feel overwhelmed, ELM is the Remedy they need. Take some time to read through the Remedies, and gently introduce them, either as a single Remedy if their emotions are intense, or in a combination bottle.

There are also other useful Brain Gym exercises you can do to help yourself have more clarity and focus. In some areas Brain Gym has been introduced into schools, with amazing results for children who find it hard to concentrate. I would highly recommend finding a practitioner who specialises in Brain Gym.

Reaching out

I recently felt I needed some outside support, and was guided towards a lady called Wendy Smith. Wendy had an accident at the age of 17, and was told she would never walk again.

She retrained herself, and retrained her mind to deal with what had happened, and now she dedicates her life to helping others overcome their deep traumas, and to become the best person they can be.

If you are struggling with a deep trauma which is impacting on your life, check out Wendy Smith at www.wendysmith.me.uk.

Reaching out for help, will help you to move beyond those feelings of feeling stuck or trapped in the past, and is a priceless step towards your recovery. Remember the more you do for you, the more you are valuing yourself, which will increase your feelings of well-being and self worth.

Do you need some reassurance or guidelines on which way to go?

In this moment, stop. Tap into, and pay more attention to your higher self, your intuition. Take a moment to stop and think of a number between 1 and 555.

Now flick through *'Free to be Me'*, and find that page number. The number you have chosen is your angel number for today. What message are you being drawn to today? Read through your chosen page, and see if you can relate to the guidance on that page.

Your chosen angel number is a simple answer from your intuition, guiding you to reach in to help yourself, or to reach out? Whichever way you are guided to go, allow yourself to go with the flow. The more frequently you trust in your intuition, your higher self, and the direction you should take, the more you will believe in yourself and what you are capable of achieving.

CHAPTER 11

BACH FLOWER REMEDIES FOR EXTREME MENTAL AND EMOTIONAL PAIN

UNFORTUNATELY, PEOPLE WHO ARE IN an extreme mental and emotional state of distress, can slip easily into their right-brain functioning, or their left-brain functioning, and get stuck there. In more extreme cases, they do not feel capable of thinking rationally about the consequences of self-harming, or other self-destructive behaviours. This state can even lead them to taking their own lives. They are stuck in an emotional and mental trap, where they see suicide as the most effective way to escape from their distress.

If ever you find yourself in an extremely distressing emotional or mental state of mind, please reach out for help. There are many professional organisations that can help you work through what you are experiencing. Contact your doctor, or reach out to someone who can help you take some appropriate action to get help. Reaching out may seem hard, but you can do it, and it will be worth it. Reaching out can be the first step to your recovery. You can find a way forward.

There are Bach Flower Remedies, and Australian Bush Remedies, which can help with these deep painful feelings, but you should seek out professional help to support you as well.

The Bach Flower Remedy for these extreme feelings of despair, and the thoughts which accompany these distressing feelings is SWEET

CHESTNUT. SWEET CHESTNUT can help bring you some relief from these painful feelings of despair, and can help you to see the light at the end of the tunnel. It can help you see solutions where you believed there were none, but please do not override the need for professional help.

The Australian Bush Remedy essence, Waratah, is for the person who is feeling utter despair, and is going through the 'black night of the soul'. It helps to bring you a sense of relief from your feelings of despair. It brings you strength and courage to cope with your crisis, and it will bring your survival skills to the fore. Waratah is available through the internet, and can be found in some health food stores.

Are you self-harming or having suicidal thoughts?

If you talking about, or are having thoughts of suicide, or self-harm there are some other Bach Flower Remedies which can help you.

CHERRY PLUM is for when you are prone to uncontrollable thoughts or irrational actions and compulsions. It helps you to let go of what you have been bottling up inside of you. It brings you calmer, rational thoughts and the courage to face your adversities.

CLEMATIS can help with suicidal thoughts when you can see no other way out, and you feel detached from reality. CLEMATIS is one of the Remedies in the Rescue Remedy.

GENTIAN is the Remedy for faith and renewed optimism. It is a comforter of sorrow and disappointments. Taking it in a crisis will bring reassurance that everything will work out in the end.

GORSE is for when everything feels hopeless, and you don't believe that anything is going to make a difference. This Remedy restores hope and faith, and is the first step towards recovery.

LARCH is for those who suffer from a lack of self-esteem. It is the Remedy for when you simply do not feel worthy of being here, or of other's love. You can feel like a failure, and that you have failed. LARCH brings renewed confidence in your abilities.

PINE is for when you are carrying massive feelings of guilt, and can hardly bear it. The pain can feel so intense, and the sense that you should remove yourself from others, and from life is overwhelming. This Remedy helps stop the feelings of guilt. There is a high chance that those who carry guilt may not even know that they do. All you will experience is an unending emotional pain that you can't seem to identify. PINE helps to bring relief from the guilt and allows you to recognise what you are responsible for, without the feelings of guilt. It brings you feelings of genuine regret.

STAR OF BETHLEHEM can bring comfort and a sense of release when someone is in a state of shock

WHITE CHESTNUT is vital. This is the Remedy for those tormenting thoughts that you can't turn off. It can help prevent and stop suicidal thoughts, especially those thoughts that are playing on your fears and self-worth. It helps to ease and block those negative thoughts, and brings you calmer and more supportive thoughts.

WILLOW. Those on the edge of self-harm or suicidal tendencies are often in a victim mode. They may feel bitter, resentful, or simply feel that their situation is not fair, and that no one is able to understand what they are experiencing or feeling. WILLOW is critical to stopping those feelings, and to help you take responsibility for your feelings and for yourself.

For these extreme feelings

When someone is experiencing such extreme feelings of despair, you will get the best results from the Remedies by taking each of the Remedies individually, and not diluting them. Place 2 drops directly on the tongue.

In such extreme circumstances, the healing powers of single Remedies will be more effective to restore calm and a more balanced perspective. If you mix them, their healing power is less powerful in these circumstances.

You may also need to take them much more frequently. I would suggest every 30 seconds until relief is obtained. Feelings of a sense of relief normally take around 2 to10 minutes to return.

When the more intense feelings subside, you could add 4 further drops to a glass of water, or a warm drink. Slowly sip the drink until complete calm returns.

The Remedies work on the vibrations within the body, and therefore they do not interfere or react with any other medication you may be taking. They are safe, non-toxic, non-addictive, gentle and effective.

Always seek the advice of a doctor or other professional person if you are experiencing any self-harming or suicidal thoughts or tendencies. Acknowledging you need help, and then reaching out, is the first step to turning your life around. If you do not feel able to reach out for yourself, please ask someone you know to reach out for you. Sometimes we all need a helping hand to lead us through the next step.

Often what feels like a breakdown, can be the beginning of a breakthrough. A breakthrough to a deeper healing and a more meaningful understanding of you, and what you are feeling. By reaching out, you are saying, 'I am ready to make some crucial changes'.

When you make this first step your emotional and mental pain will start to soften, and you will start to feel a massive sense of relief. Brighter days will come to you. Take one gentle step every day, and you will be soon be able to see a way forward.

Every small step you take will help you to feel more empowered and, the more empowered you feel, the more motivation you will have. With every step, the momentum will start to build, and the greater insight you will get into how you can help yourself. It all starts with the first simple step of reaching out.

We all need outside help sometimes

All of your healing, relaxation and grounding, affirmations, journaling and figure '8' exercise can help you work through feelings of despair and any self-harming thoughts or tendencies you may have, but please seek other outside professional help as well.

When you have someone to share your problems with, it is so much easier to find the best way through what you are experiencing. For some people, it may even be a chemical imbalance which is causing them to feel the way they do. There are many supportive agencies and professional people who can help you get an insight into what you are feeling, and help you to work through your recovery. The sooner you reach out, the quicker the support, and the results you need will come to you.

Other therapies to release stress from your mind

There are also other exercises you can do to help with stress, anxiety and traumas you may have been through. These therapeutic techniques should ideally be done under the supervision of a qualified therapist.

OHB, Optimum Health Balancing with Kinesiology

Kinesiology is a holistic approach to healthcare and well-being. The originator of OHB was Charles Benham. It links traditional Chinese acupuncture, meridians and energy balancing with Western muscle testing and anatomy and physiology. You can use it to help with your emotional problems to discover what your body is experiencing. If you would like some help to deal with some deeper trauma, or reoccurring pains in your body, I would highly recommend checking out Susanne's website, www.susannelakin.wordpress.com www.kinesiologyohb.co.uk.

EMDR, Eye Movement Desensitisation and Reprocessing

EMDR is an interactive psychotherapy technique, used to relieve psychological stress. It can be an effective treatment for trauma and post-traumatic stress disorder (PTSD). EMDR uses a patient's own rapid, rhythmic eye movements. These eye movements dampen the power of emotionally charged memories of past traumatic events. EMDR does need to be done under the supervision of a qualified therapist for the optimum results.

Hypnotherapy

I was recently guided to go see a hypnotherapist called Jason Edwards, when I kept finding myself back into thoughts of things which had happened in my past. These childhood traumas were impacting on the results I was trying to achieve, and Jason was able to help me work through, and heal these past traumas. The next day I was able to take the steps I needed to take, without fear of rejection or self-judgement. Hypnotherapy is a gentle and effective way to help you overcome traumas which have happened to you in your past. If you would like to understand how hypnotherapy can help you, check it out with Jason at www.hypnotherapy-in-norwich.co.uk.

CHAPTER 12

ARE YOU GROUNDED?

WHEN YOUR MIND IS TOO busy, and you feel stressed or anxious, you have a natural tendency to become ungrounded. Being ungrounded means you may have a feeling of detachment from the reality of what is happening in your life. In this state, you will find it hard to concentrate and remain focused.

It can make you feel disorientated, clumsy, forgetful, and find it hard to make the smallest of decisions. You can feel sleepy, and your mind can drift off to other things when you should be being more focused on the present task. You may find it hard to concentrate on the task in hand because you have lost interest in what you are doing.

This is a very familiar state for children, and adults, who may be described as being 'away with the fairies'. A lot of the time they may live in an imaginary world of their own. These people may find it really hard to focus and concentrate on what they are being taught in school, and often find it hard to remember what they are being taught.

The Bach Flower Remedies CHESTNUT BUD, CLEMATIS, IMPATIENS and SCLERANTHUS can help to remedy this state of mind. They will enable better concentration, and a calmer approach and attitude towards learning.

In schools, our creative, right-brained children need to be taught through kinaesthetic learning, which is learning through using touch and emotions, and using more creative images they can relate to, to help them retain the information. Their ability to retain information becomes easier when they can associate facts with images and emotional stories.

Try holding something in your hand to stimulate parts of your brain to function more effectively when you need to concentrate. The more creative you are in your ways of learning, the easier it is for your mind to function and retain any information it receives. Always remember short spells of learning can be more effective too.

Is your mind all over the place?

You can become ungrounded by worrying about something, even if it's somewhere in the future. If you are feeling stressed, unwell, or are in a traumatic on-going situation, you can feel detached and ungrounded from reality. This feeling can be caused by tension, relationship challenges, illness, a sudden shock or bad news, or even when you are bored and have lost interest in what you are doing. You can even feel ungrounded when you are not using your true creative potential. Being stuck in just thinking about an idea, and not putting it into practise, can take you to a place of feeling ungrounded.

Drink some water to nourish your body. Add 2 drops of the Bach Flower Remedy HORNBEAM to the water, and drink it, and then add 2 more drops, and keep sipping the water until you have completed your task.

It can be easy to confuse the state of being ungrounded, with procrastination. Procrastination is putting off doing something you do not really want to do. Procrastinating can make you feel very weary, but it is only in your mind you believe you are tired. HORNBEAM will help you to overcome this state of mind, and getting on with the task will lift this state of weariness.

Taking action to remedy feelings of being detached or procrastinating, cannot only be very productive, but it also helps you to be living back in the moment. CLEMATIS is the Bach Flower Remedy for grounding you, and STAR OF BETHLEHEM will help you deal with any shock or trauma you are experiencing.

Being ungrounded can take your mind into a state of unrealistic ways of escaping from the situation you are in. Your mind constantly goes to thoughts of, 'What if I.......' as a way out of what you are experiencing right now, with no strong conviction to follow through on those thoughts. Being ungrounded can make you feel light headed, detached and spaced out. Being in this state can often increase any feelings of fear, anxiety and stress, and can be one of the initial causes of panic attacks and extreme fears.

It can also take you into deeper feelings of helplessness and despair because you want to run away from the situation rather than face up to it, and gently nurture yourself through your experience. When you are in this state of mind it can be difficult to see practical ways to make changes. Feeling ungrounded can often be the instigating cause of irrational thoughts and behaviour. Once you are in this space it can be hard to reason with your thoughts, or bring them back to a state of harmony and balance.

CHERRY PLUM can help bring you back to a place where your thoughts become more rational, and VERVAIN can help you calm your mind when your thoughts have become fanatical and you cannot let them go. VERVAIN brings you to a place where you can mentally step back and observe what is happening.

It can be hard to get any sense of clarity, or the ability to focus when you are in this ungrounded state. Doing something creative, physically hands-on, or going out into nature, can help you be more grounded.

Increase your water intake, if you find yourself feeling ungrounded and unable to concentrate. Drinking water can help you to feel more alert and grounded.

Remember, if you feel stressed, drinking more water will help your body, and your mind, function better.

Not drinking enough water will make you feel even more stressed too.

In your healing journal, make a note during the day when you feel disoriented, detached, or forgetful.

How did you feel? What were you thinking about? What were you focusing on instead of the task in hand?

Are you constantly considering another issue whilst going about your day? Is it usually the same issue, perhaps from a different angle?

Are you answering the questions in your mind, over and over, or re-enacting an event, trying to change the circumstances or the outcome? Try adding VERVAIN and WHITE CHESTNUT to your Remedy bottle. Are you constantly thinking about something you wish you could be doing?

Are you struggling with a future event or decision? Try adding SCLERANTHUS to your bottle today.

Are you escaping a difficult current issue by retreating into your mind? Try adding CLEMATIS.

DAWN CHRYSTAL

Do you feel scattered, and unable to focus or concentrate? If you are feeling scattered, or finding it hard to make a decision, the Remedy SCLERANTHUS will help you make the right decision and feel more poised and balanced. It also helps with emotional mood swings and if you struggle with constant highs and lows of energy.

Write down the issues that are causing your mind to drift. Taking it out of your mind, and putting it on to the page can give your mind the space to be more in the moment, and enjoy what you are doing right now. It also allows you to focus on the issue, rather than allowing it to be continuously whirling around in your mind, and fogging your day. Writing things down encourages you to start taking control by focusing on the issues one by one. Writing can also help you to feel more grounded because you are doing something practical and useful. An expression we often use is, 'It can help bring you back down to earth'.

Write it on the page, break it down, and start to properly process it. Combined with the following grounding techniques, you will be able to feel more awake, more attentive, more aware and more productive. You will also see how far you have come when you look back on your notes. Your healing journal is a great place to have an on-going discussion with yourself. Always remember to make a note of how well you have done as your journey progresses.

People who are very creative, and those who are potentially creative, but are not using their creative potential, can very easily become ungrounded. This is one of the Personality Types Dr Bach discovered. The personality type is CLEMATIS, and they have a natural tendency to drift off into their daydream state when they start to lose interest in reality. Their mind detaches from what they are doing, and they can find it very hard to refocus or maintain concentration. This is the time when you need a grounding exercise.

Doing something creative, practical or physical can help you feel more connected and have more interest in the moment. It can help take you out of your mind, to put into action what you have been thinking about. Maybe you could add to the experience by walking barefoot for a while. Walking out in nature is also a great way to ground yourself. Take some time to step outside whenever you feel ungrounded. If you take your shoes and socks off, it will enhance the experience, but please be careful where you tread.

The Bach Flower Remedy CLEMATIS can help you to *become* more grounded, and CHESTNUT BUD can help you *maintain* this sense of being more grounded. CLEMATIS will help you to remain more focused, and find a lively interest in what you are doing. CLEMATIS is in the combination bottle of Bach Flower Remedies known as Rescue Remedy, or five Flower Remedy, which is available in many supermarkets, health stores and on-line.

People whose personality type is ROCK ROSE also have a similar tendency to want to escape from a situation they are not comfortable with, but instead of daydreaming, their behaviour pattern is to go inwardly and panic. The Remedy ROCK ROSE will help with these feelings of panic and terror. ROCK ROSE is also in the Rescue Remedy.

If you have a sudden, or on-going shock, or a challenging situation to deal with, you can go into a state of feeling ungrounded, detached from reality, and even panicky. And when you are in a state of shock, it can affect your behaviour, your mind, and your body on many levels. The way you feel about everything becomes more intense. STAR OF BETHLEHEM, CHERRY PLUM, CLEMATIS, IMPATIENS, and ROCK ROSE can help you to deal with the stress and shock, and bring you back into the present moment. Although this state can still feel painful to work through, the Remedies can help release some of the stress from your mind and your body, and enable you to deal more effectively with your emotions, and the situation in hand.

From the calmer state of mind you can emotionally and mentally process the stressful situation more effectively, and feel enabled to move through, and beyond, the trauma you are experiencing. Again, these essences of these Bach Flower Remedies are all in the bottle of Rescue Remedy. This combination of Remedies will help soothe you through your trauma and emotional distress.

'Coming down to earth'

A gentle and effective way to ground yourself is to sit on a chair and rub your feet backwards and forward on the ground for a minute or two. This increases your circulation, and helps you be more aware of your physical body when the tingling starts. It can refocus your mind and brings your body back into reality. Take deep slow breaths in and out, whilst rubbing your feet on the ground.

Stress can make you feel ungrounded and dehydrated. Drinking more water can also help you feel more grounded. When you are stressed, your body needs more water to help it deal with the stress you are experiencing. Being dehydrated can make you feel light headed and more stressed, and increase feelings of anxiety. Take small sips of water, slow down your breathing, and take time to feel the sensation of the water flowing through your body. When you take your attention to your body's functions, and the sensation of the water flowing through you, it can bring you 'back down to earth'. This also re-focuses your mind on something practical, to bring you to a state where you can start to make more rational choices.

Another effective way of grounding yourself down is to do a grounding meditation.

Choose to stand still, or sit down. Take your attention to your breathing, and start to slow down each breath.

Take two slow breaths into your heart, hold your breath, and slowly release.

Take a slower, deeper breath into your stomach, and slowly release.

Repeat this six times.

Then imagine a slow flow of water flowing down to the top of your head.

Imagine the water, flowing in through the top of your head, and slowly filling up your mind.

Imagine the water, slowly flowing down through your body, and then out through the bottom of your feet.

Also see the shower of water cleansing the energy field around your body.

Set the intention, to release anything you have been worrying about, through this flow of water.

The water is washing everything away.

You could imagine you are under

a shower of water, and that you are gently washing away all your stress, worrying thoughts, and any tension you may be carrying.

When the flow of water reaches the bottom of your feet, imagine the water turns into solid roots, like those of a great oak tree. See these roots coming out through the bottom of your feet.

Imagine pushing your roots down into the earth beneath you, each time you breathe out.

As you are pushing your roots down, set the intention of releasing any thoughts and feelings which no longer serve you. Imagine, and feel these old feelings flowing through your body, and out through your roots.

Have the intention, of pushing the roots deep down into Mother Earth.

With every outward breath, push the roots down deeper.

Count the roots down in 10s, to the centre of the earth.

Push them down to 10%, down to 20%, slowly push them down to 30%.

Imagine the roots spreading wider at the same time. Check your breathing is still slow and calm.

Feel your mind feeling calmer, and your body feeling heavier with every release of your breath.

Push your roots down to 40%, 50%, 60%, 70%, 80%, 90%, and 100%.

Your roots being 100% grounded has taken them right down to the centre of the earth, Mother Earth.

Imagine your roots being wrapped around a big boulder, or a beautiful crystal of your choice.

You are now grounded for today. Your mind will feel calmer and clearer, and you will feel more grounded.

When you are feeling grounded, you can take this meditation a stage further.

Take your attention back to your body, and surround yourself in a bubble of coloured light.

Imagine, as you are pushing your roots down through the earth, this bubble around you, is being anchored down, with its own roots at the same time.

This will help you maintain this feeling of being grounded, and protect you from any influences around you which could be having an impact on you, and the way you feel.

All of this needs to be done slowly, and with the intention of becoming grounded. You are giving your mind and your body a new pattern to work with; a new pattern which will help you maintain more focus and concentration. The more you practise this exercise, the more effective it will be, and the more benefits you will receive. Give yourself time to adjust to this new way of feeling.

If you do this exercise at the beginning of each day, it will help you to start your day feeling more grounded, focused, and productive. It helps bring you back into reality, and brings you more vitality and interest in what you are doing. If at any time during the day, you become ungrounded, you can take your thoughts to your 'new intention to being grounded', and imagine the energies flowing through your body, and down through your roots.

The more you practise this exercise, the more easily it will happen for you. Remember to be patient with yourself as your mind takes time to create a new pattern, but the more frequently you practise this exercise the more naturally it will flow. When it feels more natural, you will be able to tap into this grounding exercise at any time during your day when you need it. The more you use your grounding exercise the more comfortable it will feel, and the more easily you will be able to access it. Allow it to become a natural part of your day.

Remember you are creating a new pattern for your mind to work with to enhance your life. As you repeatedly practise this grounding exercise, you will soon experience how easily you can re-ground yourself. You can practise this grounding during the day when you have a spare moment, or when you feel yourself being pulled back into your old patterns.

Remember it can take sixty-six days to create a new pattern, and naturally maintain it. Start today, and it will soon start to feel a more natural and comfortable way of being.

Grounding will bring you to a much calmer state of mind, and a more relaxed and focused way of being. You will be able to accomplish so much more, and maintain a much more peaceful perspective on your life. It will also help you to have more patience with yourself, and with the process of synchronicity. Everything happens just as it should, and at the perfect time for what is meant to be for you, and for your progress.

Building on today

Write down what you did, how you felt at the beginning, and how you felt at the end. On a scale of 1 – 10, how much improvement did you feel?

Make a note of how long it took to ground yourself and feel calmer. What could you do differently next time?

Did you record the Bach Flower Remedies which helped you today?

Remember CLEMATIS is for grounding in the present moment.

CHESTNUT BUD helps you create and maintain new patterns.

SCLERANTHUS helps you make the right choices.

ROCK ROSE helps you when you may be going into a state of panic.

If you do not have the bottles of the Remedies you can use the Bach Flower Remedy healing cards I have created for you to complement this exercise.

If you find it really hard to ground yourself, and bring yourself back to reality, standing outside on the ground is a very efficient and natural way to ground yourself. Try taking it a stage further and stand barefoot on the ground, and see how quickly you come down to earth. You will feel a shiver of coolness run through your body as you are grounded down. This is an extremely quick, effective and natural way to come back to reality.

Remember though, that quickly is not always the best way if you are feeling very emotional, or in a state of shock. It would be more beneficial to go for a gentle stroll in nature to allow your body the time it needs to adjust, and your emotions to come back to a more natural state of balance and harmony.

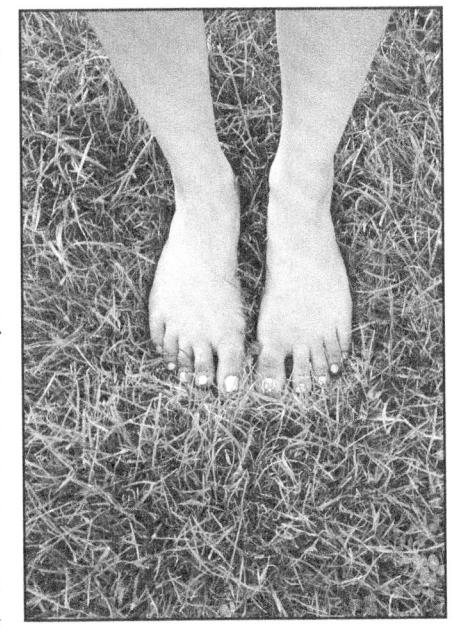

The Remedy STAR OF BETHLEHEM is beneficial for anyone who is in a state of shock or feeling traumatised, and CLEMATIS will help them to feel more centred. ROCK ROSE will help if they have gone into a state of panic, and CHERRY PLUM will help if their behaviour has become out of control or hysterical. IMPATIENS will help if you are feeling impatient with yourself, and with the speed of your progress. All of these Remedies are in the Rescue Remedy.

What is making you feel the way you do today?

Take out your healing journal and write down anything which is causing you to feel ungrounded, or in disharmony today. Start by acknowledging how you are feeling, and write it down. What are your thoughts around this?

Acknowledging what you are experiencing is always a big, brave step towards recognising anything in your life which is taking you away from your peace of mind. When you have peace of mind you will feel contented and in harmony with yourself, and you will feel more grounded and able to focus on what is happening in this moment. When you have written down your thoughts, take a few moments out, to connect with your own self, and praise yourself for the healing you are doing. Gratitude and praise will help you to feel proud of what you have achieved, and will once again help to lift up your spirits.

Give yourself and your body time to adjust to this new way of being.

Shower cleansing

Next time you go in the shower, take a few extra moments to feel the water flowing around your body, and then imagine it is cleansing the inside of your body, and all around you with healing water. Ask for anything which no longer serves you, to be washed away, as the water flows. Then imagine all the old feelings and stress flowing down into the ground below you as your roots take away all the debris.

If you practise this in the shower, and hold this as a new memory for your well-being, you could do a virtual shower cleanse for yourself whenever you feel you need cleansing and grounding. Remember your mind will respond to the thoughts you give it, and it will act accordingly by producing the wonderful feel-good chemicals.

Try singing as you shower yourself, and your energies.

You can cleanse, refresh and ground your energies, as often as you need to throughout the day. The more you use this technique the more effective it becomes, and the more energised you will feel. Take a few minutes for yourself now, and imagine you are under a shower of water, being cleansed and re-energised on the inside, and the outside. You could imagine the water as a colour to lift up your vibrations. See your roots flowing deep into the ground as you feel your body is being cleansed and grounded. Totally refreshing, and you can do this wherever you are.

CHAPTER 13

HEALING HANDS

WE WILL NOW LOOK AT other natural healing techniques you can use to help yourself. You can use each method individually or, when you are feeling more comfortable and experienced, bring them together.

At the beginning, use one technique for a few days, and then when you feel comfortable, you can start to bring in the next steps.

We all have a natural ability to help support and heal our own body. Today, you can help yourself to release your discomfort or pain naturally, with your own hands.

Do you remember the last time you hurt yourself, or had a headache? What do you naturally do? Rub the place where it hurts, or place your hand over the area where the pain is.

When you rub the area where there is pain, the blood rushes into the space, your circulation speeds up, and helps your body to start healing itself, and soothe some of your pain.

What if you could take this a stage further?

Take a few minutes to sit down to relax, and take a few deep slow breaths. Slowly breathe in calm, hold your breath, and slowly breathe out peace.

Start by recognising where you may be holding tension or pain within you.

FREE TO BE ME

Rub your hands together. Separate your hands, and hold them with your palms facing each other, about 20 cms apart.

As you slowly bring them together again, you will start to feel a warm, or tingling sensation in your hands. Sit with your hands in this position for about 20 to 30 seconds.

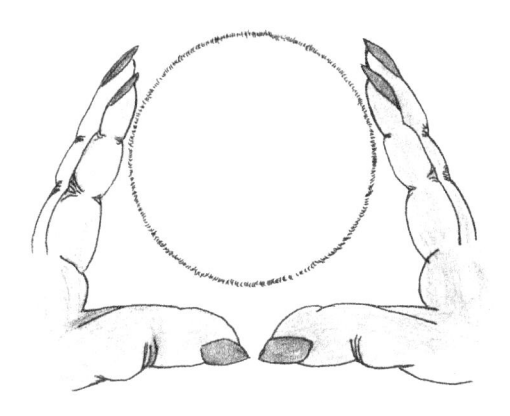

Move your hands apart, and then gently move them back towards each other again.

As you move them towards each other, you will feel like you have a ball of tingling energy between your hands.

Hold your hands at this point for about 30 seconds. The sensations in your hands will get stronger.

You could imagine this becoming a coloured ball flowing between your hands.

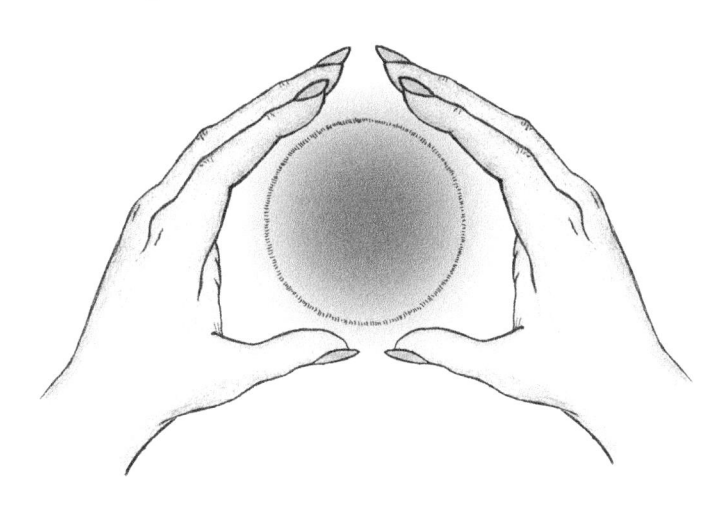

You have started your own personal healing flow within your body.

Take a few minutes to sit and relax with this flow of energy.

Bringing your attention to the flow of your breath will help you to naturally increase the flow and strength of your healing energy.

The more relaxed you are the more naturally the flow will be. Notice how the energy feels as it flows through your hands.

If your hands feel uncomfortable, take a few moments to shake your hands to release any energy trapped in your hands. Shake the energy down towards the earth.

Again, when you feel ready to progress, move on to the next step.

Did you know?

When you bring your attention to your heart space, and you send healing into that space, it increases your electro-magnetic flow, and so raises your heart vibrations.

This helps to increase your blood flow, and all of these wonderful feelings will increase your feelings of well-being, love and compassion.

Are you feeling pain in your body?

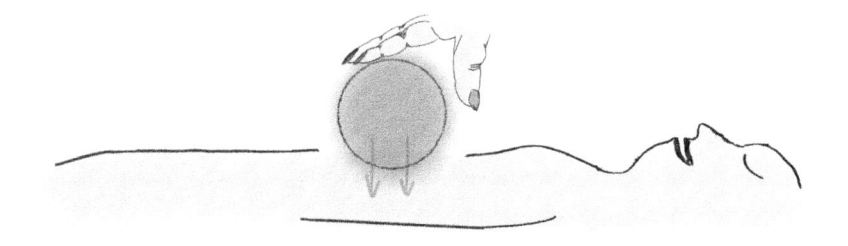

Bring your attention to somewhere in your body, where you have some tension or pain.

Place your hands over that place, and allow your hands to rest there for a few minutes. What colour do you imagine or see in your healing?

Imagine this colour flowing into your body.

You will start to feel warm or cool sensations in your body, which can help to soothe your aches. Relax with your hands there, for as long as it feels necessary.

FREE TO BE ME

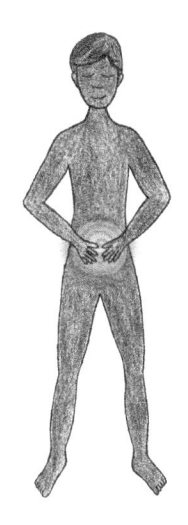

You may want to move your hands to another place on your body where if feels sore. Continue allowing the healing energy to flow, moving your hands as necessary.

Imagine any pain or tension flowing out through your feet, and down into your roots. Imagine, and feel the pain is flowing away from you and down into the earth.

The more you practise this, the more natural it will feel, and the more benefits you can receive.

Chakras

Within your body, you have energy centres which we refer to as chakras. When you are doing any form of healing, the healing energy raises up the vibrations within these energy centres.

Each of the chakras resonates at a different vibration.

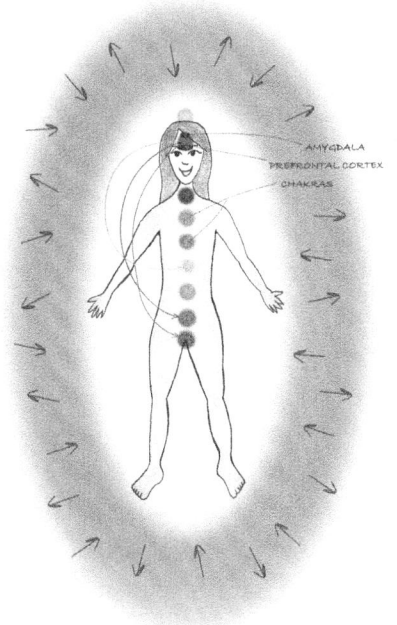

When you send healing into your body, your chakras are being cleansed, and uplifted to a more productive state. When you are healing your chakras you are encouraging your brain to send positive chemicals into your body.

If you wish, you could send healing into these energy centres to help your body feel more uplifted. Your main chakras run through the centre of your body, from the top of your head, down to below your feet.

See the healing energy flowing out into your energy field around you. As you send good vibrations out, you attract in good things.

Give your healing a purpose

Take your healing a stage further, and ask for any feelings which no longer serve you, to be cleansed away. Place one hand on your tummy, and one hand on your heart.

Give yourself some time to let these feelings flow through you, and away from you, down through your feet and into the earth. You could say 'I joyfully release any tension, and feelings which no longer serve me. I let them go now'.

With every breath out, release another layer of tension and emotions from your mind, and from your body. Feel your pulse beating as you send healing into each part of your body. Imagine, and feel all the old feelings flowing away from your precious body.

Keep allowing your hands to flow to different parts of your body, front and back. If you cannot reach the back of your body, send the healing through your body to your back.

Do not try to rush this process. Give yourself plenty of time.

Now imagine a shower of rainbow colours, and feel those colours flowing through your body, to regenerate your body. Notice the sensations in your hands. Are those sensations getting stronger? The more you use your healing energies, the stronger the healing and the sensations will become.

Keep gently breathing, as your body is filled with the healing colours. See the colours flowing into every cell, muscle, organ and bone in your body.

When the sensations in your hands stop, you have done enough healing for yourself today.

Always ground yourself, with your roots after any healing. This will help with any feelings of light-headedness or dizziness. Remember as you cleanse and lighten your energies, it takes time for your body to adjust.

Drink plenty of water to enhance the healing, detox your body and rehydrate you.

No pain today

If you do not have any aches or pains today, but would like to enjoy the many other benefits of your own healing energy, place your left hand over your heart space, and your right hand under your belly button, and allow the healing energy to flow through your body. This will help to realign your body's energies and calm your mind. Let your hands rest here for a while. You may experience tingling in your body, or see colours in your mind.

Allow the feelings, and the colours to flow naturally through your body.

Are you concerned, or worried about somebody today?

Once you have become familiar, and comfortable with these healing methods, you could take your healing a stage further.

If you have been worrying about someone else, take yourself into your relaxing healing space.

Ask for any feelings which do not belong to you, to be taken away using the following exercise.

Sometimes the thoughts you are having, can get out of proportion, or maybe you cannot see the whole picture. The more you think about a situation the more real it seems, and the more your perception strengthens.

To change the situation, you need to let go of your thoughts, your perceptions and your worries, to allow your mind to be clear, and enable you to see the reality of what is happening. This can also allow and enable you to see alternative perspectives and solutions.

Cleansing exercise to release over-concern

Take yourself into your calm healing space with your slow deep breathing.

Think of someone you have been worrying about.

Imagine all your feelings of 'over-concern' you have been holding in your mind, and surround them all in a bubble of light, filled with whatever colour comes to your mind.

Now imagine that bubble of light, filled with all those heavy feelings, flowing away from your mind and down through your body.

Imagine, and feel all those feelings flowing out through your feet, and into the ground below you.

Say to yourself, 'I am joyfully releasing all feelings which do not belong to me', and see those feelings flowing away from you, out through your hands, and down into the earth. Give yourself some time to release any feelings you have been carrying in your mind.

When you have done as much as necessary for today, sit for a few minutes, and bring your attention back to your gentle breathing to allow your body time to adjust. Take a drink of water to replenish yourself.

The next step

Now think about the person you were concerned about, and imagine them, surrounded in a shower of rainbow healing colours, or a particular colour if that comes to your mind first.

Trust your intuition, and know they will receive the healing colour they need. You are sending them the highest vibration of healing through the colours. Trust they will be taken care of, in the best way possible, for them and for their journey.

Create an uplifting affirmation you can send to them, to support their situation. 'Every day you are getting stronger. I know you are stronger every day'. When you use healing, colours and affirmations to help others, you will benefit too. You will also feel able to rise above their situation, which will then enable you to offer more constructive advice and support when the time is right.

Always ground yourself afterwards, and drink plenty of water. Give yourself time to adjust before you go back into your day. Notice how much lighter you feel.

Take some time to write in your healing journal about your healing experience, and anyone you were working with. You could write down a positive affirmation alongside their name. Maybe, 'I can see them feeling stronger now.', or whatever fits in with the intention you choose to send.

Feeling fulfilled

You can practise these exercises each day. Each time you work with your healing hands, you will feel more relaxed, and your mind will feel more at peace.

You will feel uplifted, and have a sense of fulfilment because you are now working with your own healing and your higher self, which brings you closer to your sense of real purpose. We will look more at your higher self later in your book.

A good time to practise these healing exercises is at bedtime, or if you wake up during the night. It's also a great way to start your day, or refresh your energies and lift up your spirits during the day.

If you like crystals, you could enhance the energy flow through your hands by holding your favourite crystals in your hands whilst you allow the healing energy to flow. Each crystal has its own healing properties. Use the crystals you are drawn to today.

Healing colours

This is a general guide, to help you recognise how each colour can support you. When you use the colours you may get a different insight in your mind as to how the colour will support you. Go with this insight. Your mind and your higher self will know what is best for you.

White contains all the colours of the spectrum, brings clarity, and helps you to heal on all levels.

Black also contains all the colours of the spectrum, but can indicate you need more grounding.

Indigo and violet brings insight and helps you see things through a higher perspective.
Light blue helps you speak about how you feel.
Turquoise helps you speak from the heart.
Green and pink bring you forgiveness, compassion and unconditional love.
Yellow brings you renewed confidence and self-belief.
Orange helps you release anger, and brings passion and creativeness.
Red brings you stability, trust, abundance and grounding.

The more you practise using the colours, the more you will get an understanding of how they can support you in your life. Each time you use the healing colours, you are enhancing your healing, and you are expanding your creative mind, which then enables you to see things more clearly. You are getting in touch with, and trusting your intuition, your higher self, to guide you.

When you practise working with imagining colours, you are expanding your ability to work with your pineal gland in your mind. Your pineal gland vibrates with colours, and helps to expand your deeper perception and insights. The more you use the colours in your thoughts, the more clarity you will get.

Personal Protection

If you are prone to picking up on other people's feelings, you could imagine yourself surrounded in a bubble of coloured light during your healing time. This will help you be less over-sensitive to others' feelings. You can also imagine yourself in your coloured bubble of light throughout the day to strengthen your own energy field.

It is usually natural that sensitive people are empathic, which means they can easily pick up on other people's feelings. When you are feeling vulnerable this can create even more problems for you. You become over-sensitive to others' feelings, and can find it hard to separate their feelings from your own.

Throughout the day, if you do feel over-sensitive to others' feelings, you could imagine any feelings you pick up from other people, being flushed through your body. You do not need to be resting, to allow yourself to release those feelings as you did in the previous exercises. Make a habit of cleansing your energies throughout the day, with the shower of healing colours.

Take it a stage further, and imagine your energy field around your body, your aura, being cleansed with the shower of coloured light as well. You may have one particular colour, or many colours. See the outside of your aura being strengthened. You could imagine it as a crystal, or a cloak of protection being placed around you. If you want to work on a more spiritual level, you could ask Archangel Michael to surround you in a healing cloak of protection, and imagine that cloak around you. Always say thank you for the help and the protection.

Your protection field is a sealed space where you can thrive and feel safe and protected. If you are feeling over-sensitive, you can imagine a thick perspex tube around you for protection. See the tube about 2 metres wide, and going up to a dome shape above you, with just a small opening at the top to allow your connection with your higher guidance.

Imagine your protection field around you getting stronger throughout the day. Imagine your protection field being sealed up if you find yourself feeling tired, lacking in energy or motivation, or you are being pulled into other people's stress. At the same time, take some time to imagine the coloured shower flowing through your body, just in case you are being affected by energies around you. Cleanse your energy throughout the day.

Take some time to listen to where your thoughts are. Are you thinking about, or worrying about someone? If so, you may be picking up on how they feel.

Keep cleansing and protecting your energies throughout the day, and you will find it easier to maintain your sense of well-being. You will also become more aware of which feelings are yours, and which belong to other people. You will feel more empowered because you have control over how you feel, and when you are being affected.

Take those thoughts out of your head and put them in your healing journal. When they are in front of you you can study them to start recognising if your thoughts are supporting you, or not. What alternative thoughts could you use about the situation?

Seal your aura after appointments

Do you realise that when someone comes into your energy field they can impact on your energies? They can leave a residue of their energy with you, and they can also leave your energy field open to be depleted.

Whenever you have allowed someone into your energy field, take a few moments when they move away from you to clear your energies, and seal up your aura.

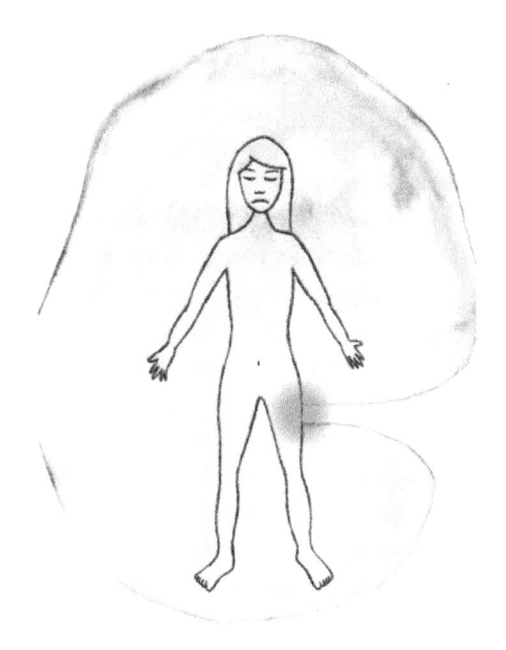

An aura which is left open will make you feel depleted in energies, and you could have re-occurring aches and pains. Make it a priority to reseal your aura throughout the day, especially if you spend time around unwell, unhappy or negative people, or have anything like a dental appointment or medical intervention.

If you feel depleted in energy, or have reoccurring aches and pains, your aura, the energy field around you, could be depleted.

Take some time to imagine yourself in a bright coloured bubble of light, and see that bubble as a sealed unit. This is your safe place to be.

DAWN CHRYSTAL

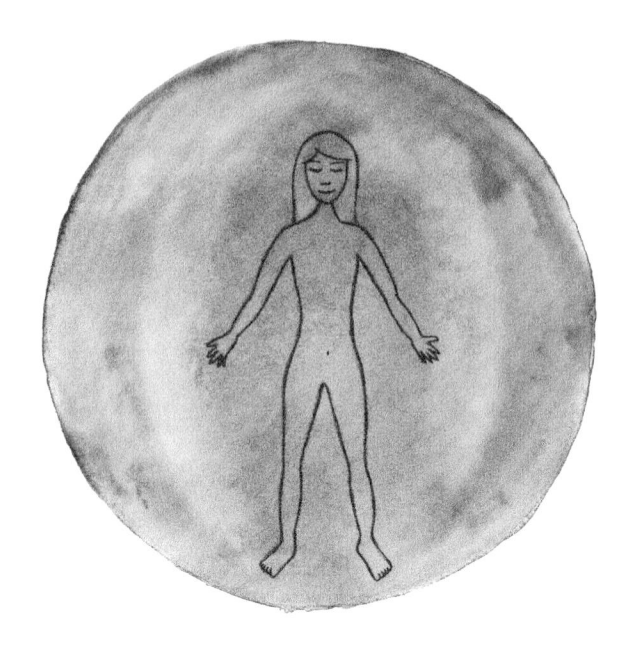

As a general rule, if you feel depleted in energy, or have reoccurring aches and pains, always check your aura is cleansed and sealed.

Always strengthen your aura before, and after any interventions to your energy field.

See the outside of your aura as a strong sealed unit to help you maintain your sense of well-being, and for your protection.

CHAPTER 14

ARE YOU FEARFUL FOR OTHERS?

ONE OF THE THINGS WHICH can frequently create stress and anxiety is worrying too much about other people. It is often a natural over-reaction to feel concerned, or fearful for others when they are going through a stressful time. Being caring and concerned is alright, but when it becomes over-care or over-concern it can create more problems for you, as well as for them.

There are some important things to consider when we are fearful for others.

The first is that you are sending them even more thoughts of fear and stress, and this lower vibration of thoughts can affect them on an energetic and emotional level. It is a form of telepathy. What you project out, is what the other person will receive in their thoughts, and so this can impact on them and compound their own thoughts of fear and insecurities.

If you are telling them verbally that you are fearful or anxious about their situation, that will add to their stress levels too. Their mind will start to process your thoughts and words, and their mind will then start to create more negative thoughts around your thinking of their situation.

Another consequence of thinking stressful thoughts about others, is that your mind cannot differentiate whether you are thinking about them, or about you. It can only recognise the stress and fear thoughts, and cannot differentiate to whom the issue refers. Your mind will produce all the reactive chemicals to help you to cope with what you are thinking about. More stress induced chemicals are produced and released into your body to help you cope with that, and you will be caught up in a perpetual pattern of feeling stress again as the process continues to spiral.

A gentle way to turn this situation around for everyone concerned is to start thinking and sending out more positive, supportive thoughts. Listen, acknowledge the situation, and then send out thoughts which will help lift the situation for the other person concerned, and for you. You could use a simple affirmation like 'I am blissfully feeling at peace with all that is happening in their life. They are confident, and have all they need to deal with this', or 'They are getting stronger every day. Everything will work out well for them' or, 'I am lovingly sending you peace and strength to deal with this situation'.

Over-concern for others

Over-concern for other people can be one of the more challenging things to deal with, especially when the concern is for those close to you. This is a good time to get in touch with your prayers. You don't need to be religious or believe in after-life to believe in the power of prayers. Just know that prayers send positive vibrations. The more you ask for help for them, and send out positive expectations that they will be looked after, the better the outcome will be. In your prayers, ask for them to be surrounded in strength, hope and comfort. If they are unwell, ask for them to be surrounded in strength, support and healing, and trust that it will be done. See them as feeling stronger and more able to deal with their situation. Remember you are lifting up their vibrations with your own positive intentions and expectations.

The Bach Flower Remedy RED CHESTNUT is really helpful to support you in sending out good thoughts for others. It helps to alleviate your fears and over-concern for others, and enables you to take a more passive, objective and supportive view of the situation. RED CHESTNUT helps you to have more uplifting thoughts and positive expectations for their situation, and their well-being.

If you are in a caring role, a good combination of Remedies for you could be CENTAURY, CRAB APPLE, MIMULUS, RED CHESTNUT, SCLERANTHUS and WALNUT. Take this Remedy frequently as a preventative, as well as to help you maintain uplifting expectations for others. This combination can also help you to alleviate any fears you may have, have stronger boundaries, cleanse your mind and body, make the right choices, and be less over-sensitive to other people's feelings.

Take some time throughout this day to recognise who your thoughts and energies are with today, and then follow it though for a few more days until you get a clearer perspective of what you need to change. Use your healing journal to keep a record of what you are observing.

Where do you spend your time with each person? In your head, on the phone, in person, on social media.

How much of your day is consumed by each person, or each situation? When you take this information out of your head and put it in front of you, it will give you the opportunity to get a clearer perspective of what is happening, and what you need to change.

Seeing the situation in front of you can help you get a reality check. How much of your thinking time, or your physical time, is being consumed by other people's needs. Can you start to see why you can feel so tired, run down and overwhelmed? Taking appropriate action to help yourself will then free you up to be able to give more quality time when you choose to. You can choose to re-evaluate each situation, and choose to take more time for you. Allowing yourself to have more quality time, enables you to start sending out positive thoughts to lift up the people and their situation, and enhances the feelings of well-being and safety for all concerned, including you.

Your brain will then start producing healing feel-good chemicals which will give you more compassion, understanding and strength. In turn, your improved mental state will enable you to feel stronger in the support you can offer. In this state, you will have better clarity and are more able to provide positive and uplifting solutions and support if you are meant to be helping them.

What thoughts and vibrations are you sending out?

Remember a time when you were really anxious about an event or a situation, and someone gave you an uplifting or reassuring comment? 'You look lovely', 'You will do well', 'It will all work out well for you'. Remember how much better you felt when you heard those reassuring words and comments?

What thoughts are you sending out? Are your thoughts helping or hindering the situation for others? Become more aware of what you are thinking about, and start to turn around any thoughts which could be detrimental to others, and to yourself. Take some time to write down thoughts you notice you are constantly using. Start to turn them around today.

Write in your healing journal, how you feel today about the situation. Why do you feel so concerned for them? How can you help, without transferring your over-concern or your anxiety onto them? What thoughts could you use instead?

It is important to acknowledge how you are feeling, or what your concerns are. You can take your supporting thoughts a stage further by saying to yourself, 'Although I am concerned for them, I am trusting they can handle this. I am sending them strength and supportive thoughts'. This will help bring you back into a state of balance, because you are acknowledging you are concerned, and are sending out positive thoughts and expectations.

Doing something practical together can help both you and them. It is often the case that people open up when they are moving about, maybe walking, in the car, or out of their usual surroundings. What respite can you bring that will help both of you?

Keep your breathing calm whenever you think about them, or you are with them.

Your affirmations for today:

'They are feeling peace in their life, they can deal with this. They are getting stronger, and all will be well'.

'I am calmly feeling at peace with my life, and all that is happening in their life'.

When someone is feeling unhappy or out of sorts, their energy within their body, and around them, can become depleted. You can take your supporting role to a more detached level, but an even more supportive role, by asking the universe for a healing colour to surround the person you are concerned about.

When you think about them and their situation, automatically bring a colour to your mind, and imagine them surrounded in that colour. Every colour has a different healing property. Trust that they will receive exactly what they need for their situation. Using colours has a beneficial effect for both of you, because you are thinking of the colour, your mind and body also respond more favourably to the healing colour you are focusing on, so it is a win-win situation for you both.

The calmer you are, the more easily all will be resolved, and the stronger you both will become. When you send out positive thoughts, and expectations, everyone will benefit. Thank yourself for being a caring person. Be proud of who you are, and the love and support that you can offer. Never underestimate the power of caring.

Your boundaries

Does your over-concern infringe on your boundaries?

One of the most common causes of inner conflict can be putting others' needs above your own. When you are concerned about someone else it is often natural to put their needs above your own. Sometimes this is appropriate or necessary, and frequently putting others' needs above your own has become a way of life. Is this detrimental to your own well-being?

How many times do you want to honour your needs by saying 'no', and yet you disregard your body's needs and give in to others' requests? If you are a full time carer, or your job involves caring for others, obviously you cannot disregard what you need to do for others. Maybe this would be a good time to start looking at ways you could invite in more help for yourself to make time for you.

Take some time over the next few days to observe how often you go with other people's needs, instead of what you need for yourself. Make a note in your journal when you recognise somewhere in your life where your boundaries are out of balance. How many times do you say 'yes' to someone's requests, when you wish you could say 'no'?

Are there particular people who seem to be taking more of your time than necessary, people who seem to constantly demand your time and your attention, whether it's on the phone, on-line, or in person? Make a note of who these people are. Start to recognise how much time you are giving to their requests or demands. Are their needs really more important than yours? If their needs are a priority, how could you get more help to support you?

Make a note of where you spend your time during the day supporting others, maybe unnecessarily. Write down the names concerned, and then start to look at how you can adjust this. Work with one person at a time, and this will often then flow into making your boundaries stronger in other situations too.

Start to re-balance your boundaries. Start to make a conscious decision to allow yourself to say 'no' when it feels right to you. It is not about saying 'I don't care', it is about saying 'my needs are important too'. If you become too tired or unwell to help, others will have to find a way to manage. Trust they will always find a way. Start now while you are still strong enough to make the right choices. The Remedy to help you reset and maintain your boundaries is CENTAURY.

By stepping back, and using higher thoughts, vibrations and expectations you are enabling others to empower themselves as you empower yourself.

An affirmation to support you could be 'I joyfully take responsibility for my actions, and my needs, and I am sending to them good thoughts and vibrations. I know they have what it takes to work through this'.

If you recognise that you do struggle with your boundaries, the Remedies CENTAURY, CHESTNUT BUD and RED CHESTNUT would be a good combination for you. You may need to take these Remedies for some time, if you have always given in to others' requests and put their needs above your own.

Or maybe, you have never considered a need to change the way things are. Listen to what your body is telling you. When someone asks you to do something for them, what is your initial feeling or thought? If it is upbeat, joyful and willing, continue to go with the flow of stepping in to support them.

But if you feel some reluctance or resistance, ask yourself why? How are their requests or needs making you feel? Make a note of your feelings and thoughts in your journal. Be honest with yourself. Are you helping because you want to, just because they have asked you, or has it become the norm for you to step up and fulfill their needs. Maybe there is an underlying reason for your actions, or your resistance.

Do you feel guilty?

Do you feel over-sensitive to what others think of you? WALNUT is for over-sensitivity, or being influenced by others. If you spend your time feeling guilty, or putting others' needs above your own, you will always feel depleted in energies. PINE is the Remedy to help you with any feelings of guilt and taking too much responsibility for others' mistakes, well-being or happiness.

Sometimes you can become too proud to ask for help. WATER VIOLET is a really effective Remedy to counteract these feelings of pride, and being too concerned what others think of you. CENTAURY will help you to honour your needs and CERATO will help you to recognise when others are taking advantage, or you are allowing yourself to be taken for granted. And CERATO will help if you constantly need their approval. CERATO helps you to approve of yourself, and trust in yourself and your intuition.

You may have convinced yourself what you are thinking is the truth. You may believe you have got to do things just because you always have. You may even think you are invincible, and it has to be done. You may become so worried what others think of you, you go overboard to help or to please. Sometimes you may even assume, or become convinced, they will be judging you if you do not oblige. CERATO is the Remedy for trusting in your own judgement, and not needing others' approval. As long as you approve of yourself, and of your choices, everything else will fall into place.

If you are feeling constantly tired or weary look at your thought patterns and boundaries. OAK is a great Remedy to help you deal with your tiredness, but you do need to address the reason for your tiredness. I believe the OAK Remedy is often needed when your soul says 'Enough is enough. I am tired of living like this'. When your body and soul are weary and tired, it is time for you to step up and take back your personal power.

Take some time to write down what you are observing in your life. Do you have strong boundaries, or is there room for improvement?

One of the greatest gifts we can give others, is our time, support and attention. This is the reason many of us are here. It is what makes us thrive and feel inspired to keep going. Giving is our way of saying 'I care about you' or 'I love you'. Caring is a way of life. It fulfills your needs as much as it supports others.

But the problem often comes when you are always putting others' needs above your own, and not listening to what you and your body needs. What is your body and your soul saying to you? Are you giving willingly and unconditionally, or has your giving become subservience or conditional?

I am not saying stop helping and supporting others, but stop and listen to your own 'gut reaction' next time someone asks you to do something for them. Is your body too tired to help? Do you feel mentally or physically exhausted? Do you need to rest at the moment? Are their needs really more important than yours at the moment?

How is your body reacting when someone asks for or demands your time? Writing down your observations in your healing journal will help you to be more aware of what is happening, and where you need to make some changes. Be proud of yourself as you work through any changes you need to make.

Consequences

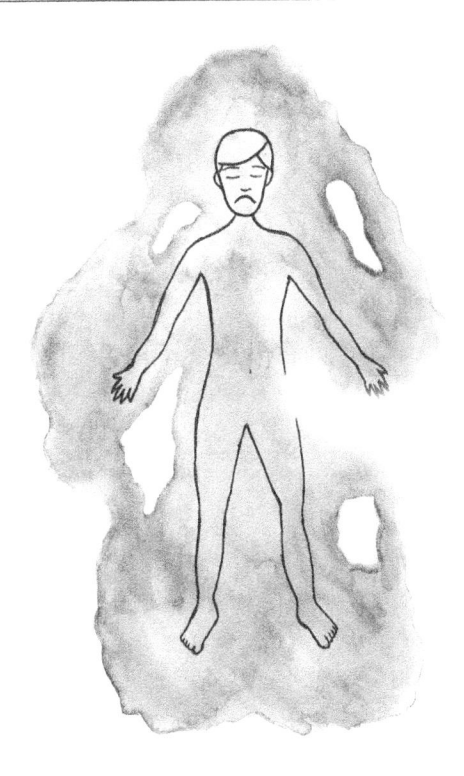

What are the consequences of not listening to your body's needs? Your body can become more and more weary, to the point where you feel unwell. Or you could end up only giving conditionally, and with feelings of resentment, which then becomes more detrimental to your feelings of well-being and harmony.

It is hard to feel caring and loving towards someone when you are feeling resentful, or you feel that they are taking advantage of you and your good nature. When you start on a spiral of feeling resentful or reluctant it affects you on all levels. Your brain produces the harsher chemicals to help you deal with what you are feeling, and your body struggles to cope with the harsher thoughts and feelings which are flowing through your body. Your mind cannot think of two thoughts at the same time, and so it seems impossible for you to feel joyful and loving when you are holding harsh thoughts.

Often a CENTAURY 'personality type', when in a subservient state, can become the VINE 'state of mind' when their boundaries have been pushed for too long. This can result in them becoming bossy, demanding and too pushy, to overcome their own lack of boundaries, and to cover up what has become their weakness. Take some time to read about these two Bach Remedies to see if you can relate to the way you feel. There is often an underlying feeling of frustration, anger or resentment which has not been addressed.

The Remedies HOLLY, MUSTARD and WILLOW can help you to work through these feelings. There is also a chapter on Forgiveness, and some meditations later in this book, to help you work through any feelings of resentment you need to release and heal. It is often not a conscious thought to start feeling resentful. It is usually a deep reaction to years of accumulated feelings which may have been out of balance. It is hard to see any good perspective within a relationship when you are holding negative thoughts towards someone or their actions. It can feel like they are doing things against you, whether intentionally or not, which then increases your feelings of disharmony and your unconscious or conscious way you feel about them.

Make a decision today, to notice if your boundaries are out of balance. Ask yourself, 'Who is infringing on my boundaries?' or 'Who is taking advantage?' or 'Where have I allowed my boundaries to become too slack?'

How can you start to address this? Start with one person at a time, and then work with the next person. Create an affirmation which supports you. Maybe, 'I joyfully respect and value myself, and everyone respects and values me', or 'I have good strong boundaries now. It's okay to say 'no', and I am happily doing so'.

Creating new boundaries can be a constant aspect of you which needs to be addressed. If you are a CENTAURY personality type, your reason for being here on this earth is to help and support others, which is a great mission. But it is when you come to a point in your life, where you have given too much of yourself, and you do not listen to how you feel, or what your needs are, that it starts to create problems for you. Being in this state can then bring you feelings of disharmony and inner conflict.

What healing colour could you surround yourself with today? Use the affirmation, 'Today I am joyfully creating new boundaries for myself, and everyone respects my boundaries'. Send this message out in your thoughts throughout the day, and it will help you set, and maintain new boundaries for yourself.

Make some time in your day to sit with your healing energies to help re-balance your well-being. Imagine the colour you see flowing through you, and filling your aura. Make the colour as strong and vibrant as possible.

This brings the best quality of life for you, and an ideal balance between looking after you, and for others.

Having strong boundaries helps everyone around you

When you have strong boundaries for yourself, you have more energy to give willingly when you wish to, and everyone around you knows where they stand with you. By stepping back, and allowing others to do things for themselves, you are encouraging them to empower themselves, and re-evaluate how they need to change. They can learn new skills, and grow in ways which would have been inhibited if you had always been the one to step in and take action on their behalf. Giving others the space to empower themselves is a priceless gift you are offering them.

Maybe your old beliefs are holding you in a place of subservience. Do you feel guilty for saying 'no', and putting your needs above others? Do you find it hard to speak about what is troubling you? Do you feel less worthy than them, or feel like you are not a good person for saying 'no'? Do you feel like you may lose them? Or maybe you feel a need to justify why you want to say 'no'. If you feel frustrated about a situation, take some time out to use your voice-clearing exercise, to release some of your frustrations. Cleanse your energies, and set about making subtle changes, one step at a time.

If you can recognise you need to make some boundary changes the Remedies AGRIMONY, CENTAURY, CRAB APPLE, MIMULUS,

PINE, RED CHESTNUT, WALNUT would be a good combination for you to work with to help you resolve this situation for yourself. Take some time to read about these Remedies to discover the best way you can find relief from these heavy thoughts and feelings which may be holding you back.

Whatever reason is behind you feeling a need to make changes, be honest with yourself, and start to create new healthier boundaries for yourself today. Everyone will benefit from your new boundaries, and the rest of your life will start to fall into place. The more empowered you feel, the stronger your feelings of harmony and contentment will be. Red is a good colour to surround yourself with, to help you feel safe and protected.

Take some time to observe what is happening in your life, and choose to make some changes. Make a note of any observations you notice, and how you intend to make those changes. How will you feel when you have made the necessary changes? Praise yourself as you go through the steps you are taking, and the things you overcome. As you strengthen your boundaries you will simplify your life.

Is it always a person's energies I am picking up?

When you are sensitive you can constantly be picking up on, and being affected by, vibrational energies around you. In time you will start to recognise how you are being affected by the energies around you. If you are feeling over-sensitive you can be severely affected by the energies you are experiencing. This can impact on how you feel each day.

Start to make a conscious effort to notice if your moods suddenly shift. Could you be being affected by the weather, the moon cycles, the planetary shifts, or the energies in a place where you go to? It may even be the energies in your home or your workplace which are having an impact on you, and the way you feel. Make a note in your healing journal if you suddenly feel a shift in the way you feel, and take the time to be more observant of what is happening around you. Looking at how outside influences impact on you can help you to prepare, and adjust what is happening.

One of the places which always seemed to have an impact on me was the supermarket. I would come away from the supermarket feeling absolutely drained. I also started to recognise how my moods and emotions were affected by the moon cycles. Recognising the impact of this helped me to be more aware of the fact it was not always something inside of me which was making me feel the way I did.

You can be affected by a vast range of energies, from other people, from the universe, from the weather, or it could be from a building. Quite often a building, or a place, can hold an energy of something that has happened there. Imagine a family has had a bad argument in their home. That energy, of the tension and distress, can be held in that place where it happened. You can walk out of that distorted energy to continue your day, feel more uplifted and detached from it, and then walk back into the distressed energy when you return. This is often why you can feel better when you move to another situation, and then feel distressed again when you return to the place of the incident.

If you start to work with clearing energies in places around today, you will soon start to recognise when the energies are not compatible with you. When you work on making significant changes, you will feel more empowered because you are taking back responsibility for how you feel wherever you go. One of the simplest ways of changing the energies within a building, is by opening all the windows and doors, and allowing the clean air to remove all stagnant energies. Playing upbeat or soothing music can also help to lift up the energy vibrations.

Some different ways to clear energies

You can use many natural ways of clearing the energies that are held within a space.

Smudging is a powerful technique from Native American traditions. When smudging, you are using natural plant energy to remove any negativity.

Sage is often used for smudging. Place some sage on a shallow dish. Light it with a match.

When the sage starts to smoke, use a feather to wave through the smoke. Then move around the room which needs clearing, wafting the smoke into the air and allowing it to clear the energies and re-energise the room.

Chime bells can be used to clear energies. You tap the two cymbals together, and then allow the vibration of the cymbals to permeate out into the room. You can walk around the room, repeatedly ringing the chime bells to clear all the corners, and then walk in to the centre of the room, ring the bells again, and allow the beautiful energies to do the cleansing for you. You can be more specific and cleanse each piece of furniture within the room. This is particularly beneficial if there is someone who is in a negative state, and spends time sitting in a particular chair. This will lift the vibration in that space, and so help the person involved too when they return to the chair. They will benefit from the uplifting energy.

Singing bowls are a very powerful way of clearing energies. You can use Tibetan singing bowls, or crystal bowls. See which one you are drawn to. They are both very effective. Gently strike the bowl with the wooden stick which comes with it. The noise vibration from the bowl will cleanse and re-energise the room. You can sit in the centre of the room and imagine the energy flowing out, or you can physically move around the room with the singing bowl to do the cleansing.

Using candles. Lighting a candle in a room can lift the vibrations. The flame helps to transmute any negative energy into a higher vibration.

Use healing colours. Think of a healing colour in your mind, and then imagine the colour flowing into each room in your home, or your workplace.

You can use this technique to cleanse any building or area where the energies have become heavy or distressed. Try using a combination of clearing techniques. Experiment with each of the methods, and see which you prefer. They are all really effective ways of cleansing energies, and will uplift the spirits of everyone who comes into the building. You can also use each of these methods for cleansing the energies within yourself, and within, and around, other people. It really does lift up everyone's spirits.

Exploring a way forward

When you feel discouraged or confused, you can lose sight of yourself, and you can start to lose belief in your own abilities. You may find yourself being unable to separate what is going on in your body and mind, from who you are. You may question who you are, and ask a million negative questions of yourself, which all lead you back to the same place.

We often ask 'What is wrong with me?', 'Why does that keep happening to me?', 'Why do I keep making the same mistakes?'. You can feel powerless to change because you cannot see a solution, or an alternative way.

If you feel like you have lost yourself, and you do not know who you really are, the Remedy CERATO will help you to start believing in yourself again. CHESTNUT BUD will help support you through making any changes, and creating new more uplifting patterns for yourself. If you combine these two Remedies with CENTAURY you will feel enabled to maintain any changes you need to make, and not worry about needing others' approval. The only person's approval you need is yours.

Acknowledge if you are feeling disharmony now

If you are struggling, or in emotional or physical pain, firstly acknowledge this. Do not try to pretend you are not struggling. Acknowledging your distress or your disharmony is an important step towards recognising what you are going through, and that you need help. There are some times on your journey when you will not feel like trying to fix your pain. And this is okay for now. Sometimes acknowledging the pain is a big enough step for today. Be gentle on yourself through these days.

When you feel ready, take gentle steps forward each day. Write down the way you feel today in your healing journal. Make a note of how often you have these days when you are low in energy or motivation. Do not judge yourself for these days. There is usually an underlying reason why you feel this way. Be gentle on yourself during these days and try to do things which help you to feel relaxed and as joyful as possible.

Do you ignore the fact that you are not happy? Do you question yourself for feeling this way? Are you too hard on yourself on these days? How does this make you feel? This is a good starting point. Write the date you acknowledged this. Do you want to address this today?

When you have lost sight of who you are or how you feel, and are feeling powerless to change this perception, anything you achieve never seems to be able to bring you satisfaction. When you feel helpless to see solutions for yourself, it is all too natural to then move your expectations of fulfilment onto other people. You expect them to bring you the happiness you desire.

You can then transfer your frustration onto those around you, and worse still, can start to inappropriately criticise and condemn them because they do not come up to your expectations. You then feel even more disharmony, and end up skipping from one state of frustration to another. You may start to question why you have this feeling, and even who you really are.

You may question your behaviour, your attitude and belief in yourself, and can even question your own personality and, worse still, you start to criticise and condemn yourself. This brings an even deeper sense of disharmony, and this inner distress can bring feelings of anxiety and more stress, which can even lead to feelings of deeper stress, anxiety, depression and feeling totally lost or not belonging.

Signs of emotions being out of balance

Feeling sad, disillusioned, angry, rebellious, guilty, impatient, intolerant, agitated, frustrated, holding tension, stressed, feeling anxious, tearful, sadness, depression, loneliness, isolating yourself, withdrawal, not feeling good enough, apologising, having suicidal thoughts, ideas of wanting to escape, not being able to rest or to sleep. There are a multitude of other symptoms which show themselves when you are feeling emotionally confused.

Be gentle on yourself when you start to acknowledge what is going on, and recognise that you are at a crossroads, and you can turn it around.

WILD ROSE is a great Remedy to help you find inner motivation again, and SWEET CHESTNUT will help you to see light at the end of your tunnel. Please reach out if you cannot work through transformation by yourself. Any step you take will feel like a massive step forward. Keep taking lots of small baby steps and you will find your peace of mind and the clarity and strength you need.

What is your ultimate goal today?

Your ultimate goal is to be able to move your state of mind from the confused and busy state to the relaxed state, so your mind and your body can enjoy the calm and peace you need to thrive and have a good quality of life. It is difficult to think well when you feel tense, are rushed, or doing too many things at once, or are thinking about too many things. A calm state of mind brings you the ability to have, and maintain, a sense of well-being. It enables you to deal with anything you are currently experiencing, or anything which comes along.

The most effective thing you can do for yourself is make a new decision, a new choice, to take simple steps to create or increase this feeling of well-being, one step at a time.

Every step will bring you the ability to make the most of your life today, not only in how productive you can be, but in also being able to maintain your sense of calm and peace within. We will take the time to look at ways you can help yourself to achieve this. The most productive step you can take, at any time of the day, is to recognise when you are feeling mentally, emotionally or physically stressed, and take your thoughts to your breathing.

Starting to incorporate the gentle, slow, deeper breathing techniques into all of your day-to-day activities will help you to achieve a more relaxed state of mind. If you practise using your deeper gentle breaths to relax your body and your mind, after a while it will feel more natural. This will help you to not react, and so maintain your composure. You are retraining yourself, so that when you have a stressful situation to manage, your brain, mind and body will all respond in the best way possible. It will also help you maintain your inner strength and a calm state of mind.

By using a combination of the breathing techniques, affirmations,

Bach Flower Remedies and lessons learned throughout your journey, you will obtain a powerful result. Drink plenty of water to help you maintain your new calmer state of mind and body. Your brain will naturally produce the feel-good chemicals, which will help you maintain your ultimate composure and energy levels. Take time to stop and relax when it feels necessary.

In this way you are creating a new, more beneficial way of living for yourself, and a gentle way to help you deal with any stress, traumas and anxiety. This will give you a refreshing new perspective on whatever you are dealing with. It will also give you the opportunity to see what is happening in your behaviour.

When you have a better understanding of yourself, and how some of your detrimental patterns have been created, it gives you a better insight into how you can start to turn things around for yourself. Take one step at a time, and you will be able to undo patterns which are creating distress and chaos in your mind. Be gentle but persistent, both with yourself, and with the process of changing. With tenacity, self-appreciation and renewed hope, anything is possible.

GORSE is the Remedy to bring you renewed hope, and is the first step towards your recovery. IMPATIENS is a great Remedy to bring you patience with yourself, and ROCK WATER helps you to be gentle on yourself and honour your needs. CENTAURY will help you stay strong in your intentions to make changes, and CHESTNUT BUD will help you maintain those changes.

Always remember. Every small step will make a big difference. Every step is a step forward. When you keep following the stepping stones, you will reach your goal. Celebrate every step you take forward. You will soon start to see your real potential.

When you feel more contented in yourself, and accepting of who you are, your true happiness will soon follow. Take time at every stage to acknowledge the steps you are taking. Take time to acknowledge how well you have done. Praise and thank yourself. Take time to enjoy the moment.

What is causing your stress today?

There are so many things that contribute to stress in your body, and in your mind. Some things are really obvious, and you are probably already aware of what is causing you to feel stressed. List the causes in your healing journal, and make a note of the date you start to work with each pattern.

Thinking and worrying about things in your past can keep you in a similar state of stress to what you went through in the actual incident.

Take a few moments to think of something which brings you happiness, and then, using your fingertips, gently tap on the centre point on your forehead, just above your eyebrows. Keep thinking of your happy thoughts. Continue tapping and breathing until calmness comes.

Take it a stage further by gently tapping on your thymus point, the space between your heart and your throat, to increase your energy flow.

Now take this to a practical visual level, where you can keep your mind clearer and more uplifted. Create a prayer board, where you write the things which worry you, and the people and situations you are concerened about, and take some time to pray for those each. Everything which is worrying you can be added to this board each day. Keep moving the things which have been resolved or healed to your gratitude board.

CHAPTER 15

RAISE UP YOUR VIBRATIONS WITH CHANTING AND SINGING

WHEN YOUR EMOTIONS HAVE BECOME out of balance, it can impact upon you on many levels. Your whole body can feel affected. It affects the way you feel, and can even cause physical pains and a sense of feeling out of balance.

A gentle way to re-align your energies within your body is with chanting. Chanting is gently repeating out loud something repetitive to yourself. You can change and raise the vibration of your chanting healing by changing the tone and pitch of your voice. Experiment with different sounds. You can chant at any time. You could combine your chanting with doing something you enjoy, or take some time out to relax whilst you chant. Chanting is like a gentle singing, with a soothing vibration which lifts up your spirits. Introduce a soft gentle tune with your chanting.

A really simple chant to use is repeating the vowels A E I O U out loud to yourself. Chanting the vowels can help to release any trapped emotions you have in your body. This will then help to realign your energy centres and the chakras within your body. The more you chant the vowels to yourself, the higher your vibration will become. Gently lower your voice, and repeat the vowels out loud to yourself. Notice the effect it has on your body. You will feel different sensations within your body and your mind. Keep slowly chanting until you feel calm and more empowered.

Allow a change in the tone of your voice each time you repeat the vowels. Let your voice flow naturally. Sometimes your voice may sound gruff and deep at the beginning. If you have been feeling stressed or uptight, or you find it hard to express how you feel, it may seem hard to get a long tone out through your voice. Keep repeating the chanting with whatever sound comes out. Do not judge how it feels, or how it sounds. You are releasing stress from your body, and that may not always sound pleasant!

If you have been through some shocks or traumas, or you have found it hard to speak up for yourself, you can often feel like you have a lump in your throat. You can hold trauma in your body in many places, but the throat is usually the place where it seems more evident. It can feel hard to clear this feeling of tightness to talk about what has upset you. When you are holding shock or trauma in your throat, it can also feel like you have a heaviness in your heart and your stomach feels uneasy.

Chanting will help you to clear your throat and your voice, which then allows you to clear tension from the rest of your body. Do not think about, or try to alter, the sounds which come out, just keep doing it until you feel free of tension. As your tension is released, the tone, the sound, and length of your chant will change.

Chanting helps to realign your emotional energy centres in your body, and can be the first step to calming your mind. It can also help you connect with your higher self. Chanting can be a great step towards your spiritual development and feeling empowered to speak your truth. When you feel ready to speak your truth, you are speaking from your heart, not your head, so it is essential that this channel is open and clear to speak. Chanting helps to empower your voice and your ability to speak with sincerity, and with total conviction.

Try chanting with your fingers in your ears, so you can get a more profound experience. The next time you have a bath, try chanting A E I O U to yourself with your ears under the water. The noise will be much louder, and you will get a real strong sensation of cleansing within your body, as well as a profound healing experience in the water.

You may need to ground your energies down after your chanting experience, and drink plenty of water as your body is having an amazing healing experience and needs time to adjust. Be gentle on yourself after your chanting session. Many people find it hard to meditate, so use chanting to take them to a more relaxed state by concentrating on the sounds and vibrations. Chanting allows you to escape from your thoughts, and can help you when you cannot focus. It can take you to a similar peaceful place as meditation does. You may find it easier to meditate after some chanting, or you could combine the two.

Chanting 'Ohm' helps relax your mind and your body. Your blood pressure decreases, and your heart beats with a regular rhythm which is good for the health of your heart. Chanting not only benefits you, but everyone around you with the wonderful vibrations you are chanting out. It is a great way to lift up the spirits of those around you whilst helping yourself too.

The more you chant, the more uplifted and relaxed you will feel. Experiment with different chants to find which one feels right to you today. Try putting your fingers in your ears to get the full sense of the chanting vibrations resonating through your mind and your body. Maybe you could bring in a musical tune to accompany your chanting. Choose to make chanting something you use to lift up your spirits at any time throughout your day. Try chanting outside in your favourite place in nature to see how much more impact chanting can have. You could even do it barefoot to make a stronger connection with your grounding.

Take it a stage further. Think of a colour, and breathe that colour into every cell of your body as you chant.

There is a wonderful Buddhist chant 'Ohm Mani Padme Hum'. You can find it on Google. The meaning of this mantra can be translated as 'The jewel in the center of the lotus'. I like to think that the lotus is referring to the heart chakra, and the jewel is the energy of compassion. The mantra 'Ohm Mani Padme Hum' is a mantra which can be used for protection, healing, and many other positive attributes, including communication with higher realms of consciousness. But most powerfully, it is a mantra used to generate compassion. When people chant or listen to this mantra, they seem to have the element of compassion manifest within them.

Every day, your body and soul will be going through a new journey. Whichever way you choose to raise up your vibrations today will be right for you. Be led by your intuition, and allow yourself the privilege of going with the flow. Each time you chant will be a new experience for you.

Remember to drink plenty of water afterwards, and ground yourself if you feel light-headed. Make a note in your healing journal of anything you experience during your chanting experience. Which method felt most effective for you? How did you feel afterwards? Make a note in your healing journal, of any insights you received, and the date you received them.

If you do recognise you are holding any feelings of trauma within your throat or your body, the Bach Flower Remedy STAR OF BETHLEHEM is brilliant for helping you to release any emotional and mental trauma you may be carrying. It can seem impossible to identify what you are feeling when your body is holding shocks or traumas.

Use the STAR OF BETHLEHEM by itself for a few days to help you release trapped feelings from your precious body. Be gentle on yourself and write down any thoughts and feelings which come up. Add the Remedy AGRIMONY, if you find it hard to talk about your feelings, and WHITE CHESTNUT too, if your mind keeps going over and over things which have happened.

Add other Remedies as necessary, but please do not rush yourself through this releasing and healing period. Drink plenty of water to help you release old feelings and keep your mind and body flowing more smoothly.

Please reach out for help and support if you are struggling to process feelings which come up for you.

Use your chanting to release and soothe you, and to then lift up your emotions. Chanting will then help to re-energise your mind and your body on all levels, Chanting can help to lift up your vibrations and still your mind. From this wonderfully calm place, you are often more able to tap into your true potential. The more you chant, the clearer things will become for you.

If you do not feel like chanting today, put on a favourite piece of music. Music lifts up your heart, and can help you to feel more joyful. Often the words within the songs you choose resonate with how you are feeling today.

Have you ever been listening to the radio, and suddenly you are drawn to a song which is playing? Sing along with the song, and you will start to feel more uplifted. There is so much healing power within the music and the words you sing. The words and the music vibrate through, and lift up, every cell of your body. Even if you do not have some music playing, sing to yourself to lift up your spirits. Choose songs which are upbeat and with an uplifting melody. You don't have to be good at singing to get the benefits of the musical vibrations flowing through your body.

Keep chanting and keep singing, and notice how quickly you start to feel more joyful and energised.

Create a vision board and a gratitude board

When you have some time to spare, put on some of your favourite music, and take some time out to start to create a vision board and a gratitude board.

On your vision board, write down some of the things you would like to achieve and create in your life. Cut out some pictures which represent your dreams, and your goals and inspirations. Put the board somewhere you pass by frequently. Every time you pass the board, glance at your vision board, and know that the universe will be working behind the scenes to help you achieve your dreams and goals. When your mind sees the goals you are aiming for, it starts attracting towards you new opportunities, and creating a mind-set which will help you to achieve what you are aiming for.

On the second board, create a gratitude board. On this board you can add some of the things you have already achieved, and as you accomplish things in the future you could move those achievements from your vision board, onto your gratitude board. Every time you look at this board, you will feel proud of yourself for what you have accomplished.

If you don't have any boards at the moment, maybe you could use a cupboard door, or a wall space where you could start to create your list and pictures of your motivations and dreams.

CHAPTER 16

HEALING YOUR INNER-CHILD

WHEN YOU HAVE HAD TRAUMATIC experiences in your life, those experiences can affect you on so many levels, and you can hold muscle memories of those traumas, not only in your mind, but in your body. When the past memory is triggered, you can usually recall exactly how you felt emotionally about the incident, and your body may even react physically to that memory. You may even feel like you are reacting as that younger you would have reacted.

A gentle way to heal those painful memories is to work with healing your inner-child. When a past memory keeps coming into your mind, it is usually because on some level the memory is affecting you in some way today. This memory may be being triggered off by something which is happening in your life at the moment, or it may just be that this is just the perfect time for you to be able to release these feelings and memories from your precious body and mind.

For some people, this exercise will need to be done only once with each memory, but for others it may need to be done more often. It depends on how deep the pain is. The more you practise this inner-child healing the more benefits you will gain on many levels.

For many years I have worked with, and been observing how people who have had past traumatic experiences react to things in their life in the here and now. I believe that many people who are diagnosed with mental illness, personality disorders, or are suffering with severe mood swings, are actually reacting to things which have happened in their past, and cannot escape from the mental and emotional impact of those memories.

My understanding is this. Assume for a moment, that you never have any traumas, or things happen to you which make you feel traumatised or emotionally affected. You would go through your life in the calmest and most happy state of mind. I believe we are all born with the potential to be happy, and this is the true state of mind we start off with. We respond to everything in a natural way, and our personality is as it should be.

But just imagine for the moment, that you start off that way, and then something upsetting or traumatising happens to you, which affects you mentally, emotionally and maybe even physically on some level from that day on. This is a 'reset' to the way you now start to react to anything which is similar, or resembles this initial traumatic event.

My understanding is that once you have had something happen to you which affects you on all those levels, it can take the smallest of things to send you back into the feelings, and reactions you felt when this incident happened. You can revert back to the 'younger you' in a moment.

You may come back to a plateau of calmer feelings again, but then, a while later, your old memory is triggered again by something else, so you go back into those old feelings and ways of acting again.

It can feel like you have two personalities. One personality, which is calm and logical, and the other personality, which is highly strung and over-reacts to what is happening around you today. The longer you keep slipping backwards and forwards into these different Personality Types the more they become a part of who you are, and the harder it is to separate and recognise which is the real you.

So many of us are affected emotionally and mentally by things which trigger off emotional reactions every day. How many memories can you recall that you still feel emotionally attached to? Take some time to take out your healing journal and write down any memories which you recognise have impacted on the way you act, or react to things. You can come back to these later to work with your inner-child healing.

It may feel like you are living in a constant roller-coaster of emotional mood swings. You may even question who you really are.

A doctor may have given you a diagnosis to help you understand what you are experiencing in your emotions and in your mind. I can see how easily a doctor diagnosing what you are experiencing can be an answer, but the cause of the underlying trigger problem does not often get looked at, or sorted out. You may even come to a belief that the diagnosis is the answer you need because it fits with the way you feel about yourself and your behaviour.

I must say at this point, if you are taking any medication for mental illness, or any other emotional imbalances, please do not stop, or alter this medication. Contact your doctor and talk to them about what you are exploring and working through. Any changes in medication you need to make must be under the supervision of your doctor. Some people may have a chemical imbalance, or their disorder may be genetic. There may be a need for your medication to support you. If this is the case, you can still do all of the exercises I recommend and use the Bach Flower Remedies, and they will help you to work through healing your emotions and your past.

Medication may be suppressing or calming some of the extreme feelings you are having, and removing that medication could bring up other emotions and behaviours you are not ready or able to deal with on your own. Your doctor will be able to gently work through any changes you are ready to make when the time is right. Always keep your doctor informed about what is happening. It is imperative you look at supporting and healing yourself from every angle.

If you feel like you are trapped in your thoughts and feelings that you have been experiencing, take the Remedies CHERRY PLUM and WHITE CHESTNUT for a few days. They can help you find more calm and a release from those trapped feelings. These Remedies can be taken straight from the stock bottle or diluted in water. Take them frequently throughout the first few minutes until you feel calm resuming, and then take them consistently throughout today, and for as long as you feel you need them.

Please be aware that the underlying feeling of the negative CHERRY PLUM state can be anger, so please don't be surprised if anger does come to the surface.

When you start to experience any feelings of anger, jealousy, rage, or wanting to lash out, the Remedy HOLLY will help you to gently release these feelings of anger, and come back to a calmer more loving state of mind. Keep taking the HOLLY until the anger subsides. Once again, you can start by using the HOLLY undiluted and frequently. Use it about every ten minutes for a couple of hours, until your feelings of anger feel soothed.

If you feel like you are in a state of shock take STAR OF BETHLEHEM.

If you start experiencing feelings of resentment, and that life isn't fair use WILLOW.

HONEYSUCKLE can help you to release the past, and enable you to move on.

ELM will support you to cope with one thing at a time if your emotions feel overwhelming.

LARCH will bring you renewed confidence in your abilities.

CERATO will help you start trusting and believing in yourself again. It helps you to start to identify who you really are.

CRAB APPLE will help you to start accepting yourself, and even loving yourself again.

Back to healing your inner-child

Set aside some time for yourself when you will not be disturbed.

Take yourself to a comfortable place to sit or lay down. Have a glass of water ready to drink.

You could add 4 drops of Rescue Remedy to your glass of water, to help you release and heal any emotions you experience.

Take six deep, slow breaths into your tummy, and slowly release.

Notice any tension in your body, and let that tension start to melt away.

Continue to take deep slow breaths in, and out, until your body feels relaxed.

Set the intention that you are going to help to heal your inner-child today.

Bring into your mind, a memory that keeps troubling you.

Think about how old you are. It can be any memory at any age.

It may even be something that happened recently.

Whatever age you are, for the purpose of this healing, we are going to refer to the past you, as your inner-child.

Back to the healing exercise:

Imagine you are standing in front of yourself, like a mirror image, but you are the age, at which the traumatic situation happened.

Imagine this younger you, your inner-child, standing in front of you.

You reach out your arms, to welcome your inner-child.
As you smile, and gently beckon the child to come towards you,
Talk gently to them, reassuring them, and telling them that they are safe.
As your soft voice reassures your inner-child, they gently step towards you, and you gently wrap your arms around them in a soft, but firm healing embrace.

Take a few minutes to gently talk to, and reassure, your inner-child as you hold them.
Tell them how proud you are of them, and that you understand the pain they have been through.
Reassure them that they are safe, and that you love them.
Let them know that they will be okay, and that you have confidence in them, and their ability to heal their pain.
Maybe you need to say 'sorry' to your inner-child, or you would like to forgive them, or ask for forgiveness from them.
Tell them, you believe they can heal from the experience they have been through. Tell them again, how much you love them, and that you can heal this together.
Keep gently holding them, and reassuringly talking, and loving them. Hold this embrace for as long as you need to.

You may feel emotional, and want to cry. You may feel vulnerable, and that is okay. You are safe. Let the tears and the emotions flow. This is an essential part of your releasing and healing process. You are releasing feelings which have been trapped within your body since the day this incident happened.

When the emotions subside, take a deep breath in, and say to yourself, 'I am joyfully feeling safe to let this go now'. 'I am ready to feel whole, and to feel healed again'.

Imagine your inner-child melting into your body, and now filling every cell of your body with love and compassion. You feel like your body is being filled with the most beautiful healing gift.

You can imagine a wonderful vibrant colour flowing through your body, as your inner-child blends with you.

Hold this embrace in your mind, as you breathe your chosen colour into every cell of your body. Take a few minutes to embrace this wondrous feeling of calm and healing.

Say, 'It is done. Thank you' to your inner-child, and to yourself.

Now, gently imagine your roots going out through the bottom of your feet, and into the earth below you.

Say to yourself, 'It is done, I am safe, and I am whole again. I am love'. Thank yourself, and thank your inner-child.

Take some time to embrace, and enjoy this new feeling. Enjoy this new experience of feeling complete, and at peace, with yourself and your inner-child.

When you feel ready, bring your attention back to your breathing, and take a few deep gentle breaths.

Gently start to move your toes, and wriggle your feet. Stretch out your legs. Then gently start to move your fingers, your hands and your wrists.

Slowly, stretch out your body, and become aware of your whole body as it stretches and relaxes back into a calmer space. Very slowly, open your eyes when you feel ready.

Drink plenty of water, and keep drinking more water throughout the following few days to help flush out the old feelings. Be very gentle and compassionate with yourself over the next few days. You may feel exhilarated, and a sense of inner peace and freedom, but it will take a few days for your body to adjust to this new lighter feeling.

Keep working on your grounding and cleansing exercises throughout the following days if ever the memory pops back in. This is a natural part of the releasing and healing process. You are releasing cellular memories from every part of your body, and this can take some time. Each time the memory pops in, or you have any thoughts or emotions around the incident, please take a few moments to re-assure your inner-child, and yourself that you are safe, and that you are loved.

You can revisit this inner-child healing exercise as often as you wish, with the same memory, or with other memories which come to the surface to be healed. Do not try to rush this process of healing. Any cleansing and healing can feel tiring, and it can take time to get used to this new way of being. So please allow your mind, your body, and your emotions, time to release, adjust and heal. The greatest gift you can give yourself is to release the past and the pains you have been carrying in your precious body and soul.

Do you need to work with forgiveness?

If you are finding it hard to forgive yourself for your actions, or someone else, for the way they have treated you, please take the time to work through the forgiveness meditation which is further into your book.

Work through this process at your own pace, and you will heal yourself and your inner-child in the best way possible. You will be ready to heal when the time is right. If you do not feel ready for this at the moment, that is okay. There will be a perfect time to heal your inner-child and any painful memories you have been carrying. You will know when the time is right. You can use your inner-child healing with anything which is troubling you. You can even use it with things which are happening at the moment in your life. We are all the result of what our inner-child has experienced, and is feeling today. Allow them to both heal and to feel whole again.

Use your healing journal, your affirmations and Flower Remedies to support you through. If you are struggling to come to terms with what has happened please reach out to someone you trust, and if necessary seek out some professional help too.

It can seem alarming, and a shock to your system when you start to realise the impact past experiences and people have had on you. Nurture yourself through any feelings you have, and you will come out the other end feeling renewed. STAR OF BETHLEHEM is the Remedy for intense feelings of shock or grief which come up to the surface. Use your healing journal as a confidant. The clearer your mind is the more clarity you will get. The more you release from your body and your mind the calmer you will feel. The calmer you feel, the more energy and motivation you will have. Take some time out to talk to someone you trust.

The Bach Flower Remedy ELM helps when you feel overwhelmed by your emotions, or what you are dealing with. It helps you to feel you can cope, one step at a time. It can bring back your confidence in yourself, and lift that heavy feeling of weariness you have been carrying.

HONEYSUCKLE helps you lay the past to rest, and enables you to start again.

WALNUT helps you to adjust to the changes you are making, and be less-oversensitive or affected by any past influences. WALNUT is the link-breaker which breaks through, and helps you release ties and influences from the past, enabling you to move forward.

CHESTNUT BUD will help you to learn from the past, to learn from any experiences and mistakes you may have made, and to make new more uplifting and constructive patterns. It will help you to maintain these patterns too, and recognise when you may be starting to make the same mistake again.

When you have healed the past, you will get a greater insight into the lessons, and the gifts within each situation and challenge you have been through. What has happened to you in your life has made you who you are today, and often the most painful experiences you have been through, are where you have become the stronger version of who you are meant to be. It is almost impossible to get this insight, or see those hidden gifts, when your mind is tormented by your past.

As you work on healing yourself, you will come to a place where you can see the way the past has impacted on you, and how it has helped you to grow. As you heal your inner-child, you will come to a place where you will feel enabled to let go. When you move beyond pain, you are more able to see how your past has given you inner strengths, and the wisdom you need to move forward.

Keep using your Bach Flower Remedies to support your healing.

CHAPTER 17

ARE YOU ANXIOUS ABOUT SOMETHING COMING UP IN THE FUTURE?

TAKE SOME TIME TO THINK about the situation ahead, and then take yourself into a calmer space in your mind.

Gently slow down your breathing, until your body feels more relaxed. Take yourself into a healing space, with your gentle breathing. Feel the healing energy in your hands, and then visualise a colour flowing through your body.

Bring to your mind, the situation which is causing you to feel concern. Think of a colour to support you, and imagine the colour surrounding the situation. Each colour has a different healing vibration. Trust that your higher self will know what colour you need to focus on.

Imagine the situation flowing smoothly in front of you, and everything working out calmly, and productively. Put yourself in the picture, and see yourself accomplishing what you set out to do. Feel how good this feels, and hold this sensation within your body. Hold this image and these feelings in your mind and your body, and keep coming back to this vision frequently, to create the outcome you desire.

Create an affirmation, which confirms that you have confidently done what you set out to do. Write your affirmation down. Maybe you could start with, 'I am confidently celebrating I can…..' What would your affirmation say about you, and this impending situation? Make a record of the affirmation you choose, and the outcome you achieved. Know it will work out for you, and you will feel empowered. You have everything you need within you to make it happen.

If you go to my website, there is a meditation called Withinercise, which you can to help your mind overcome challenging situations. This exercise will help expand your creative mind, to enable you to start seeing your true potential. Take some time out for yourself, and stay optimistic, as your thoughts will influence the outcome.

Did you know? Worry, not only keeps you stuck in the problem, but it stops you seeing potential opportunities. When you worry, your brain produces cortisol, which increases your tension, and so causes you to worry even more. Choose to turn your life around today, by changing your thoughts, and your expectations.

Take a few moments to think of something which brings you happiness, and then, using your fingertips, gently tap on the centre point on your forehead, just above your eyebrows. Keep thinking of your happy thoughts. Continue tapping and breathing until calmness comes.

Take it a stage further by gently tapping on your thymus point, the space between your heart and your throat, to increase your energy flow.

Using a combination of techniques to help yourself can be highly effective. You are seeing your healing needs as important, and this increases your feelings of value and self-worth.

Looking deeper at what is causing your stress?

Now you have had a chance to work on yourself and clear away some of the old layers of your feelings, we are going to look again at what may still be causing you to feel any disharmony today. This process can be repeated as often as you feel necessary as you progress on your journey. Anything which is keeping you in a state of disharmony, or keeping you from experiencing true joy, needs to be addressed.

There are so many things that contribute to stress in your body, and in your mind. Some things are really obvious, and you are probably already aware of what is causing you to feel stressed at the moment.

As you peel away some layers of emotions, you can start to see things more clearly. This enables you to delve deeper into any other cause of confusion or unrest you may be feeling. Remember, some things will take longer than others to rectify. If you have not resolved those issues yet, please be patient with the process and gentle on yourself. You are on a journey and it is important to recognise that. The more you work on helping yourself the easier it will be to resolve anything which is out of balance.

List the things which are affecting you in your healing journal today. Remember to add the date.

Could it be? Worrying too much. Being subservient. Working too many hours. Lack of time for you. Pushing yourself when you are tired. Cannot switch your mind off. Not getting adequate rest or sleep. Stressful situations at work or home. Insufficient money. Feeling pressured with deadlines, or others' expectations. Feeling tired, worried, anxious, overworked. Tension and lack of body care. Worrying too much about other people. Not eating properly.

Often what we believe to be the cause of the problem is not the whole picture. The more you work with this observation process, the more clarity you will get. The more you work on helping yourself, the more you will get a feeling of well-being and feeling empowered.

What are your constant stress triggers?

There are also underlying stress triggers, which we often overlook, that you may not be aware are causing you stress.

Feeling angry, resentful, being critical of yourself, or not believing in yourself, feeling jealous or life isn't fair, feeling sorry for yourself, ashamed, holding regrets, intolerance, being judgemental, lack of boundaries, not standing up for yourself, not trusting in yourself, grief, loss, lack of love towards yourself or others, loss of identity, overwhelmed, disappointments, setbacks, feeling helpless, loneliness, fears and insecurities, feeling guilty, not feeling important, not being heard, not having your feelings honoured or validated, not feeling in control, not feeling like you fit in, not respecting yourself, not being validated, not feeling respected, not feeling appreciated, not feeling worthy, not feeling good enough, always at others' beck and call, not enjoying your work, being over-worked, not taking time for you, not doing things you enjoy, having negative thoughts or beliefs, being critical of others, feeling people do not care, not being able to relax, being fearful for your safety or for others', and post-traumatic stress.

At different times in your life, you may be experiencing the stress of dealing with one, or many, of the emotional imbalances mentioned. For every emotional imbalance that is not addressed, it can create a small amount, or a great deal, of stress constantly throughout your day.

We are all different

Everybody's stress triggers will be different. Please do not compare yourself to what other people are going through, and do not undervalue how you are feeling right now, and what is causing you to feel out of sorts or out of balance. Where one person may deal with something easily, another person may feel like they are going through a major dilemma. Each person, and each personality, will react differently. And also bear in mind, that the way your life has been in the past, can have an impact on how you react to stressful situations today.

If there is any stress, minor or major, your brain produces cortisol and adrenaline, which enables you to keep functioning through your daily life. Whilst this can be fine for short spells, after a while your body can feel more constantly or frequently under attack from the continuous flow of adrenaline and cortisol. When there is too much adrenaline and cortisol flowing through your precious body you can feel constantly stressed. You can feel unable to control your feelings, or even feel anxious or panicky when something happens to trigger more stress.

You can go from feeling stressed to anxious or panicky frequently, without any prior notice. Start to work on gently calming down your breaths today, and take back control of what is causing you to feel distressed. Anything you do for yourself will benefit your emotional and spiritual well-being. Lots of people I know have turned their lives around by taking control of their anxiety and stressful panic attacks. They decided they wanted a better quality of life, and needed to make some simple changes.

A breakdown can be a breakthrough for you

Frequently, a breakdown within your body can be turned into a breakthrough. You can turn your life around, one gentle step at a time. When your body has been carrying stress for too long, it can seem like you cannot take any more. You can feel like you are carrying a heavy load, or your moods are constantly ready to explode. This is your body's way of saying 'Stop, you need some help'. Never underestimate the power of reaching out. Having someone to share your load can make a real difference, and can be a big step towards your recovery.

Check out which Bach Flower Remedies will help you at this moment. Start by reading about CHERRY PLUM, CLEMATIS, ELM, GENTIAN, GORSE, and SWEET CHESTNUT.

We all need a little boost sometimes, and the Remedies can bring you that uplifting state of mind which will help you to move forward. Take some time to look at what is causing you to feel anxious and what are your trigger points today.

Take a few moments for you

When you have acknowledged things which are causing you tension or stress, take some time out to breathe, and shake out any tension you may be holding at the moment.

Take a few deep slow breaths into the base of your spine, to help you feel safe making these changes. Imagine the base of your spine, your base chakra, expanding as you breathe into it.

Start to work on forgiving yourself for the way things have been, and how things may have become out of balance. Say to yourself 'I forgive myself for this', or 'I forgive myself for this irritation I have been feeling', or 'I forgive myself for getting so uptight'.

Whatever you feel you need to forgive yourself for, this is the perfect time to start to work on letting yourself feel forgiveness. Needing to work with forgiveness, does not mean you have done anything wrong. It is about recognising harsh and painful feelings you may have been holding, and knowing this is the time to start to let those feelings go. The more you release any feelings of unforgivingness the more uplifted you will feel.

Follow this through with 'I am feeling love and compassion'. You could add something which feels right for you like, 'I am loving and I am peaceful', or 'I am loving and I am compassionate'.

There is a meditation for forgiveness on a deeper level on my website. If you feel a need to do some deep forgiving for yourself, you could go to the chapter on Forgiveness to help you work through the process.

One of the most valuable lessons you can do for yourself, is to release old hurtful feelings from your body, to allow more love and compassion to flow. When you start to work with forgiveness you will start to see a whole new perspective on your life and what has happened. You will find your life purpose within you as you heal yourself.

You could also use the 'Ohm Mani Padme Hum' chant, to help you heal your feelings and raise your vibrations.

Remember reaching out to heal yourself is a sign of inner strength, and says you are ready to make those changes.

But I am too busy to take time for me

Procrastination. This was my safety blanket. Procrastination is putting off doing something we need to do because we have a deep underlying fear it may be difficult or impossible to change. When you are unhappy within yourself, you can end up skipping from one unhappy situation to another, without ever understanding or resolving what is causing your inner conflict.

These avoidance tactics are often a natural way of trying to find happiness and harmony, but this often ends up creating more problems because you are not facing up to the reality of what is making you unhappy.

Within this state of disharmony, we can go into avoidance of acknowledging what is creating the problem, and so distract ourselves by flicking from one thought to another. We go from one task to another, one relationship to another, one job to the next, one holiday to the next, one unnecessary purchase to another. Only to find that none of these things resolve the issue, and so do not bring the happiness we were seeking. Instead we have masked the issue, and allowed this to become more deeply buried. Our frustration becomes deeper, and we feel more lacking in vitality and confidence in our own abilities.

Our happiness becomes a fleeting moment in time when we feel like we have made it. Only to return to the place of disillusionment when we feel like that person, that purchase, that holiday, that job did not come up to our expectations. And even if it did, we still have this deeper sense of there is something not quite right within us. It can feel like a sense of heaviness, loss or sadness. We have a constant state of searching for something outside of us to bring us the inner happiness. We feel limited in the choices we have.

It is often through this inner conflict that we can become angry, and feel like our life is out of control. We can internalise that anger by becoming hardened, or critical of ourselves. Nothing we do ever seems good enough. And it is usually when these feelings become ingrained in our way of being, that we start to take our anger and frustrations out on people around us. This then brings even deeper feelings of disharmony, and brings greater problems in all areas of our life.

Quite often we cannot see that our feelings and behaviour have become out of perspective, and we can find it hard to identify what we are really feeling. If you were to try to think about the situations causing you disharmony, you would just go deeper and deeper into the confusion because your mind cannot see an alternative perspective.

It is quite natural that we have a reluctance to make changes, because with any new change comes new responsibilities. Sometimes, we may even feel a strong sense of justification to hold onto our old ways of being. We are going to explore the ways in which these false feelings come about, and how you can unravel your feelings and emotions from this day forward.

Be honest with yourself

Through your healing journey with this book, you will go to a place of deeper insight, and a place of honesty with yourself, where you can identify and transform your situations which are out of balance. Through this honesty and integrity, you will find the answers that will help you to find your inner peace, harmony and true happiness.

HORNBEAM is the Bach Flower Remedy which will help with your procrastination patterns. You may also need a fear Remedy to support you. HORNBEAM will help you to stop procrastinating, and enable you to start to accomplish the tasks needed to make the necessary changes. HORNBEAM brings you renewed vitality and confidence in your abilities.

Did you know that putting off doing something can cause you to feel even more stressed? Think about something you are putting off. On a scale of 1 to 10, how stressed does it make you feel when you are just thinking about what you are putting off.

Getting yourself in motion with your task, or starting to work through your situation, will start to lighten your stress levels. The task is never as difficult as you believe it is. Making changes can seem scary, but resisting will bring more intense feelings, and will drain your vitality.

Put 4 drops of the Bach Flower Remedy HORNBEAM in a glass of water and drink it. Then add 4 more drops in another glass of water, and sip it whilst you are doing the necessary task. HORNBEAM is one of my favourite Remedies, and has helped me shift through many times when it would have been easier to sit in my discomfort!!

Take out your healing journal, and write down what you want to work on first. Take some time to look at the benefits of making those changes, and how much happier you will feel when you have started to get the situation resolved. One simple step at a time can bring a whole new world of possibilities. Start to take action. Once you have started on making the necessary changes, re-evaluate, on a scale of 1-10, how much more relaxed you feel.

I ask again, 'Where would you like some help today?'

Is it smaller things like getting the paperwork sorted, tidying up the cupboard, or making that phone call? Or maybe you are struggling with bigger transitions in your life. Have you suffered emotional disappointments, setbacks, a trauma, loss, grief, or unhappy relationships, and cannot see beyond those situations, or let go of them. This is the day you could start to make a change. Maybe you are in a situation which is on-going, and causes you to feel unhappy, anxious or deeper disharmony.

Maybe you have not had people to encourage you or make you feel good about yourself, and you have adopted the beliefs you have been given by others. Anything you are resisting changing will cause you to feel disharmony within your precious body. This is often the root cause of feelings of frustration, stress and anxiety, and can even be the underlying cause of depression.

Nothing you do, or try to do seems to bring that complete feeling of satisfaction or inner peace. Then you can lose your joy in things you should enjoy, and even your life. It can feel hard to get any clarity of the bigger picture. You may struggle to see the good within yourself, anything around you, and sometimes within people too. All this happening within you, can bring you even deeper confusion.

If you are feeling anxious, stressed, or are having difficulties moving past an upsetting situation or traumatic time in your life, stop now and address your situation. Take a few deep breaths in and out, and drink some water. Stress of any kind is draining on your body, and water can help to replenish your energies. Take a few moments to think of something which brings you happiness, and then, using your fingertips, gently tap on the centre point on your forehead, just above your eyebrows. Keep thinking of your happy thoughts. Continue tapping and breathing until calmness comes.

Take it a stage further by gently tapping on your thymus point, the space between your heart and your throat, to increase your energy flow. Remember the more you do for you, the more empowered you will feel. You are seeing your healing needs as important, and this increases your feelings of self-worth.

The Remedy SWEET CHESTNUT can help you rise above your situation, and bring you more clarity and strength, and GORSE can bring you renewed hope, and is the first step towards recovery. If the changes feel too overwhelming, ELM is the Remedy which will help you to cope, one step at a time.

Work through the steps to help you address the issues that you may be struggling with. Work gently through each step, and allow yourself the space and patience to enable the changes to support you. Every day is a chance to start again and make some changes. The gentler you are on yourself through these transitions, the more easily things will flow for you.

The Bach Flower Remedy WALNUT helps you adapt to changes, and to be less 'over-sensitive' to other people's influences and ideas. HONEYSUCKLE will help you lay the past to rest, and feel enabled to move on. It doesn't matter how big or small your challenge is right now, you can turn it around. Remember too, age is never a barrier to transforming your life. Whether you are 8 or 80, you will find this book at the perfect time of your life. Today is your chance to start again.

Always day one

You have taken important steps. Congratulate yourself that you have recognised that something is out of balance and you are ready to remedy this. Each day, turn your attention back to yourself. Do not ask why did this happen to me. Ask, 'What can I do for me today. How can I help myself?'. See the good with yourself, and have respect for the beautiful person deep within you, your very soul. This is the person who you were born to be, who is needing to be acknowledged, respected, nurtured and loved right now.

Each day, start to build a new relationship with yourself. Your needs and your feelings are waiting to be heard. This is your time to be nurtured and encouraged. And it begins with you, and the choices you make today.

Each step will help you find more inner peace and happiness today. From this place you will find renewed faith in yourself. Your renewed faith will bring back feelings of love and compassion, for yourself and for others, and a greater sense of understanding of who you are. The feelings of self-love will grow within you.

You can have the life you were chosen to live, and these feelings of love will then flow into every area of your life.

When you feel confused or unsure of who you are, it is easy to lose sight of all the wonderful qualities you have within you, and the good things and blessings that you do have within your life.

Many of us can lose faith or confidence in ourselves, or in the likelihood of finding our inner peace and harmony. Being mindful of your thoughts is always a good start point to turning around any situation you are dealing with. If you have these feelings of discontent stirring within you, take time to stop and listen to your inner self, your feelings and your thoughts. What can you do for you today? How can you get yourself back to a place of inner peace and happiness?

Take some time out today, and go into the stillness of your mind. The answers, and the happiness you seek, are within you. Take time to listen.

Stay consistent with your writing

Write your current thoughts down in your healing journal. You probably have already noticed how much your thoughts are changing, and how your perception is changing.

Before you do anything else, stop and take 6 deep, slow, gentle breaths in and out. Breathe in calm, and breathe out peace. Feel the calm and the peace start to flow through your body.

Drink some water, and repeat this gentle exercise several times throughout the day. This is the simplest and most effective way to start to change any stress levels you experience.

Set your intention

Every day is a new beginning, and a chance to start again. It does not matter if you went off track yesterday; set the intention to start again today.

From the moment you wake up each day, every action you take will make a difference to the quality of your day.

Simplify your day by resetting your intentions whenever you feel you have gone off track. Be gentle on yourself through this time. Remember it takes time to create and maintain new patterns.

Get up slowly

Give yourself the privilege of having ten minutes for you, before you move into the rest of your day. Gently increase this amount of time you dedicate to yourself at the beginning of each day. The more time you dedicate to yourself the more benefits you will feel.

Take a few deep slow breaths in and out. Stretch out your body, smile, and take a few minutes to count your blessings. Yawn if necessary to expand the air right down into the bottom of your lungs.

Think of something you would like to achieve today, and using an appropriate affirmation, repeat it to yourself.

When you are ready to move out of your bed, slowly sit yourself up and move to the edge of your bed.

Place your feet on the floor, and take some time to stretch out your body.

Drink some water to re-hydrate your body and your mind.

Take a few moments to rub your feet backwards and forwards on the floor to stimulate your circulation before you start to move. This can also help ground your energies down.

Repeat your affirmation to yourself, and flow slowly into your day.

Think of a song, and start to sing to yourself.

Keep bringing your attention back to your breathing, and your song if you start to feel any stress or tension as you go through your day. Use your affirmation frequently throughout the day.

Shake any tension out, and move forward with more clarity and a sense of purpose.

CHAPTER 18

CREATE YOUR NEW LIFE WITH AFFIRMATIONS

EVERY MOMENT OF EVERY DAY you are feeding your mind with thoughts, and these thoughts will dictate your actions. They will also affect how you feel, and the way you act throughout your day.

Have you stopped to consider whether your thoughts are helping you, or not? Are your thoughts supportive and uplifting, or are your thoughts negative and detrimental to you?

Every thought you have does affect the way you feel, and the way your day unfolds. So is it any wonder you can feel low or confused if your thoughts are negative or detrimental to your progress. The thoughts you use today may be influenced by the way you have been taught to think, or based on past experiences. Some of these thought patterns could be helpful and supportive. But for the majority of people, who are unhappy, tired, stressed, anxious, depressed, or feeling out of sorts, those thoughts are probably negative, derogative and far from the truth of who they really are.

A simple rule to remember: what you think about, you are sending out to the world, and what you send out, you attract back towards you.

You need to be able to recognise when your thoughts are not helping you, but this can sometimes be difficult when you have been in those thought patterns for a long time. A simple and effective way to overcome your old habits of thinking is to start using repetitive affirmations.

An affirmation is a simple statement which says what you can achieve. So, for example, if you are lacking in confidence, your affirmation would be 'I am feeling confident in all that I do; my confidence is getting stronger every day'. If you were feeling you never have enough money, your affirmation could be 'I am happily attracting the abundance of the universe. Money is coming to me. I have all the money I need'. If you would like a more loving relationship you could say, 'I am enjoying a more loving relationship. The love is flowing between us now' or, 'A loving relationship is flowing towards me now'.

As you repeat your new affirmation, your brain will respond accordingly by producing the chemicals relating to what you are saying. Your mind cannot tell the difference between whether what you are saying is true, or not, and it cannot tell the difference between whether the idea is in the present or the future. It will start to produce the uplifting chemicals which will support your new way of thinking.

These new chemicals will lift up your spirits, and give you the tenacity to move on to attract and create what you need. As you raise up your energetic thought vibrations, you attract towards you what you are thinking about. Your mind will believe it is true because these are the instructions you are giving it. It is often referred to as the law of attraction. You attract what you think about.

Your emotions create memories

We only tend to remember incidents from the past, which are associated with the emotions we felt about what happened.

You can start to correct the way your mind works for you, by giving it new thoughts and feelings to focus on.

When you have uplifting emotional thoughts, which are happy and encouraging, your brain produces chemicals which help you to feel good.

We have a tendency to remember things in our past which have emotions attached to them. Whether the emotions are good ones, or not good ones. It is these emotional triggers which trigger the amygdala to produce the chemicals which created the emotions we felt when we had those experiences. And it is these emotions which help us retain those memories and the way we felt about the experience.

A good example would be when you went to a birthday party and fell over in front of everybody. You felt embarrassed, and so your mind remembers that incident because of the emotions you felt on that day. Maybe you struggled in school, and did not feel like you were clever enough, or felt embarrassed to ask for help, or maybe you were ridiculed or bullied. All of these negative emotions you felt are what have triggered you to retain these memories. Or, another example could be when you had an argument with someone, and you felt really angry and disappointed. Your emotional response is what triggers your brain to remember this situation.

These are examples of negative responses, but your positive emotions also trigger the amygdala to produce chemicals which create the feelings you feel when you have experiences, and it is these emotions which help you retain the memories. So, the happy time you had with your friends, the day you received your qualification, or the day you fell in love. All of these positive experiences trigger your mind to remember how you felt, and therefore the memory is imprinted in your mind as a feeling associated with the experience.

If there was no emotion attached to the incident you are less likely to remember what happened back in your past.

What may be a good experience for one person, may not have been a good experience for someone else. It is how you *felt about the experience* that determines how you perceive what happened, and whether or not you remember the incident.

Take it out of your mind

Take some time to recall experiences from your past. Write down the memories you can remember at the moment. Look at the emotions you felt around each situation.

How did you feel? How do you feel about this now?

Can you see how your emotions have been triggered, and why you remember each situation?

We have a tendency to remember the negative experiences more than the good ones. These are often the experiences which have had the greatest impact on you. They could be experiences which have affected the way you feel about things in the past, and what is happening now in your life. These memories can even impact on the way you feel about yourself and how you perceive yourself and your abilities today. We will look at this in more detail in the chapter 25, 'Exploring a new way of understanding you'.

It is extremely common, that we can develop what is called 'false memory syndrome', where what we believe to be true about a situation in our past, has become confusing or distorted. When we are feeling stuck in the emotions of the past, it can still feel very emotionally real to us today. In your mind, the incident can feel as intense as when you went through the situation, regardless of how long ago it happened. Often the deeper you have tried to bury the memory, the greater impact it can have on you. The incidents may have been so traumatising, you cannot even remember the memory, but the way you react today can still be influenced by what happened to you, and the way your deeper unconscious mind has processed the event.

If the emotions you felt are very painful, it can be hard to separate the past from this present moment, and can make you feel confused and out of balance. The emotions you felt back then can seem just as intense as if you are now going through the situation again. If you are feeling stuck in incidents from the past, it can impact on the way you are, or react within your daily life today.

You can start to heal these past memories

Find someone who you feel you can trust to help you work through any painful experiences you cannot let go of. Talking things through can bring you a massive release of feelings, and can be a big step towards releasing what is holding you back.

Choose someone with whom you can genuinely be honest, and you feel safe to confide in; someone who will not judge you and will respect you for sharing with them. Maybe they can help offer some constructive advice when you are ready. If you do not have someone around you who you can trust, maybe this would be a good time to seek out some professional help. Remember, doing something for yourself will lift up your spirits, as well as taking some of the burden away from you and helping you to feel supported. There are many support systems you could access through your doctor.

Holding heavy emotions within your body and your mind can feel extremely emotionally and mentally draining, and can wear you out. Alongside talking to someone, take some time to write down memories, and your emotions which come to the surface. If you have lots of memories, write down as many as you can for the moment, and keep adding to memories as you remember them. Be gentle on yourself as you start to explore this healing for yourself. It can be very emotional and tiring. Take some time out if you need to. What can you do for yourself? Maybe this would be a good time to do some self-healing with colours to help you release some of the feelings you have explored.

Exploring how your emotions have impacted on you can also be extremely enlightening. It can bring you a better insight and understanding into why you react the way you do, and how you perceive yourself and your life.

Can you start to see how your past has had an impact on who you are today? You could take some time to read about the Remedies which could support you today. Having more knowledge about the effects of the past, and how you can release those feelings, can be empowering and bring you a renewed sense of inner strength and confidence. As you use the Bach Flower Remedies, your past feelings will start to feel less painful and, after a time, you will be able to get a new insight into your past and how you have grown as a person.

Remember, every experience you have been through has helped to shape who you are today. A lot of your old patterns may have come from peer pressure, others' opinions, influences and expectations, false beliefs, and comparing yourself to others. If you are not happy with some aspects of you, the Remedies will help you to alter and adjust those patterns you need to change.

Read about HONEYSUCKLE, AGRIMONY, WHITE CHESTNUT, CHERRY PLUM, GENTIAN, GORSE, HOLLY, SWEET CHESTNUT, VERVAIN, WILD ROSE and WILLOW. Recognising, and acknowledging how you have been feeling, and looking at the positive states of mind you can achieve will bring you a renewed sense of who you really are. Where is your mind today?

You can use a combination of up to 7 Remedies together. The Remedies will help you to move through and beyond those thoughts and feelings which have been holding you back.

Create an affirmation to support you

Create an affirmation which fits with the emotion you are working on first. So, for example, if you are working on not feeling happy, your affirmation could be 'I am feeling happy and loved', or 'I am happy with who I am today'. Start with a simple affirmation, and then adapt the affirmation as you go. Your follow-on affirmation should include an emotion and a verb, a doing word. Including the emotional word triggers the amygdala to start releasing the feel-good chemicals, which will help you feel more uplifted and emotionally strong. Adding the verb will bring in the feeling of movement. It will give your mind the guidelines to start you moving forward.

When you say 'I am happy', this works on your mental level. When you say 'I am happily making changes', your mind triggers the emotional response, and starts acting on your instructions. Your mind and body responds to the instructions you are giving them, and the emotions you are feeling.

If you are feeling tired and unhappy you could say 'Although I am feeling tired, I am happily making changes'. By acknowledging how you are feeling, or what could be your reason for resistance, you are reassuring your mind and your body that you are listening to what is going on within you. You are acknowledging that what your body is experiencing is important to you, and you are caring for yourself. Your amygdala response centre will reciprocate by producing even more healing chemicals. When you start to respect and care for yourself, everything else will start to fall into place. Adjust your affirmation as you grow.

Try this affirmation for a few days to see how it helps you. 'Even though I am tired, I am happily empowering myself'. If this doesn't feel quite right, you could adjust the words to suit your feelings and your intention. Experiment with different variations of your affirmation, until you find one which flows smoothly for you. The more you use your affirmation, the more successfully you will achieve your goal. Remember, it takes sixty-six days to create a new pattern, so the more persistent you are the better your results will be.

You can choose to adjust your affirmation as your feelings change. Write down in your healing journal which affirmation you are choosing to use today. Add the date so you can remember when you started working on this new pattern. Your intention when using your affirmations, is to help trigger your brain to produce the feel-good chemicals. These chemicals then start to create new uplifting feelings and thought patterns, which will help you move beyond your old feelings and patterns of thinking. This will empower you to move forward with more clarity and courage. The more you use your new affirmations, the easier it will be to heal and override your old patterns of thinking.

This is where I believe the Remedies are invaluable. They help you gently and subtly heal your old feelings and emotions. They work on your behalf to help you shift through the changes.

Take some time out to write

Take a few minutes to write down the thoughts you use during each day. Acknowledge if they are not helpful and may be holding you back. Create an affirmation which will help you to over-ride your old thought pattern. Your affirmation will start your mind working on a new pattern of thinking.

Every time you hear yourself saying your old thought, acknowledge it, and turn it swiftly around by saying your new affirmation. The Bach Flower Remedy CHESTNUT BUD will help you change old habits, and create and maintain new patterns of thinking. GENTIAN will help you when you have a setback. It will also help you to be more optimistic and expect good results.

Do something for you

Any emotional or mental healing can be exhausting. Acknowledge if you are feeling tired. Maybe it's a good time to rest, or you could go for a walk. As you are resting or walking, shake off any old feelings which no longer serve you. Take some time to stretch out your body to release any tension you may have been holding.

Drink plenty of water to help with any stress. Be kind to yourself, and remember to thank and praise yourself for the great work you are doing.

You are creating a new habit, a new pattern

When you smile, sing, walk in nature, or think of something that makes you smile, your brain produces serotonin, which brings you happiness and joy.

Remembering, imagining, or thinking of a loving moment, produces oxytocin, which brings compassion.

Reliving, or thinking about, a success or an achievement, produces dopamine, which brings feelings of success.

Thinking of a memory, or the intention of bravery and courage, produces endorphins, which brings you feelings of confidence.

Write down one pattern you recognise you would like to change each day.

Write the negative words you use, so you can stay focused on what you are working with. Immediately you hear yourself using a negative thought, stop and turn it around. Use your new affirmation to help you refocus your mind. Repeat your affirmation three times.

Choose an affirmation which is appropriate to what you want to change in your life today. Write the affirmation down. Keep repeating your affirmation throughout the day. You could enhance the power of the affirmation, by writing it on notices all around your home and work place, so that every time you see the affirmation, you can repeat it to yourself.

You could put an affirmation on your bedside cabinet. Start your healing as soon as you wake up, and use your affirmation with your deep breathing exercise. It could be something as simple, yet profound, as 'I am breathing in calm, and I am breathing out peace', or 'I am respecting myself, and everyone is respecting me', or 'Everything is flowing smoothly today'.

Your mind and your body will start to work with your new affirmation, and it will start to produce the chemicals which will enhance and support your new way of thinking.

Combining affirmations with breathing

Combining your affirmations with your new breathing techniques will help you to relax, as well as help you maintain your new way of thinking. At the beginning, your mind may want to contradict the new affirmation you are giving it, as it may seem untrue to you.

Keep using the affirmation anyway. Your mind cannot think of two things at the same time, and you are giving your mind a new pattern of thinking. The more you persist with your affirmation, the stronger your new ways of thinking and your beliefs will become.

If your thinking goes off track, repeat your affirmations three times again to get you back on track. Remember you are creating a new mind pattern, and this takes time. Persistence will pay off.

Be gentle and patient with yourself as you start to create your new ways of thinking. The more you use your breathing techniques and affirmations, the stronger and more determined you will feel.

If you find yourself feeling impatient with yourself, or the process you are working through, take the Bach Flower Remedy IMPATIENS, which will bring you patience with yourself and the pace of your transition. If you find yourself being too hard on yourself, the Remedy ROCK WATER will help you be gentler on yourself and set realistic expectations. These two Remedies will bring a gentle understanding that things work out as they are meant to, and in the perfect timing of synchronicity. Everything really does happen when it is meant to. Be proud of the steps you have taken.

When you use your affirmation regularly throughout the day, your body will feel more supported, and so your brain will produce more of the feel-good chemicals to support you, your mind, your body and your spirit.

After a while you will not want to return to the old way of feeling because you know what the truth is now.

You can change your affirmation when you have achieved the results you need and, if necessary, re-use the previous affirmation if ever you feel a dip in your emotions. Some goals will take longer than others to achieve, but stay persistent, and know you are on the right track. The more you use the affirmations, the stronger you will become, and the better will be your results. You will ultimately see the results in the new way of life you are creating, and this will bring you the success and happiness you desire.

When you have achieved your desired goal take some time to acknowledge how well you are doing. Make a note of your successes in your healing journal, and the affirmation which helped you the most. Then create a new affirmation for the next step of your journey, and follow the process through again. The more affirmations you use, and the more frequently you use them, the more readily your mind will start to create the new patterns of thinking.

'Today, I am joyfully discovering joy and contentment'. 'Today I have a feeling of joy and contentment'.

'Today I am happily embracing all that I have achieved'.

Praise yourself frequently for the progress you are making, and keep a record of your achievements. Thank yourself for the changes and things you have achieved. Remember your mind responds to kindness, whether it comes from outside, or from you. The more persistent you are, the better results you will achieve. Remember it takes sixty-six days for your brain to adapt to this new concept you are giving it, and for this new pattern to become natural.

Create a stronger pattern today

Combining your breathing techniques with your affirmations, will bring you more mental calmness, and will support your brain to start creating new patterns.

Start each day as you wake with a simple affirmation of something you would like to achieve during the day, something as simple as:

'Today I am celebrating feeling more assertive, I am confident in what I do,' or 'I am joyfully respecting myself and everyone is respecting me.'

Or maybe, 'Everything I am optimistically setting out to do today, I can achieve'.

Choose an affirmation which feels right for you today.

Set the intention that you will notice times in the day when your affirmation comes into play and supports you.

Take a few minutes to say 'Thank you' to your mind for responding to your affirmation, to the things and people you feel grateful for today. The more you do this, the more things you will start to recognise, and the more you will attract good things towards you. Do remember too, self-praise is a priority.

Become more aware

Throughout the day set the intention to recognise when you do things which are not productive. This is your new plan for today.

Set the intention to turn around any negative thoughts today. Start to be more aware of times when you could be more self-orientated, and choose to do things for yourself and your well-being.

Notice the words you use to talk about yourself, your work, your day, and your life. Are your words destructive or demoralising?

Notice how they make you feel. Choose to use more constructive, encouraging thoughts and words about yourself and what is going on around you….. take out capital R

It will take time to maintain this new way of treating yourself, but keep working on it.

Do not get frustrated with yourself if you forget. Do not be critical of yourself. Be gentle, patient, and encourage yourself.

Do not give up or stop trying. Nurture yourself and be persistent. Use self-praise frequently. Acknowledge how far you have come.

Take some time to write down your plan for today and the words you are working on changing. Thank yourself for noticing that this needs to change. The more you encourage and nurture yourself through changes, the more easily transformation will be.

Do a random act of kindness for yourself and for others throughout the day. The kinder you are the more of the love and compassion chemical you will produce, and the more loving and compassionate you will feel.

Love is the only true emotion which should be flowing through your body, and you are the one who can make that happen.

Read about the The Bach Flower Remedy CENTAURY, CERATO, CHESTNUT, GENTIAN, HORNBEAM, LARCH AND WALNUT.

Gently but persistently make changes

Choose to eat more healthily each day. Change a few things at a time because it takes time for your body to adjust to new ways of eating.

Choose to be slightly more physically active each day until your body gets used to more exercise. A gentle walk is a good way to start improving your physical activities, or if you cannot get out, do a virtual exercise routine in your mind. Or do some gentle movements by rotating your ankles and your hands, and gently moving other parts of your body. Any movement will be beneficial to your circulation and your feeling of well-being.

You could do some gentle dancing to your favourite music to lift up your spirits and give your body some feel-good chemicals. Dancing and music nourish your soul. Music is a powerful healing vibration which resonates with everybody. Every person feels the music differently, and every person gets the healing they need from the music they choose. Which music could help you today?

Some of my favourites are The Climb by Joe McElderry, The Greatest Love of All by Whitney Houston, The Man in the Mirror by Michael Jackson, Something Inside So Strong by Labi Siffre.

Take some time out to listen to the powerful words, and the beats of these songs, and then choose some of your own to add to the collection. The messages in the words resonate with my very soul. The music goes straight to your heart, and can change the way you feel about yourself, your situation and your world. Upbeat music really is one of nature's magic healing tools.

Before you start. Make a note of how happy you feel, on a scale of 1 to 10. 1 being really fed up, and 10 being exceptionally happy.

As you listen to the music, smile to yourself, and gently start to move the parts of your body that you feel able to, and then increase the amount of movements you do.

Start with your fingers, and then your hands and your arms. Then start to gently swing your arms. Let your body gently sway with the music, as you gently start to move the other parts of your body.

Anything you change needs to be done gently, and in moderation, so your body can adjust. Maybe you feel like singing, or laughing to yourself. Go with whatever feels right for you.

If you have not done exercise for a while, or have any medical conditions, please consult a doctor before starting any new physical exercise.

After each song, how happy do you feel now, on a scale of 1 to 10? Notice how your feelings start to change when you go with the flow of the music.

Always recognise at the end of each day how you have helped yourself, and the changes you have achieved. Give yourself some praise, and thank yourself for the steps you have taken. Acknowledge, and make a note in your journal, of how well you have done today. Go to bed pleased with yourself, count your blessings, and start the process again tomorrow.

When you feel your affirmation has served its purpose, choose a new one. Maybe 'The abundance of the universe is mine, I am gratefully attracting all I need now,' or 'I am surrounded by people who are willingly helping and supporting me. Everyone is respecting me and my needs now.' You could prepare a list of affirmations for future days.

Every time you use your affirmation, you are creating a stronger foundation for the life you desire. The way you think, and feel about things is the link between what you desire, and what you receive.

I have produced some Bach Flower Remedy cards which will give you some guidelines on affirmations you could work with each day. The Remedy cards will help you to recognise the emotions you are feeling, and give you an affirmation to support you as you work through your emotions and adapt to the changes. The affirmations are guidelines. Adapt the affirmation to suit you. Include an emotion and a 'doing' word to trigger your brain to start responding to your requests. See next chapter for more information.

You can use the cards, by placing the photo of the Remedy picture against your heart, and take some deep slow breaths, as you repeat your affirmation. This allows your heart to resonate with the card you have chosen. Hold the card against your heart as you breathe.

When you have taken sufficient breaths, and the Remedy card has helped to realign your emotions, you will feel a shift in your energies.

This often comes as a feeling of a deep sigh, a yawn, or a tingling sensation going through parts of your body. This is a gentle way of helping your body to release any emotional stress you may be feeling, and realign you with who you are meant to be.

Say 'thank you' to your body for the shifts and changes it is allowing to happen. Remember, the more gratitude you embrace, the more your body will start to flow with the feelings of love and compassion.

Another way to lift your spirits is by playing soft, soothing music or a favourite soothing song. Always have some of your favourite music standing by, ready to use whenever you feel like you need a little bit of soothing or motivation.

You could record some of your favourite music, and mix it with some affirmations between tracks so you can pick them up to use whenever you need them.

Not feeling very active today?

There may be times when you do not feel like doing any movements, dancing or exercise.

Be gentle on yourself and recognise that it's okay to not feel like doing exercise at the moment, or maybe you recognise your circumstances do not allow you to do exercise.

Virtual exercise

Take yourself to a comfortable place, and sit or lay down. Take a few deep gentle breaths in and out.

In your mind, start to think about a favourite form of exercise you like to do, or would like to do.

Imagine you are carrying out that exercise in your mind. Make the virtual experience as vivid as you can in your mind. See the colours, imagine where you are, and how you feel. Maybe you see yourself dancing and gently moving to your favourite music or song.

FREE TO BE ME

See yourself starting off slowly, and gently increasing the speed of the exercise. Smile to yourself, and see yourself as really happy and pleased with yourself. Praise, and encourage yourself through your virtual exercise.

You may even want to start to physically move parts of your body, as if you are actually exercising or dancing. You could enhance the experience by imagining what is around you, the breeze, the sun, rain, colours, people, the ground beneath you.

My favourite exercises are dancing, swimming or cycling, so I imagine I am cycling to the swimming pool, and then gently gliding through the water. I imagine I am laying on my back, and gently moving the water with my hands. The sun is shining, and I am totally chilled out and relaxed. Then I imagine I am dancing around in the garden, and all is well in my world.

In reality, I am not such a great dancer, but in my mind anything is possible! And maybe, one day my body will start to be as agile as the images I see in my mind. I certainly feel more uplifted, and have more energy when I come out of my virtual exercise meditation. Anything is possible when you believe. Change all starts with a single thought, and today is the best day to start to create the changes you desire.

When I have finished my virtual exercise session, I feel as refreshed and energised as if I have had a good work out.

Why does this help you?

Your mind cannot tell if you are actually doing the exercise, or if you are imagining the exercise routine.

Your brain will start to produce the same chemicals as if you are actually exercising, and so your body will also receive the benefit of the flow of chemicals surging through your body and your muscles.

It is highly beneficial to your feelings of well-being, and a lot less stressful on your body if it is hurting or unwell. Doing a virtual exercise is a soothing form of meditation. It helps to relax and de-stress your mind, and establish a new way of thinking and feeling. Reassure and encourage yourself as you do this exercise. Anything you do for you will make a difference to the way you feel.

You can do this exercise as often as you need to. Next time you need some exercise but don't feel like moving right now, take some time to take your creative mind and your body through a virtual exercise trip. It is a great way to lift up your spirits whilst your body is resting and being re-energised.

Virtual exercise is a great way to prepare your body for a real exercise routine too. If you do a relaxation meditation before your physical exercise, you have already created muscle memories to warm up your body for the real thing.

Even athletes do it

Many athletes now use meditation as a way to prepare themselves for their races and games. Former athletes like John Howard and Chris Montgomery have said that relaxing through meditation changed their results for the better.

Meditation is a wonderful way to increase your body's energy flow. It helps your body and mind to relax, helps you to concentrate, gets rid of nervousness and removes distractions from your mind. Meditation can improve your performance, and helps you have more endurance.

Imagine how you can increase your stamina and performance in daily tasks if you take twenty minutes to meditate on the tasks in your day ahead.

Meditation also helps you to sleep. Sleep is very important for relaxation and for your feelings of well-being. Rest and sleep helps in regeneration of worn out cells, and meditation helps to free your mind so you can have a better quality of sleep.

On days when you do not feel like doing anything else, rest and sleep as much as you can. You are supporting and healing your body whilst you rest. When you bring in some meditation and virtual exercise time your body will reap the benefits on many levels.

CHAPTER 19

BACH FLOWER REMEDY HEALING CARDS

THE BACH FLOWER REMEDIES ARE a natural, gentle way to help you work through your emotions and challenges in your life.

If you do not have access to the bottles of the essences of the Bach Remedies, you could use the Bach Remedy healing cards to help you rebalance your emotions.

The cards are available through my website.

The Remedy cards can help you recognise emotional blockages you need to work with, which will enable you to achieve greater clarity and happiness.

The Remedy cards can be used as a healing vibration to help you gain a greater understanding of how you are feeling, how the Remedy can support you, what to expect from taking the Remedy, and an affirmation to help you rebalance your emotions.

How to use your Bach Flower Remedy cards

Shuffle the cards, and fan them out in front of you. Pick one card you are drawn to.

The card you have chosen will give you three things:

Insight into how you are feeling at this moment (your negative state of mind).

What you can expect from using the Bach Remedy card you have chosen (your positive state of mind).

An affirmation which can help you move gently through the negative emotional state, to find renewed inner peace and inspiration.

The affirmations are guidelines for you. Adapt the affirmation to suit you. Include an emotion with your affirmation and a verb, a 'doing' word, which will enhance your affirmation and trigger your brain to start taking action.

The card you have chosen represents the feelings you can relate to most at this moment, the feelings which are most prominent.

When choosing the Remedy card for you for today, you are learning to use your intuition to guide you. The more you use your intuition, the more you will start to believe in yourself and the choices you make. Your intuition will get stronger as you let go of any stress.

If you do struggle with trusting your intuition, the Remedy CERATO will help you to start trusting in your intuition. CERATO could be a good healing card to start your healing process.

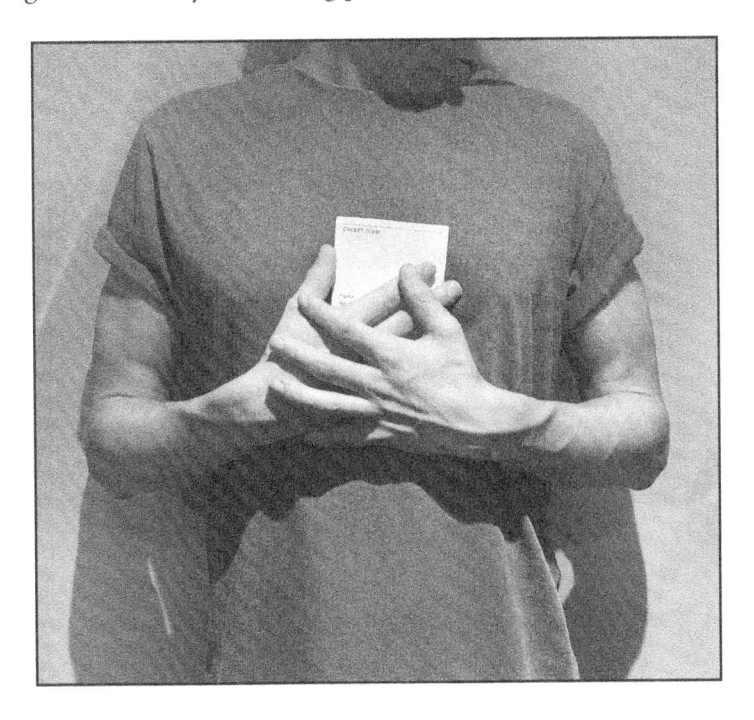

Gently place the chosen card over your heart space, with the picture side against your body.

Take some gentle deep breaths in, and out, as you repeat the affirmation on the card. Adjust the affirmation with an emotion you would like to attach to your changes.

You can work with your card, and your gentle breathing, until you feel a calmness start to flow through your body.

Use your name with the affirmation, and adapt the affirmation slightly, to suit your own challenges at the moment, e.g. 'I am confidently embracing, that I have all the confidence I need to follow this through'.

Maybe, 'I am lovingly and confidently moving forward', 'I am joyfully bringing this to fruition', or 'I am joyful and confident, and everything is falling into place'. Or 'I am happily trusting in myself now and the choices I make'.

Create your affirmation with lots of loving, joyful and supportive words, alongside words which bring in a feeling of moving forward.

You could use words such as moving, embracing, celebrating, trusting and achieving. Choose words which sit comfortably with you. Your healing cards will give you the suggestion of what you are aiming for, and you can adapt your affirmation to make it personal to you.

Start with the simple affirmation, and expand it to suit your circumstances after a few days. Keep adjusting your affirmation until it feels just right to you.

Continue breathing, and holding the card over your heart space. As you focus on your heart space, you are increasing the vibration within your heart. Let your heart open up to the beautiful healing of your Bach Flower Remedy card. Then breathe deep down into the base of your spine for three breaths, to help you feel safe to make these changes.

When you have taken sufficient breaths, whilst repeating your affirmation, you will feel a shift in your energies. This often comes as a feeling of a deep sigh, a yawn, or a tingling sensation going through parts of your body. This is a gentle and effective way to help you release any emotional stress you may have been feeling.

Drink some water. Take a few more deep breaths in, and out, and then go gently into your day. Increase your water intake throughout the day if ever you feel stressed or weary.

Use your affirmation cards as often as you need to

You can repeat this gentle healing process a few times throughout the day, until you feel you have worked through the process of shifting your state of mind from a negative imbalance to a positive state, and are able to maintain your new way of thinking.

The more you use your affirmation and your healing cards throughout the day, and the night if you wake up, the more effectively your mind will start to adopt your new pattern, and your new way of thinking.

Repeat the healing process with your card, whenever you feel overtaken by any negative thoughts or feelings.

The more you use the Remedy cards, the calmer your mind will feel. Your brain will produce the chemicals which will enhance and support your new way of thinking. You will have more clarity, and a feeling of well-being, satisfaction and feeling empowered.

You can choose to work with more than one card at a time, but you may find it more effective if you work with one card. Experiment and see what suits you. Repeat your affirmation to yourself frequently throughout the day. If you have the Bach Flower Remedy essences, you can use the Remedy cards with the essences.

Remember anything you do for yourself, will trigger your brain to produce the uplifting feel-good chemicals.

The Bach Flower Remedies and the healing cards can help you, but if you do not have access to them at the moment, just reading about the negative and the positive aspects of the Remedies can be helpful to get you on the right track to creating changes.

If none of the above are available at the moment, the other techniques in your book can be equally effective. Each person will find their own most appropriate methods for helping themselves.

Remember, when you focus on your heart space, you increase the vibration within your heart. Visualise your heart space becoming brighter and brighter, as the healing energy of the card permeates into your heart space.

CHAPTER 20

NOT EVERY DAY WILL BE A GOOD DAY

YOU DO NEED TO BE realistic, and recognise that however much you try, some days will not feel like good days. Some days, you may wake up feeling flat, sad, tearful, angry or even depressed at the beginning.

Maybe you have a long-term disability or unwellness which you struggle to come to terms with, or an on-going situation which is draining you. On those days when you feel like your emotions are overwhelming, try not to berate yourself, or be too hard on yourself. These are days when you need to rest more and nurture yourself. On these days, it is okay to have a dressing-gown day. It's okay to wrap yourself up in your quilt and not do very much. Acknowledging you are not in a good place is an important step forward.

It is okay to sit around and not feel like doing anything. Often this is your body's way of showing you that it is needing to release emotions and stress, or that you have pushed yourself too far. Acknowledging your weary body is often all you need to do for today. You need to recognise, acknowledge and learn to accept that sometimes you just need to be.

This could be a day when you do not want to make anything feel better, or to improve the way things are, and that is okay. Rest, and allow your body to start to regenerate itself. Resting and sleeping is nature's way of healing your body.

Maybe you could use some soft music to soothe you through this time, or to just relax and sleep. It is essential that you are not hard on yourself during these days. Each cell of your body has a consciousness, and if you treat your body, your ailments and your unwellness with kindness and gentleness, you stand a better chance of dealing with the situation, or starting to feel more at peace and hopeful within the situation you are dealing with. On these days, you may not feel like reaching out for help, and that is okay too. Be gentle on yourself and frequently take some deep, slow and gentle breaths in, and out, to release any tension in your body.

Nurture yourself with warm foods and drinks, use kind thoughts and words about yourself, self-praise and whatever makes you feel comfortable on these days. Nurturing yourself is a top priority when you are not feeling so good. As you nurture yourself, your brain will start to produce the feel-good chemicals to support you. If you find it hard to just switch off and relax there are Bach Flower Remedies to support you on these days. Read about the Remedies VERVAIN, WHITE CHESTNUT and ROCK WATER.

Always remember, when you are resting, your body is working through its own natural ability to adjust, heal and support you.

CHAPTER 21

SIMPLE MEDITATION

IF YOU WANT TO CHANGE the way you are feeling today, doing a simple meditation about a place in nature, can be a gentle way to help you release heavier feelings and find some emotional relief. It can help to change your mind-set too. Your brain cannot tell if you are imagining your favourite place, or activity, or are actually there. It produces the same feel-good chemicals which helps lift up your spirits.

I have created several relaxation meditations if you would prefer to listen to a guided meditation. They are available as downloads through my website.

Simple meditation

Take some deep gentle breaths in and out. Breathe in peace, and breathe out love.

Feel the peace and the love fill every cell of your body with each breath.

Now take your attention to your heart, and feel your heart fill with love and harmony. Feel your heart expanding, and filling with love.

Although we talk frequently about your mind being the trigger for how you feel, your heart is the centre of your soul. As you calm your mind, and fill your heart with love, you will get more in touch with your true feelings.

As you heal your heart, your soul can heal.

You mind may instigate your thoughts, but your heart is the centre of your soul, and from this sacred place, is where you feel you fit into your world.

Tense your body, and then gently start to stretch out your body, one piece at a time. Let your shoulders drop.

Feel your body sinking deeper into the chair. If you have any tension in your body, feel the tension gently easing away with every breath.

Feel the love flowing through your heart, and into every tiny cell of your body. Now breathe deep down into the base of your spine for three breaths.

Think of a place outside where you love to go or, if you don't have a favourite place, imagine a place in nature.

Imagine you are gently getting up, and starting to walk. You are feeling the breeze against your skin, the warm sun on your face. Listen to the gentle sounds of nature as you walk. Feel the ground beneath your feet. Notice if it is firm or soft. Imagine you are gently strolling along, with no sense of urgency. Look up and see the clouds and the sun, feel the warm sensations running through your body. How does this make you feel?

Feel it, see it, touch it, and become what you are experiencing. Enjoy this feeling and all the sensations which go with this wonderful feeling of freedom. You are free.

You start to notice the colours around you. You keep gently deep-breathing as you walk.

If you feel any tension, or stress flowing through your body, shake your hands and release it out, through your fingers, through your feet, and through your breath. Shake your hands, and your arms, to release the tension and the stress.

Breathe into any thoughts in your mind, and allow them to flow down, through, and out of your body. You feel totally relaxed, and at peace with yourself. You are feeling healthy, radiant and feel comfortable in your own body. You find yourself smiling, and taking in even deeper breaths.

Your body feels relaxed and energised. Your mind is calm and clear. You are feeling contentment, peace and joy.

You are feeling empowered. You feel healthy and energised. You have renewed vitality now.

You notice the colours around you are more vibrant now. You notice a particular colour you feel drawn to. Think of that colour, and breathe the colour into every cell of your body. As you breathe in that colour, you feel more alive and refreshed now. Give yourself plenty of time, to enjoy this wondrous feeling. Keep strolling, breathing, and unwinding until you gently drift off to sleep.

Or, if this is during the daytime, when you are ready to come back, bring yourself back gently, moving your fingers and toes. Take in some deep breaths as you open your eyes. Drink some water, and go gently into your day.

You could expand this exercise by introducing your virtual exercise routine. Introduce whatever makes you feel good. You could record this meditation on your phone, so you have it ready to listen to when you need it. The more you use this meditation, the more energised, calmer, and more at peace you will feel.

Remember, your mind cannot tell if you are thinking about something, or actually doing it. Your brain will produce the same feel-good chemicals, which will flow into the muscles in your body. So not only are you relaxing in your comfortable place, your muscles feel like they are having a workout at the same time. When you are using your imagination to visualise, you are expanding the creative part of your brain, to enable you to start seeing possibilities through visions and insights.

Create an anchor

Give yourself a word that you associate with this simple meditation. We are going to call this your 'anchor'. If your imaginary place is walking through trees, your word could be 'tree'. If it is walking in the flowers, your word could be 'purple flower'. If it is walking on the beach, your word could be 'pebble' or 'sand'. Choose a word that reminds you of your meditation experience.

By thinking of this word, your brain will start to create a similar calm feeling within your body, as if you are actually out walking in nature. Again, your mind cannot tell if you are actually doing the exercise, or just thinking about it. When you use your 'anchor' word through the day, your brain produces the gentle supporting chemicals which bring you a feeling of well-being and joy.

If you have a stressful situation to deal with through your day, or you feel deflated or confused, say your 'anchor' word to yourself, as you take a deep slow breath in, and release. Your mind will associate your 'anchor' word, to the feel-good feelings out in nature, and start to produce the gentle healing chemicals to support you. You may experience a tingling sensation, or a warm, or a cool feeling flowing through your body. Allow it to naturally happen. This is your body being flushed with the healing chemicals you need to calm your mind and your emotions, and at the same time, invigorate and energise your body.

It is natural, it is so simple and gentle, and it will make a big difference. You are tapping into your own natural healing abilities, and creating a new way to deal with and overcome stress, tension and other emotional feelings which can weigh you down. You are creating new, more uplifting thought patterns and muscle memories within your mind and your body.

Using touch to support you

Take it a stage further, and pick up something which you associate with your place in nature. It could be a pebble, a pine cone, an acorn, or anything which you feel attracted to.

Hold your item in your hand and let your fingers gently move over the item you have chosen. This triggers off the kinaesthetic system in your body, which brings in the sensation of moving through using your touch sensors.

The item you have chosen to hold is your connection to your natural healing. This is your healing gift. From today we are going to call this your 'gift'. Your gift is now your trigger to moving forward and having emotional calm.

Feel the texture of your 'gift' on your fingertips. As you are touching your 'gift', you are stimulating increased energy to flow through energy meridians in your body, and also stimulating parts of your mind to start activating feel-good chemicals to support you. The more you use your sense of touch the more uplifted you will feel. Use this alongside your 'anchor' word, and you will be increasing your body's natural ability to heal itself.

You are creating new memory patterns, for your mind to work with to support you. Keep repeating your 'anchor' word to yourself. The more you repeat it, the stronger your new associated healing pattern will become. Every time you touch, or think of your 'gift', your mind will create a natural flow of healing chemicals through your body.

Take it outside

When you go outside for a walk, be more aware of the sensations against your skin, feel the breeze, the sun, the warmth or the coolness. Hold your 'gift' in your hand, and run your fingers over it, to encourage your mind, and your body to get in touch with the wonderful healing sensations which will flow through you. Take off your socks and shoes, and feel the ground beneath you; notice how it feels.

Take some slow deep breaths in, and slow breaths out, to release any tension or stress. If thoughts pop into your mind, breathe into those thoughts, and slowly release them out. Continue gently breathing, walking and releasing.

Take some time to really feel how this feels to you. What feelings and sensations are you experiencing? The more you can be in touch with your feelings, the more easily you will be able to learn to understand, override and heal any emotions you experience on your journey.

If you have been stressed, out of sorts, or unwell for some time, you can lose touch with how you really feel. Your logical mind is constantly trying to work out what is happening, and your emotions can switch off. You become detached from how you feel emotionally because you are stuck in your mental thinking patterns. When you get back in touch with your awareness of touch, and feeling sensations, you can get more in touch with your emotions, which then allows you to be able to process your thoughts and emotions for healing.

Did you know that when you are by the seaside, or out amongst trees in woodlands, you are embracing the same vibrational healing energy as if you are having a Reiki healing session.

Both the energy in the woodlands, and at the seaside, are the most uplifting and refreshing places to go if you want some calm and peace.

When your body has been uplifted by this healing energy, you will feel refreshed, your mind will be at peace, and you will feel more energised.

It does not matter if you cannot get outside at the moment. As you imagine and manifest the feelings of being outside, your brain will respond by producing the feel-good chemicals. So if this is one of those days when you cannot get outside, encourage your imagination to take you to a place of calm and tranquillity.

Hug a tree

Next time you go out in nature, find a tree, and give that beautiful tree a long hug. As you hug the tree, you are triggering all the feel-good chemicals in your brain. You will feel more calm, content and grounded by the calm healing energy of the tree.

As your hands touch the bark of the tree, you are triggering your kinaesthetic senses to calm your mind and your body. Take some time to imagine you are blending into the tree, as you hug her.

Imagine your roots beneath your feet going down into the ground, and blending down through the solid earth with the roots of your tree. The longer you stand there, the more at peace you will feel. Hugging a tree brings you natural calm healing.

Trees have wonderful healing properties. When you hug the tree, you are enjoying the wonderful healing essence of your tree.

Many of the Bach Flower Remedies were created from the essences of trees. Take some time to read about the Remedies which were made from the tree essences, and next time you go out in nature, seek out the tree you are drawn to. You can receive a gentle and profound healing experience, just as you would from taking the essence of the Bach Flower Remedies Dr Bach prepared for us. Hugging a tree can be an invigorating and healing experience.

When you do your next meditation, you could incorporate the hugging of your tree within your meditation. Remember your mind cannot tell if it is a physically real experience, or you are thinking about the experience. You will receive similar healing benefits. Your senses will trigger your brain to produce the healing chemicals, to lift up your spirits, and your feelings of well-being.

Kinaesthetic learning

Using your sense of touch, which is also called kinaesthetic learning, helps stimulate parts of your mind which may have become stagnant. Through touch, you are stimulating your mind to get back in touch with your feelings, which enables you to see and feel possibilities, where perhaps you could not see a way forward because your emotions had become out of perspective, or even closed down.

Kinaesthetic learning helps you get back in touch with your natural ability to see solutions, and it can help you feel more settled within your own body and mind too. It can help you when you feeling restless, or are finding it hard to concentrate. It is a great natural way to stimulate your mind and your body to feel more stimulated and yet restful. Try holding your chosen 'gift' when you are meditating or relaxing.

You can use all of these natural techniques, to help anchor you back into your physical body when you feel stressed or out of sorts throughout the day. The more you use these techniques, the more easily you can tap into your natural healing abilities, and the more swiftly your mind and body will respond to the new patterns of relaxation you are creating. As your 'anchor' word, and your sense of touch become stronger, you will get a deeper feeling of well-being, which brings you more clarity, and a sense of feeling empowered. The more you use these gentle techniques, the more you will be in touch with yourself, and who you are meant to be.

Carry something with you that becomes your stabilising anchor today.

Always remember, it is not how you think about the world, but how you feel about your world, which will make a difference.

The more you get in touch with your feelings, the better you will feel.

The better you feel, the better the world will feel to you.

CHAPTER 22

HOW YOU CAN LIFT UP YOUR SPIRITS NATURALLY

IF YOU FEEL A NEED to do something for yourself, but don't have much energy, you could gently massage your hands and your feet with a favourite lotion, whilst playing your favourite music. The hands and feet are both parts of your body which are accessible, and by nurturing them, you are helping your body to feel nurtured. Pampering yourself helps you and your body to feel soothed.

Do not worry if you can't reach your feet – working with just your hands can be enough. In reflexology, points on the hands and the feet are relevant to different parts of the body.

The parts of your hands and feet which feel sensitive or sore reflect places in your body where the energy is stagnant. You don't need much more information about this at the moment, but just know that this is a simple way you are helping yourself and your body's feeling of well-being.

Hand and foot massage is an effective gentle way to soothe your body and help you relax too. It also helps to increase your circulation. This could be a simple nurturing routine to bring into each day as part of your new self-care programme. Expand the massaging up into your arms, your shoulders, and your neck. Then gently massage your legs, knees, thighs, hips, and going into your stomach and chest.

Using gentle circular and sweeping movements will help to increase your circulation, and your body will start to feel soothed and comforted. Massage is a great way to release tension and relieve some of your pain. And just in case you are wondering, yes, men need nurturing too.

Have some favourite movies set by for those days when you do not want to move or think about anything. Choose movies which are uplifting and take your mind out of the situation you are in.

It may not always seem appropriate when you are feeling down, but listening to and humming a favourite tune, or singing can lift your spirits quickly. We sing from the heart, and music is a great way of lifting your spirits whenever you feel you need a boost.

Have some books nearby which you could dip into whenever you feel ready, or some knitting or a jigsaw puzzle. Anything simple that you can get into without too much preparation.

Make some time in your day to pray for help. When you start to ask for help, miracles really can happen. When you are dealing with emotional or physical pain or illness, it can be extremely debilitating. Anything you do for yourself can help your body to feel supported, and your body will start to feel the benefits of the gentle endorphins which will start to flow, which will in turn lift up your spirits and can help to reduce some of your pain.

Drink plenty of water through your relaxation days to keep your body hydrated. Remember stress can cause you to feel dehydrated.

When you feel ready, open up some windows so you can breathe in the fresh air and clear the energies in your home.

When you are ready, reach out for help

Talking to someone really can help you to relieve some of your feelings of worry, distress, stress and anxiety. Talking things through with someone you trust can be a major step towards healing and understanding what you are going through. You may not need someone to give you answers or solutions. You just need to voice how you feel.

By talking things through, you can often get a greater understanding of what you are feeling, and a sense of relief when you have unburdened yourself of your thoughts and your feelings. We all have a need to be validated, and being heard is a powerful way of starting a chain-reaction of deep healing.

Have a list of people nearby who you can call on when you are in a space where you need a chat or some extra support. If you don't have people who can help you, maybe it is time to reach out to a stranger, to somebody outside your circle. Your doctor's surgery will have contact details and leaflets of places where you could get support.

This is something you could start to explore on days when you are feeling stronger, so you are more prepared on days when you need help. If you cannot get out, it is worth making a phone call to your doctor's surgery to ask if they could recommend someone to help you.

Reaching out for help is often one of the things most of us struggle with. Set a new intention to feel able to reach out. You could use a new affirmation which says 'I am now surrounded by people who want to help me.' Keep repeating the affirmation to yourself through your stronger days, and hopefully by the time you do need the help again, you will have found the people to help and support you.

Do not try to rush yourself through days when you are low in energy and spirits. These are days when your body is healing, or coming to terms with whatever you are dealing with right now. Maybe this is your day to rest.

Although you may not always feel an immediate need to use the Bach Flower Remedies, know they are always there for you to use at times when you feel low, and when you are not feeling emotionally strong.

Do not rush to use them as soon as you feel a dip in your emotions. Sometimes, we need to feel the fullness of the emotions we are working through, and how we feel about them, but MUSTARD is a great Remedy to help lift gloomy moods where you feel frustrated with your situation.

Take some time to read about the Remedies CLEMATIS, GORSE, OAK, OLIVE, MUSTARD, SWEET CHESTNUT, WILD OAT and WILD ROSE, or would HORNBEAM help you?

Medical intervention

Remember to reach out for medical or professional help if you are feeling low or depressed. In some deeper states of turmoil and extreme emotions, you may need extra help as well, or some medical support. Needing to ask for help is never a sign of weakness, or an inconvenience to others. It is a sign of inner strength, and can be the first step towards recovery. We all need some extra help and support sometimes.

Reaching out may seem hard right now, but please know that this will be the best step you ever take. Please acknowledge how you are feeling, and reach out for help. If you are feeling like you need help today, ask somebody you know to support you. Maybe they could make those initial calls for you. Tell somebody that you genuinely need help, and let the help come towards you. The sooner you start to reach out, the easier it will be for you. Asking for help can be the most empowering thing you do for yourself today.

Your doctor is often the best source of help for emotional support. They can put you in touch with other beneficial support systems. It is important to honour what you are feeling, and approach your healing from all angles.

The Bach Flower Remedies and healing techniques can support you on many levels but, for some people, if they have a chemical imbalance or are in deep pain, they may need some medication to help them work through their recovery. Your doctor is the best person to advise you with this.

The Bach Flower Remedies should not be seen as a replacement for any medication or medical intervention you need. Medical support works alongside the natural Remedies and techniques. The more support you have, the more smoothly you can heal your emotions.

Learning can lift up your spirits

Reading and learning about something new can help to lift up your spirits, because you are expanding your mind and increasing your knowledge. You can learn a lot about yourself by reading about the Flower Remedies and identifying Remedies which will support you. When you feel ready, read through the pages of the Bach Flower Remedy section of this book, and start to choose and use the Remedies which feel appropriate for the way you feel right now. Or you could use the Remedy cards to support and rebalance your emotions.

If this is one of those days when you feel down, but you are ready to deal with and start to heal your emotions, this would be a good day to start working with your Bach Remedies. They can help to lift your emotional discomfort, and bring back a feeling of renewed hope and inner strength.

They will help to renew your confidence in yourself, and in your ability to rise above your situation.

At the beginning you could pick 1 or 2 Remedies which feel most prominent.

Take 2 drops of each Remedy, and put them in your drinks over the course of the day. Continue to do this until your mood starts to lift.

As your mood lifts, you can usually get more clarity and motivation to make some changes.

If you have already explored the Remedy pages, maybe you have recognised some of the moods and emotions that you struggle with. You could make up a combination bottle of Remedies to have as a standby.

This is where reaching out can be a real gift for you. Maybe this is the time when you could reach out and ask Dawn, the author of this book, to help you, or reach out to a friend, or a family member, who could support you through this. Ask them to read through the Remedies with you, to help decide which ones would help you. Sometimes people around us can see how we are feeling, when we can't really understand ourselves.

Always remember, being gentle on yourself brings better results. Start using your affirmations when you feel ready. Praise yourself for the steps you are taking, however small they might be. Think of a song, and start to sing.

Use your Bach Remedies frequently and consistently. You will start to feel emotionally stronger. Consistency brings better results.

Keep checking whether you need more Remedies, or if you need to move on to another Remedy, or combination of Remedies. Setting the intention to help yourself, is the biggest step of all. Every journey starts with a single step. You are on your own journey of self-discovery, and taking steps to explore your true potential, by taking care of yourself. If you cannot access the Bach Flower essences you could use the Remedy cards.

Reality check

I am very aware that some situations, illnesses and disabilities are not going to go away. All of the techniques will still be beneficial in supporting your body and your emotional well-being. They can help bring you to a place of emotional balance.

This will enable your brain to produce the feel-good chemicals which can ease some of your discomfort. Anything you do for you will help to change your perception of yourself and what is happening to you. The more you work on helping yourself, the more ease you will feel.

One of my favourite books is You Can Heal Your Life, by Louise L Hay. This book was one of my earlier inspirations to changing my life. I would highly recommend it to anyone who is struggling with any emotional, mental, or physical ailments or illness in their body.

When you start to use the Bach Flower Remedies, they may start to trigger some of the deeper emotional hurts you have experienced, and this is a natural part of the healing process. Your body brings the old emotions to the surface for you to release. Your body is letting go. Be kind to yourself as you go through these periods of growth, and the harmony will soon resume. Drink plenty of water to help your body release.

Always remember that these feelings of more intense emotions are temporary, as your body is going through a time of great transformation. And also remember, this process should not be rushed.

Honour what you are feeling and experiencing, and make a record of your feelings in your healing journal. Know that this time will pass, and you will soon start to feel the benefits of these healing times of transformation. This would be a good time to reach out to a friend to share your feelings. More calm, clarity and peace of mind will follow, alongside your body feeling more at ease.

CHAPTER 23

VISUALISING YOUR FUTURE

MANY OF US HAVE VERY busy minds, and we constantly repeat thoughts over and over to ourselves during the day, and sometimes throughout the night too. A valuable step towards healing your emotions, is to focus on clearing and calming your mind, and then to give your mind a new way of supporting you.

It can seem unrealistic at the beginning to expect you to blank your mind completely. One of the ways you can start to heal your emotional state of mind, is to give your mind something else to think about. Your mind cannot think two thoughts at the same time, so to heal your mind you need to aim to give your mind something new to focus on.

Retraining your mind will enable you to rise above your current situations, and to find inner peace, and is another way to deal with your emotions and challenges in your life.

At first you may not always see the full benefits of the following exercises. But when you persist in practising them and bringing them into your daily life, you will soon start to reap the rewards of a clearer, calmer, and more focused mind. You will discover a new way of dealing with your emotions and situations you need to work through.

Practising Withinercising, (going into your mind and retraining it), helps you create new, more supportive patterns of thoughts and, ultimately, a new way to create the future you desire. Ideally, you need to the following

'Withinercise' exercise at least once a day, until you feel the benefits of what you are visualising and aiming for in your daily life.

Your Withinercise meditation

It can take time to create a new pattern in your mind. The more willing you are to use this technique, the better the results will be.

When you use your Bach Flower Remedies alongside Withinercising, the Remedies will help you to flow more easily through the changes you are creating, and maintain those changes. A Withinercise meditation is available digitally through my website. You could record a Withinercise exercise on your phone, then listen to it whenever you wish.

It does not matter if you fall asleep when you are listening to this exercise. The messages and suggestions within the affirmations are for your sub-conscious mind, which does not need you to be actively participating. You are reprogramming your deeper sub-conscious mind, and your conscious mind does not need to hear what is being said. The more you do this exercise, the deeper and deeper the messages will go into your mind.

You can create your own Withinercise meditation by taking yourself into a relaxed meditation space, and then think of something you would like to achieve. Bring to your mind something which represents what you have achieved. It could be an image of you in your perfect setting, or a holiday you will reward yourself with. Talk yourself through the scenario. How does this vision make you feel. Use positive affirmations to encourage yourself to achieve what you set out to do.

Always praise, and thank yourself every time you take action to create changes in your day. Acknowledging your successes helps your brain to produce the dopamine chemical and the endorphins, which then stimulates more acts of self-belief, confidence, bravery and success.

Make it personal to you

Thank yourself for the opportunity you are allowing to happen. The more grateful you feel when you choose to relax, the easier it will be for you. You are setting the intention for your mind to be more content and receptive to what you are doing. You can choose the scenario which is appropriate to you and your needs. You can choose to use words to fit with what you desire to achieve.

Always finish your meditation by saying 'I am confidently moving forward now.'

> BACH FLOWER REMEDIES
> AND LIFE-CHANGING SKILLS
>
> # TRANSFORM YOUR LIFE
>
> DAWN CHRYSTAL
> HELPING YOU TO HELP YOURSELF

Each time you come back to this place, you now feel stronger and more empowered. You now have more belief in yourself, your abilities, and what you can achieve. You are feeling proud of yourself and the dignity you feel.

Notice your breathing. If necessary, slow down your breaths, and breathe deeper again.

Take some deep, slow breaths in and out. Notice how relaxed you feel. Hold in your mind the vision of you, and what you have achieved in your future.

You have accomplished everything you have set out to do. You have emotional intelligence now.

You are feeling emotionally strong. You are feeling powerful. You are successful. Whatever comes your way, you have the ability to deal with it.

Hold this vision, and let yourself relax into it for a while.

Notice how strong, empowered and how confident you feel.

How does it feel to have accomplished what you set out to do? See it, feel it, become uplifted with these feelings, and take some time to enjoy these sensations running through your body. This is your new way of feeling and experiencing your life. Enjoy this vision, and the way it makes you feel.

'I am feeling healthy and comfortable in my own body. I have renewed vitality now'. 'I have the power to create the life I desire'. I am feeling successful. I am a success'.

'I am now free to explore new opportunities which are sent my way, and I have everything I need within me to make things happen'.

Say to yourself, 'I am healthy, energetic, joyous and I am free. I have good health and peace of mind'.

How does this feel, now you have created and received what you wished for? See it, feel it, touch it and enjoy it. You have created what you deserve. Enjoy this new feeling. You are now free.

You are successful, you are wealthy, and you are free. You have emotional well-being and you can create anything you desire.

You have created the life which brings you contentment and joy. Take some time to enjoy this vision, and this wonderful feeling.

Thank your mind for this vision, and the potential is has brought to you.

From this day, every time you think of your vision, your mind will help you to start working towards what you want to accomplish.

Come back slowly

When you feel ready, bring your attention back to your physical body. *Slowly start to move your fingers and your toes. Take a few deep, slow breaths.*
Come back gently into the room, and open your eyes.
If you do this during the day, come slowly back to the present time, slowly starting to move your fingers and your toes. Thank your mind and your body for the experience you have had.
Stretch out your body and open your eyes. Slowly drink some water and feel the water flowing through your body, saying 'thank you' as it flows. When you feel ready, go gently into your day.
If you do the 'Withinercise' exercise at bedtime, drift into a peaceful sleep, holding the image of you in the future.
Keep retraining your brain to expect success. If you find yourself keep slipping back into old patterns of thinking and acting, take some time to do a Withinercise meditation for yourself. As you visualise, and send out your intentions, you are working with the universal law of attraction. You attract to you what you think about.

Always finish with gratitude

Always say, 'thank you' for any visions and insights you receive. Take some time to record your intentions, and your insights. When you acknowledge what you have received, and what you are working on, you are giving your mind a new focus, and a new plan of action.
As your vibration of expectation and gratitude vibrates out into the universe, you are also triggering the deeper part of your brain to resonate and co-operate with your desires and intentions. The stronger your intentions are, the more your brain, your body, and your emotions will resonate with the intentions you are sending out.
As everything in the universe resonates on a vibrational frequency, what you attract is relevant to what you are thinking about, feeling and sending out. Raise up your expectations with your words, intentions and visualisations, and see how the universe responds to your requests.
In my recorded Withinercise meditation, which is available through

my website, I have included a music track which will help your mind to resonate on a higher frequency, and get in touch with your emotional state of mind. The combination of words and uplifting music will help you to attract what you desire in your life. The music track is called Ascension. It helps you to rise up above your current situation, and attracts to you what you deserve. There is also a shorter daily Withinercise to help you keep on track. When you have created your vision in your mind, and experienced it a few times, you can do the short visualisation for about 5 minutes each day. The more you use your visualisation the more powerful it becomes.

If you cannot access these meditations at the moment, you could create your own Withinercises. Record your own meditation on your phone. Add your own name, positive affirmations, and use your imagination to create new visions of the future you desire. You could add some soft music in the background, to enhance the experience.

Remember, gratitude will keep you in the flow of receiving, so please thank yourself for the precious work you are doing for yourself. Every step is a success, and every step needs to be acknowledged. The more you acknowledge your successes, the more tenacity, passion and motivation you will have.

Your confidence, self-belief, and feelings of self-worth, will grow with every step you take. Well-being is a state of mind, which will increasingly grow as you put in the foundations of your successes.

CHAPTER 24

FINDING JOY IS YOUR PURPOSE

REMEMBER, FINDING JOY AND HAPPINESS for you is your purpose, and through this joy, you will find passion and inner happiness, and you will find you.

Take some time to read through the following pages, to give you a greater understanding of you, and how you may have accumulated your patterns of thinking. Give yourself some time to process how this information fits in with you and your life. Use your healing journal to process your thoughts.

Frequently take some time out to rest when necessary, and do something which brings you joy each day. This will allow your mind time to relax and process what you are learning. When you come back to the next stage of your learning, your mind will be more open and receptive to the next step.

The answers you need will often come when you are least expecting them, because you are allowing your mind the space to process the information, and not thinking about it. You are simply being.

How does it get so confusing?

In an ideal world, our capabilities would never be questioned, our behaviour would always be ideal, and we would never question our values and beliefs or who we are. Our identity would be unquestionable and our sense of purpose would always be on track. We would totally understand, and know our true spiritual selves. We would all be confident, content and motivated.

But we don't live in an ideal world. We live in a world full of constant challenges, influences and stress. A sense of uncertainty and foreboding follows many of us around. These uncomfortable feelings usually start within one of the environments we live in.

If your environment has been unhappy or incompatible with your true self, you may question your capabilities, which in turn results in inappropriate behaviours. It can lead you to question your beliefs and values, and ultimately your own identity and sense of purpose.

This deeper confusion, or conflict within, can arise from the variety of environments you live within: your home environment, your extended family environment, your work environment, your social environment, your spiritual environment.

According to what is happening within each environment, and what is expected of you there, you can take on roles, some of which are what you have learnt, or have been forced upon you through your earlier life.

Some confusion may have arisen from the expectations others have of you, and some are based on different parts of your character. The way you react or respond will depend on who you are, and on how you feel within each situation.

Are you content, and at peace within each area of your life?

I believe the further from your true self you are, the more uncomfortable you can feel. This can often manifest as extreme mood swings, mental confusion, or even depression or illness. You may find it hard to separate how you are feeling, and any unwellness you are experiencing, from who you really are. Deeper disharmony you are feeling, can often come about when you associate your sense of identity with who you are when you are in a negative state of mind or behaviour.

The environments you live in, constantly change during your life, and it is often, not until you are more mature, that you start to recognise the impact of what has happened in the past. It is often through pain and disharmony within your precious body, that this confusion becomes apparent.

It is often not until we become unwell, that we start to look at how different things have affected us. It is usually through this wake-up call we start to look at making radical changes.

We come to crossroads in our lives, when we start to recognise that the impact of what has happened in the past is affecting us at the moment. It can be through this insight that we can start to have a deep desire to want to make radical changes, in not only ourselves, but the world around us.

Thank your mind and your body for being receptive to the information you are going to process, and take some time out as you go to digest and acknowledge what you are feeling. Confide in your healing journal, and acknowledge the progress you are making. Remember to count your blessings at the end of each piece of information you are processing, and allow yourself time to adjust, and be comfortable in this new understanding of yourself. Do a random act of kindness for yourself whenever you need it.

Are you tense?

As you read through, and process the following information in this chapter, keep checking on the tension you are holding in your shoulders.

On a scale of 1 to 10, how much tension are you holding in your shoulders at the moment? If you are tense, you are often holding your shoulders high up near to your ears. The more tension you are holding, the more stress you feel.

Start to calmly slow down your breaths, and lower your shoulders. Think of a colour in your mind, and see your mind filling with that colour, surrounding all your worries, and all your stress. Feel the tension releasing, as your shoulders drop.

Feel, and imagine your chosen colour, with all the things which have made you feel tense, flowing from your mind, down through your neck, your shoulders, down your arms, your hands, and out through your fingertips.

Gently shake the stress, and the tension off, as you shake your hands. Notice the sensations flowing through your fingertips. Acknowledge how this feels.

You carry a lot of tension in your shoulders, and it is hard to be relaxed when your shoulders are raised up and tense.

Let your shoulders drop, as you do your slow breathing exercise, and breathe out all of your tension. Feel the stress gently flowing away from you.

This can help you to have less stress, better concentration, and enable you to feel more able to process the information, in relation to you and your life. On a scale of 1 to 10, how tense do you feel now?

Take it a stage further. Gently rotate your shoulders to loosen up your muscles, and then shake out your hands again. Now, notice where else you are holding tension. Is your jaw tense and rigid? Tighten up your jaw as you breathe in, and as you breathe out, let your jaw gently drop.

Take a big long yawn, and stretch out your arms as you breathe out again. Let your shoulders drop, as you shake any tension out through your hands and your fingers.

How tense are you now, on a scale of 1 to 10?

De-stress your whole body, bit by bit

If you notice you are holding any tension in other parts of your body, tense that part of you as you breathe in, and then let the tension flow away, as you breathe out. Gently stretch, jiggle, and move your body as you release any tension.

Finally, take a nice big, slow, deep breath in, and feel the energy gently flowing through your body, from your head, down through your body, and out through your feet to the ground below.

On a scale of 1 to 10, how tense do you feel now? Keep gently releasing the tension throughout your day. Notice how much more relaxed you feel.

Take a few moments to thank your body for the tension you have released. Take some time to enjoy this new feeling.

Make a note in your journal

How long does it take to de-stress your shoulders each time?

Each time you this, you are encouraging your body to enjoy this new, more relaxed way of feeling. The more you practise this, the easier it will be for you to move into a more relaxed state, and the more able you will be to adjust your levels of tension.

Notice how much easier it is for your body to relax, when you have done this a few times. The more relaxed you are, the easier it is for your mind to concentrate.

During the day, become more aware if you are holding tension in other parts of your body. Thank your body for showing you the tension you need to work on. Pain is often a way of your body showing you where it needs more attention.

Start to gently focus on the place where you are holding the tension. Tense up the muscles, and then gently move your body to release the tension. Then give your whole body a gentle shake, to encourage your circulation to flow.

The more you practise this, the quicker your body will respond to releasing stress when a stressful situation comes up. Trying to concentrate and absorb information when you are tense creates more tension for your mind and your body.

Deep breathing, stretching, and shaking it out, is a gentle way to soothe your body, and allow it to go into a more natural flow. This can be an effective way of combatting and soothing many forms of stress or anxiety. You are giving your mind something practical to focus on, as well as acknowledging and releasing stressful tension in your body.

Acknowledging, and thanking your body for the changes it is making, helps you go with the flow of feeling compassion, gratitude and ultimately love. The more you encourage and appreciate you, and the steps you take, the more easily these feelings will flow. By empowering yourself, and slowing down your breathing, you are adjusting your tension levels. You are helping your brain to start to release gentle healing chemicals. This will help you to get a clearer perspective, and a greater span of concentration. Your mind is more receptive when you feel relaxed.

Overload of information?

If you feel there is too much information to process at the moment, walk away, and give yourself some time to process how the information fits in with you and your life. As you are walking, shake your arms and hands, and feel all the tension flowing out, and away from you. As you are walking, let your mind relax, to allow it to process the information and your feelings. Giving yourself some gentle exercise allows your mind time to reflect and process what you are learning and feeling.

Do not try to rush through all of the information. Give yourself time to explore how the information fits in with you, and how you feel about what you are learning. When you are ready, make some observations in your healing journal about the information you are learning, and the impact it has on you.

As you release your tension, can you start to recognise how different things in your past have influenced you?

Maybe, this would be a good time to take ten minutes to lay down, to allow your energies to flow smoothly through your body, and up into your head.

Take ten minutes to lie down to practise your deep, gentle breathing. Feel the healing energy flowing into your hands, and your fingertips. What colour is your healing for today? Place your hands over your body, and feel the healing colour flowing into your body.

If you do feel overwhelmed by your emotions, or the changes you are making, ELM and WALNUT will help to support you, and bring you the strength to work through one step at a time and gently adapt as you go.

Where do you start today?

Be honest with yourself. What do you need to change today?

Use your healing journal, to record any insights you get, and be grateful for the steps you are taking to make changes. At every step, take some time to acknowledge your progress and give yourself plenty of praise as you go. Recognise just how important these steps are to your growth. The desire to change and improve your life will keep you motivated to keep working on yourself. Acknowledging your desire to change, will help to encourage your brain to create more uplifting ways of supporting you.

Recognising your growth, and thanking yourself at every step, will bring you feelings of recognition and self-approval. The more you approve and encourage yourself, the more empowered you will feel. Your feelings of self-worth will grow and blossom as you learn to respect yourself and the progress you are making.

The ultimate goal is to be happy and at peace in every area of your life. So how do you get there?

Continue to make small, but important changes each moment of each day. Continually count your blessings throughout the day. Set small realistic goals each day, and act on those intentions. There are so many simple ways you can help yourself. Make a note of your intention for today, and keep it with you through the day.

The Bach Flower Remedies can help you to work through those changes, and help you find and maintain your inner peace and certainty. With this, will come the confidence and strength of character to achieve anything you choose. The Remedy LARCH is for confidence, and CERATO will help with approval of yourself, and trusting in yourself again. CRAB APPLE will bring feelings of liking yourself, and even loving yourself. It helps you to see beyond any imperfections, to enable you to see your own inner beauty.

When you are more certain of who you are:

You will have fewer irregular and fluctuating moods and emotions.
You will be less confused and have less conflict within your mind.
You will believe in your capabilities, and your behaviour will be more balanced. You will be as true to yourself as you should be, and you will be strong in your beliefs and values.
You will have a strong sense of your true identity, and you will feel more empowered. You will have a greater understanding of how things have impacted on you.
You will have more clarity about the relationships you have experienced.
You will have more clarity about changes you need to make.
You will have a greater understanding of your purpose on this earth.
Wherever you go, you will always know who you are.

You will be feeling confident, content, and able to make the right choices.

When you know you are free to make the right choices, you will feel at peace.

Remember to acknowledge and be grateful for the steps you are taking, and praise yourself at every step. Give yourself time to adjust, and take the next step when you feel ready.

Time out is a reward for the amazing work you are doing. Keep up the good work, and keep telling yourself 'Well done', and thank yourself for every precious step you have taken today.

We all need approval, but the most sincere and lasting approval comes from within you. Approving of yourself is a major building block to creating the foundations of everything in your life. The more you approve of you, and the choices you make, the more tenacity you will have and the more you will feel able to achieve.

The more you value yourself, the more easily you will attract to you what you desire, and you deserve. You are the driving force behind everything which happens in your life from this day forward.

Why do you question yourself?

Each and every one of us has chosen to come to this earth with an intention to work through challenges and lessons. These experiences and lessons are to help us grow, find the person we are destined to be, and to be the best we can be in this lifetime.

But are you happy with the place you find yourself in right now? Are you happy with yourself and who you have become?

Are you happy with the choices you have made? Do you embrace the challenges you have been through?

Those experiences and challenges have made you who you are today. If you are not happy at the moment, what would you like to change? If you are not happy with an aspect of yourself today, again you can start on a new gentle yet profound journey of healing and discovery. Every day is a new opportunity to start again. As you are growing, you are peeling away layers of you which no longer serve you.

As you reveal new things to work on, praise yourself again for what you are acknowledging you are ready to change. You are a beautiful person. It is your patterns of thinking and behaviour which need to change, not you.

You may have allowed others to influence who you are and, in turn, have taken on board their opinions, beliefs, influences and values. Over time, you have taken these as your beliefs, adopted these ways of thinking, and made them your reality, the way you see your world. It can take time to reveal these patterns. You will recognise where you need to make changes, at the perfect time for you. When you are prepared, and armed with the tools you require to make those changes, you will get the insights you need, and you will feel able to gently adjust what is necessary as you move forward.

Do your beliefs serve you today?

You may have been questioning yourself because of your thinking, and you do not really know who you are. You may have been having conflicting thoughts about yourself, your behaviour, and even your life. Often these patterns accumulate slowly over years, and you do not even recognise the impact they are having on you.

Keep studying your thoughts

Are your thoughts helping or hindering you today? Now, it is your patterns and beliefs we are going to look at, to help you understand how you may have lost your way.

Wherever you start your journey with the Bach Flower Remedies, they will help you gently peel away the layers of false beliefs and values you have accumulated, to reveal your true identity. It is when you live within this reality, this awareness of yourself, that you can appreciate your sense of who you truly are, and your purpose on this earth.

As you reveal the lessons, and grow through them, you will recognise how the past has helped you to grow, and how it can shape who you become in the future.

No challenge or lesson has ever happened by coincidence. It has all been part of the plan to help you to create you, and who you are destined to be.

At any stage of your journey, you can choose to be free to overcome any false beliefs you have accumulated during this lifetime, and maybe even lifetimes before this. You can have the freedom of choice to reach for the realms of possibilities you were born to achieve.

As a general indication of whether you are in your true character or not at the moment, pay attention to how your moods feel. If you feel happy and uplifted, you are being true to yourself. If you are feeling low, anxious, stressed or constantly tired, you may be acting in contradiction to your true self.

If ever you find yourself acting outside your true character, or feeling out of sorts, take the time to step back and identify how you are feeling, and then explore which of the wonderful Bach Flower Remedies can help bring you back into harmony and balance. The more you work with the Remedies, the greater understanding of yourself you will achieve. It is never too late to start again.

Whenever the environment around you feels uncomfortable, you will in time learn to identify what is causing your disharmony. For every state of imbalance you feel around or within you, there is a Bach Flower Remedy, or a combination of Remedies, that can help you restore balance and harmony.

It is often, not what is going on around us that causes the problem, but the way we feel about it, or react to it. For every emotion, or state of mind you are feeling within you that is out of balance, there is a Remedy or a combination of Remedies which can help you. It will take some time and patience, but the Remedies will help you find greater strength and enable you to take back your personal power.

Take some time out to read through some of the Remedies you feel drawn to. Maybe you could intuitively open your book at one page of the Remedy section, and see which Remedy is calling you. Your intuition can be a great leader in helping you to move forward. Read about CERATO, LARCH, GENTIAN and SCLERANTHUS

Is your mind working for you?

Each and every one of us has a unique ability to create anything we wish to. So why don't we? We are such complex creatures, and there is so much going on in our minds and bodies which we are oblivious to. Your mind is an amazing piece of machinery. If you are in charge of your mind, it can manifest for you anything you desire. So why do we get stuck in situations which are unsuitable for us, and cause us to feel disharmony?

Every moment of every day, you feed your mind with thoughts. If these thoughts are negative or condescending towards yourself, you will feel disharmony within yourself. Constantly trying to control these negative thoughts and feelings can wear you down. They can make you feel stressed and anxious. When you feel run down or out of sorts, the desire to understand yourself and why you react the way you do, often seems out of reach.

Use your healing journal to process what you are learning about yourself and how things have impacted on you. When you write down your thoughts and feelings, you are listening to, and acknowledging what is happening within you. We all need to be heard and the best person to acknowledge this is you. Listen carefully to what thoughts and feelings you have, as you process each piece of information.

Thank yourself for recognising what is happening, and count this as one of your blessings as you go to bed tonight. When you acknowledge what is out of order, you are on the path to deeper healing of yourself.

Become true to yourself

One of the initial driving forces behind making changes is recognising and acknowledging that how you feel is not who you really are, followed closely by the realisation that you have lost your way. But the greatest driving force of all is the desire to find peace, happiness and a sense of well-being.

If every thought you have determines your reality, what is going on in your life at the moment? Do you like what you are manifesting for yourself today?

Dr Bach's philosophy was simple: 'When there is a void between your thinking and what is your true self, is where 'dis-ease' sets in.'

Many of us have been living for so long in a false sense of who we are, we have become disillusioned about the truth of who we truly are. The disharmony comes when we associate our sense of identity with who we have become, when *actually our behaviour reflects how we have become, rather than who we truly are. The result is we cannot separate the two.*

We are really blessed that we live in a time when we have more choices. We all have a choice to change our lives by changing our thinking about how we see ourselves. I believe the Bach Flower Remedies are the greatest gift we could have been given to help us with this.

The Remedies help you gently rectify your thoughts by gently moving them from a negative state to a positive one, and can help you to maintain this state. They also help you get a greater understanding of yourself. It is often not the situations around us which cause us grief, but the way we react to them. Do you always feel in control of your emotional responses?

If you can change your thoughts, you can change your emotions. You can have more control over how you think and feel about situations, and then you will start to feel better about yourself and your life. You can then choose to determine your own destiny. The Remedies will help you move through these changes. They will help show you the way forward, with more clarity and understanding.

What you believe can come true

You will achieve what you first perceive in your mind to be true. We all have so many choices. When we have choices we can change things.

You will achieve what you see in your mind

Your initial driving force behind making changes in your life, is recognising that how you feel has become uncomfortable, and that you have a desire to change it.

What are your thoughts saying to you now? Are you happy with your thoughts at the moment?

Being mindful of your thoughts and how they make you feel is powerful. This awareness is key to helping you make changes as the need arises.

It does not matter how many times you need to bring your awareness back to this thought process. If your thinking has become negative or detrimental, it needs to be addressed to allow you to move forward into a state of harmony.

Do you have emotional confusion or emotional intelligence?

Emotional confusion comes from knowing the emotions you are experiencing are not really who you are, but not knowing how to change them.

Emotional intelligence comes from recognising where the emotions come from, how they have come about, acknowledging you need to change them, and the consequences of not doing so.

With this knowledge, you can then work on understanding your emotional reactions and how you can turn them around. From this place, you can make new choices. From this place, you can feel more empowered to make changes. Having all of this understanding brings you inner strength, tenacity and a feeling of emotional well-being.

Emotional strength comes from knowing how to make the necessary changes, and being prepared, willing and able to make those changes.

Maybe, you have come to a plateau where you are feeling content. If this is so, please take some time out to celebrate this new experience you have achieved. Praise yourself for the journey you have taken. You do need to be realistic, and realise that you may not be able to change everything immediately you set your mind to do. Your mind and your body need time to adjust to your new way of being, and so do the people and circumstances around you.

Take some time out to observe how you do feel, and enjoy living in this new sense of being. Take time to enjoy this new-found sense of who you are. Take some time to record in your healing journal how this new experience feels to you. Make a note of the date when you recognise you feel content.

Move on when you feel ready

You can move on to more learning and healing when you feel ready. The urge to make more changes often comes as another feeling of unrest within you, or something may happen which triggers you to react and feel uneasy in yourself again.

If you have recognised that you are not feeling totally content and at peace today, there is more work to do. This is a chance to reset your triggers again to what is causing your stress.

To change your day, and your life, you need to start to observe your thoughts again, and look at what is happening within today. Maybe this is the time to look at, and to change your thoughts again. It can be so easy to fall back into old ways if you do not monitor what is happening. Be gentle on yourself, and please do not beat yourself up for slipping backwards.

GENTIAN is a good Remedy to help you if you have had a setback, and ROCK WATER will help if you are being too hard on yourself. CHESTNUT BUD will help you maintain new patterns of thinking.

Whenever you choose to start again, your intention and your new thoughts will start to rebuild your new way of life, which will ultimately be the significant motivational driver of your success and happiness. Always go back to the basics, and remember, anything is possible when you are honest with yourself, and you keep taking steps forward.

It does not matter how many times you need to restart your healing programme. This is a massive learning curve for you. Some parts will flow more easily than others. Be gentle on yourself, and start again whenever you recognise you have gone off track. This is your unique journey, and the more you nurture yourself, the more easily it will flow for you. Remember to be your own best friend.

PRENTAL you throughout every day

Praise, respect, encourage, nurture, thank, acknowledge, and love yourself every moment of every day. When you become your own best friend your world will take on a whole new meaning.

This is your action plan for each day to help you value yourself.

I attach to the emotions I feel today, but I am so much more than this

The confusion can come from knowing that the emotions you are experiencing are not really who you are, but you do not know how to change them. The more intense the emotions are, the deeper is the hurt you can feel.

Many of us cannot identify how we are feeling, but know we have a general feeling of discomfort we label as unhappy, feeling stressed or suffering with anxiety. It is good to acknowledge and identify what you are dealing with so you have a foundation to work from. Denying what you are experiencing and feeling can lead to even deeper problems.

Your thoughts are your driving force

The more power you give to your thoughts, the more real they will become. If you keep telling yourself you cannot do something, how do you think your body will respond? It will respond to the commands you are giving it, and act accordingly. Your mind will go searching deep inside your old patterns and beliefs, and find ways to help you act on your commands. You have given your mind instructions to say you cannot do it, and it has no choice but to follow those commands. It doesn't know any different. It is simply following your orders.

When you decide to change a thought, you are deciding to give your mind a new way of working, a new set of instructions. You will need to follow your new thoughts through, with constant uplifting and encouraging thoughts, until you create your new way of being, and it feels natural for you.

Unfortunately, sometimes the old thoughts may return, and take you back into an old pattern of belief. For me, this was a constantly recurring pattern, until I discovered the Bach Flower Remedies.

The Remedies helped me to shift through this process of change, until I could maintain the new way of thinking. By consistently taking the Remedies, and constantly working on my new thought patterns, I started to feel more confident and empowered. The Remedies seemed to be giving me a new lease of life, and a real sense of who I was.

The Remedies seemed to be giving me a calmness and a space where I could see things more clearly and take bolder steps forward. In time, I was able to reflect on how my old thought patterns had led me to feel so disorientated, angry, anxious and depressed. The more I used the Flower Remedies, the stronger I felt, and it became more apparent in my thoughts I was using about myself and my life.

It wasn't long before I felt more content, and at peace with who I had become. With the peacefulness I felt came more insight and clarity into how I had lost my way, and become so far from my true self.

CHAPTER 25

EXPLORING A NEW WAY OF UNDERSTANDING YOU

WE ARE NOW GOING TO be exploring a new way of understanding you. Sometimes you need to look back at your life, to enable you to get a greater understanding of what is affecting you today. I am going to simplify some of the processes your thought patterns go through, to help you explore some of the things which happen within your mind.

To help you understand in as gentle a way as possible, I want to share with you my simplified understanding of the way in which your body reacts to any stressful situations you experience. I know there are more technical medical explanations available, but I prefer to try to keep it as simple as possible.

I do understand that when you are feeling stressed or out of sorts, it can be hard to take on board too much information. If this information is too much to digest right now, please come back to it when the time is right. Take some time out to do something you enjoy.

Looking deeper

Every time you have a thought, there are many underlying responses or reactions to each thought. Take some time to read through the following few pages. See how much of the information fits in with you and your life. I want to give you some simple insights into how you may have lost your way or, maybe, how you have settled for an unhappy pattern or even a life which no longer brings you joy and happiness.

Go slowly through the following pages. Take some time to write down relevant things you recognise have affected you and your life. Make a note of the date you start to recognise these observations, and maybe memories which pop into your mind. How do these memories make you feel? Notice how you can start to get a greater understanding of yourself, and your behaviour pattern. Maybe you can see where your ways of thinking or your beliefs have come from.

You may not always like what you see, or feel comfortable with your new perception, but please remember, you cannot heal something you cannot see, and once it reveals itself, you are on the path to recovery. Some of your greatest lessons about yourself will come from the parts you do not like, and you may even want to resist addressing these issues.

When emotions and situations come to light, thank them for showing up. Thank these aspects of yourself for showing themselves to you, and gently set about processing what you have learnt. Again, this is another blessing revealing itself to help with your growth and healing.

CHAPTER 26

YOUR NEUROLOGICAL LEVELS

READ THROUGH THE FOLLOWING PAGES. Keep using your journal to process what is being revealed to you, and remember to add the date. As you read, you will gain insights into different things which have influenced you and your life. You will be amazed how far you have come, and how much you have grown when you look back at these notes in the months ahead.

As you are processing this information, you may feel overwhelmed by what you discover. ELM is the Bach flower remedy for feeling overwhelmed, and CLEMATIS will help you to feel more grounded, and at peace with all that you are processing.

How do we accumulate our emotions?

Identity, beliefs and values, behaviours, capabilities, environment
Read this section with reference to the list of the five neurological levels above.

From the time we are born, we have many environments within which we need to exist in our lives. At the beginning of our life there may be just one environment, our home environment, or maybe two or more, such as a hospital or extended family environment.

How we feel in each of these environments can have an influence on the thought patterns we start to create for ourselves, and ultimately on how we feel. Was it a happy, comforting experience or was it an inhospitable, unwelcome experience?

Did you have a combination of good and bad experiences? Did you feel loved and nourished? Did you feel safe? Did you feel confused or unwelcome? How did the environment feel to you? What are your memories as a youngster?

At the beginning of your life, there could have been a huge range of experiences, and all of these will start to influence the way you, as a baby, start to feel about yourself and your world. As you grow up, you are given other circumstances to contend with, some happy places, and others not so easy. You are introduced to many more people who can all have an impact on you, with their words, teachings and behaviour towards you.

Some people will adapt easily to all the circumstances in their lives, while others may feel extremely uncomfortable. For some, it can be very confusing, and have a serious impact on how their world starts to look and feel. How you feel within each environment can have a major impact on the true or false identity you start to take on. Or do you feel as though you have more than one identity, a split personality?

The older you get, the more outside environments you are introduced to. Some are good, some are bad, some feel easy, some you may struggle with, and with some others you have no idea how you feel about them. The environment you are in can impact on the way you see your capabilities, how you behave, your beliefs and values, and ultimately how you identify yourself.

If we had only one environment to deal with, life would be much simpler. But most of us have many environments to deal with each day: our pasts, our home, our family, our work, our friends, our social and our spiritual environment. We can take on a different identity within each one, if we are not sure of our own identity and capabilities. Can you recognise how different environments in your life have influenced your personality and your life?

The beauty of working with the Bach Flower Remedies, is they can help you work through, and beyond all these old influences. The Remedies can help you to be yourself within every environment you encounter, regardless of what has happened in your past.

If you have lost your way, and are not sure why you feel the way you do, the Remedies can help you peel away the layers of false beliefs. With consistent use, they will help you to be true to yourself within every environment in your life. They will help you recognise your true self, and help you maintain this wherever you go. You are influenced by so many outer circumstances of your life. Let us look more closely at this.

Your fundamental state of being is your individual character, in relation to your true character. Dr Bach identified this as your personality type. This state of being affects how you communicate to the outside world and the environment around you. But there is so much more to you. What you show to the world today is sometimes an illusion of accumulated thoughts and beliefs which neither belong to you nor serve you.

If you are at peace and in harmony with your individual true self, positive emotions such as love and kindness, courage and strength will evolve. But if your fundamental state of being is blocked by negative emotions, the way you react to your environment becomes distorted, which causes negative emotions such as anger, arrogance, impatience, stress, anxiety, depression and fear. If these emotions continue to build up, it can lead to other problems, and you can start to feel the deeper pain within your emotions, and often within your physical body too.

If you do not recognise or comprehend this impact, and do not learn to communicate to yourself or to others in a positive way, your true self then tries to compensate for this fault.

This can happen in various ways, often causing more negative states. For example, if you are unsure about something or someone, you might try to compensate through different methods of trying to be in control. You might appear confident, but also be domineering or arrogant to try to compensate for your insecurities, or you may become withdrawn, rather than dealing with the situations you meet.

In this way, you can often develop a false attitude of mind, and your beliefs and values about yourself are affected. You may feel a need to justify what you do, and you develop basic characteristics to justify your behaviour, and how you do things. It can also affect how you see your capabilities. You can convince yourself that your current beliefs, your ingrained thoughts, are the absolute truth. When thoughts have become so ingrained they will feel like the truth to you, whether they really are or not.

Every thought you have, becomes an emotion within your body, whether it is negative or positive. You attach to the emotions you feel, and act accordingly. If the emotions are intense and painful, the more emotional pain you can feel. The longer you hold these painful feelings and emotions, the more distorted and distressing your emotions can feel.

These feelings often erupt, in a way which is contrary to your true nature, and can be very distressing, and inappropriate to you and the way you feel about yourself. They can erupt as emotional outbursts, or simmer away gently inside you. Often distorted emotions can result in other feelings, which are not really the real cause of your distress.

The deeper the emotions are buried, the more distorted they can become. Although you may not recognise how this happens, the result of buried emotions often turns to anger and resentment, either towards others or towards yourself. The deeper the anger becomes, the more distorted and even despairing you can feel.

Take a few minutes out for you

Take a few moments to think of something which brings you happiness, and then, using your finger tips, gently tap on the centre point on your forehead, just above your eyebrows. Keep thinking of your happy thoughts. Continue tapping and breathing until calmness comes. Take it a stage further by gently tapping on your thymus point, the space between your heart and your throat, to increase your energy flow. Using a combination of techniques to help yourself can be highly effective. As you value you, your feelings of self-worth will grow.

CHAPTER 27

ANGER CAN MAKE YOU FEEL SICK

ONE OF THE UNDERLYING DEEP feelings we can all experience, and recognise is anger. When we feel angry, we can feel emotionally, and often physically, unwell. It can make you feel sick in your stomach, and affect the way you eat. Anger can cause stress and tension in many parts of your body, and impact on your feelings of well-being.

When you are holding feelings of anger, it can completely change your perspective of your life, of your relationships, and the way you see your world.

Anger is the absolute opposite to the true emotion of love which should be the only emotion flowing through you. Your body can only hold the anger for so long, before it feels ready to explode, and unfortunately the anger often gets released in the wrong way, as inappropriate emotional outbursts.

Anger is often felt as a result of underlying emotions and thoughts which have not been expressed. Anger is often the result of other distressing feelings which have been out of balance, and going on for a long time.

Feelings of anger can be transferred onto the wrong subject because it has not been expressed and addressed to the appropriate root cause. The Bach Flower Remedy HOLLY is the Remedy to help you release your anger, and come back to a place of feeling more loving and compassionate.

HOLLY is a catalyst Remedy, and can be taken alone to help you work through your issues of anger. Never tell someone they should not be angry, or they will feel like you are invalidating them, and the anger will intensify.

If you recognise you are feeling lots of confusing emotions, but the underlying cause is feeling angry, take the HOLLY by itself for a one week or two, to help you ease through some of the anger you are holding. When the anger has considerably subsided, you can slowly introduce other Remedies to support you.

AGRIMONY can help you talk about how you feel, and enable you to confront the person, or persons concerned, so that the issues can be resolved and healed. It is important to acknowledge your feelings of anger, or they become deeper and could manifest as despondency and despair.

Because these feelings of anger are so far from your true self, and are heavy as a result of other negative states you have accumulated, your deception cannot be maintained forever, without manifesting inwardly or outwardly in some way. Holding false beliefs of anger can be draining on your body and soul. It can make you feel detached from the reality of who you are, and what is really happening. Speak about how you feel with someone you trust.

I believe this is where dis-ease often sets in, and it can even be the root cause of mental and emotional unwellness, such as depression and mental illness. As Dr Bach said, 'When there is a void between our thinking and who we truly are, is where dis-ease sets in'.

It is essential to recognise and treat extreme psychological states, which have been out of balance for a long time, very gently. Sometimes, there is a need for other therapies, and always for recognising the potential need for medical intervention. The person's environment and extreme states must be acknowledged and taken into account, otherwise successful healing will remain incomplete.

Be very patient and gentle with people in these extreme states. Introduce single, or a minimum number of Bach Flower Remedies at the beginning, and introduce further Remedies later when appropriate. A slow, steady rate of recovery will be far more effective.

A light-bulb moment

During an anger-management workshop I attended, a lady spoke about a Japanese author Masaru Emoto who wrote a book called The

Hidden Messages in Water. He said that human consciousness has an effect on the molecular structure of water. He claimed that when a glass of water was subjected to positive emotions, and words which invoke positive feelings, the water molecules change into beautifully shaped structures.

He did some experiments with glasses of water, subjecting half of the glasses of water to harsh hurtful words, and the other glasses of water to kind loving words. Then the water was frozen, sliced and examined under a microscope. The water molecules of the water, which had been subjected to the harsh negative words morphed into harsh distorted shapes, and the water molecules which were subjected to the kind, loving words had formed into beautiful symmetrical shapes.

This concept really resonated with the learning I was doing with the Bach Flower Remedies, and the Reiki healing. I was intrigued by his findings and the book he wrote. His theories were apparently never confirmed, but I could really see the sense in what he was saying.

If every cell in your body responds, or reacts to the words you say or hear about yourself each day, is it not worth considering changing those words if they are not encouraging and uplifting, so that your body can resonate to the higher vibration of kind and loving words. If you are using, or hearing angry hurtful words, could this not contribute to your mind becoming confused, and you feeling out of sorts?

Next time you say harsh angry words, take a few minutes to resonate with how you feel about those thoughts. How do those words make you feel? Where do you feel those words in your body? Is it a coincidence, that if you are with someone who says harsh angry things, you feel low in energy and your moods are affected? Use your healing journal regularly to help you work through your insights, understanding and healing process.

Next time you pick up a drink of water, take a few minutes to say kind loving things to the water before you drink it, and notice how much better you feel.

Be gentle on yourself

When your emotions have been out of balance for a long time, the patterns of belief can become so ingrained that they may take longer to shift. Be patient with the speed of progress, consistently take your Remedies, and you will achieve the results you desire.

Remember too, that anger can be a very powerful energy to help you create change when it is used constructively. It's okay to feel anger, but use it to create important changes in your life. There is a beneficial state of mind beyond anger. It is called motivation and taking action. Use your anger to make changes, and then work on calming and soothing your anger. You can use the remedy HOLLY to help ease you through these feelings of anger as you start to take action.

ROCK WATER will help you if you are too hard on yourself. It will help you to be more gentle on yourself, and set realistic expectations of yourself. ROCK WATER also helps you to have more flexibility in your thinking and beliefs, which is important when you are going through changes. IMPATIENS will help you to be more patient with yourself, and the speed of your recovery. It helps you recognise the need for synchronicity, and that everything happens at the perfect time. Your healing is not a race, it gradually happens as you gently work on helping yourself.

BEECH will help you when you want to verbally lash out. BEECH will help you to feel more tolerant, and be able to see things from the other person's point of view.

Someone who has been in an imbalance of emotions for a very long time can appear to have very fixed beliefs. It is important to remember that the things you have been saying to yourself will seem like absolute fact in your mind.

Do not spend time trying to convince yourself that your thoughts are wrong, or that your perspective is wrong. It's okay to acknowledge you feel anger.

The Bach Flower Remedies will help to gently move your thoughts from their fixed beliefs, to a more positive and balanced state of mind. Remember this takes time and patience. When you have released some of the anger feelings you have been experiencing, you will be more able to see a different perspective, and start to understand how your thoughts have impacted on you and your feelings of confusion.

If you keep ingnoring the anger, you can go into a state of despondency because you are suppressing the anger, and the feeling of anger will have a greater impact on you and the way you feel. Unfortunately, if you continue to suppress and ignore your feelings of anger, it can seriously distort the way you act, and feel. You can move into the negative VINE state of mind, or a negative CHERRY PLUM or BEECH state.

When anger has been suppressed for a very long time, you can feel like you are stuck in a negative state of WILLOW, and it is hard to move away from feeling that life is not fair. In any of these negative states it can seem impossible to see a way out, and can lead to a feeling of despondency. This is where the above remedies can be invaluable in helping you to peel away the layers of trapped emotions. The more you use the remedies, the easier it will be for you to move into a state of calm, clarity and joy.

Remember this too when working with other people. What they say to themselves in their mind, and the way they feel about situations seems absolutely real.

Do not spend time trying to persuade them that their thinking is wrong, nor detrimental. Offer them the remedy HOLLY to help them start to release their anger, followed by other remedies they need, and in time the right time will present itself for you to guide them.

You could then, gently help them to see how they have come to the understanding they have through their belief system, and how their thoughts, and others' thoughts and actions have influenced them.

Do not tell someone they should not feel angry, or that being angry is wrong. If you do not allow them to express there anger it will have a detrimental impact of them. They can go from a state of anger to feeling despondent, and invalidated, and in time this anger will erupt in other ways.

When a positive mind-set is achieved, it is easier to reflect on, and talk about, how their state of mind was before. Always remember, each person, and each personality, may need to be approached differently, depending on their state of mind, and their past and present circumstances.

Anger can be constructive

Remember that anger does not have to be destructive. Anger can be a powerful energy when it is used constructively.

If you use your anger to create changes in your life, you will come through the situation feeling much more empowered.

You can use your techniques and the Bach Flower Remedy HOLLY at any time, to help soften the feelings of anger before it starts to impact on your well-being, your health and your peace of mind.

Take some time out to explore your anger. Look at why you feel this anger. Is it justified, or is it necessary to keep holding this feeling?

What can you do about it? What could you put this energy into to help you make changes? Is there something you could do which is constructive and productive at the moment?

My son used to make me smile when he saw I had the vacuum cleaner out. He said he always knew when I was angry about something, because I would blitz the house, and clean it from top to bottom. He was right. Although I didn't like being angry, I knew it was far more productive to do something positive when I was in this state of mind, rather than dwelling on what had happened, and getting more and more angry.

Whilst I was cleaning, my mind was processing what I was feeling, and quite often I would feel ready to make some big changes when I had calmed down. And I had a lovely clean house! A win-win situation. As I have gotten older, and less prone to getting angry, I find myself cleaning out a cupboard whilst I process what I am feeling. It doesn't have to be something huge, but choose to find something constructive to do whilst you process your anger or frustration.

You may prefer to go for a walk or a gentle jog, go to the gym or shout at the top of your voice to get your feelings out. These are your feelings. Honour them. Do not push them down. Use that energy to do something useful or productive.

What could you do for yourself to help you process your anger and frustration?

Remember to keep taking your HOLLY and other remedies regularly and consistently, until the calm resumes.

CHAPTER 28

THE CONSCIOUS-COMPETENCE LEARNING LADDER

AS WE GO THROUGH LIFE, we are on a constant journey of discovery. Life is a never-ending process of learning, with many ups and downs. But overall, our progress as we learn can be thought of as a learning ladder.

I am using the Conscious-Competence learning ladder, which was developed by Noel Burch of the Gordon Training International organisation in the 1970s. I am using it as a visual aid, to help you understand the natural steps of learning we can all go through when we are setting out to do something new.

It is vitally important for your improved feelings of well-being and growth that, at whatever stage of your progress you are, you continually nurture and be kind to yourself. Give yourself time to adapt, adjust and re-adjust if necessary, as you go. It is a natural process to go through the different learning stages.

Know that not every step will go to plan. If you have setbacks, take some time out to process what is happening. Praise yourself for recognising you may have gone off track. Remember to give yourself some time out if necessary. Things often look different when you have had some time out. Giving yourself some quality time gives your mind the space to find different solutions.

When you feel ready, return to your goals and take slow, steady steps forward.

```
    Your Goal
    ―――――――――
    Unconscious
    Competence
    ―――――――――
    Conscious
    Competence
    ―――――――――
    Conscious
    Incompetence
    ―――――――――
    Unconscious
    Competence
```

When you are going through life, you can be totally oblivious to the fact that you are *unconsciously incompetent* in some aspects of your life. You are blissfully unaware of what you cannot do, which often keeps you in a state of harmony, a state of *unconscious competence*. You feel at one with yourself.

It is when you decide to step out and try something new that you can become *consciously incompetent*. When you start out on any new venture, however big or small, you begin to realise what you cannot do. You can feel awkward about the things you cannot do, and need to make more of an effort to learn.

Initially, you might work through a process of learning until you feel competent. You continue to move up the ladder, gaining experience and confidence in your abilities, so you feel good about your achievements and yourself. You start to feel *consciously competent*.

The more you work in this *conscious competence,* the more natural it feels, and the more naturally things flow, until one day you do things without having to think too much about what you are doing.

As you continue to gain in confidence, you start to be aware of how confident you feel about yourself, and your abilities. In time, you start to accomplish the things you were struggling with, with no thought of how you are doing things.

This is when you have moved into a state of *unconscious competence*. Everything is naturally flowing as it should, things seem a lot easier, and you feel good about yourself.

Ways to help yourself on each step of your new venture

Unconscious competence. At this first stage, focus on the benefits of learning the skill, not on the process of learning.

Conscious incompetence. At the second stage, help yourself by working through your plan of learning. At this stage, many things may go wrong, as well as go right, and that is okay. It is all part of your growth.

Conscious competence. At the third stage, give yourself lots of tips, tricks, and techniques to help yourself achieve some successes.

Unconscious competence. At the fourth stage, praise yourself and reinforce the learning you have gained.

Take time to embrace every stage, regardless of what is happening. Remember setbacks are often learning curves, where you need to re-evaluate, not only what is happening, but how you are thinking about what is happening. Remember to use your healing journal to write down your goals, and your step-by-step plan.

Working through any challenges you come across on paper, will help you be more objective, and get a clearer perspective.

What if it doesn't go to plan?

You can often feel out of your depth, and unable to achieve what you were initially aiming for. The intention and desire to accomplish something becomes diminished, and you can give up on what was to be the next step forward.

You can then feel as though you have failed, and start to have negative thoughts about your competence and your intentions. In these circumstances you can even start to question your abilities, and even yourself. You can feel like you have lost your way.

Instead of seeing just the single setback, your mind will go off into a series of old negative thought patterns and beliefs, which bring up old feelings and emotions around anything else where you feel as though you have failed.

These are the times when the Bach Flower Remedies can support you in achieving your intention. When you start to question yourself because of your inability to achieve your goals or your needs, the Remedies can bring you renewed confidence and clarity, with fresh hope, motivation and stability.

It is natural that past inhibitions, experiences, influences and failures can affect both your ability to achieve and your perspective on yourself. The Bach Flower Remedies can gently bring back your personal self-belief, and help you to move beyond your old limiting beliefs with renewed insight.

The Bach Flower Remedies you choose will help to move you through any old patterns of belief to create new more supportive patterns of thinking.

Read about CERATO, CHESTNUT BUD, ELM, GENTIAN. GORSE. LARCH and SCLERANTHUS, and introduce which Remedies you think will support you at the moment.

You don't have to be stuck in the old patterns. You can change these old ways of thinking.

Keep reaffirming how well you are doing. Visualise yourself doing well.

Use positive affirmations throughout the day to help keep yourself on track. You are changing the neurological patterns in your mind, and this takes time, patience and.

It is an important time to keep supporting these changes with your positive affirmations and visualisations of how you will feel, and how life will be for you.

CHAPTER 29

FREUD'S THEORY

Higher self, ego, superego: Why do you act the way you do?

SIGMUND FREUD DEDICATED MUCH OF his life to looking at the way the mind works. He came up with theories which he believed explained the way our mind processes what happens, and how we react to every experience we have.

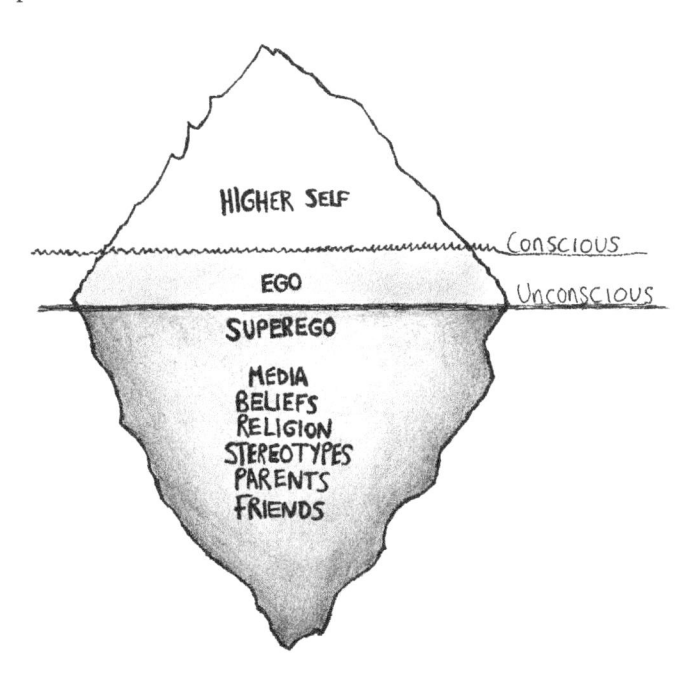

Although on some level I understand his point of view, my understanding varies slightly from his perspective. Since Freud's discoveries and writings, other perspectives have come to light.

My simple understanding is, from the time you are born you hear, and are influenced, moulded and affected by, the words and guidelines from the people around you. It could be those close to you, or other influences such as school, technology, social media, television or radio.

These words and guidelines may have been encouraging and uplifting guidance, or they may have been negative and detrimental, or a combination of both. Regardless of their validity, you can take these thoughts and inputs on board as your own way of thinking and perceiving things around you, and even yourself.

Your mind cannot tell the difference between what is the truth about yourself, and what is false. From an early age, you can start to associate these words with how you feel about yourself.

Although you may intuitively recognise that some of the words are not really connected to you, or do not feel comfortable to you, you can adopt these words and thoughts as if they are the truth about you and about the world around you. These words you consistently think of, and use throughout your day, can influence how you think about yourself and your life.

The workings of the mind is complex, but my simple understanding is, every thought you have is kept somewhere within your mind, usually in the pre-frontal cortex. As you continuously use these thoughts they become ingrained as your reality, your beliefs. They become your belief system about who you are.

To simplify this concept, we are going to refer to these accumulated thoughts and patterns as 'your old memory cabinet' for the moment.

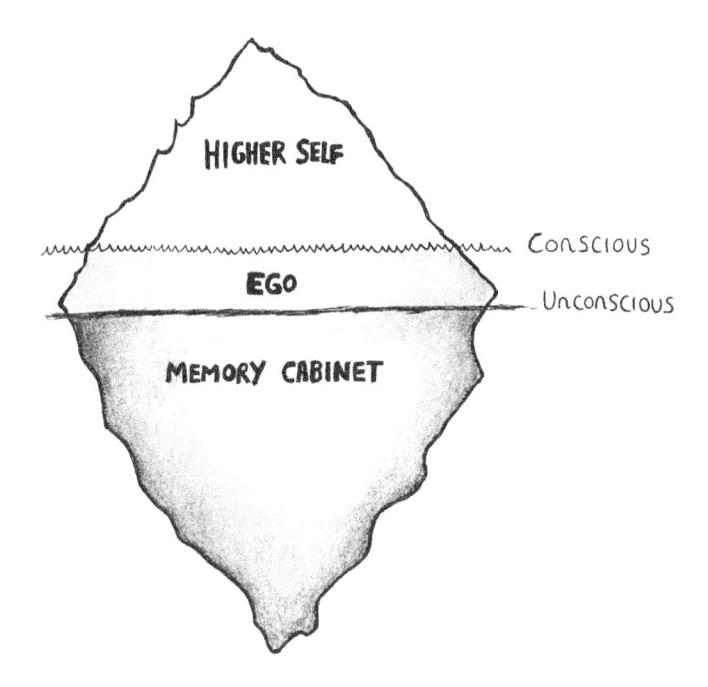

Diagram: An inverted iceberg divided into three sections — "HIGHER SELF" at the top (above the waterline, labeled "Conscious"), "EGO" in the middle (at the waterline, with "Unconscious" below), and "MEMORY CABINET" in the lower, submerged portion.

You can think of this memory cabinet as a filing cabinet in your mind, full of all the thoughts and experiences you have accumulated throughout your life.

These thoughts and experiences may be your own, or those imposed upon you from outside. They may be good, exciting, loving, uplifting, helpful, supportive, detrimental, bad, horrendous, scary, real or imagined.

The deeper part of your mind gathers all of the experiences you have been through, even those you would not necessarily have chosen to retain.

Freud described these old thought patterns as your superego, but I am referring to them as 'your memory cabinet' to bring you a simpler understanding of how, I believe, your mind can become confused.

Are you being led by your old memory cabinet?

My understanding is, that every old experience, word and belief you have accumulated, can influence the way you react or respond today. When you are going through a situation today, your ego, the negotiating part of your mind, will negotiate between what are your old patterns of thinking and belief, and your new intention. And it is from this place you can make decisions based on those old experiences.

My perspective is that your 'higher self' is your true identity. It is the child-like part of you which believes you can do anything, and is always looking to be acknowledged and pleased.

This is your inspirational self, which is constantly trying to guide and inspire you. It knows the truth of who you really are, and what you can achieve. If you listen to your higher self, it can lead you to achieve anything you set out to do.

Compare yourself to the picture of the iceberg. Your higher self, the top of the iceberg, can be the way the world sees you, and often, how you see yourself.

It knows your true potential, but you cannot always access this potential. This is just a small part of who you are, and what you show the world is not the whole picture.

Below the surface of yourself, are years of accumulated information and beliefs. Through your lifetime, you will hear countless ideas, thoughts and opinions, and you can lose touch with the truth about who you are and what your real potential can be.

Through negative input or stressful experiences, these negative thoughts can become overriding, often to the detriment of your growth and your progress.

Your memory cabinet stores all of this old information. Every thought you have, every experience, good or bad, correct or incorrect, is stored in your 'memory cabinet', what Freud called your superego.

When you set out to try something new, your 'ego', the mediating part of your brain, negotiates between your higher self and your memory cabinet, looking for ways to help you move forward. Your ego's intention is to help you to take action, so you can move on to make suitable changes in your life.

The problem can come if you have a really strong, negative, overriding memory cabinet, full of detrimental thoughts and beliefs, and you continually listen to these thoughts and beliefs. Your mind can react to what you are trying to achieve, based on the patterns of the negative experiences you have had. Then you will unconsciously listen to this inner voice of negative beliefs, and may fall into detrimental habits your 'old memories' see as correct.

Remember, your 'memory cabinet' cannot tell the truth between what is right or wrong, good or bad. The patterns and habits may not be in your best interest, but your mind cannot tell the difference between good or bad guidance. It all seems appropriate for this new project. If your beliefs and thoughts in your 'memory cabinet' are in control, you may continually repeat the same mistakes. You can find it difficult to make a new decision and stick with it, or you will repeatedly make bad decisions.

When you venture out to start on a new project or journey in your life, you can make a really good decision, and you know within yourself it is the right one, and that you can achieve it. You get a real strong sense of what you can achieve. You have every intention of following through on your desires. This is your higher self talking to you.

Some people are fortunate, and can complete their mission. But for many of us, it is a different story. We often struggle, and become anxious when we get caught up in the old 'memory cabinet' patterns. It can bring you that 'sinking feeling', a downward spiral you don't know how to escape from.

When we have a setback, or things don't move as swiftly as we anticipated, we often dip back into our old negative memory patterns and beliefs to remedy the situation we are dealing with. But, unfortunately, those old negative patterns can only give us more of what we have already not achieved.

A downward spiral

As you act on these old patterns in your 'memory cabinet', they can seem more comfortable, and you can soon get stuck here again.

When the negative aspects of your past override the intention of your higher self, you start off with great enthusiasm, and then talk yourself out of the decision a short time later, and you can then lose that initial inspiration, excitement and motivation.

You could go into a place of disappointment, fear and anxiety, and start to berate yourself. This can be very detrimental to your new decisions and your new venture. When this happens, your old thoughts have overpowered your new way of thinking and acting, and it can feel hard to get in touch with your original incentive, your passion, or your motivation.

Hard to start again

Once again, now the thought of doing something new can start to trigger old feelings of anxiety. The amygdala, the deep subconscious, emotional part of your brain, triggers the stress responses that produce the adrenalin and cortisol that can, in turn, result in you feeling anxious.

Your body and your mind then revive and relive the familiar old stress patterns because you don't feel safe. In this state it is natural to want to back away from the challenge that triggered the stress response. It is not long before you are back in a place of disillusionment, which inevitably brings you back to a place of negative thoughts about yourself and, ultimately, the way you feel about yourself.

This can lead to a feeling of discouragement and despondency towards your new project, and then towards yourself. In this state of mind it is really easy to talk yourself out of the inspirational idea you originally had. This is when stress, low self-esteem, shame and anxiety often start to set in.

This is when we can often go into a state called the dark night of the soul. A place where we feel extremely emotionally distressed, lost, disorientated, agitated with ourselves, and cannot see a way forward. The Bach Remedy SWEET CHESTNUT can help revive you from this state of mind, bringing you light at the end of the tunnel, and renewed insight, tenacity, motivation and clarity.

ELM can help if you feel overwhelmed, and LARCH can bring you renewed confidence to try again. GENTIAN can help you recover from your setbacks and be more optimistic, and GORSE can help you if you feel helpless to make changes. It brings you renewed hope, and can be the first step towards recovery again.

Inner conflict often sets in because you have a deep inner knowing that you need to, and can create the changes, but you have lost the ability, or the will to work through the negative mind-set which is holding you back.

You end up with a conflict within your mind, and this then starts to impact on your emotional well-being and belief in yourself and your abilities.

This is where the Bach Flower Remedies are invaluable. The Remedies can be a great emotional support for you. They can help you retrain your amygdala response centre to feel safe, and your mind to create new patterns which will support you through any changes you choose to make.

By using the Flower Remedies to emotionally strengthen yourself, and to calm your stressful feelings which may arise, and by using positive affirmations and visualisations, you can create new patterns. The Remedies will help to sustain your confidence and motivation. Your brain then produces the endorphins, and other chemicals which help you deal with any stressful situations. This then brings you feelings of contentment and happiness.

When you have this more uplifting feeling of well-being, you feel safer, stronger, and more motivated. You will feel more empowered to be able to accomplish your intention.

Take some time to read about the Remedies you are drawn to. Look at CERATO, ELM, LARCH, GENTIAN and WILD ROSE. Can you recognise the patterns of thinking you slip back into? Take some time to write down any Remedies you can relate to, and bring those Remedies into your healing journey today.

Keep on top of your emotions

Always remember that your old thoughts, your old 'memory cabinet beliefs', can very quickly overpower your new way of thinking and acting.

Make a conscious decision to recognise the downward spirals you are prone to, and make a decision to maintain the changes you would like to achieve. Listen to your thoughts, and what your body is telling you, and rectify your thoughts as soon as possible. Be gentle on yourself. Speak kindly to yourself, and give yourself plenty of reassurance.

Choose the correct Bach Flower Remedies, and take them consistently until the balance and harmony comes back. Continue to take them throughout the changes you are creating.

Start using the Remedies before you start your new project, and keep updating them as you progress. If you find yourself slipping back into old patterns, the Remedies can bring you clarity, with renewed hope and confidence, to accomplish your desires.

When you have an inspiration you wish to act on, the appropriate Remedies will help you face up to, and overcome, any challenges you encounter. They will help you maintain an uplifting and encouraging state of mind.

Write in your journal about what you would like to achieve. If you slip back, recognise the pattern you have slipped back into.
Use affirmations and your Bach Flower Remedies throughout the day.
Make a note of the Remedies you choose, and note how they help you.
Do you need to add more Remedies to make the necessary changes?
Remember to use your journal as an 'I am a winner record' as well.
What was good about your day?
What was better than yesterday?
How did you help yourself today?
What did you achieve today?

Remember a small step is a big achievement, and many small steps will get you to your desired destination.

Simplify your life with one thought at a time

What thought do you need to change today? If you find yourself saying, 'This is hard', ask yourself what it is that you are finding hard? How can you turn this around tomorrow?

Choose to work with one thought pattern today.

Are you ready to change your potential with your thoughts?

Write down the good changes you recognise you are aiming to change today. What will be the positive outcome of making this change today? When you study your thoughts, you will start to learn a lot about yourself, and what you need to change.

When you have an insight into parts of yourself, be gentle on yourself. Make a note of your potential alongside anything you need to change.

Use your positive affirmations throughout the day, and visualise yourself as succeeding.

Remember, self-praise is imperative.

Keep focusing on your goals. A desire to do something will help your mind find the way to achieve it.

Renewed hope and inspiration

When I saw Freud's 'iceberg in water' diagram, it triggered within me lots of deep, provoking thoughts. I could really relate to the way I had repeatedly tried to make changes, and every time I bobbed my head up above the water, something or someone had tried to push me back down.

After a while, I started to realise it was often my old thoughts which were dragging me down. I also realised the impact people around me were having on me. I recognised that if I was going to change my life, I would have to take control of my thoughts and, ultimately, my life.

I created my own diagram, to help simplify the way I believe we are affected in our thinking, and our beliefs.

For me, this was where the Bach Flower Remedies were invaluable. The Remedies helped me to feel more uplifted and rise above my old fears and beliefs. The more I used the Remedies, the less impact the past seemed to be having on me. They helped me to recognise my old patterns and beliefs, and enabled me to move myself into a new place of clarity and self-belief. I was more able to recognise when my old beliefs were starting to overtake my new intentions.

If I did take a downward slide, I realised how much it affected my feelings. This usually manifested as a lack of energy and motivation, feeling agitated with myself, as well as a feeling of heaviness and disappointment.

Two of the Remedies I found really effective were GENTIAN for optimism and setback, and MUSTARD for frustration and some unrecognised anger.

ROCK WATER was invaluable in helping me to be gentle on myself and honour my own needs. LARCH was helpful for renewed confidence in myself, and CERATO helped me to keep trusting in myself again and again.

CENTAURY helped me to stay strong in my intentions, and CHESTNUT BUD helped me to maintain my new ways of thinking. The more I used the Bach Remedies, the stronger I became. The stronger I became, the more I was able to accomplish.

If you slip into old patterns of thinking or behaviour take a moment to study what you are thinking. Write your thoughts down, and study the Remedies to see which ones would help you to override your old ways of thinking. Create an affirmation for yourself, use it throughout the day, and visualise your goal working out.

Retraining your mind with visualisations

If you find yourself keep slipping back into old patterns of thinking and acting, take some time to do a Withinercise meditation for yourself. As you visualise, and send out your intentions you are working with the universal law of attraction.

As your vibration of expectation vibrates out into the universe, you are also triggering the deeper part of your brain to resonate and co-operate with your desires and intentions. The stronger your intentions are, the more your brain, your body and your emotions will resonate on the intentions you are sending out. As everything in the universe resonates on a vibrational frequency, what you attract is relevant to what you are sending out. Raise your expectations with your words, intentions and visualisations and see how the universe responds to your requests.

The more you use this exercise, the more effective it will be. Remember, it can take sixty-six days to create a new pattern, and maintain it naturally, but you will start to reap some of the benefits soon after you start working with this. It takes time but it will be so worth it.

Everything you do for you today is a step forward.

Keep adding things onto your vision board to motivate you, and remember to move them onto your gratitude board when you have achieved what you set out to do.

CHAPTER 30

ARE YOU A SPIRAL OF NEGATIVE EMOTIONS?

MANY OF US ARE FAMILIAR with the 'sinking feeling' of going into a negative spiral of feelings about something that happens to us, or about the circumstances around us.

But how many of us can stop that process, before it gets the better of us? We can change a downward spiral by changing our thoughts.

Each thought becomes an emotion

Most of us live in a spiral of emotions, which impact on us continuously throughout the day, and often during the night too.

Each thought you have becomes an emotion. Your thoughts then determine and influence your emotions, the way you feel about your circumstances and yourself, which then affects your behaviours, and what the outcome will be.

Then we often criticise and judge ourselves based on the outcome.

You become a spiral of emotion, and these feelings you carry are contagious. The more you live in these feelings, the greater impact they have on the way you act, the way you feel, and the way your body reacts or responds to what is happening. It can also influence the outcome you create, and ultimately the way you see yourself in the world.

```
        NEGATIVE
        THOUGHTS
        AND BELIEFS
HOW YOU
SEE YOURSELF
              NEGATIVE    NEGATIVE
                          EMOTIONS
  NEGATIVE
  OUTCOME       NEGATIVE
                BEHAVIOUR
```

When you hold thought patterns for a long time, they become your beliefs, and it is these beliefs which can create deeper confusion if the thoughts are negative or not true to the nature of your personality.

This brings more negative emotions, which brings negative behaviour, which creates a negative outcome. You then question yourself, and you are back to your old negative thoughts and beliefs.

Constantly having negative thoughts, or false feelings and trying to control them can be draining. Your mind and body can feel worn out, which then leads to deeper stress, which brings deeper hurts and an even greater imbalance.

Is this the spiral you were living in?

Do you recognise your pattern of thinking?

Do you like the way it makes you feel?

As we said earlier, your body can only hold false beliefs for so long, before you feel tired, weary, disorientated or out of sorts. When you hold positive thoughts and beliefs you feel uplifted, confident, safe, motivated and valuable.

The blessing is, you do have a choice. Get ready to make some changes today.

Your thoughts are your driving force

As we said earlier, the more power you give to your thoughts, the more real they will become to you. Your thoughts become your beliefs. Your beliefs then create your patterns from which you make decisions you live by each day.

If you keep telling yourself, 'I cannot do it,' how do you think your body will respond? It will respond to the commands you are giving it, and act accordingly. Your mind will search deep inside your old patterns and beliefs, and find ways to help you act on your commands. You have told your mind to say you cannot do it, and it has no choice but to follow your commands. It doesn't know any different. It is simply following orders.

POSITIVE THOUGHTS AND BELIEFS → POSITIVE EMOTIONS → POSITIVE BEHAVIOUR → POSITIVE OUTCOME → HOW YOU SEE YOURSELF → **POSITIVE**

When you decide to change a thought, you are deciding to give your mind a new way of working, a new set of instructions.

You need to follow your new thought through, with constant uplifting and encouraging thoughts and affirmations until you create your new way of thinking.

You are retraining your mind.

Unfortunately, sometimes the old thoughts may return, and take you back into an old pattern of beliefs. The Bach Flower Remedies will help you work through this process of change, until you can maintain your new way of thinking.

By consistently taking the Remedies at the beginning, and returning to them when your circumstances change again, you will start to feel more confident and empowered. The Remedies will help you maintain your new patterns of belief. Be gentle on yourself as you work through any time of change, and constantly reassure and praise yourself as you go.

The Remedies will bring you a new lease of life, and a real sense of who you are. In time, you will be able to reflect on how your old thought patterns have led you to feel so disorientated, anxious, stressed or depressed. The more you use the Flower Remedies, the stronger you will feel, and this will become more apparent in your thoughts about yourself, and about your life.

You will soon start to feel more content and at peace with who you have become. With this new sense of self, will come more insight and clarity into how you may have lost your way.

Remember. When you change your thoughts, you can change your perspective and your emotions, and ultimately your life. Working with this thought alone can be life-changing. Use your Withinercise exercise frequently, to help re-programme your mind and create the life you desire.

Write some affirmation notices around your home to remind you, and to inspire you. The more you do for yourself throughout the day, the easier it will be to stay on track.

'Today, as I am gently changing my thoughts, I am lovingly changing my life'. 'I am feeling more in control of my life'.

You can be back in control of your life.

Smile as you go

Throughout your journey take some time out to smile, and laugh at some of the things and experiences you have been through. When you can learn to laugh at yourself, and find some humour within the experiences you have had, you will be heading towards a more uplifting and enlightening way of life.

When I learnt to lighten up, my whole world seemed a lot lighter. My son used to say to me, 'Lighten up Mum'. At the time I did not recognise that I was so uptight, or that I was being so serious and intense. Sometimes it used to irritate me when he said that, because I thought it was unjustified. It wasn't until I had moved beyond the state of being so uptight and stressed, that I could see the sense within what he was saying.

Stress and tension really can affect the way you feel, and the way you are. Learning to smile more, and laugh at myself for some of my crazy ways, really did help me to lighten up, and start to see the lessons within my crazy experiences.

Sometimes, we do need someone else to point out to us how we need to change, and that's okay. If someone does make a comment about some aspect of your behaviour, take some time to assess what they are trying to tell you. Is there something about you which you need to adjust today?

Start to see the funny side of what is happening. Being gentle on yourself, and gently adjusting what is necessary, will help you to see the lighter side of your life, and who you are.

When you learn to laugh at yourself and your experiences, the whole world becomes a happier place to be.

During my journey I was introduced to a lady called Beverley Bishop, who did a therapy called Laughter Yoga. She explained how laughing, and the sound of laughing, creates a nearological feeling of well-being. At first, I must admit, laughing felt a bit false when I really was not feeling happy, but I had nothing to lose so I carried on with the session. Just listening to the other people laughing made me smile, and it wasnt long before I was joining in without it seeming false. I found myself smiling

After just one session I started to feel lighter in myself, and from that day I started to see the funnier side of things which had been bothering me. The more I started to laugh about things, the easier it felt to actually be happy.

Laughing is a great remedy for healing all sorts of emotions in your life, and I would highly recommend checking out Beverleys website, www.beverleybishop.co.uk or contact her for a chat at bishop-bev@hotmail.com. She even does sessions on-line so you dont need to leave the comfort of your home.

It you do not feel ready to take this step yet, choose to do things which make you laugh. Choose to spend some time with someone who is upbeat, and makes you laugh and feel happy.

Even if you have to force a smile or a laugh at first, your mind will respond by starting to produce the feel-good chemicals you need to lift up your spirits. Your mind cannot tell if you are pretending to laugh, or you are really laughing. Laughter triggers a whole chain reaction to helping you feel good. Laughter is a great release for stress and tension, and can even help with pain relief, anxiety and feelings of loneliness and depression.

Always remember, anything you do to support yourself will increase your feelings of being supported, and increase your feelings of self worth. Whatever situation you are going through, your mind responds to laughter, and the more you do for you, the stronger you will feel.

CHAPTER 31

THE PRE-FRONTAL CORTEX: DO YOU REALLY HAVE CONTROL?

IN THIS PRESENT TIME, WHEN life has become so highly evolved, how come we are all still struggling with stress and anxiety?

When something happens, and you start to feel stressed, it is because the stress triggers a part of your brain, the primeval survival part of your brain.

Your thoughts start in the pre-frontal cortex, which then triggers the amygdala, the emotional response centre, to react by producing chemicals which enable your physical body to react to be able to survive.

This stress trigger happens whenever we are, or we feel, threatened.

In primeval times, we generally felt threatened by an animal attacking, or by feeling separated from our tribe. We all had a real need to stand and fight, freeze or run away from a threatening situation.

This stress response enabled us to survive. Added to this, in order to survive, we needed to be with other people, as we couldn't have survived alone.

We are all descendants of these survivors, still using the same stress responses triggered by our daily circumstances.

Why is this still happening now?

What is happening in the present day is that the same stress response is being triggered on a minor level, almost constantly throughout every day, by various situations in your life.

Do you know what your stress triggers are? You may have just one stress trigger, or an endless list of them. Start to recognise your stress triggers, and make a list of them.

Your primeval reaction is being triggered constantly. All of your stress triggers create a continuous, minute level of the stress response in your body. So the physical dynamics of that stress response haven't caught up with our technological life and the way we live today. It has become an inappropriate imbalance.

When a fearful or stressful situation happens, as we perceive pressure, threats or danger now, it triggers a physiological response. When we feel pressured, or under threat, and our survival is at risk, it triggers an amazing internal dynamic response within the body, which we have evolved to create.

Your body's response

To help you understand, I want to share with you my simplified understanding, of the way in which your body reacts to any stressful situation you experience. There are more technical and medical explanations available, but I like to try to keep it as simple as possible.

As I have said earlier, I do understand that when you are feeling stressed, or out of sorts, it can be hard to take on board too much information. If this information is too much to digest right now, please come back to it when the time is right.

Natural reaction

The pre-frontal cortex in your brain, starts to create a neurological reaction to anything emotional or stressful which happens in your day. The sympathetic nervous system, the 'fight or flight' system, in the amygdala takes over, and your body reacts accordingly. This is a subconscious, automatic reaction, and we can feel like we have no control over this reaction.

With each neurological response, cortisol and adrenalin start pumping round your body. This delivers more energy to your heart, which beats faster to pump all the blood needed to your muscles, so they can work faster, enabling you to run away from the situation, freeze or stand and fight back.

This natural process still kicks in today, and gives you the ability to deal with and survive stressful situations today.

When we experience something difficult or challenging, our thoughts go into that place of fear, of being threatened. This is often aggravated when we feel alone, when we feel disconnected, or when we notice a difference between ourselves and others, and are comparing ourselves.

So, when we start having stress thoughts that aren't supportive, and we feel under threat, we still go into the primeval feeling of fear, which impacts on the way our body reacts and our energy flows.

Today, this still triggers that very same stress response, and the survival response is as it was in our primitive ancestors. The blood is pumping faster to our heart, which beats even faster, which pumps more blood to our muscles, and we go into the fight or flight, or possibly the freeze response.

When we are in that stressed and anxious state, the blood is diverted away from the stomach, which is why so many people nowadays struggle with stomach upsets and other digestive problems when they are anxious or stressed. Their ability to digest effectively and efficiently diminishes, so they can feel physically, and often emotionally unwell.

The ability to think clearly also diminishes, as the adrenalin and cortisol energy is focused on the heart, and pumping the blood to the muscles. Part of the brain shuts down, which is why it can seem hard to make decisions when you are stressed.

When you are in this stressed state, energy is also diverted away from the logical thinking part of the brain. When you are in stress mode, the adrenalin and cortisol are rushing round the body, and you cannot think straight. Your ability to make rational decisions is often diminished.

Remember, your mind cannot think of two thoughts at the same time, and in a stressed state your brain's focus is in a stressed survival mode.

How can we compare this to something which could be happening today?

Just imagine for a moment:

You are walking down the street. It is late at night, and you are suddenly aware of footsteps behind you.

The footsteps seem to be getting faster and closer to you. You do not want to turn around. You start to quicken your pace, but the footsteps are getting closer. Your heart is starting to race. You realise you are starting to feel more anxious as you start to walk even quicker.

You turn the corner and see your house in front of you. You race towards the door and you notice the footsteps are getting closer, and someone raises their voice to get your attention. By now you are at the door and frantically fumbling to find your keys. As you are turning the key in the lock you suddenly feel a hand on your shoulder. Your heart feels like it is going to explode, you feel light-headed and in a split moment you realise you are actually shaking inside. You want to scream out, but nothing comes out of your voice.

You feel frozen to the spot. A gentle voice says 'Excuse me, but I think this is yours. You dropped it near the bus stop as you got off'. It takes what seems like an eternity, but it is just a brief moment, before you can turn around to see an elderly gentleman standing there holding your orange scarf in his hand.

A massive sense of relief comes over you, as you thank him, and watch him walk slowly away. A moment in time suddenly feels frozen, as your mind goes to a blank space, and you start to chuckle to yourself. 'What on earth was that about? What on earth possessed me? That doesn't make any sense.'

As you turn the key in the lock and start to push open the door, you have an overwhelming feeling of not knowing if you want to laugh or cry. Your heart is still racing, and you feel hot and bothered yet cold and shivery.

As you go to sink in the chair you realise your legs are shaking and you are still breathing rapidly. As you close your eyes for a moment you have this overwhelming feeling of calm, yet confusion flowing through your body.

FREE TO BE ME

What has happened to you?

You have gone back into what is your primeval state of survival. Your body is using the same coping mechanism it would have used a thousand years ago, to help you survive a real threatened attack.

'But it wasn't real', I hear you say to yourself. 'I wasn't really under attack. My mind just went crazy and I started to feel panicky'. And this is what often happens in your life. You are constantly creating and reliving in your mind situations what you believe to be true. Your mind cannot tell if what you are thinking about is actually happening or, if you are merely thinking about what is happening, or could happen.

When your mind starts to think about a situation under which you feel stressed or threatened, it kick-starts your natural primeval state which is to help you survive. It can seem like you have no control over this. This is partly true, on some level you are not in control of this reaction. Your mind is working on your behalf and instructing your body to act on its most primeval instinct. To freeze, fight or run from the situation you feel is threatening you.

Is it real, or is it not?

It may be that you really are under threat, in which case you have within you the tactics and the ability to defend yourself or run away.

But more often than not, the threat is merely in your mind. It may seem like others are attacking you with their words or their attitude. It may seem real that others are trying to put you down, or make you feel guilty or inadequate. And yes, sometimes this may be the case, or has been the case in the past. But more often than not, the perceived threat is really just in your mind, and your mind is trying to help you deal with the situation you are thinking about.

When you feel stressed or are worrying, your brain starts to produce the chemicals adrenaline and cortisol which help you to work spontaneously through what you are experiencing. When you are constantly feeling under stress your body is naturally producing these chemicals to help you to cope. It has no choice; it is merely reacting to what you are thinking about.

More often than not the things we worry about may never happen

How much of your thinking time is consumed by things over which you have believed you have no control or may never happen?

The more you think about something, the more emotionally attached to the event you become, and the more real it feels to you. Stop and study what you are thinking about. How can you help yourself today, by simply acknowledging and correcting your thoughts?

The prefrontal cortex is the more evolved part of your brain, and it is important for access to all our resources, memories, experiences, and learning. It is where you create from, the place where you think about things and problem-solve from.

So what is happening nowadays is that when you are constantly in a state of stress, the adrenalin and cortisol go round on a smaller level, but constantly, in your body. This stressed level can diminish access to a healthy, flowing digestion, and can even damage your immune system. It can also create many of the other diseases we hear about, which are partly related to stress.

So, if technology has evolved, why haven't our stress responses?

Many of us have been caught up in this busy, fast-paced, technological world, and we don't take enough time to be away from the things which induce the stress responses. And then, when personal or work circumstances bring us yet another challenge, we are already in a state of stress, and not in the right frame of mind to deal with things appropriately. The stress levels continually go up, and we start to feel the effects of what is happening in our emotional and physical well-being.

Part of your brain shuts down

I would like to share my simple understanding of what happens. When you become stressed, part of your brain becomes overwhelmed. The part of the brain called the thalamus shuts down, and so the entire picture of what is happening cannot be stored in your brain.

Instead of forming specific memories, of the full event of things which have happened when you have been traumatised in the past, you remember flashes of images, sights, sounds and physical sensations. It is how you felt about the situation, which creates the memory. These flashes create sensations which become triggers of the past, which can be triggered whenever you go through anything stressful or traumatic now.

The brain becomes wired, to be on alert for things which seem dangerous or stressful. Your brain creates an emotional memory system which, when triggered by stress in the here and now, causes you to react as you would have done in the past. This activates your old emotional states, which is why it can seem impossible to separate what has happened in the past, to what is happening in this moment.

Please recognise it is not that your emotions are necessarily so extreme in this moment, but your mind cannot separate the past from the present. When you are feeling traumatised or stressed, you can often flick back to old memories which seem to be extremely raw. This is your body's natural way of trying to help you deal with stress. Your mind will be connecting with these past incidents, and trying to use the same coping mechanisms as it did in the past. The cortisol and adrenaline will be released to help you deal with what you are experiencing.

Your body can feel like it is under attack, and you can feel extremely emotional and vulnerable. It is often normal that you can feel more threatened than you really are. Whenever you go into this vulnerable space, it is important to acknowledge how you are feeling. Do not try to push your feelings away. By acknowledging your feelings, you are starting to acknowledge where you need healing on many levels.

Take some time out to write down how you are feeling. Writing can help you process layers of emotions you may not have recognised you are feeling.

The Bach Flower Remedies, can be extremely beneficial in helping you to peel away these layers of emotions, and will help you find more balance and harmony.

As you peel away one layer of emotions and thought patterns, underlying thought patterns will show themselves. If your emotions have been intense for a while, start by choosing Remedies which feel most relevant to how you feel at the moment.

Take the Remedies regularly for a few days to give your emotions time to adjust. Remember, it is often more effective to take a single Remedy, or a minimum of Remedies together, if you do feel extremely uptight or stressed.

If you do not know how you are feeling, use your pendulum to ask which Remedies would help you with this feeling you have today. (See later section on using a pendulum in the Bach Flower Remedy section.)

Sensations and emotions can feel more intolerable, because you can feel like they will never come to an end. The Remedies will help ease you through the emotional pain you are experiencing. When your mind knows that this pain will come to an end it can bring a great sense of relief, and your whole attitude and perspective can change.

Always remember, that whatever you are going through right now, there is a way you can work through this moment in time, and find a better quality of life for yourself.

Take a few moments to think of something which brings you happiness, and then, using your finger tips, gently tap on the centre point on your forehead, just above your eyebrows. Keep thinking of your happy thoughts. Continue tapping and breathing until calmness comes.

Take it a stage further by gently tapping on your thymus point, the space between your heart and your throat, to increase your energy flow.

Using a combination of techniques to help yourself will be highly effective. Never underestimate the healing power of doing something for you.

Be gentle on yourself, as you work through any stressful or challenging times. Being patient and respectful of yourself, and what you are experiencing, will help you feel more supported. When you are stressed it is often natural to have an emotional over-reaction to situations. This is your body's way of dealing with things which are causing you to feel out of balance, based on your past experiences.

Unfortunately, far too often, you will associate how you see yourself as the behaviour you display. This can bring a false sense of who you really are. This needs to be addressed. It is important to be able to separate your behaviour from who you are. Your behaviour patterns are just an aspect of who you are; they are not who you are.

How can you naturally support yourself today?

Thinking of something that makes you smile produces serotonin, which brings happiness and joy.

Remembering, imagining, or thinking of a loving moment produces oxytocin, which brings compassion.

Reliving, or thinking about a success, or an achievement produces dopamine, which brings feelings of success.

Thinking of a memory, or the intention of bravery and courage, produces endorphins, which bring you feelings of confidence.

Doing things for you can lower your stress and lift up your spirits.

The figure '8' exercise will help you to process what you are thinking about.

Take some time out, to cover your eyes for a few minutes, as you gently take deep breaths right down into the base of your spine.

Meditation and visualisations will help you to get a clearer perspective.

Chanting and singing will help to lift you above what you are experiencing.

Talk to somebody about how you feel.

Give yourself a hug to start the flow of oxytocin in your body.

Anything you do for you will make a difference, because your mind feels like it is being supported, and your emotional response centre, the amygdala, produces more of the feel-good chemicals to bring a feeling of well-being.

Feeling more adventurous

There are times on your journey when you will need to reach out for help. Some of the other therapies I have turned to are Emotional Freedom Technique (EFT), Optimum health balancing with kinesiology, hypnotherapy and counselling. The EMDR therapy can help to desensitise you from the traumas you have experienced in the past. Or, if I needed some physical stress relief, or my body felt out of sorts, Reiki, Indian head massage, massage, reflexology, crystal healing, and acupressure are all great ways to help me find relief from tension and stress.

Doing something creative like painting, drawing, writing, baking, listening to music, singing, dancing, gardening, walking or swimming, can be a great way of giving your mind some space to process what you are experiencing. When you come back to the situation, you will be in a better place to re-evaluate what is happening, and so create a more favourable outcome. If you are not feeling very energetic or inspired, gentle breathing exercises, meditating, chanting and sleeping are all ways to give your mind some much needed space and rest time.

Whatever you feel drawn to right now, give yourself some tender quality time to explore something which will help you get back in touch with your true self. The more you look after yourself, the easier it will be to work through any situations you feel challenged by.

Some people thrive with stress

When you are dealing with a stressful situation, some people can thrive for long periods, and the extra flow of adrenalin and cortisol helps you to accomplish what you need to. It can give you the boost of energy you need for daily tasks. Some people can live in this state of hyper-tension for long periods. But for the majority of us, constantly pushing our bodies to this place of extreme exertion can become more and more tiring and draining.

CHAPTER 32

WHAT IS YOUR STATE OF MIND?

Out of balance

IT IS NOT ALWAYS APPARENT that you are stressed when you are in an on-going situation. It is normally the after-effects you notice, the extreme tiredness, headaches, stiff neck, achy body, feeling uptight and agitated, poor digestion, restless nights. This is your body showing signs of being pushed too hard. If you are experiencing any of these symptoms, you may need to start to listen more carefully to your body, and adjust some things in your life.

So how can you alleviate or adjust this, in a world where you don't seem to have any control? You need to take time out, to stop the process of the cortisol and adrenalin being constantly fired up. You need to give your body some respite from the constant feelings of stress and tension. Anything you do for yourself which you enjoy, will encourage your mind to start to produce the more soothing healing chemicals into your body.

Your brainwaves

> ***Gamma brainwaves*** – Higher mental activity, including perception, insight, problem-solving and consciousness.

Beta brainwaves – Active, busy thinking, active processing, active concentration, arousal and knowledge.
Alpha brainwaves – Calm, relaxed, yet alert.
Theta brainwaves – Deep meditation, relaxation, inspirational ideas, rem (rapid eye movement) sleep.
Delta brainwaves – Deep, dreamless sleep, loss of body awareness.

In this fast-paced life we live, we usually spend the majority of the day in the beta brainwaves state of mind, which is necessary to be able to do the day-to-day things to thrive, and often survive.

But the problem comes, when we are in the beta state of mind for longer and longer periods. When we are constantly pushing ourselves, we are constantly in the beta state of mind. When we are using technology, we are in the beta brainwave state, and often we get caught up with our mechanical gadgets for longer periods too – for example, watching television, texting on mobiles, using computers right up until bedtime – and then our brain cannot switch off from the beta state of mind.

You can find it harder to switch off your thinking or worrying, which ultimately can cause you restless sleep, and can result in a weary mind and body the next day. For many of us, this pattern keeps going on day after day, and we become more and more stressed because we haven't given our brain the chance to relax into the deeper states of alpha, theta and delta brainwaves.

We need to retrain ourselves, to be able to achieve a deeper state of relaxation throughout the day, to encourage the mind to be able to switch off, and especially before our sleep time.

Is it any wonder you feel confused?

With all of these things going on in your mind, and with all of the outside influences, no wonder you can feel so disconnected from your true self.

Is it any wonder, when you have a new, or stressful situation to deal with, you can feel confused about how to react or respond?

Thankfully you do have choices. You can start on a new journey of healing today, by making a few simple changes and introducing the Bach Flower Remedies into your life.

If you have not already started, choose to start your new way of life today. Discover who you really are.

Your ultimate goal should be to be able to move your state of mind from the busy states to the relaxed states, so your mind and your body can enjoy the calm and peace you need to recharge yourself. And this will bring you the optimum ability to make the most of your life, not only in how productive you can be, but also in being able to maintain your sense of calm and peace within you.

Adjusting your sleep patterns

We are led to believe that we all need a consistent block of sleep each night. If you are struggling with your sleep patterns, firstly recognise that we are all different, and we all need different amounts of sleep.

Does not getting a good night's sleep cause stress?

Lack of sleep can create extreme stress for some people, but not necessarily for everyone.

It is the way we think about our sleep, or lack of sleep, which can cause us to feel more stressed than necessary.

Maybe if you have restless nights, you would get more benefit from two blocks of three hours of sleep, rather than trying to force yourself to be asleep consistently throughout the night. Keep a record of the times you sleep, the times you wake up, and the times you are restless or awake. Then you can start to gently adjust some things, to help you be more at peace with what is happening. Try writing down anything you have on your mind, before you lay down to rest.

If you practise your breathing exercises before you go to sleep at night, you can achieve a more restful sleep. If you wake in the night do the exercises again, until your body relaxes back into a restful sleep. Try the exercise where you cover your eyes to shut the world out. This is a great way to switch off your busy mind.

Breathe in slowly, deep inner peace, and slowly release. You can combine this with your figure '8' exercise to calm your mind.

The aim is, as you calm your breathing, your mind will start to calm. As your mind calms, your brain will start to produce the chemical melatonin, which your mind and body need, to help them relax and drift off to sleep.

Night time can be a creative time

What can you do for yourself at this time? Start to accept that when you wake up, maybe there is a reason for this. As you wake up, your subconscious is more receptive to suggestions and inspirations.

Meditation and breathing exercises will help release tension from your body. Write down any thoughts which are going through your mind. You may even get some inspirational ideas. Write these down so you can remember them in the morning.

Take some time to do some self-healing before you go to sleep, and again when you wake up. The more you support you, the more your brain will produce the calm and relaxing melatonin to help you feel rested. Combine your meditation with some self-healing.

Did you know that between the hours of 2am and 5am is a very creative time, when your mind could be exploring new creative ways to express itself. The majority of this book was written and designed during the night.

Acknowledging, and accepting, that you have had enough sleep for the moment, helps you to not get frustrated, so stopping you from getting stressed. Your brain will continue to produce the soothing and relaxation chemicals as you maintain a more relaxed state of mind. This helps you maintain the calmer state of mind needed to replenish your body. Often resting calmly can be as beneficial as sleeping.

It can be far more effective for your body to have one block of sleep, then do something productive, and then have another block of sleep. Keep a record of the new patterns you try, so you can adjust them until you find a sleep pattern which suits you.

Take some time before you go to bed, to make a list of things you need to do tomorrow. Maybe you could write down things which you are worrying about too. Anything you do to clear your mind will help your mind be more relaxed. When you have written things down, you can often wake up with new insights and solutions.

Try a gentle breathing and visualisation exercise before you go to sleep. Thinking of something relaxing and enjoyable can help your mind to release the relaxation chemicals.

Try wearing socks in bed. This can assist the body's internal temperature regulation. It can help you get to sleep faster. It can also help your body's internal temperature stay regular during the night. We often wake up because the temperature of the body can slightly drop whilst we are asleep. Waking up can be a natural way to stimulate your body to start moving to warm you up again.

Are you waking up hungry? Maybe you need to adjust your eating patterns to help you get a more restful sleep. Maybe you could take a light snack to bed with you.

Are you waking up thirsty? Take plenty of water to bed with you. If your body has been stressed, it can be dehydrated, and you can wake up with a very dry mouth frequently during the night. You could add your Bach Flower Remedies to your water, and sip them when you are awake.

Are you waking up because you are too hot? Try sleeping with just a light cotton sheet, and have a light blanket nearby in case you need it during the night.

I remember when I was going through the menopause, I would wake up constantly throughout the night feeling hot. I would drink plenty of water, calm down my breaths, and talk reassuringly to myself.

When your body is going through big changes, you need more reassurance that what you are experiencing is natural. When you have an understanding, you can cope with the changes you are going through. You will know that you are safe. Feeling agitated, or fearful of the hot flushes, or even fearful of not sleeping, can fuel the flushes, and make them feel more extreme and prolonged. When you are agitated or fearful, your brain produces more cortisol, the worry chemical, and this fuels the hot flushes.

Calmer breathing, self-reassurance, and a cool bed can really make a difference. Maybe change the bedding you are using, and make sure your room is as quiet and as dark as possible.

Light in your bedroom will inhibit the secretion of the hormone melatonin which helps to promote natural sleep. Melatonin is produced primarily in the pineal gland, which helps regulate your relationship with light for the daytime and darkness for the night time. When you are producing melatonin you are more likely to drift into a natural sleep. Your body is programmed to sleep when it is dark. When you sleep in complete darkness, your levels of melatonin can increase. This helps your mind to relax, and so you get a better quality of natural sleep.

Try sleeping alone

Over the years of working with people, I have found one of the biggest causes of sleepless nights is sleeping with someone. Each person has their own body clock, and ways of sleeping. Some people are very still when they sleep, whereas others can be very restless, or tossing and turning all night. We all have a tendency to naturally move during our sleep time.

Some people are very noisy when they sleep, and some people are very hot. All of these factors can affect the quality of sleep you get, especially if you are a light sleeper. Maybe try sleeping away from your partner for a few nights, to find out if you get a better quality of sleep. If you do sleep better, it may be worth exploring having two separate beds. It doesn't mean you don't care for your partner, it just means you are making your need for a good night's sleep as a priority. When you get a good quality of sleep, it can make a big difference to the way you feel during the day, and it can even help to improve your health.

Make a note of the methods you use to help yourself. When you feel tired or agitated, your mind forgets some of the logical steps you need to take. Having a record of the changes you make, and what works for you, will give you an easy reference for future days, and you will be able to see more clearly what you need to adjust.

The Bach Flower Remedies can help you too. Try AGRIMONY, ASPEN, ELM, CHESTNUT BUD, WHITE CHESTNUT and VERVAIN.

Be realistic if you have not been sleeping well for a long time. It can take time for your mind and body to adjust. Keep a sleep diary, and start to gently adjust your bedtime routine and sleeping arrangements. Be patient and gentle on yourself at bedtime, and know the changes will soon come.

Take time out through the day

If you feel tired throughout the day, make a record of the times when you feel low in energy. This could be the time when you need to do more of your relaxation techniques, or take a few minutes out to do a mini meditation. Meditation can be equally, or more beneficial than a longer period of sleep. It can relax your mind and body, and re-energise you on many levels. When could you fit in a relaxing siesta for you in your day?

How do you start your day?

All too often, we start the day feeling agitated, or worrying about things in our mind. When you wake up complaining to yourself about the lack of sleep you have experienced, you are setting yourself up for a less productive day.

If you start the day with a negative mind-set, you will probably find yourself feeling disheartened before the day starts. Maybe you could say, even if you didn't get enough sleep, 'Thank you for the adequate sleep I have had. I feel calm and relaxed, and my relaxation techniques will see me through'. Follow this through with your 'deep inner-peace' breathing technique. An alternative affirmation can be, 'I am thankfully feeling refreshed, and ready for the day ahead'. What you tell your mind will start you off on the right track.

Write in your healing journal about your sleep time-keeping.

Is your bedroom cool and dark? Do you go to bed at the same time each night? Do you relax before sleeping?

Did you use your breathing techniques? Did you do your gratitude blessings? Did you try a meditation?

Are you sleeping too much during the day, so you're not tired at night?

If you need to sleep during the day, try to do so before 2pm, so you are more tired at night time. Try to see if you can adjust the sleep you take during the day. If you do need to sleep during the day, try setting an alarm before you lie down, and listen to a meditation to calm your mind and uplift your spirits as you relax or sleep.

How can you help yourself today?

When you get comfortable starting your day, in a more upbeat and productive way, you really will make a difference to the quality of your day. Even if you do wake up feeling tired, you can start to take some control over two simple things in your life: your breathing and your thoughts. Taking gentle, deeper, slow breaths in and out, can start to alter your stress levels.

Release tension in your neck

Place your fingertips just below your ears. Move your fingers gently towards your spine at the back of your head.

Very gently massage those muscles between your ears and your spine, just below your skull. Use soft circular movements, to gently ease away the tension you are holding.

This exercise can be done at any time of the day, when you recognise you are holding tension in your neck and shoulders. It would be highly beneficial when you first lay down at bedtime, or when you start to do your meditation exercises.

Slow down your breathing, and you are taking more control over any stressful situation. You will help your brain to start to release gentle healing chemicals, and these will help you to regain your composure. As your breaths calm, so will your mind, and you can then get a clearer perspective on any situation.

In touch with your intuition

When you release tension in your neck and shoulders, it can bring a calmer mind. A calm mind can bring you more clarity, and an insight into an alternative way of sorting things out.

When you have a calmer mind, you are more able to listen to your intuition, your higher self.

With this insight and inner peace will come a feeling of well-being and inner contentment. The more you learn to be at peace within your mind, the better quality of life you will have.

Take some time out of your day to do nothing but gently focus on your breathing, and encourage your body to relax. The more familiar your body gets with this new state of peacefulness, the more natural it will become. Your body needs this calm state to be able to replenish itself.

CHAPTER 33

DO NOT QUIT

IF A SITUATION DOES NOT feel right, look carefully at it, and see what you are being shown. Learn from it, and be prepared to move on. Not every opportunity presented to you will flow as easily as you would like it to. Listen to your intuition and your 'gut' reaction. If it does not work out, what can you learn from it? This journey will start to run smoothly for you, if you allow it to. It will start to feel light, exciting and enjoyable.

The pieces of your life which are sent to challenge you are often the situations where you need to face your inner turmoil. Stand up strong and turn them around. Don't try to resist the challenges. If you are feeling tested by something in your life, please stop thinking of it as a test, and see it as an opportunity to grow. Challenges are often where things may not run smoothly, and you are being given an opportunity to work through something which may have been holding you back.

If you are feeling challenged by a situation, this is often an essential growing time for you on your journey. This may be the right time to adjust an old habit which you need to work through, to help you to become stronger, and work more within the true essence of who you really are. Work through the challenge step by step. Believe me, you will come out the other end stronger, and with a greater sense of determination and strength of character. Your resolve will win through.

The right opportunities will be sent to you, to help you to grow at a time when you are strong enough to deal with them. It is a constant learning curve, and will take you gently, but boldly, towards your wishes and your visions. Continually keep sharing your troubles with your journal, and asking your higher self for the right guidance. You will find your true self, and be led towards your dreams. It is a time of great transformation in your life. Allow yourself to grow through these transformations. They will bring you great rewards.

You are a winner. Stay true to you

You have made a decision to change your life. You do deserve the very best. Never back down on your decision to be true to yourself.

It does not matter how many times you have to take time to stop and rest, or stop to reassess your situation. Take the time to process what you are experiencing. A winner bounces up one more time. Keep bouncing!

Hugs help with your healing

When you hug someone, oxytocin is released into your body by your pituitary gland, lowering both your heart rate and your cortisol levels. Hugging can help lower levels of stress hormones like cortisol, bringing you a better quality of rest and sleep, and a feeling of harmony and well-being.

Cortisol is the hormone responsible for stress, high blood pressure, and heart disease. It is often known as the 'worry' chemical, which is responsible for even more stress.

Scientific research shows that hugs boost your happiness levels. Basically, a good hug is the fastest way for you to get oxytocin flowing in your body. Oxytocin, also known as the 'love drug', calms your nervous system, and boosts positive emotions. In addition to releasing Oxytocin, 'the love hormone', hugs also stimulate your brain to release dopamine, the pleasure hormone. Increasing the pleasure hormone helps to decrease the harmful effects of stress, increases human bonding, and helps you feel loved and supported.

It lowers your blood pressure, which is especially helpful if you're feeling anxious. Some reports have even shown hugs can reduce pain levels. A twenty second hug can signal the end of a stress cycle you have been going through. A twenty second hug takes you to a calmer place where you feel loved and supported. When you are in a calmer space you can make more rational decisions. Hugging can increase your social connections, and bring you a sense of belonging.

Because of these findings, it might be no surprise that studies have also shown that couples who hug each other more are more likely to stay together.

So why wouldn't you hug?

Hugs make you happier, healthier and more relaxed, and improve your relationships.

For the maximum benefit it has to be a good hug. This means it has to last at least twenty seconds.

Holding hands

Did you know that just holding someone's hand for ten minutes can help with stress? When you hold their hand, you are stimulating the same chemicals which help them, and you, to feel loved and safe. So if it feels inappropriate to hug someone, holding their hand could start a healing chain reaction.

Take time to talk and to listen

When you are talking your problems through, or are listening to someone who needs help, you are both having the benefits of an increase of your feel-good chemicals. Imagine how much healing can take place, if you take time out to stop, listen and chat, whilst you hold someone's hand, or give them a hug.

No-one to hug today

Getting a hug is a wonderful feeling. It can instantly lift your mood, making you feel safe and appreciated. Sometimes, however, there may be no one around to give you that hug you need. When you're having a bad day, experiencing some sort of pain, or simply craving a bit of affection,

FREE TO BE ME

why not give some love to yourself? Hugging yourself is the perfect way to boost your spirits, and to remind yourself that you are loved.

Wrap your arms around yourself

Bring your left arm across your chest, and place your left hand on your right upper arm. Then bring your right arm across your chest, placing your hand on your left upper arm.

You may find a point on your arms where it feels sore or tender to touch. This is the place to hold. Apply a comfortable firm pressure with your fingertips on your arms. Relax your shoulders, and hold your arms comfortably. Sit like this for as long as it takes for you to feel comforted, but for at least 20 seconds.

This encourages the oxytocin and dopamine to start flowing through your body. Unfold your arms, and cross them the alternative way across your body.

Bring your right arm across your chest, and place your right hand on your left upper arm. Then bring your left arm across your body, placing your left hand on your right upper arm. Relax your shoulders, and hold your arms comfortably. Does it feel different this way around?

Hold whichever way feels most comfortable for you today. Tomorrow you could try the previous way of hugging yourself.

Give yourself a nice big squeeze

Press both arms into your body. Use the pressure that you feel when you get a reassuring hug. Don't squeeze so hard that it hurts, but use just enough pressure so that you feel secure. If you are in any physical pain, hugging yourself can help reduce the pain. Crossing your arms in a self-hug can influence the brain to produce the soothing, healing chemicals which can help minimise the sensation of pain.

Hold your hug for as long as necessary

Sometimes a quick hug is all you need, while other times you might want a lingering, gentle hug. The great thing about hugging yourself is controlling exactly how long the hug lasts. Nothing is awkward when you're hugging yourself! Keep holding your hug until you feel a sense of calmness flowing through your body. You can repeat this as often as necessary.

Take it a stage further, and firmly rub your hands up and down your arms, between your shoulders and your elbows. This can help you release the relaxation chemicals which calm your mind and body.

When you return to the situation which was causing you to feel distressed, you will feel more uplifted and able to see things with a clearer perspective.

Use your gentle deep breathing exercise at the same time, to increase the flow of feel-good chemicals. You could use an affirmation to support you such as, 'I feel loved and supported. I am feeling safe'.

What benefits will you feel?

When you are doing something that makes you feel happy, your brain and mind will respond accordingly, and produce chemicals which enhance the relaxation and healing process. You will start getting some respite from the stressful feelings you have been living with.

When you are happy, and doing something which fulfils your needs, you are also creating new uplifting thought patterns for yourself, and increasing your feelings of self-worth. The new patterns in the pre-frontal cortex then enable you to work through situations in your life, to bring you a better perspective, and a more productive way of sorting things out.

It is within this space that you can get more clarity and insight into how you can make changes, and what your true potential can be.

As you support yourself, your mind and your body starts to work with you in a more supportive way. You will start to experience a sense of inner-peace, well-being and feeling more empowered.

Choose to take some time out to do some self-pampering

It's amazing how much more relaxed you can feel if you sit with your feet in a warm bowl of Himalayan salts, or your favourite oils. Ten minutes of simple pampering can refresh and revive you. Maybe each evening, you could give yourself a gentle hand massage to stimulate your circulation, to help you feel pampered and relaxed. Massaging your hands helps stimulate the circulation in the rest of your body.

The more self-indulgence you give yourself, the more you can lift up your spirits. This would be a good time to do your gentle breathing exercises, to bring yourself into the alpha or theta brainwave state.

Put on some of your favourite relaxation music, or something upbeat, depending on what time of day it is. The more you do for yourself, the more gentle healing chemicals your brain will produce.

Did you know? When you are drifting between more relaxed states of mind, is when your mind is more open to inspirations and ideas. This state allows you to be more receptive to opportunities, and to your true potential.

Expand your self-indulgence time by a few minutes each day, and notice how much better you feel. When you return to your day, you will have a whole new perspective of your day, and a feeling of well-being, with a more peaceful mind.

CHAPTER 34

HOW DO THESE TECHNIQUES WORK ALONGSIDE THE BACH FLOWER REMEDIES?

WHEN YOU START TO MAKE changes in your life, you can start off with good intentions, but often within a short time you can slip back into old patterns and stressful ways of life. As Dr Bach said, 'When there is a void between your thinking and your true self, this is when dis-ease sets in,' and often what you have believed about yourself could be far from the truth of who you really are. But these thoughts have become truly ingrained into your way of being.

Feeling stuck in, or keep revisiting these old thought patterns, is often where the sense of feeling out-of-sorts, or not liking yourself, can come from. You can feel like a roller-coaster of emotions, and even feel like you have a split personality. The feelings of frustration towards yourself accumulate again, and you go round in another debilitating cycle of emotions.

The Bach Flower essences gently help change the negative state of mind you have been living with, into a positive, uplifting state of being. The Flower Remedies work on your behalf while you are working through the necessary changes, to help you, not only change your mind-set, but to help you maintain your new way of thinking and feeling. CHESTNUT BUD is the remedy to help you create new patterns, and maintain them.

When you start to change your emotional state, the Remedies can work on other aspects and perceptions of yourself at the same time. The more you do for yourself, the better you will feel about yourself. When you start on this journey of healing and self-discovery, your body will start to respond accordingly, by producing the gentle healing chemicals, which will help your body and your spirit to feel uplifted, energised and motivated.

The more you do for yourself, the sooner the results you desire will happen. When you treat yourself as a priority, and as someone special, and act accordingly every day, your emotional feelings of well-being will increase, and you will have a more uplifting state of mind.

The Remedies will help you to gently undo the false beliefs you have been living with, and will move you into your true sense of who you are. Keeping a record of your progress in your healing journal, is a good way to recognise what you need to correct, and how well you are doing. As you monitor your progress, remember to thank and praise yourself for the remarkable steps you are taking. The Remedies will help you to move gently through the emotional shifts you need to make. They will help you gain, and maintain new emotional and mental patterns of thinking.

Living in the present

When you are not happy in your present circumstances, your mind often flicks forward to the future, or back to the past, so you have little or no interest in the present. When your mind is in this constant fluctuating state, it is hard to find enthusiasm and joy for the present moment.

Try to let go of yesterday, for you cannot change it, and do not worry about what might happen tomorrow, for you have no control of that.

But you can take control of this moment. It is a special gift, which you cannot exchange or claim back.

Each moment is a chance to start again. Be happy, be content, choose to move forward and, most of all, be true to yourself.

It does not matter where you have been, or what you have done.
It does not matter what you are, it's who you are that counts.
Be the best you can be and you will have no regrets.
Life is precious. Treat it as the special gift it is,
And treat yourself as the special and unique person you are.
Do not waste time condemning, or comparing yourself.
Do not waste time searching for recognition of your work.
Be content with all you have achieved.

Recognise yourself as the special and unique person you are.
And that, my friends, and that alone, is your special gift to the world
Believe you are the best
And deserve the very best,
And you will receive the very best of the best.

By Dawn Chrystal

CHAPTER 35

FORGIVENESS

HOW MANY TIMES A DAY do you find yourself agitated by feelings you wish you could let go of? Do you hear yourself saying 'Why do I keep thinking about that, why can't I let it go?'

You are not alone

You truly are not alone in the way you are feeling. The majority of people are walking around carrying heavy grievances on some level. Thoughts of feeling like life isn't fair, I have done wrong, or that someone has wronged me. Many of these feelings could originate from back in your past, or are from your present circumstances. What has happened to you in your past, and the way you feel about what happened, can have a major impact on how you feel about yourself and your life today.

As you read through the following pages, take some time to look at what you say or think about during the day, and ask yourself if your thoughts and beliefs are actually true now. Start to be even more aware of how you need to make changes from this day. The Bach Flower Remedy for resentment is WILLOW. It helps you release feelings of resentment, and allows you to take responsibility for yourself and your emotions.

Why is this a problem?

With every negative or stressful thought you have during the day, your brain will work with you, to help you to process and deal with your experience. Your brain will produce chemicals which will give you courage and the ability to work through your challenge to the best of your ability. When you are actually going through the experience, these chemicals are highly beneficial. They give you what you need, to enable you to cope, thrive, or to survive.

But the problem often comes when you are beyond the situation, and are still thinking about what has happened. Your mind cannot differentiate between what is really happening, or if you are just thinking about it. Your brain produces the same stress chemicals, regardless of how long ago the scenario actually happened. Your brain assumes you are still working through the stressful situation at this moment in time.

Whilst you are thinking about a past experience which upset you, you are keeping your mind and your body in a similar level of stress, and often emotional distress, as when you were actually experiencing the challenge. You can feel constantly troubled, or even tormented, by these old thoughts and feelings. This stress can often settle, not only in your mind, but also in parts of your body where you felt the hurt when the situation occurred. If this is left unaddressed, it can lead to longer term pains in your body. It can cause discomfort like stomach problems, or reoccurring headaches. It can be the cause of tension and pain anywhere in your body.

This pain may start off with a restless mind, feeling agitated, a low mood, or a cramping, or sick feeling in your tummy, which can then lead to other complications. It can make you feel like you cannot eat, or you eat excessively to try to comfort the feelings in your tummy. It can bring you restless nights, which then rob you of sleep and energy for the following day.

It can bring you confusing feelings of fear, anxiety, anger, stress, confusion, rage, jealousy, resentment, being critical, judgemental, angry or condescending. It can make you feel like you have been wronged against and that life is not fair. You may be having feelings of shame, not liking yourself or feeling guilty. You may randomly, or constantly, feel agitated, despondent, or berate yourself for things you wish you could have done differently.

All of these heavy thoughts can drain you of enthusiasm and motivation. They can even bring you to a place of apathy and lack of joy, with a lack of trust of yourself. It can bring you to a place where you have difficulties trusting other people and situations in your life. Remember, your mind cannot tell when the event occurred, and will assume these feelings you are thinking about are current. These old thoughts and feelings can cause even more deeper complications, in that they can rob you of any feelings of joy and true clarity within your current relationships, both with others, and with yourself. Old feelings and thoughts can influence the way you feel today on so many levels.

When you are holding old feelings of grievances, it is often natural to bring old feelings of hurt and resentment into new conversations, friendships and relationships, and recreate the old pattern time and time again. When your mind-set is in such a negative state it can be hard to see the good within anyone, or any situation in your life. You can come to the mind-set and belief that this life is unfair, and that everything is against you.

If you find you are feeling trapped in what seems like 'irrational thoughts', try the Remedy CHERRY PLUM for a few days. CHERRY PLUM helps bring you to a place where you have more rational thoughts, and you can see things more calmly and clearly. CHERRY PLUM can help you to peel away the layers of irrational thoughts, to reveal the underlying feelings you may have buried. Then you can start to use other Remedies to soothe and transform your underlying feelings.

It is difficult to feel total joy in one aspect of your life, when you have issues of unforgivingness or torment within your thinking. Your mind will ultimately keep coming back to the same belief that you have done wrong, or are being treated unfairly.

For every thought you are having, your brain will be working on your behalf, to help you deal with what you are experiencing. Your brain produces the chemicals which give you the courage and ability to work through the challenge you are thinking about.

If you currently find yourself dwelling on situations which have upset you, and left you feeling emotionally or mentally confused, this would be a good time to address these issues.

There is so much sadness created, and precious time lost in looking back on parts of your life with regret, and wondering what you could have done, but did not, or maybe could have handled differently.

You can choose to turn this around today. All is not lost. Start to let go of pain, guilt, blame, resentments and regret, and start to feel the love in your heart, and in your precious body.

This is your perfect time to change the course of your life. This is your opportunity to create the best in you.

Take some time over the following days, to be observant of memories which flick into your mind, as you work through addressing your thoughts, and processing where the thoughts have manifested from. Notice what thoughts and feelings you have around your memories. Use your healing journal to start to process any changes you would like to make. Be honest with yourself, but please be gentle on yourself as you make changes.

Remember, you cannot change the past, but from today you can start to heal it, and you can move forward, with a greater understanding and compassion for yourself, and for others.

Are you being true to yourself?

As a general indication of whether you are in your true character or not today, pay attention to how your moods feel. If you feel happy and uplifted, you are being true to yourself. If you are feeling low in energy, sad, anxious, impatient, stressed, angry, tearful, vindictive, disillusioned, depressed, self-harming or constantly tired, you may be acting in contradiction to your true self, the beautiful person you were born to be.

If you are experiencing any of the above, on any level, I want to help you explore your reason for feeling this way. It does not matter how large or how small your grievances are, they are important to you. If they are making you feel any mental or emotional disharmony, then this needs to be addressed. Addressing these emotional hurts can bring you to a place where you will feel more at peace, and in harmony within every aspect of your life.

We will look at where you are now, the reason for your hurt and unhappiness, and ways that you can go about understanding, coping with, and changing this. We look at ways to help you understand and heal your emotions and your mind, so you can move on with clarity, calm and a renewed sense of purpose. If ever you find yourself acting outside of your true character, or feeling out of sorts, take the time to step back and identify how you are feeling.

Take some time to write in your journal about how you feel. Where do these feelings come from?

Healing with the Bach Flower Remedies

When you feel ready to explore some solutions, go to the Bach Flower Remedy section at the back of this book, and start to explore which of the negative states within the Remedies relate to you at this moment. The negative state of each Remedy is how you become when you are not in harmony with your true self. The negative states are how we become when we have been influenced by outside circumstances, and have taken on different characteristics which are not true to who we should be.

Dr Bach said, 'When there is a void between your thinking, and your true self, is when dis-ease sets in'. Can you identify with this at the moment? Can you recognise some of your thought patterns, your patterns of behaviour, within the negative states? Which of the negative thought patterns, or emotions within these negative states, can you identify with at the moment?

As you read through the different Bach Flower Remedies, write down the Remedies you can identify with at the moment. Put a date with them. Then read the positive states of the Remedies. This is your true state, the real you, and your true potential. Make a note of the positive states. These positive states are where the Remedies will take you to, your real potential, the real you. The Remedies help restore your faith in life, and in yourself and your abilities.

If you are unsure where to start, read about the Remedies AGRIMONY, CHERRY PLUM, CRAB APPLE, HOLLY, MUSTARD, PINE, VERVAIN, VINE, WILD ROSE and WILLOW.

Do you recognise your feelings within the negative states of these Remedies?

Please always remember, the negative state of mind is not a reflection of you as a person. The negative states are the way life has made you feel right now, and the patterns you may have adopted from others as a coping mechanism.

Now, look at the positive states of each Remedy you can relate to. This is your real potential. The beautiful person you have deep inside of you.

The Remedies will help you move subtly and gently from the negative states, to the more positive, uplifting ways of being you.

Explore which of the wonderful Bach Flower Remedies, can help bring you back into harmony and balance. Which negative states within the Remedies can you relate to the most at this moment?

These are the Remedies which will be most supportive for you right now.

The more you work with the Remedies, the greater understanding of yourself you will achieve. It is never too late to start again.

You can use single Remedies, or you can make a combination bottle of up to 7 Remedies together. See page 384, making a combination bottle.

Be gentle on yourself as you work through this period of transition. And always remember, whatever patterns of behaviour you have accumulated and adopted, this is all part of your growth and your learning.

From this day, if it does not feel comfortable or right to you, you can make a choice to turn it around.

If you do not have the bottles of Remedies to use, you can use the Bach Flower Remedy balance cards to support you, or you can write down the positive affirmation you can relate to on a piece of paper, and then place it over your heart centre. Adjust the affirmation to suit yourself, including loving, encouraging words.

Repeat the affirmation out loud to yourself as you take some deep, gentle breaths, in and out.

After a few breaths, you will start to feel a sense of relief, and you may even experience some tingling sensations within parts of your body. This is a natural way of your body showing you how your body is releasing the emotions which have been trapped within your body. The more you work with this, the lighter your feelings will be, and the more peace and clarity you will have.

Today is the perfect time to stop judging your thoughts, your emotions, how you act, and who you are. Remember, your thoughts are not wrong. It is just the way you have been seeing yourself and your life.

Set the intention today to start to simply acknowledge and rectify your thoughts, and the way you have been talking to yourself. Remember to always treat yourself, and anything you observe of yourself, with compassion. Be grateful for the things you acknowledge, and set the intention to be able to resolve what you recognise is out of balance.

The more you work on you, the more easily the balance and harmony will come to you. When you support and encourage yourself, your body will support you with its natural healing chemicals.

Journal healing

Take some time to write down the things which you are acknowledging. Your feelings, your thoughts, and any situations you have been dwelling on which are causing you disharmony.

For this moment, choose one aspect you would like to work with. Which thoughts are your priority to change at the moment?

Record the date you started to work with these thoughts, so you can see your progress when you look back.

Which Remedies would you choose today? Which affirmation would help you? What will be the positive outcome of your new thought pattern?

Take some time out to do a Withinercise exercise, to help reset your thinking.

Start now

Every day start again. It does not matter what happened yesterday. This moment in time is the best time to start again.

Whenever someone, the situation, or the environment around you feels uncomfortable, take some time out to explore how you are feeling, and what thoughts may be causing your disharmony in this situation you are in. For every negative thought or state in your mind, there is a Bach Flower Remedy, or a combination of techniques and Remedies that can help you restore balance and harmony. Remember, the negative state of mind is how the situation is making you feel. This is not your true self.

Your true self is the positive state. This is the real you, your real potential, the person you were born to be. Taking the Remedies will help to shift you gently back into your true self, and your true personality. Make a note of any Remedies you choose for yourself, and the date you start to take them.

Look at the affirmations, and choose which one you are going to work with today. You can add an emotion to the affirmation to give it more meaning for you, and a verb which brings you the feeling of movement. One example could be 'I am happily moving forward now'.

You could write down your true potential that you are aiming towards. This will help keep you on track if ever you wander off. Keep going back to your healing journal daily, and make some notes about anything which is causing you disharmony.

Can you identify what you are feeling? It can be natural that you may not be able to recognise how you are feeling at the beginning. Remember, your disharmony can start with your thoughts about yourself. Make a note of your thoughts. Or, your disharmony can be triggered by your thoughts about a situation or person, and the way you felt they have treated you, or are still treating you.

If you cannot get in touch with your feelings, take some time to write down your thoughts about each situation or each person concerned that you feel is affecting you. Writing down your uppermost thoughts, can help you start to identify your underlying feelings about the people or situation concerned.

Do not worry if you cannot get in touch with your feelings at this stage. This is quite natural when the feelings have been buried for a long time. As you work through other methods of healing yourself, you will start to get more clarity around your feelings, and things which have impacted upon you. The Bach Flower Remedies will help to bring you more clarity when they start to take effect. You could use your Bach Flower Remedies and Remedy healing cards to help rebalance your emotions. Look at ELM, HOLLY and STAR OF BETHLEHEM.

Take some time to acknowledge the steps forward you have taken, and praise yourself.

Always remember, it can be tiring working through making changes. Give yourself time to process what you are working through before you take the next step.

You could give yourself some quality time, such as a walk in nature, some pampering or a meditation. Anything you do for you will help your body and soul to feel supported.

What do you say about you?

For reasons that we often cannot comprehend, nor justify, many of us spend a lot of the day thinking negative or condescending thoughts about ourselves.

Do you criticise yourself, the way you look, your behaviour, the way you have dealt with something?

Or, worse still, do you label yourself with words such as 'I am so dumb, I always make mistakes, I have no confidence, I am to blame, I was wrong, I am hopeless, clumsy, I am too fat, thin, or I am so fed up with myself'?

CRAB APPLE helps you to start liking yourself, and ultimately start loving yourself, and ROCK WATER helps you to stop being so critical of yourself. It helps you to start being gentler on yourself.

How many times a day, do you chastise yourself for making a mistake, or for something which goes wrong, or for something you have said or done? How many times during the day do you repeatedly go over conversations, or situations in your head, wishing you could change what you said or did?

How many times during the day do you feel guilty or to blame for something, or someone else's situation or unhappiness? Do you constantly feel responsible for others' problems, and are constantly trying to fix them?

Read about the Bach Flower Remedies CERATO, CRAB APPLE, PINE, RED CHESTNUT, ROCK WATER and GENTIAN. How often do you set expectations for yourself, and then feel disappointed with yourself when you don't reach those expectations? Are those expectations realistic for you?

How often do you feel disappointed with yourself, compared to someone else? Do you keep feeling like you are not as good or as able as others? How often do you seek someone else's approval, and feel disappointed when they do not acknowledge you, or your actions?

How many times a day do you not listen to your own needs, and feel agitated with yourself when you are tired? How many times a day do you allow your needs and your boundaries to be compromised?

How worthy do you feel today? Are you being your own worst critic?

The good news is, if it does not feel right, you can turn it around

Be aware of when you are using condescending, critical or damaging thoughts, and start to turn them around today.

Your thoughts about yourself often reflect the way you feel about yourself deep down inside and, if you continue to use detrimental or derogative thoughts about yourself, your mind will keep you feeling stuck in the thought patterns you constantly use.

This will lower your self-belief, your confidence, your feelings of worthiness, your self-esteem, and your ability to make any changes. You can constantly be feeling tired, drained, disillusioned and even stressed, anxious or depressed. It can take away your joy, your contentment and your inner peace.

Quite often you do not even realise you have come to believe the thoughts you say about yourself.

Do you like the way your thoughts make you feel? Take a few minutes to reflect on the way you talk to yourself throughout the day. Write down the thoughts you have or say about yourself. Are these helping, hindering, or even damaging you, and the way you feel about yourself?

Being too hard on yourself, criticising, compromising, and comparing yourself, is so damaging. It conditions your mind to believe that you are in the wrong, that you are not a good person. Your brain produces more of the stress chemicals, and then you feel more agitated and continue going in a downward spiral of emotions, followed by more negative self-talk.

Repeatedly thinking negative thoughts during the night and upon waking can often disturb your sleep, which adds to your emotional distress, bringing you even more disharmony, and even lack of energy and motivation for the day ahead.

Your mind and your body are only reacting to the instructions and the thoughts you are giving it to act on. Your mind does not have the ability to change these for you, until you decide to make that change.

FREE TO BE ME

Every day choose to start again

Set the intention today to start to acknowledge and rectify your thoughts, and the way you have been talking to yourself. Remember to always treat yourself and anything you observe with compassion and gratitude. Your brain will help you by starting to produce chemicals which will take you into the more soothing feelings and supportive patterns of belief about yourself.

Forgive yourself for the thoughts you have been using. Do a forgiveness exercise throughout the day, and the forgiveness meditation as soon as you have time. Go to my website for your forgiveness meditation. This will help to let go of old hurts, and move you into a more uplifting state of mind today.

Start today by saying, 'I am lovingly forgiving myself for the harsh thoughts I have used about myself', or 'I am lovingly forgiving myself for the irritations I have been holding towards myself'.

Always finish by saying, 'I am love'.

Create a list of more helpful, supportive words you could use. Praise yourself, and use affirmations to support you throughout the day. Every moment of every day be aware of how you are treating yourself. Only you can really turn this around, and help yourself to feel loved.

The Remedies will help you to shift subtly through the changes you wish to make, and help restore your faith in yourself, and in human nature. Take some time to give yourself a gentle hug to lift up your spirits. Do not rush yourself through this healing process. It can take time. Remember, you can be healed one step at a time.

Take some time to read about BEECH, HOLLY and WILLOW. Choose a Remedy, or a combination of Remedies, which fit with how you are feeling right now. Use these Remedies until you feel calmer and have more clarity. When your most intense feelings have subsided, you can add other Remedies to support the new plateau you have come to.

If your underlying feelings come from anger, use just HOLLY for a few days until the anger subsides, and then slowly introduce more Remedies, to a maximum of 7 Remedies mixed together.

So what is forgiveness?

One dictionary defines the word 'forgive' as to 'stop feeling angry or resentful towards someone for an offence'. There is another definition where it is necessary to 'pardon somebody for an offence in order to forgive'. I am fully aware that some of you will have been subjected to bad treatment, or a series of events for which there can be no pardon, and no excuse for the person that has deliberately inflicted pain onto you. At the moment, I am not asking you to pardon anyone for mistreatment that has been intentionally inflicted upon you, or is continuing now.

You can start to heal your emotions by working on you

As you forgive yourself, start to love yourself, and treat yourself with kindness, with more respect and, as a valuable person, you will automatically start to feel a sense of healing going on within you.

This could be all of the healing you need to do right now. What each person needs for their healing will be different. Your healing process will be unique to you. Some emotional, mental and physical pains may scar you for a lifetime, but the more you work on you, the easier the torment and pain can feel.

If you need some extra help to work through your situation of your mental and emotional torments, there are many professional organisations available to help you. If you are not feeling strong enough to search for the help at the moment, you could ask a friend to help you find the right organisation for you. Your doctor can recommend good sources of support where you can get help.

If you or your dependents are being subjected to any form of abuse or misuse, there are organisations who can help to move you out of harmful situations. You have the strength within you to make your life better, but we all need extra support sometimes. Please reach out for help if you are struggling. Sometimes you may need someone objective to be able to help you through. Having someone to talk to helps you to release some of the emotions you are experiencing. And it can help you to process what is happening. Being listened to, helps you to feel more nurtured, and enables you to start taking bolder steps forward. Never underestimate the power of having someone to talk to.

Healing happens at the right time

Some people are thoughtless in their actions, and seem oblivious of the consequences of their actions which inflict emotional and physical hurts, confusion, or pain onto others. It is okay to say I do not want to forgive them at the moment. Ask your higher self for more healing. Start to forgive yourself for what you have been through, and any feelings you may have been holding towards anyone who has hurt you. Do as much as you feel able to heal, and reach out for help if you are struggling with this.

If you are being subjected to painful or abusive behaviours at the moment, please reach out for help. Reaching out is a sign of strength, and shows you are ready to take back control of your life.

Start to work on your forgiveness healing meditation, and you will start to feel more compassion for yourself, and re-ignite feelings of love within your precious body.

I am also very much aware that many of you will have been subjected to unintentional harm, perhaps through continual chastisement or put downs in a relationship or situations in your life. There could still be people in your life who have, or are subjecting you to, criticism or judgement, or do not take your feelings into account. There may even be people who may undermine you, or make you, your feelings and your needs feel unimportant. They may even ridicule you for having such sensitive emotions, and make you feel that it is wrong to feel emotional and hurt. They may constantly make you feel like you are in the wrong, and this can seriously impact on the way you feel, and your ability to stand up for yourself.

The term which is often used for someone who is constantly harming, ridiculing or putting others down is a narcissist. They believe they are always in the right, and cannot see that there is anything wrong in the way they treat others. Do not wait around for them to change, or try to sway them to see how they make you feel. You will be wasting valuable time which you can be using to repair you.

If someone has hurt you in any way, they may never be ready to admit they have done wrong, or to say they are sorry. Acknowledge this, and be prepared to start working on helping yourself to heal. As you heal yourself, the pain you feel will soften and you will start to recover.

Did you know that one of the underlying traits of someone who is a narcissist is weakness? They use their arrogant, domineering or condescending ways to maintain control, because inside they are not feeling strong in their own boundaries. The Remedy for the state of mind which surfaces is VINE. Read about the negative state of the VINE Remedy and the HOLLY Remedy, and see if you can recognise these traits in others.

When someone's boundaries have been ignored, pushed and manipulated for long enough, they can shift from the positive CENTAURY personality type to the negative VINE state of mind. It is important to try to remember that when someone is in a negative VINE state of mind, it is because they have been severely affected by circumstances in their life. They probably are totally unaware that they have lost sight of who they really are.

The person in a VINE state of mind often does not intentionally go into the negative state they are in. This negative state is often as a result of years of other negative experiences they have been through where they have not felt in control. To maintain some feelings of control they go into a state which shows up as anger, dominance, dictatorship, and often aggression and condescending attitudes. Remember, these negative states are only brought to the surface because they do not feel in control. Often their negative behaviour has become about because this is the way they have been treated.

When someone is in the negative state of VINE, it is hard for them to see the good within anything, or anybody. Whatever you do for them, or how ever hard you try, it will never be enough. They are usually angry with the world, and all that it happening around them. They can become hard-hearted, and feel out of touch with their emotions of love. It is hard to feel love and compassion when someone is in this state, and they cannot see, or comprehend that the problem lies with them.

Being around someone who is in this state, can feel very intimidating, and can create barriers within relationships and work places. They can alienate people around them, and become unapproachable and unreasonable. There is no point trying to reason with them if you are in a vulnerable place right now. They will throw all your attempts to reason with them, back to you.

Heal yourself, and then you will be in a better place to deal with the person who is in this negative VINE state of mind. You can still send them love and compassion to bring yourself into a better and stronger place. As you let any feelings towards them go, you will feel more uplifted, and there will be a time when you can stand up to them if you choose to. For the moment, it is better to step back, and work on helping yourself by getting stronger. Know that when the time is right, things can change for them too.

If you recognise that the behaviour of someone in a VINE state of mind has impacted on you, use CENTAURY to help you create new stronger boundaries. CENTAURY will also help you to stand up for your beliefs and your rights, and to stay strong-willed in your intentions.

Love and compassion can heal most situations, but it may not be the right time for you to work on helping everyone. As you become stronger, you will recognise where you can help, and if you are meant to. Having this information, and getting a greater understanding of the VINE state of mind gave me great inner confidence, helped me to lift up my feelings of self-worth, and empowered me to make massive changes in my life.

I consistently took the Remedies CENTAURY with GORSE, to help me reset and strengthen my boundaries. And in time, when I was feeling more assertive and hopeful, I started standing up for myself, started being more assertive and resetting my boundaries. This was a major turning point in my life, and empowered me to start to recognise how my feelings about myself had become so out of balance.

I always find it interesting that the Remedy VINE comes into Dr Bach's category of 'over-care for others'. When someone is in a negative VINE state of mind, they genuinely believe that the way they are acting is appropriate. They genuinely believe they are acting for the good of others. This state of mind can be turned around, but it can take time if someone has been in this state for a long while.

We can all slip into this negative VINE state of mind at times, when we feel like life has been unfair, and our boundaries have been pushed beyond their limits. Remember, it is not a conscious act. Your mind is reacting in this way because your boundaries have been pushed out of balance and you feel like people have taken you for granted, or even harmed you in some way. If ever you find yourself becoming too bossy with others, or even with yourself, take the Remedy VINE until the balance starts to resume. A person in the positive state of VINE has good leadership qualities. They can be great teachers, and lead others by inspiring others to follow. There is no need for control. They set the example, and others will naturally follow them.

If you find yourself caught up in a relationship where you feel like you are being mentally, physically or emotionally tested or abused, take some time to read about the Bach Flower Remedies CENTAURY and VINE. See if you can recognise how these two roles fit into your life, and the patterns you have been living with.

The Remedies will help you to become stronger. CENTAURY will help you to start standing up for yourself, and AGRIMONY will help you to start talking about how you are feeling, and confront the person, when the time is right. If you feel like you have gone into the VINE state of mind, take the Remedy VINE, to help you start to feel more in harmony with your inner strengths and leadership qualities.

I found Reiki healing and the Optimum Health Balancing also really effective ways of recognising and clearing some stuck patterns. Take some time to do some Withinercise visualisations, where you see yourself getting stronger and standing up for yourself. The more you do this exercise, the stronger you will feel.

Use your affirmations, to start reprogramming your mind to expect things to change for you. You could say, 'Every day in every way I am getting stronger and stronger. Everyone respects me now'.

If you are struggling within a relationship because you are constantly being put down, ridiculed or harmed in any way, please reach out to someone who can help you to turn your situation around. Having someone to listen to you and to support you is priceless. They can bring you extra strength and comfort, and the support you need to make the necessary changes.

Some people are insensitive

Some people may have deliberately, or inadvertently, ridiculed you or put you down. This behaviour can be a reflection of how they feel about themselves. Some people do seem to get pleasure out of making others feel inferior or inadequate, and there are some who will not recognise how they are behaving, and just how sensitive you are. They will be totally unaware of the impact they are having on you, or have had on you.

There may also have been enormous life events and traumatic events that you can acknowledge have caused you to feel resentful, like an illness, a disability, the loss of a loved one, or the loss of your job or home. You may also be one of those people who has been putting you down, and being too hard on yourself, with your own actions, thoughts and words you use about yourself.

Wherever your disharmony comes from, this would be a good time to start to observe and to acknowledge what you would like to change today. This is your time to transform your feelings of self-worth, and the way you feel about yourself, by addressing anything which is detrimental to your emotional well-being and your growth. Separate each issue. Write down what you feel is happening, and work through the issues you feel ready to address. Work through one issue at a time. As you start to heal one situation, it can start to heal other issues too. The more you work with forgiveness, the stronger you will feel, and the more in touch with your real uplifting feelings you will become.

Take your time to gently work through forgiveness. Choose to work with issues that you feel you are able to work with at this moment. As you get stronger you will feel more able to work with other issues and situations which have caused you deeper hurts. If you feel emotionally traumatised by the thoughts which come to mind, STAR OF BETHLEHEM can help you to release the trauma, and ELM can help if you are feeling overwhelmed by your emotions and are finding it hard to cope with them. ELM brings you the ability to cope, one step at a time.

CERATO will help you to start trusting in yourself, listen to your higher self, and approve of yourself and the choices you make. CERATO helps you release the need for other people's approval. WILLOW can help relieve you of feelings of resentment and that life is not fair. It helps you to recognise that you can take responsibility for yourself, and for your emotional well-being.

Help to bring back the balance

Say to yourself, 'I forgive myself for this', or, 'I forgive myself for this resentment I have been feeling', or 'I forgive myself for getting so angry and bitter'. Whatever you feel you need to forgive yourself for, this is the perfect time to start to work on letting yourself feel forgiveness.

Follow this through with 'I am love'. You could add something which feels right for you like 'I am love and I am peace', or I am love and I am loving'.

Lack of forgiveness can manifest as anger

Unfortunately, when you hold on to the resentment towards people or incidents, you will find a lot of your energy is being used to deal with those feelings, and the pent up feelings may inhibit your ability to move forward. Feelings of resentment can simmer away inside you, and can often manifest as anger or unwellness at a later date. Be very kind and patient with yourself, and recognise that there will be a perfectly appropriate time to start to let go. Acknowledging you are feeling any resentment or anger is a bold step. Having compassion towards yourself, and the thoughts you have been having is a big step towards healing you today.

From an early age we are taught, or we choose to adapt to, the circumstances around us, and to the wishes of others. Over the years, you learn to adapt to whatever is happening around you, and take on board more influences and opinions. If these influences are not in harmony with you and your personality, they can impact on the way you feel, and cause you to have irrational moods. If these feelings are not expressed, they can result in confusing feelings like anger, jealousy, resentment or rage. HOLLY is the Remedy to help you deal with feelings of anger, rage and jealousy. WILLOW can help with feelings of resentment.

These feelings often start off as churning thoughts in your mind, which can become your inner conflict, which can then cause feelings of tension and illness in your head and your stomach. The Remedy AGRIMONY can help you to start to bring harmony and balance back for you, and WHITE CHESTNUT can also help calm your repetitive thoughts. If you are struggling with extreme emotional anguish, the Bach Flower Remedy SWEET CHESTNUT can help bring you a sense of relief from those heavy emotional feelings and thoughts. It brings you a great sense of relief and light at the end of your dark tunnel.

If you have come to a point in your life where you start to question who you really are because of your behaviour and reactions, CERATO will help you start to trust in yourself again. HOLLY, MUSTARD and WILLOW can help you feel relieved of old feelings of frustration, resentments or anger. They will bring you back to the place of being able to see, and hold love and compassion within you.

CHERRY PLUM would be extremely helpful if your behaviour has become irrational, and you do not feel in control of your emotions or moods. It can also help when you have lost your courage and do not feel in control of your life, or your thoughts and your feelings. PINE will help you feel relieved of feelings of guilt, and CRAB APPLE will help if you have been holding thoughts of not liking yourself for the way you have been acting. GORSE will help you if you feel helpless to make changes. It brings you renewed hope and faith to be able to try again. CENTAURY, CHESTNUT BUD and CLEMATIS will help you stay strong in your intentions and maintain new patterns you are choosing to create.

Start to peel away the layers to reveal who you really are

Starting to let go of the anger and resentment you have been holding, will help you feel more balanced, and stronger within yourself. It will help bring you a new perspective on the past, and what is happening at this moment in your life. It will help you get a clearer perspective on why you react the way you do. If you do feel consumed by old hurts and resentments, the forgiveness meditations can help with your healing, and the Bach Flower Remedies are a powerful and efficient way to soothe and heal your emotional pains.

This will enable you to start re-building your new way of life. You will have a more uplifting state of mind, you will feel stronger, and you will feel more able to work through the changes you need to address. Your whole perspective of your life will start to change.

When I am asking you to start working with forgiveness for others, I am asking for you to start to release feelings of anger and resentment you have been feeling towards the people who have done wrong towards you.

I am not asking you to say their behaviour was appropriate or justified, I am asking you to let your mind and body be free of the feelings which have been eating away at you.

Use your healing journal

Take some time out to write down any feelings of anger or resentment you may be feeling at the moment. Leave some space after each feeling you recognise so you can explore more about these feelings later. As your journey progresses, and you feel stronger, you can explore deeper feelings which come to the surface. In time, you will be able to look back through your healing journal and start to see, and understand, how these feelings have been accumulated, and how they have impacted on you.

As you become emotionally stronger, you will be able to reflect on how far you have come. The more you explore your feelings, the stronger your emotional intelligence will feel. The more you heal, the more empowered you will feel, and the lighter your emotional pain will feel. You will come to a place where you will have more clarity and feel able to let go of old feelings which no longer serve you, and anybody or anything which has been holding you back. Take some time out to talk to a friend about your feelings, and what you have discovered.

Why would you want to forgive?

On a deeper level, your mind cannot tell if you are angry with yourself, or with someone else. Your brain produces the cortisol and the adrenaline to help you deal with the thoughts and feelings you are experiencing, which can keep you mentally and emotionally in the place of anger and resentment, regardless of whom the anger and resentment is directed at.

Your mind hears the thoughts you are using, and assumes you are talking about yourself. It acts accordingly by producing the toxic harsh chemicals to support you. The hurtful thoughts have the same draining effect on you and the way you feel, whether you are thinking these thoughts about yourself, or someone else.

So holding on to the hurt, pain, resentment and anger can harm you far more than it harms the offender. Again, I am not asking you to condone the person, or accept their behaviour was fair or reasonable, I am asking you to start to let go of the anger and resentment you are feeling, to gently release and start to heal your old hurts and emotional pains on many levels.

This will take time, but it will start to relieve you of any mental and emotional heaviness, anguish and pain you have been feeling. Letting go and working with forgiveness will enable you to have more compassion for yourself, and enable you to feel more at peace within your mind and within your heart and your soul. Every step you take to heal yourself is valuable. It is a step towards addressing any anguish or distress you may have been feeling. The more you work on you, the more your feelings of well-being will increase, which will help to raise your self-esteem, and your feelings of self-worth.

Every step you take is a step towards empowering you.

Remember to use your healing journal, to help you work through your thoughts and feelings. It is a lot easier and more effective to help yourself when you see the issues in front of you in writing. You can start to be more objective instead of emotionally attached. Your healing journal is a safe place to offload and explore how you feel about things, and discover new ways to help yourself.

After you have written down your thoughts, take some time out to allow your mind time to process what you are working with. Do something that brings you joy. When you have released thoughts from your mind and have chosen to do something special for you, you are giving yourself the space to see new perspectives on what you believed to be true. Giving yourself some space can bring a new insight into how you can heal yourself, the benefits of doing so, and a sense of feeling more empowered.

Create an affirmation which confirms the wonderful work you are doing for yourself. One example could be 'I am joyfully releasing all the old feelings I have been holding. I am feeling empowered and peaceful. My heart is filled with love'.

Take some time to lower your stress levels with some tapping. Think of something which brings you happiness, and then, using your fingertips, gently tap on the centre point on your forehead, just above your eyebrows. Keep thinking of your happy thoughts. Continue tapping and breathing until calmness comes. Take it a stage further by gently tapping on your thymus point, the space between your heart and your throat, to increase your energy flow.

Let us work together

Together we can start to create the new future for you, without the burden of the hurt and pain the past has caused you. There will come a point on your journey when you will feel ready to work with forgiveness of others but, for now, if you are not feeling ready, keep showering yourself with lots of forgiveness, love, kindness and doing things which help you feel good about yourself.

Work on forgiving you and, as you do so, some of the old hurts will gently start to subside and you will start to feel more contentment, gentleness and compassion towards yourself. You will start to have more compassion towards those around you, and will start to feel lighter and whole again. When you are acknowledging your emotional hurts, you are listening to yourself, and giving you the support you really need. Your mind and your body will respond accordingly because you feel more supported. You are recognising just how important you are.

The Remedy to help you release anger is HOLLY. It helps bring you feelings of all-encompassing love. WILLOW helps you release deep hurts and resentments, and brings you to a place where you can feel more fairness and compassion. It helps you feel more prepared to take back responsibility for yourself and your well-being. It helps you recognise you can choose to feel resentful, which brings you more unhappiness, or you can choose to feel compassion and feelings of love.

PINE will help you release any feelings of guilt you may be holding towards your past actions, and CRAB APPLE will help you be more accepting of yourself. It will start to bring in feelings of self-acceptance and self-love.

ROCK WATER will help you to be gentler on yourself and honour your needs.

Forgiving yourself

Over the years, I've found that the person myself, my clients and friends, have found hardest to forgive, is themselves. So many people feel they cannot forgive themselves for something they have done, or did not do.

We have a tendency to hold onto memories of things which have caused us to feel emotional pain. This is the way our brains are wired to help us to deal with things which cause us to feel emotional. This helps us to work through, or even survive the incident.

When we are going through an experience and we feel emotionally affected by it, whether it is in a good way or a bad way, that memory triggers off a neurological response or reaction.

It is this emotional reaction, how we feel about the situation, which our mind holds onto, and keeps recalling after the situation has passed.

The hardest time to forgive yourself can be when there is no opportunity to go back and change or re-do that action, to make it right, perhaps after a person has died, when a child has grown up, or when you've left a job or moved away from a relationship. Remember, your mind holds onto and remembers anything with which you have had an emotional memory with an emotional reaction, whether they are good memories or bad ones.

You may have been thinking of times when you have said hurtful things, or have done things you regret. Maybe the time when you created an upsetting situation, or you made some bad choices. The list goes on.

Allow yourself to feel forgiveness

You can gently work on letting those events and feelings go today, alongside any feelings of resentment, guilt or hurt. Remember, no matter how many times you re-live the event or the situation, or the period in time of your life, there is only one certainty. You cannot go back and change the event, or that moment in time. When you keep re-living those events in your mind, your mind cannot tell whether the event has passed, or is still happening. It keeps producing the stressful chemicals, which will keep you feeling stressed, anxious or emotionally and mentally attached to the old situation.

The emotional pain can feel as deep as it did when the past event happened. It is hard to feel totally joyful and at ease in what you are doing now, when your mind is constantly being bombarded by old thoughts and emotional hurts. Start tackling those thoughts and situations now.

Remember, the more you think about something, the more your mind will keep re-inventing the scene, and how you felt about it every time you bring it to your attention.

Your brain then brings in the harsher chemicals, which is a natural and necessary response, to help you deal with what you are focusing on. This will impact on your emotions on this current day, and your thoughts can then affect the way you perceive other people, and things which are happening on this day.

It is hard to feel joyful when you are dwelling on an upsetting event from the past. This will constantly be taking you into a state of disharmony.

Make a choice to turn this around today

Your mind cannot make a decision for you, to make any adjustments or alterations to your thinking. You have to make the conscious choice about what you are thinking. Set the intention for today, 'I am calmly choosing to work on forgiving myself today. I am choosing loving and uplifting thoughts'.

Take a few minutes out to heal yourself

Say to yourself 'I am lovingly forgiving myself for this', or 'I am lovingly forgiving myself for any thoughts I may have been holding'. 'I am lovingly forgiving myself for this irritation I have been feeling' or 'I am lovingly forgiving myself for what I have been through'.

'I am calmly choosing to work on forgiving myself today. I am choosing loving and uplifting thoughts'. What would your affirmation be for today? Every new choice you make will help you to feel more uplifted and empowered. Whatever you feel you need to forgive yourself for, this is the perfect time to start to work on letting yourself feel forgiveness, and having more compassion for yourself. You could add something which feels right for you, like 'I am being loving, and I am feeling healed', or 'I am being loving, and I am feeling empowered'.

Remember, an affirmation confirms not only your intention, but that you have accomplished what you set out to do. You are giving your mind a new set of instructions, a new way of thinking. This brings you a whole new way of feeling.

Why is it so hard to let go of old hurts?

We tend to remember memories from the past when they have emotions attached to them, whether the emotions are negative experiences, or positive ones.

When there is an emotion attached to the memory, it triggers the amygdala to produce the chemicals, which then helps our body to react or respond to, and deal with what we are feeling.

It is these feelings which can keep us trapped in the old memories, and how we felt about what happened in the past. If there are no emotions attached to the memory, we have a tendency to forget the event.

Whether your regrets are small ones or large ones, this would be a good time to start working on letting them go. If you do not make a conscious decision to let go and fill your mind with more positive information, your mind will continually drift back. You may constantly feel like you regret your actions or inaction. These feelings of regret can cast a shadow, like a dark cloud, over anything else you are doing in your life. When you are having a great time, or are relaxing, the guilt and the regrets can flood in, and spoil that moment for you. This often comes with a feeling of heaviness and sadness.

It can feel like you cannot get in touch with your joy and contentment. Three good Remedies to help with these heavy feelings are MUSTARD, PINE and WILLOW. They will help you to release feelings of guilt and resentment, and lift that dark cloud. But the underlying cause does need to be addressed, to enable you to be totally healed, and able to maintain the feelings of joy and compassion.

Holding painful thoughts and feelings can often result in feelings of not liking yourself for the way you think of others, or not liking yourself for the feelings you are having. CRAB APPLE is a great Remedy to help bring you back to a place where you are accepting and liking yourself again. When your old painful and detrimental feelings surface, this is your sub-conscious breaking through the usual barriers that you put up to block the thoughts.

When those thoughts come to your conscious mind, it is those blocked feelings which can continually cause confusion to your emotional and spiritual well-being, which can ultimately impact upon your health and happiness. This needs to be addressed and changed, to enable you to find more peace and inner harmony.

Please choose to start letting go of those old feelings today. Regrets weigh far too heavily on your precious body. And always remember, your mind cannot think of two thoughts at one time. When you are holding regrets, you are blocking yourself from feelings of joy and contentment. It also overshadows any good memories you had. Take some time to remember the good memories, and let go of things which you cannot change. Starting to lovingly forgive yourself will enable you to move on without the heaviness of regrets.

Loss can be time for a new start

Almost everyone I know, who has been affected by the loss of a relationship, or a sudden death of a loved one or a friend, has some regret about what they did, or did not do or say. Choose to let this be the day when you start to heal, and let go of the old hurts and pains you have been carrying. Instead of keep thinking about those times which weigh heavily on your mind, stop now and write down what happened. Write down what you feel about each situation. Then really think about it. Within the situation, knowledge and abilities you had at the time, could you have handled it differently? Maybe or maybe not. How do you feel about the way you handled the situation back then?

Be gentle on yourself, and start to work with forgiveness of yourself. You did the best you could do within the situation, with the ability, experience and knowledge you had at the time. What can you learn from the situation on reflection? How could you handle similar situations differently in the future? How did you grow through the situation you went through? Write down each unresolved issue, and any feelings this creates for you.

Remember, every experience has thoughts and emotions attached to it, and it is these thoughts and emotions which will keep your body in the same vibration as if you are actually going through the situation right now.

It is these feelings which can ultimately make you feel stuck, stressed, anxious or even depressed. They can even cause you to feel a need to self-harm. You are constantly working against yourself, and the life you should be living in this moment.

Writing things down helps you bring the thoughts from your subconscious mind to your conscious mind, and this can help you see things in a different perspective. When you are writing down how you feel, you are changing the vibrations within your body. You are starting a process of releasing and healing. The feelings start to flow through your hands, and onto the paper. You are transferring the emotion onto the page so it can be transferred to a safer place, and transformed into a way of gaining a greater understanding, and a relief from the heavy feelings you have been carrying.

Are you ready to let go now?

Maybe you could write down the feelings on a separate piece of paper, and burn the paper. This is an effective way of releasing the feelings, and transmuting them into a higher vibration of forgiveness. You can do this process as many times as you need to. Each time you will feel a sense of relief, followed by a feeling of lightness of spirit.

I have created a meditation called 'Fire cleansing and inspiration' to help you with this healing process. It is available through my website.

Please do not struggle alone. This could also be a good time to talk to someone you trust about your feelings, to help you further release and process the experiences you have been through.

Maybe this would be a good time to seek out a friend, confidant or professional person to talk to. Having someone to listen to you, can bring a massive sense of relief, and help you process what you are experiencing. The more you talk, the easier it will be to start making changes for yourself.

Another way you can desensitise yourself from experiences of the past, is with Reiki healing, EMDR therapy, or with OHB healing.

It is often natural to get stuck in the past

When clients first visit me for a consultation, they each have different situations to address. They are either dealing with loss, confidence issues, frustration, break down in relations, being bullied, a traumatic event in the past, illness, or they may be struggling with an on-going situation. Or, they may just have a feeling of unrest, and are feeling unhappy with themselves. But, as we chat, it often transpires that the feelings they most wish to address, are those from long-standing feelings of old hurts, and emotional and mental pains and resentments.

Some of these feelings they have been holding onto go right back to their childhood. They are not deliberately wanting to feel stuck within these memories, but they have found it hard to let them go. Often, it is not until they can talk about what is upsetting them at the moment, that they can start to reveal what is really concerning them. By talking through the layers of emotions, they can start to recognise and explore what has been causing them to feel what they have really been feeling.

When they start to talk about things they have been holding onto, it is like a 'light-bulb' moment for them. It helps them to realise this is a big issue for them. The more they talk, the more upset they can become, and this is often the moment when they start to realise just how much hurt and pain they have been holding onto, and the impact it has been having on their feelings and their lives.

Talking helps them to realise just how much mental and emotional pain they have been carrying. Talking things through is an amazing way to release pent up feelings, and brings relief on so many levels. They may have been struggling to alter the way they feel about people in their past, past situations or events. The past hurts keep dragging them down, and preventing them from moving forward. They are being constantly tormented by their feelings of torment or unforgivingness, and usually find it difficult to separate their old hurts from the relationships they are in at the moment.

Can you relate to this?

It is often not what is going on around you that causes the problem, but the way you think about what is happening, and the way you feel about it, or react to it.

For every emotion or state of mind you are feeling within you that is out of balance, always know there is a natural way you can turn it around. It will take some time and patience, but you will find your greater strength, and be able to take back your own personal power. You need time to process what you are thinking and feeling, to get a better understanding of what you are really feeling. Please give yourself some precious healing time whenever you need it. You are not putting anything off, you are merely giving yourself time to adjust, and your mind and body time to process what you are experiencing.

Looking at your thoughts is a good starting point to identifying what needs to be changed. You will in time learn to identify what is causing your disharmony, and how to correct it for yourself, whether it is by using the new thought patterns you create, the support of the Bach Flower Remedies, or a combination of both.

It may seem like I am repeatedly saying this to you, and that is true. I am repeating this advice time and time again, because I believe not addressing your thoughts is usually the underlying cause of many states of dis-ease within your precious mind and body.

Remember, every stepping stone you take is a step forward. It does not matter how long it takes, or how many times you need to retrace those steps. Every time you make a decision to do something for yourself, you are taking a step in the right direction. Every step is an achievement.

It is a beautiful cycle, which starts with you recognising and understanding that you can change your life, and then choosing to use the natural techniques and Remedies to help you through each new step you take. In time, you will achieve a greater understanding of who you truly are. You can be free of tormenting thoughts, and you can have a calmer and more peaceful life.

Take some time to embrace this new plateau you have come to. From this place, you can start to change your life, and create the life you desire. Do not try to rush this healing process. You need to take time for you, to allow your mind and body to process and adjust to what is happening. The kinder you are to yourself, the more smoothly your healing journey will be.

You may even question yourself

When you are feeling tormented by the past, and by your confusing thoughts, you may question yourself.

It can be hard to be objective about situations when your mind is so cluttered. It can seem impossible to separate what is actually happening to you, from the thoughts of what you believe is happening. To add to the confusion, much of the time we can have a tendency to associate our behaviour with who we are. We identify ourselves as the behaviour we project.

This may be because you have lost sight of who you truly are at the moment, with all these false thoughts running around in your head. This is the day to stop judging your emotions, who you are, or how you act.

Set the intention, to start to acknowledge and rectify your thoughts, and the way you have been talking to yourself. Remember to always treat yourself, and anything you observe, with patience and compassion.

As you clear some of your more prominent thoughts, old memories will naturally start coming to the surface for you to address. This is a natural and gentle way of your mind working though the layers of your healing process. You are gently going deeper into your emotions, and peeling away the layers of false emotions, to reveal the underlying causes of your disharmony.

Take some time to write down these new observations and memories. Ask yourself directly, how do you think the past has had an impact on you? Write down how this makes you feel. In what way have you been influenced? You may need to re-read some of the information in the previous chapter; looking back to see a way forward, to help you achieve a greater understanding. Can you recognise any traits of behaviour you are uncomfortable with? Do you recognise where these patterns come from? How have they impacted on you?

How do you feel about these patterns of your behaviour?

Using the techniques you have already started to work with through your healing journey, how could you turn these feelings around? How can you change these patterns? How can you change the way you feel about these patterns? If, at the moment, you cannot see a way to make changes, that is okay. Emptying your thoughts and feelings onto paper is a really big step forward. It can take time to process your feelings, and start to understand what is happening.

You cannot change overnight. It will be a gradual process. It is imperative that you be gentle and compassionate with yourself, as you go through any process of change and healing. It takes time to process what you are experiencing, and it takes time to adjust. The more you work on yourself, and the more love you give yourself, the easier your transitions will be. When you are writing in your healing journal, leave some space for your observations and the insights you receive as you go forward.

Take a few minutes to do some deep, gentle breaths in and out, and release any tension you may be holding. Breathe in deep inner peace, until you feel the calm flowing through your body. Think of a healing colour, and see your body being filled with your chosen colour as you release any stress from your body. Visualise any stress flowing down through your body, and out into the ground. Imagine your roots, carrying all the stress and tension away from your body, and down into the earth. Keep breathing and releasing, until your mind and body feel calm and clear of tension.

Whenever you feel caught up in your mind in negative thinking, take some time to do a healing meditation. Use the healing energies to fill your body up with the highest possible vibration. Turquoise and blue are good colours for communication, and blue is for healing the throat, and enabling you to express feelings you have not spoken about.

Remind yourself

There will be times when you cannot get clarity or insight into a situation or the feelings you are going through. Be patient and gentle on yourself whenever you cannot get clarity. The answers will come at the correct time for you, at a time when you are more able to deal with them. You could create a poster of the following verse for yourself, and put it up in places around your home. Whenever you are trying to make things happen, as opposed to allowing them to happen, recite this verse to yourself.

Please grant me the serenity to accept the things I cannot change, courage to change the things I can, and the wisdom to know the difference.

Moving through your forgiveness process

One of the things which can keep us stuck in a state of disharmony is lack of forgiveness of others, and of yourself. Forgiveness can be one of the harder issues to work with on your healing journey. Forgiveness of people who have hurt you may seem out of the realms of possibility right now. And that is perfectly okay. There will be an appropriate time to work with forgiveness of others.

Forgive yourself first

You can start your own healing process by starting to work on forgiving yourself. As you release old hurts, and detrimental patterns you have been using towards yourself, or harsh feelings you have been holding onto, you will feel more at ease within every aspect of your life. You will feel more compassion towards yourself, feel calmer and be more at peace. You will start to get more clarity, and feel enabled to deal with people and situations in your life, in a stronger, more appropriate and meaningful way.

It will feel like you have lifted a dark veil off of your life, and you will feel able to see things in a new compassionate and meaningful way.

Meditation for forgiveness of yourself

Your forgiveness meditation is a gentle, effective way of helping you to release any old or unhelpful thought patterns and feelings you have been holding on to. It can help you to start to create new, more uplifting ways of thinking. The meditation can also bring you mental, emotional and physical healing on all levels. You will receive the greatest benefit by doing the following meditation for twenty-one days. The more you do it, the more effective it will be.

Taking time for you to meditate starts your body moving towards natural healing. It helps to break down the self-imposed barriers your mind has created. It can help you change the old automatic pre-programmed ways of thinking. Using your affirmations throughout the day will also help re-programme your mind to a more supportive way of thinking.

Taking time for you to meditate

Drink some water before you start, to help with the cleansing and detoxing process, and have a glass of water ready for after the meditation session. This meditation is available digitally through www.dawnchrystal.com

Take yourself gently into a more relaxed space, with your deep, slow breaths. Set the intention that you are going to work with forgiveness of yourself, and release any pains attached, on all levels.

Breathe gently into your heart space for six breaths, and release.
Slowly breathe deeper into your tummy, for six breaths, and slowly release.
Feel your body start to relax as your breath slows down.
Bring into your mind, the behaviour you want to forgive yourself for.

FREE TO BE ME

Hold the intention to forgive yourself.

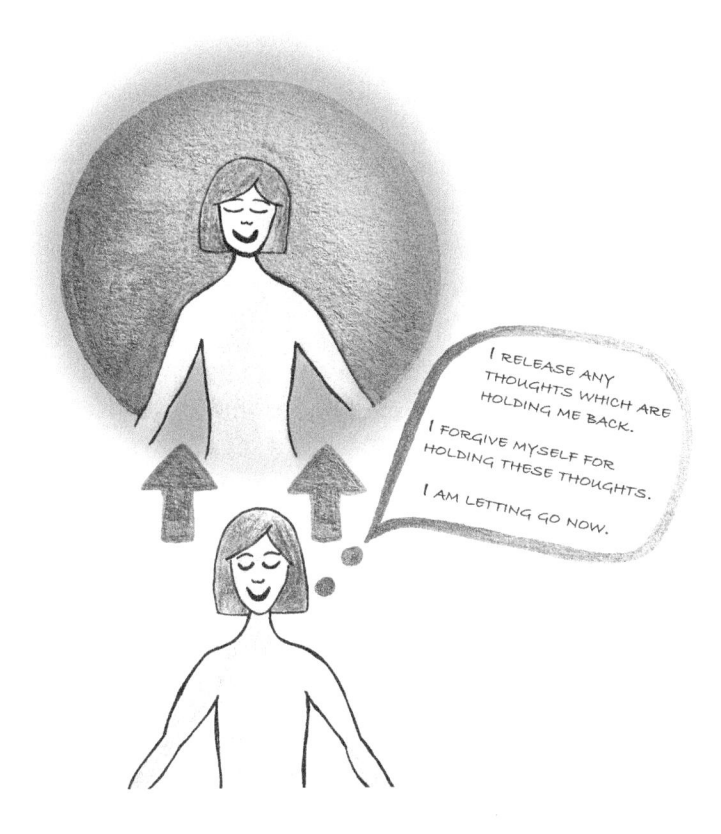

Imagine up above you, an image of you, surrounded by a ball of golden light.
This is your higher self, who is now ready to assist you with your forgiveness healing.
Imagine, or see a cord of white light, going from your heart space to your higher self, up above you.

Focus on the issue you are ready to forgive yourself for.

Send out the intention, you are ready to release any thoughts which no longer serve you, up through to your higher self.
Say to yourself, 'I forgive myself now, for holding these thoughts, these actions, and any thoughts and feelings attached to this situation'.

'I am joyfully embracing, I am ready to let go',
'I am lovingly forgiving myself, and I am feeling ready to let go'.

It may be gentler on you if you work with one situation, or one pattern of thinking at a time.

If this involves another person, send up the thought, 'I am calmly learning to forgive them, and myself, for what happened between us'.

Say 'I am lovingly setting the intention of letting this go now'.

You can be specific about what happened, and how it made you feel.

If you need to raise your voice or shout, then do so. You are releasing the painful emotions from your precious body.

After you have spoken, take some more gentle, slow breaths into your heart space, and send the message of forgiveness up to your higher self.

'I forgive myself, I am letting go'.

Visualise and feel any heavy emotions, thoughts and feelings flowing from your body, up to your higher self.

Give yourself some time to allow your feelings to be released.

When you feel you have released as much as you can for this moment, ask your higher self to shower you with a golden shower of healing.

Imagine, and feel a shower of golden light flowing into your heart space, and down through your body.
Feel the golden light shower flowing into every cell of your body.
Give thanks to the golden light, and your higher self for the healing.
Thank yourself for allowing the forgiveness and healing to happen.
Do not try to rush this process.

It may become uncomfortable

When you are working through the process of forgiving, you may experience some dull, or sharp physical pains in your body. You may feel emotional.

Acknowledge the pain you are experiencing. This is your body's way of showing you where you have been holding emotional pain.
Set the intention of letting these hurts, and this pain, go.
Take your attention to where the pain is, place your hand over where you are holding the hurts and the pain, and breathe into the place of the pain.
Imagine a colour in this space, and see it slowly getting brighter and brighter, and then flowing out into the organs and muscles around that space.
Keep slowly breathing into this space, until the pain gently subsides. It may take some time, so please keep breathing into the pain as it releases.

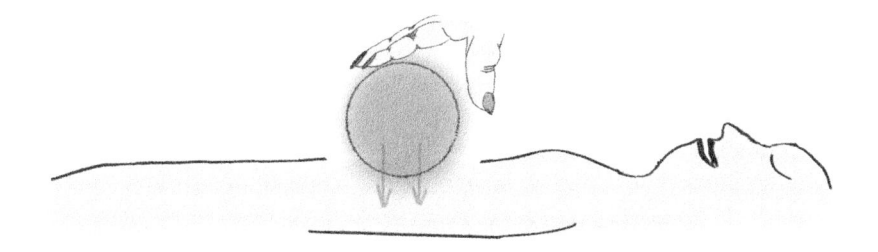

Forgive yourself for the pain you have been holding.
When the pain subsides, say 'Thank you' to your body for releasing the pain, and then say, 'It is done. I am love, and I am free'.
You may have thoughts or memories pop into your mind.

Breathe into those thoughts and memories, and let them go. Acknowledge it is safe to let them go.

Acknowledge you are forgiving whatever happened, and now you are ready to let go.

Say 'Thank you, for the forgiveness. It is done. I am love'.

Go back to your deep, slow breathing process. Breathe deep into your heart space, and then into your stomach, and repeat for as long as you feel necessary.

Imagine the image of 'healing through your higher self', and continue to send away your old thoughts, and receive the forgiveness with the golden shower of light.

When you have finished, say 'Thank you' to yourself, and 'It is done. I am love', and let it go.

Remember, it is not your responsibility to know how the healing takes place within your life. Know the healing will be done.

Take some deep, gentle breaths in and out, repeating 'I am joyfully breathing in love, and breathing out harmony and peace. I am love and I am feeling compassion'.

Bring yourself slowly, back into the awareness of your physical body, and drink some water. Take some time out to relax, and process the healing you have experienced, or go very gently into your day. Drink plenty of water to cleanse and refresh your body.

STAR OF BETHLEHEM

If at any time you feel like you are emotionally affected or traumatised by the forgiveness healing you have done for yourself, use some STAR OF BETHLEHEM or Rescue Remedy to help you feel soothed, and to help you to gently adjust.

If you find yourself keep going over and over things in your mind, or you are continually thinking about somebody and you cannot get them out of your mind, the Remedy WHITE CHESTNUT will help you, and CHERRY PLUM will help if your thoughts have become irrational, and causing you irrational mood swings or behaviour.

Feelings and old emotions coming to the surface, is a natural part of your healing process. This is temporary. These feelings will subside, and it will get easier. Be gentle on yourself for a few days. It will take time to adjust to your new lighter way of being. The Bach Flower Remedies STAR OF BETHLEHEM, WALNUT, WHITE CHESTNUT and WILLOW will support you through this.

You can do this forgiveness meditation for yourself each night, until you feel like you have cleared enough emotions and gained clarity as you take back responsibility for your emotions. The more frequently you do the meditation, the better your results will be. Revisit this meditation whenever any new awareness of painful emotions comes to the surface.

Remember, anything you do for yourself will help you to feel supported, and enable you to move on. Each day you will be in a more loving and compassionate place in your life. This new place will bring you to a place of more joy and greater insight into your true self. Imagine where you will be after doing this meditation for 21 days. When you are ready, take some time to write in your healing journal about the memories, the experience, and the emotions you have cleared, alongside today's date.

Praise, and thank yourself for the great work you have done.

Dealing with old hurts and on-going issues

It is so natural and easy to feel anger, hurt and resentment when someone hurts you. From today, set the intention of starting to let the hurts go. By setting this intention you will start to feel lighter, and your soul will be free to move on beyond the mental and emotional pain. From today, when you see something in someone else that irritates you, you do not like, or you feel like you are being treated unfairly, take some time to write down what is happening. Why is that upsetting you?

It may not be just what they are doing today which upsets you, but the way your mind is reacting to their behaviour. Or, it could be a combination of both. Is their behaviour triggering off old memories and patterns?

Get out your healing journal. Ask yourself, 'What are they triggering in me?', 'What do I need to work on for myself today?' They may be triggering off deeply buried emotions, and allowing you to have an opportunity to heal things for yourself, on so many levels. Thank them for showing you the feelings and behaviours you need to work on for your growth.

Sometimes what you see as irritating in others can be a mirror reflection to what you need to work on for yourself. How can you heal and improve yourself, to enable you to deal with this, and any similar future issues which may arise? It may seem harsh to say, but if you are reacting to something outside of you, maybe the person concerned is triggering some pattern you need to address for yourself. They may be showing you where your weaknesses are right now.

I am not saying they should be excused for their behaviour if it has been inappropriate, but look at how you are reacting, and ask, 'How can I work on this, to change the way I feel about what is happening?'

Compassion

It may be that, at this moment, you need to go to a place where you can hold compassion for yourself and, maybe if you feel ready to, you could send them compassion, instead of reacting to what has happened. By doing this you are rising above the situation, and you will both benefit from the feelings of compassion you are sharing. By having more compassionate thoughts, you can often diffuse the situation, and also give your mind the space to process what is happening, so you can get a new perspective on the situation.

Always try to remember, negative thoughts bring negative feelings, and are harmful to you as well as them.

Looking at me to heal the situation

I know I can be very impatient at times, and sometimes forget to respect my own boundaries and needs. I remember recently feeling agitated with someone, and saying to myself, 'I feel like she's trying to mould me into something I'm not. She is so impatient'. I couldn't understand why it was bothering me so much. I started to feel uptight and agitated with her. I found myself reacting with hurtful words instead of dealing with the situation more appropriately.

My old pattern would have been to walk away from the situation, rather than address it. On this occasion this would have been the wrong course of action. My understanding is, that if I walk away from a challenge instead of addressing it, I will keep meeting the same challenge again and again, until I take more control of what I need to address. This was a very familiar pattern for me, and I knew I needed to change it right here and now.

When I put the situation in writing in front of me, and looked at it the next day, I realised I felt I was allowing myself to be pushed into a corner, and I was being impatient with, not only her, but with myself too. I had allowed my needs to be disregarded, and the woman's behaviour was reflecting back to me what I was feeling, and really needed to address it for myself.

I used the Remedies AGRIMONY, CENTAURY, CERATO, CHERRY PLUM, CHESTNUT BUD and IMPATIENS for a while, and then wrote down how I wanted to address the problem, and the outcome I needed. I did my Withinercise visualisation, seeing the best outcome for us both. The next time I met with the lady concerned, I was able to tell her, tactfully, how I felt, and reset my intentions, and my boundaries. The situation was resolved, and we both had a clearer perspective on how we had gone wrong, and how we could resolve the situation as we moved forward.

Write a healing letter

Writing things down, helps you to release some of your frustration and emotions towards the situation, and helps you to detach from it for a while. If you write a letter, it can help you vent some of your feelings, and give you some time to re-evaluate the situation, so you can get a better outcome. You do not need to send the letter. When you are writing, the healing process for both of you is already starting. You are becoming more objective about what is happening, and setting intentions for the healing to take place.

Healing has no time restrictions

It does not matter if you are healing the past or the present, or if you are forgiving yourself or someone else. Even if the person has passed to spirit, you can still heal any unresolved issues. You will benefit on so many levels, and so will the other person involved. You are opening up a healing space for you both.

Your intention is always the same. Your intention is always to release you and the other person from any unresolved hurts and pains, and bring in forgiveness. This will enable you to see things more clearly, which will bring you a whole new insight into why this lesson has been given to you. The ultimate gift is that you will soon start to be able to see situations, people, and challenges from the perspective of love and compassion. You will receive a profound healing on so many levels. You will grow as you are healing.

Speak kindly to yourself

Create new gentler, forgiving ways of speaking to yourself throughout the coming days. Nurturing yourself with your words will have a profound impact on how you feel about yourself.

Maybe something as simple as, 'I lovingly forgive myself, and let these old feelings go now', or 'I joyously speak my truth', or 'I gently release all the feelings which have been holding me back'. Any positive words you consistently use will help you create new thought patterns, and your brain will continue to produce all the wonderful feel-good chemicals. It is a win-win situation. Start telling yourself how proud you are of yourself, and say 'thank you' to yourself for the amazing healing work you are doing. The kinder you are to yourself, the better you will feel, the more energy and motivation you will have, and the more you can achieve.

When you start to stand up for what is right for you, the whole dynamics of your life will start to change. Be patient and gentle with yourself as you adjust to the new way of seeing your life. And allow others time to adjust too. They may take longer than you to adjust, because they have no understanding of what you are doing for yourself. The healing will happen as it is meant to.

Every step you take for you is a step in the right direction. Your spirits will be lifted, because you know you are on the right track to creating the new you.

Your affirmation for today could be, 'Today I am joyfully integrating all the lessons I have learnt, so I can achieve my highest potential. I am love'.

Quick healing release for you

There may be on-going times, when you recognise you are holding harsh, unhelpful feelings towards yourself. This may come as a sudden awareness, when you just randomly get a negative thought of feelings about yourself, or something you are doing. It may be something as simple as 'I'm so clumsy', or 'I am so stupid'.

It may be just a flippant remark but, remember, every thought you think will have an impact on the way you feel from this moment on.

Your mind cannot tell if you are being serious, or you are joking, or if you are just using those words without being aware of their impact. It reacts to what you are saying about yourself. Using harsh words towards yourself can bring in a feeling of heaviness in your emotions. Become more aware of how you are emotionally re-acting to the thoughts you are using. As a simple general rule, if your moods feel low, or you are fed up, there is something you need to adjust.

Turn it around

As soon as you have an awareness of the negative thoughts you are having, or holding, bring to your mind the image of you and your higher self. Immediately send the message of, 'I am happily releasing these thoughts now', up to your higher self.

Say in your mind, or out loud, 'I lovingly forgive myself for these thoughts and feelings I am using about myself. I am joyously letting this go now'. Then visualise, and feel yourself, being showered with golden light.

And then carry on with your day. Notice how much lighter you feel, and how much more pleasant your feelings are. Does this reflect in the way people are now responding to you, and you are responding to them?

Make a note in your healing journal, to remind yourself how well you are doing. Thank yourself, and praise yourself for the amazing progress you are making. Once you start to have an awareness of your thoughts, and the impact they have on you, you will never want to go back to the old way of thinking and feeling. As a general guideline, when your moods feel uplifted you are on the right track.

Take some time out

Take the time to stand up. If you can, go outside, and stand barefoot on the ground or the grass.

Set the intention for any emotions, and any energies, which no longer serve you, to be released.

Take some deep breaths in, and release your breaths.

Imagine a shower of golden colours, flowing through your body.

Gently start to shake off any tension, and any stale feelings from your body.

Start by gently shaking your fingers, and your hands, and then your arms, and your shoulders.

Feel the tension flowing away from your shoulders, and your neck. Gently rotate your neck, and slowly move your head around.

Keep shaking your hands, and arms and shoulders, as you gently start to move all the other parts of your body.

Let your whole body gently move and flow, as you shake the tension out through your hands.

With every breath, imagine this old tension, and these old feelings being flushed through your body, and being released through your fingertips, and down into the ground.

Imagine those old feelings flowing deep down into the earth through your roots.

Say to yourself, 'I am lovingly letting this all go now'.

You can work on specific issues, or you can just allow your body to gently release anything, and everything which no longer serves you. Your body will know just how much you can cope with releasing at this moment.

Your legs and your body will start to feel tingling sensations as you release. Give yourself plenty of time to allow this to happen.

When you feel you have cleared enough for the moment, your healing is done for today.

This is a great way of grounding your energies down, to release you from emotional distress and confusing thoughts. You will feel lighter and much more grounded. Drink plenty of water, and go gently into your day.

You can do this gentle exercise at any time of the day, to help take you to a new plateau of forgiveness, calm and compassion.

Getting closure

If you are unable to speak to the person concerned, maybe because they have moved away, or even passed away, would your loved ones have really thought you should, or could have, done things differently? Are they still blaming you? Even if there was more you could have done, what would they truly have said to you? If, maybe, your actions were genuinely inappropriate, go to the forgiveness meditation for yourself, and start to release these old harmful feelings now.

Please remember that you are not super-human. Could you have really changed the event or the outcome?

We can all do things which are hurtful or inappropriate. This lifetime is a journey of learning, and unfortunately we may not always get it right, but thankfully today you have a choice to turn your thinking, your feelings and your life around.

Maybe their behaviour, or their actions, were truly inappropriate. We all have regrets, but we cannot turn back the clocks, or change what has happened. But you can choose to start to release those harmful, heavier feelings from your mind and your precious body today.

Be gentle on yourself

Often the feelings you carry from the past are unjustified, and sometimes they may feel justified. The important thing to be aware of, and to acknowledge, is they can still seriously impact on your life today when you are thinking about them, and for as long as the issues are unresolved in your mind.

Hopefully in time, you will be able to recognise when you have been, or are being, too harsh on yourself. Would others be as harsh on you as you are being on yourself? Where are all these harsh feelings coming from? Why do you think that you continue to cause yourself this harm with detrimental thoughts?

Would you say these harsh thoughts to your loved ones, or your friends? Write down the thoughts you recognise you have, which are about anger, resentment, being too hard on yourself, feeling guilty, and any thoughts where you find it hard to let go of feelings and thoughts of resentments. Please write down as many thoughts as you can which pop into your mind.

Take some time out to sit quietly, and close your eyes.

Imagine a colour in your mind, and focus on that colour as you slow down your breathing.

As the colour flows through your mind, it will help you feel more at peace with your thoughts and feelings.

If you feel like it's an overload of information and clearing, please take some time out for you. Use the above exercise, and then take some time to pamper yourself, and maybe get some fresh air.

Healing can be tiring and feel heavy at times. Give yourself some special time out to allow your mind and your spirits to be lifted and cleansed.

Feeling guilty?

One of the heaviest feelings which can weigh heavily on your mind, and rob you of your feelings of joy, is guilt. Do you spend time feeling guilty about things? Do you constantly worry if you have done wrong, or you have upset someone, or you should have done more? Do you feel responsible for others' happiness or unhappiness? Does your mind keep flicking back to memories where you wish you could have done things differently?

What are you really guilty of? I expect the answer is, when you really look at the situation, that you should not be feeling guilty at all. Is it really necessary for you to be having so many regrets? The feelings of guilt we carry are often unjustified. But even if these feelings are justified, this is the ideal time to start working on letting them go. Feelings of guilt often go alongside feelings of being too hard on yourself, and taking more responsibility than necessary for what has happened.

Write down things you feel guilty about. The Bach Flower Remedy to help you release feelings of guilt is PINE. It helps to turn your feelings into genuine regret, and to recognise who is responsible for what has happened. Take out your healing journal. Start with today. What has happened that you regret, or you are upset about?

Start with some of the things which are most prominent in your mind, and when other things come to mind, work through them one at a time.

Eliminate some of the most obvious things you are holding onto, and that will help you get in touch with the causes of your deeper emotions which are out of balance. Have these feelings manifested into other emotions, such as anger, detachment, not liking yourself, or your behaviour, or even self harm?

How heavy is your load today? What have you said, or done, that you regret? How could you have handled each situation differently? What can you learn from this?

Simple things can also weigh heavy on your mind. Think now about all the things you believe you could or should have done recently, but didn't. I imagine there is a long list. Write down anything where you wish you could have done better, or sooner, or times when you wish you could have acted differently. Take it a stage further, and write down the reasons which come to mind for you not taking that action, or for not doing as well as you believed you could have. I expect there are many reasons. Remember, you cannot change the past, but it can weigh heavy in your mind, your emotions and in your heart, if you do not choose to let it go. Start to release these feelings of regret today.

Maybe you acted inappropriately, or said something hurtful. Start to let it go now. And always remember, some outcomes are just not meant to be any different to what they are. But the feelings you are carrying towards the past, are what can be impacting on your feelings of unhappiness, low self-esteem or lack of self-worth, and even lack of well-being. However large or small your regrets are, if they are affecting you, they are impacting on your feelings of well-being. If they are heavy, and causing you disharmony, they are impacting on your motivation, and they will influence the way you see and feel about everything in your life at this moment.

Feeling guilty, feels like being smothered in a feeling of sadness. It robs you of your joy, and can rise up within you at the most random of moments. It can feel constantly like you are trying to lift yourself up above a feeling of torment that you cannot quite put your finger on. Let this be your time to turn this around. Your disharmony needs to be addressed now, to allow you to move to a place of greater harmony and peace of mind.

When you really think about these life events, I expect there were really good reasons for your actions. Think back to the time, or times, that you say you should or could have done more, or you should not have said this, and you could have said that. Now apply that logic to the times when you believe you should have acted differently, and that you blame yourself for. Is it really logical and fair for you to be still blaming yourself?

Read up on the Remedy ROCK WATER. Do you think this will help you to be gentler on yourself?

How confusing is your mind right now?

Often your thoughts have become out of proportion, and out of perspective. Your mind believes what you are telling it and cannot reason, or change, this point of view, until you give it a new way of thinking about the situations involved. Your mind cannot see any alternative ways of thinking, because it is stuck in the patterns of thinking you are giving it. It has no choice. And to add to the confusion, your mind hears your thoughts, and always thinks you are talking about you in this moment! Even when you are not.

Is it any wonder your emotions feel confusing, and your moods and energies low, when your mind has so much to deal with? This is an exhausting state of mind to be handling every day and every night. Feeling guilty for things can be a real underlying cause of despondency and despair which, when left unchecked, can lead to feelings of depression, and even isolation or loneliness. With so much confusion going on in your mind, is it any wonder it is hard to find total joy and contentment, and feel fully present in your life?

How are you treating you today?

Choose to become your best friend. Speak kindly to yourself, and start to work with the healing of forgiveness, to give yourself the best chance possible. PINE is the Bach Flower Remedy for feeling guilty. It brings you genuine regret, and the ability to recognise what parts you are responsible for, instead of feeling guilty. ROCK WATER is the Remedy to help you to be kinder to yourself, and to release tension and rigid patterns of thinking.

Sing to lift up your spirits

There may be times, when you recognise you are holding heavy feelings, and need a quick fix to help you rise above what you are feeling. Singing is one of the easiest ways to lift up your spirits. Try singing along to your favourite songs, and have an awareness of how your moods start to lift.

Doing something uplifting gives your mind a break from what you are thinking. Having a break from your thinking can feel refreshing, and allow your mind the space to see things more clearly. These will all help your amygdala to produce the serotonin and endorphins to soothe you, and help you to feel better.

Chanting is another way to change your feelings, and so is thinking about something which makes you smile. Maybe this would be a good time to watch a comical movie, or a musical. If your mind feels too busy or overwhelmed, take a few minutes to cover your eyes with your hands, to help calm your mind and alleviate any fears or worries.

Why forgive?

When you can find a way to let go of your emotional pain, you will have found a way to live and thrive with more peace and harmony. You will have more love, patience and compassion for yourself, and gain a whole new perspective on your life. The next time you take some time to work with forgiveness, talk to your heart and send healing love into your heart. Your heart is the place where we should be holding love, but it is hard to connect with those feelings of love when you are hurting.

I am asking you to forgive yourself, for whatever you feel you did, or didn't do. Practising forgiveness means that you are working on making peace towards yourself, and your actions. And you are healing the past, and any people or any incidents in your past. Practising forgiveness sends out the intention, and the message, that you are feeling ready to let them go now.

Forgiveness is not something you do for others – it is something you do for yourself.

Take some time out to do some self-healing. If you do not forgive yourself, you will continue to feel trapped in the situation which is filled with bitterness and bad feelings. You are harming and punishing yourself for something over which you feel you have no control. Not forgiving yourself is a very painful experience, and affects every feeling you have about yourself, and how you feel within other relationships in your life. Forgiving allows you to have improved emotional and mental health.

Forgiveness brings you to a place where you have less anxiety, stress and hostility, lower blood pressure, fewer symptoms of depression, a stronger immune system, healthier relationships with yourself and with others, and, most importantly, improved self-esteem, more self-worth, and a feeling of well-being. Forgiveness brings you renewed harmony in all aspects of your life, and enables your soul to start to flourish naturally. Being in a state of forgiveness brings you peace, joy and compassion, and a greater understanding of who you truly are. Take a moment throughout the day to stop, forgive, and heal yourself.

How can you forgive someone who's hurt you emotionally or physically?

Forgiveness of yourself comes on many levels, but it is frequently mixed with feelings of being unable to forgive others. You will know when the time is right to work with forgiving others. You will get a feeling deep inside you, an inner strength, and a knowing that the time is right, which enables you to start releasing.

Don't try to rush yourself when you start to work with forgiving others, and be very gentle on yourself whilst you work through this healing process.

When someone has hurt you, allow yourself to feel the emotions you are experiencing.

Getting in touch with the emotions may seem more painful at the beginning, but it can bring you inner strength, and more compassion and resilience.

When you have acknowledged the hurt and pain, ask for an understanding of why you need to let it go.

Take some time out to process this information. Writing down how you feel can free your mind to receive some new insights. If the situation is on-going at the moment, how can you start to take steps to deal with this? Even if it is on-going, this healing process can help you to start to heal.

FREE TO BE ME

Consider how this hurt affects you. How does it make you feel today? Are you ready to let go?

If not, come back to this issue to work with it when you feel stronger.

If you do feel trapped in a situation where you feel you have no choices, please reach out for professional help. Any step you take will lead you to the healing you need, and help you to feel more empowered. Remember, that forgiveness can be possible at the right time. Would the Remedy CHERRY PLUM help you?

Acknowledging your feelings is often the first step towards helping you to release them and let them go. You will feel able to let go when the time is right. The more you work on healing yourself, the stronger you will feel. The right time will show itself when you are ready. To start forgiving anyone, we must first acknowledge that forgiveness is possible. There may be a less painful situation you can work with for now. If you feel ready to start to forgive today, set the intention to choose to start to forgive.

Write in your healing journal. Write today's date, and what your intention is. List all your emotions, all your feelings, and your desired outcome. Make the decision to start to let go.

When you have acknowledged and expressed your pain, you will know when the perfect time is to work with forgiveness. Talk to your mind, your heart and your body, and reassure them that you are working on their healing now.

At times in the past, when I didn't feel ready to forgive someone, I wrote down how I felt as if I was writing them a letter, and then each day I would rewrite the letter until I felt I had released most of my emotional pain and anger onto the page. Between each writing session, I left the letter on the table with a rose quartz crystal on top of it. The rose crystal was symbolically holding the healing in a place of love, until I was ready to deal with it.

What would you say to the person, or people, who had hurt you? Take those thoughts and feelings out of your mind, and put them into writing. Keep rewriting your letter until you feel you have adequately released as much as you can, or need to. Leave your letter, with a rose quartz crystal on top of it, and start to feel your pain dissolving. Rose Quartz is the crystal of unconditional love, and can hold a healing space for everyone concerned. You are taking back your responsibility for your own well-being. You are no longer a victim of your past circumstances. You are strong, and incredibly courageous. You are taking back your own personal power. Be proud of that, and praise yourself at every step.

Being able to forgive will bring you healing on so many levels, and help you recognise who you truly are.

Focus on where you are today, and how you've worked through this book to help yourself. Look at how far you have come, and what you have achieved for yourself.

Be proud of yourself, and be proud that you have made the right decision to heal yourself, and your life. Take a few moments to sincerely thank, and praise yourself before you go any further.

Let the techniques help you right here and now, so you can move beyond those feelings which are causing you pain. Reach out for help. Reach out to friends, family, a stranger, a charity, myself, or ask your qualified doctor, and other support services, to help you through if you need more support.

Be aware that when you reach out for help, you will not be the first, or the last, to have these feelings and pain. There are many professionals who work in this arena, and they will be able to help you. When you reach out to a friend, or a new person to support you, you will automatically start to feel some sense of relief.

Set the intention to let the emotional pain go. When you set this intention, your mind will start to work with you. Set the intention to start to work with forgiveness. The best place is to start with you.

This is a big step towards healing your life. When you start allowing healing to come in, you are going with the flow of supporting, loving and valuing yourself.

Through forgiveness you will find true joy, inner peace and lasting happiness.

CHAPTER 36

A MEDITATION TECHNIQUE TO AID FORGIVENESS OF OTHERS, AND HEAL YOUR SOUL

WHEN YOU WORK THROUGH FORGIVENESS, you will start to have more compassion for yourself, and for others. It is often when you are able to move beyond blame and anger, that you can get a clearer and truer perspective of yourself, your behaviour and thoughts, and what has happened.

Your higher self, can then show you the greater lessons in all that you are going through, and what you have been through. And then, everything can be healed on an even deeper level. When you this technique for yourself, please remember, it is not your responsibility to know how another person receives, or heals, the situation within themselves. Whether the healing is for you, or for another, know the healing will be done in the most appropriate way for everyone's higher good.

Meditation for forgiveness of others

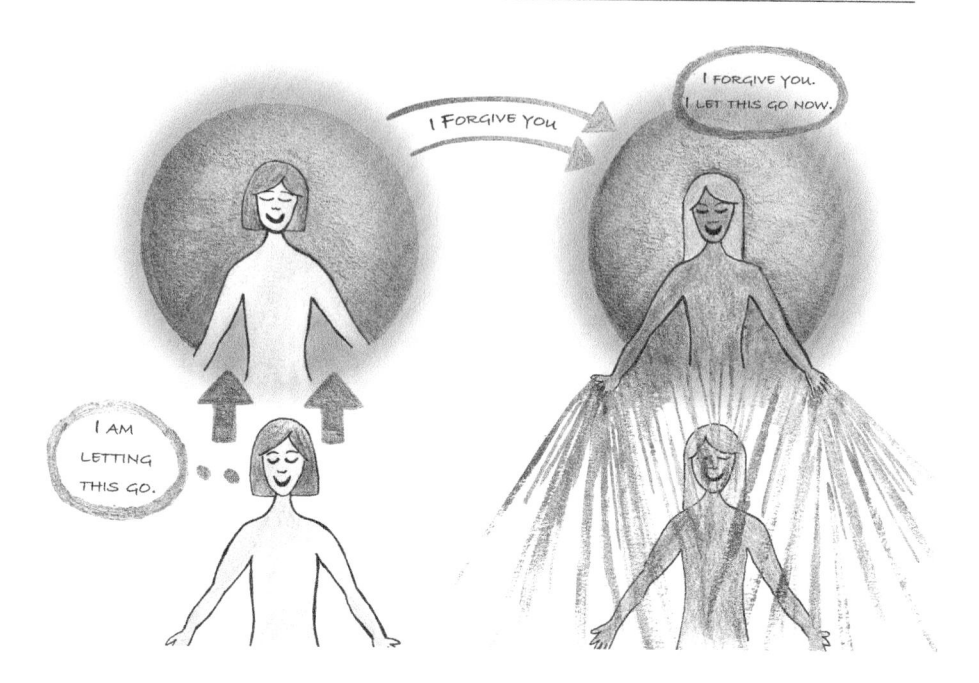

Take yourself gently into a more relaxed space with your deep, slow breaths. Set the intention that you are going to work with forgiveness, and release any pains attached, on all levels.

Breathe gently into your heart space. This is the space from where you are sending your message of forgiveness. This is the centre of your soul, and ultimately the place from where you need to forgive, to allow you to heal and to feel true love.

Let your body relax as you take some deep, slow breaths into your heart and then your tummy, and release.

Bring into your mind the person you want to forgive, or ask for forgiveness from.

Imagine them, and hold the intention to forgive.

Imagine, or see, a cord of white light going from your heart space to your higher-self, that is surrounded by a golden light up above you.

Then imagine the other person concerned, and their higher self, sitting above them, also surrounded by a golden ball of light.

Send your thoughts of forgiveness up to your higher self, and across to the other person's higher self.

See the cord of light flowing across to the higher self of the person concerned.

Then the cord, with your healing message, is sent down to the person's heart space, as they are showered with healing light.

Say, 'I am lovingly forgiving you for your actions.' (You can mention specific actions, and say their name).

The message of forgiveness is being delivered to the other person, through your higher self, and their higher self. This stops any miscommunication or judgement about how the healing should, or will, happen.

The higher self always works in the highest and best interest for everyone concerned.

All healing will be done with unconditional love for both parties.

Ask for the 'healing space' to be opened, to allow the healing to take place.

Tell the person you are ready to forgive them, and yourself, for what happened between you.

You can be specific about what happened, and how it made you feel.

If you need to raise your voice or shout, then do so. You are releasing the painful emotions from your body.

After you have spoken, take some more gentle breaths into your heart space, and send the message of forgiveness up to your higher self, across to their higher self, and down into their heart space.

When you are working through the process of forgiving, you may experience some dull, or sharp physical pains in your body. You may feel emotional too.

Acknowledge the pain you are experiencing. This is your body's way of showing you where you have been holding emotional pain. Be gentle on yourself as this happens, and do not try to rush this process.

Set the intention of letting this pain go.

Take your attention to where the pain is, place your hand over where the pain is, and breathe into the place of the pain. Feel the love and healing flowing into where you are releasing your pain.

Keep slowly breathing into this space until the pain subsides. It may take some time, so please be gentle on yourself, and keep breathing into the pain as it releases.

When the pain subsides, say 'Thank you' to your body for releasing the pain, and then say 'It is done. It is done. I am love'.

You may have thoughts, or memories pop into your mind.

Breathe into those thoughts and memories, and let them go. Acknowledge it is safe to let them go, and send them up to your higher self.

Acknowledge you are forgiving whatever happened, and now you are ready to let go.

Say, 'Thank you, for the forgiveness. It is done, I love you. I am love'.

When you feel ready, say to the other person, 'I am gently forgiving you. I am releasing you, and any thoughts and feelings I have been holding towards you. It is done'.

Go back to your deep, slow breathing process. Breathe deep into your heart and your stomach.

Breathe in deep inner peace, and gently release.

Imagine the image of 'healing through your higher self', and continue to send the forgiveness.

When you have finished, say 'Thank you' to yourself, and 'It is done, I love you. I am love'.

Feel yourself being showered with the golden healing energy from your higher self.

Remember, it is not your responsibility to know how the other person receives, or heals the situation within themselves. Know the healing will be done.

Take some deep, gentle breaths in, and out, repeating, 'I breathe in love, I breathe out peace'. 'I breathe in love, I breathe out compassion'.

'I am ready to forgive now'.

See yourself being showered with the golden healing light.

Imagine breathing the healing light into every cell of your body.

Take some time to sit in this new gentle energy of love and compassion.

Say 'Thank you. It is done'.

When you have done all the healing you need to for today, always bring yourself very gently, and slowly, back into the awareness of your physical body, and come slowly back to full consciousness.

Drink some water, and go gently into your day. Drink plenty of water throughout the day to flush out any old feelings.

After any meditation for healing, you could take some time out to go outside, and do your barefoot grounding exercise if you do feel emotional or light-headed.

Be gentle on yourself throughout the day, as your body is working through a time of release, and this could bring in other feelings like regret, grief, sadness or anger.

Acknowledge what you are experiencing, and gently work through those feelings. Do not try to rush this process. The more you work with your forgiveness meditation, or forgiveness process throughout the day, the more at peace you will start to feel.

If the feelings you have been holding have caused you deep pain, you may need to revisit this meditation for several days to get the full benefit of the healing. Some wounds will take longer to work through, and heal. Do not try to rush this process. These wounds have hurt you deeply, and may take time to release. Talk gently to your body as it releases the pain.

Drink plenty of water throughout the following days to flush the old feelings out of your body.

This meditation would be more beneficial if you do it regularly for about twenty one days.

As you are working on your feelings of being able to forgive, this is the energy you are now living within in every cell of your body.

It is also the loving energy you are resonating in within your mind, your deeper consciousness, and what you are sending out to the universe.

As you continue to resonate on this new gentle energy, you will attract towards you people who respect you, and bring you everything you need.

The more you heal yourself, the more benefits you will feel on all levels.

Keep the healing flowing

Whenever any thoughts, memories, or feelings come to you around the person you have worked with forgiving, bring into your mind the image of 'forgiving through your higher selves', and swiftly release any feelings which have been brought to your attention.

You can do the same healing process for anyone else, or any other situation where you need to forgive. Breathe gently into your thoughts, and release them through your higher self. Imagine the image for healing forgiveness through your higher self, and send the intention of forgiveness out. Ask for the forgiveness to be sent to the person concerned.

Trust the healing process will happen in the best way possible for you both, and say 'Thank you, it is done'.

Repeat the affirmation 'I joyfully breathe in love, I lovingly breathe out peace'. 'I lovingly breathe in forgiveness, I joyfully breathe out compassion. My heart is filled with love. I am love'. You can adjust your affirmation if you wish.

Feel your higher self-showering you with healing light. Feel your heart and your body being filled with love and healing. Repeat to yourself, 'I forgive myself, I am love, I love myself'. Say 'It is done. I am love'.

You may find the need to go to the toilet more often, as your body processes the healing. Drink more water to help with the clearing process, and take more time for you.

Take some time to work through this healing process of forgiveness. It is not a process to be rushed. It takes as long as it takes. You can do it as often as you need to. The deeper the pain has been, the more you may need to work with the forgiving and healing process.

You may need to work on some issues for several days, to feel able to fully release feelings you have been struggling with. Working with your forgiveness meditation for twenty one days, will allow you to get the full benefits of the healing process on your mental, emotional and physical levels.

Who is next?

When you feel ready, do your forgiveness healing with anyone else who you are holding detrimental feelings towards. Over the next few weeks, work with forgiveness with the next person, and the next, until you feel you have done enough. Revisit this forgiveness meditation to heal anything else which comes to the surface throughout your healing journey. Be gentle on yourself as you work through any process of release and forgiveness. It takes time for your mind, your emotions, and your body to adjust. Emotions coming to the surface are a natural part of the forgiving and healing. Release any emotions as they come up.

If you feel overwhelmed by your emotions as they come to the surface, please seek help from family, friends, medical professionals or a counsellor.

You can also use the Bach Flower Remedies

AGRIMONY helps you talk about your feelings, and calms your thoughts.

CENTAURY will help you set new boundaries for yourself, and maintain them.

CERATO will help you have more belief in yourself, and trust in your gut feelings.

ELM is the Remedy for when you feel overwhelmed by your feelings. It brings you to a place where you have more confidence in your ability to deal with things, one step at a time. Writing down your thoughts and feelings can help you too.

GENTIAN will help you feel optimistic about the changes you are creating.

GORSE will help you if you feel helplessness or useless. It brings you renewed hope and faith.

WHITE CHESTNUT helps with constant repetitive thoughts, and brings you a calmer mind so you can get more clarity and peace of mind.

HORNBEAM is a great Remedy if you keep putting off making the changes you need to. You could add a fear Remedy as well to support you. Read about the Remedies in the fear section of this book.

The more you read about the Remedies, the more easily you will start to recognise the emotions you are experiencing, and what your real potential can be.

Quick healing release for you both

There may be on-going times when you recognise you are holding harsh or unhelpful feelings towards someone. This may come as a sudden awareness, when you just randomly get a negative thought, or harsh feelings about someone, or it may come when you are in the presence of someone.

Either way, as soon as you have an awareness of the negative thoughts you are having or holding, bring to your mind the image of you, your higher-self, and the person with their higher-self.

Immediately send the message of, 'I am joyfully releasing these thoughts now. I lovingly forgive you and myself for these feelings I am holding. I let it go. I am love'.

And then carry on with your day. Notice how much lighter you feel, and how much more pleasant your feelings are. Does this reflect in the way people are now responding to you?

Make a note in your healing journal to remind you how well you are doing. Thank yourself, and praise yourself for the amazing progress you are making.

Make a note if you recognise a difference in the way people are being towards you too.

Once you start to have an awareness of your thoughts, and the impact they have, you will never want to go back to the old way of thinking and feeling. You are opening up a whole new world filled with compassion, loving feelings, and a greater understanding of who you really are.

CHAPTER 37

PSYCHIC ATTACK

NOW YOU HAVE EXPLORED WAYS of forgiving yourself, and others, I want to give you some insight into why it is so important to do so.

When you start to let go of emotional pains and things which have hurt you, you will get a sense of relief. This feeling will help you feel lighter and more uplifted. Your body will be flowing with more uplifting and healing chemicals, and you will be able to see more good within yourself, and those around you. Always remember, what you think about, is what you will feel inside you. So if you are thinking or saying negative things about yourself, it will keep you in the feelings of disharmony.

When you are angry, disappointed, critical or resentful towards yourself, you are lowering your vibrations within your body. Your mind will reciprocate, by producing chemicals which make you feel even more stressed and uptight, and this results in more negative feelings, and more stress and anxiety. It is a vicious cycle, which never seems to end. This is a form of psychic attack. You are attacking yourself, and your body has no defence against this constant pattern of destructive thoughts. It can seem almost impossible to rise above these thoughts.

It is like being constantly criticised by someone else, and having no way of fighting back, or repairing the damage. It weighs heavy on your mind, and can seriously affect how you feel mentally, emotionally or even physically. Acknowledge that you need to address this. It is exhausting, both mentally, emotionally and physically.

Start creating thoughts and affirmations which are more supportive and forgiving of yourself. Maybe, 'I am lovingly forgiving myself for all these thoughts and experiences. I am choosing to let them go now. I deserve the very best. My heart is filled with love', will be a good place to start.

The more you work on forgiving, and being kind to yourself, the more uplifted and nurtured you will feel. When you have done some healing on forgiving yourself, you can then start to heal other situations around you when you are ready.

A new perspective

Notice how you look differently at those around you when you have started this healing process.

Notice if you still feel a need to react, or not. How do you feel now about them?

Make a note in your healing journal. How does this make you feel now you have released these feelings?

Psychic attack hurts everyone, including you

If you are feeling angry, hurt, or feel resentful towards someone else, or if you are critical of them, your mind cannot tell who you are thinking about. Your mind cannot tell if you thinking about someone outside of you, or if you are talking about yourself. Your mind reacts to the words you are using. If those words are hurtful, painful or derogative, your mind assumes you are talking about you. Your mind reacts appropriately to what you are saying or thinking.

The more you dwell on those thoughts, the more discontent you feel within you. Please remember, any negative thoughts you use about others, will have the same impact on you, and the way you feel. Your mind cannot tell the difference, and so assumes you are talking about yourself.

Your mind thinks you are being derogative towards yourself, and this brings you feelings of disharmony and discontent. These feelings are often the source of depression and anxiety, because the situation hasn't been resolved.

The feelings haven't been expressed, and the inner conflict keeps getting more and more intense. The more intense the feelings become, the heavier and more unhappy you can feel. The longer this goes on, the harder it is to see the situation in any other way. These thoughts really can wear you down on so many levels. Because there is no end to the hurt you are carrying, and the conflict within you, it is hard to see any solution or resolution to the way you are feeling. You cannot see any alternative perception of the situation concerned.

This is where the healing potential of the Bach Flower Remedies is invaluable. They help to shift you from the negative state of mind, to a more uplifting state, where you can see things through a different perspective. It is important to address your thoughts as well though, or you may keep repeating the same pattern.

Lowering their vibrations

Another challenge negative thinking creates towards other people, is that it can lower their vibration and impact on the way they are feeling, or feel about themselves. The way they feel, or see themselves, may be affected by what you are thinking of them. This can cause them to feel emotional disharmony, and sometimes even physical pain. It can affect them mentally too.

We all have an innate ability to sense what is going on in others' thoughts, and transfer our thoughts to other people. If your thoughts towards them are negative, derogative or condescending, this can bring them into a state of confusion and disharmony.

Have you ever been thinking about a friend, or had a thought to ring somebody, and a few minutes later they ring you. Is it a coincidence, or a form of telepathy?

Now, take it a stage further. Assume every thought you send out, is being telepathically picked up by the other person concerned.

What you are projecting out, is how they can start to think and feel. They cannot separate your projected thoughts, from the thoughts they are having about themselves. It can become very confusing.

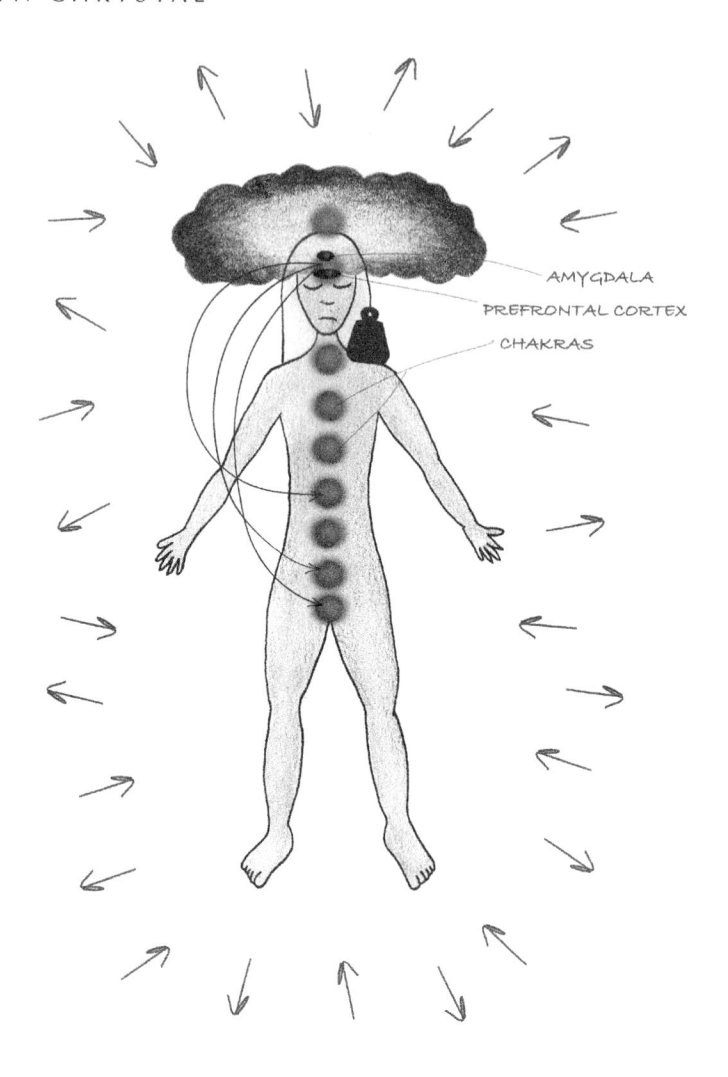

The other consequence of sending out negative thoughts is, as that person picks up your thoughts, they could project those thoughts back to you, and that can make you feel even more emotionally and mentally confused or hurt. The way they perceive you, may now be based on how you are thinking about them. When you are feeling overly sensitive or vulnerable, it is hard to separate their projected thoughts from your own. This form of psychic attack can be very detrimental to any form of relationship or healing that you are working on.

If you are projecting negative thoughts out, whether it is intentional or not, it will create a feeling of mistrust within you, and with the relationships around you. If you have any grievances, choose to start to heal them, and it will turn your life around. Start to let any feelings of disharmony, and resentment or hurt go, and start to see the good within yourself and within people around you.

I do understand that some pain and situations you have been through will be extremely raw and painful. Acknowledge your pain, and start to heal yourself today. Do it for you, and in time you will be in a place where you are ready to work on forgiving others. Start the healing process just for you, and allow yourself to be comforted and soothed, by letting go of the pain and anger towards the things you have been through.

Be very gentle on yourself when you are working through this process of forgiving, as it can bring up unexpected emotional and mental pains which need to be cleared. Seek out the help of a really good friend, or loved one you can confide in, or a professional person who can help and support you. Writing down your feelings can help you to start to release them and see situations more objectively.

The Bach Flower Remedies CRAB APPLE, HOLLY, PINE, ROCK ROSE, ROCK WATER, STAR OF BETHLEHEM and WILLOW can support and soothe you.

Remember, your mind cannot focus on two things at the same time. It reacts, and gives power to the thoughts that you give most attention to, and if those thoughts are harmful, this always results in you feeling disheartened, in a state of disharmony, and out of sorts.

When you start to look at and appreciate the good within yourself, and see the good instead of the negative aspects, you can start to see everything in a new and far more uplifting way. When you have grievances with others, and you are constantly seeing negativity within them, it is hard to see any good, and then your mind attaches those feelings to other aspects of your life too. It cannot comprehend or separate where the feelings belong. It is quite common that when you are focusing on the negative aspects of someone, you can only see negativity in other situations which come your way.

And please remember, your mind thinks you are talking about you. It can seem hard to feel any joy when you are in this state of mind, and there can seem like there is no end to your torment.

What are you seeing?

When you see things within other people which frustrate, or annoy you, sometimes they may be mirroring something in you, or triggering something within you which needs to be addressed. Take some time to write down how you feel about them, and the situation. Is this something you need to address for yourself? What are they triggering in you?

Do you feel disharmony within this relationship? Is this disharmony with yourself, or with the other person?

Where did that begin? What feelings are being brought up for you? What can you do to change that?

What thoughts are you having about this person? Be honest with yourself.

Are these negative feelings keeping you stuck in your heavy emotional state, or keeping this relationship at arm's length?

Look at your issue to be addressed, and break it down. Take some time to write a letter to them, telling them how you are feeling. You do not need to send the letter. You are merely processing how you are feeling, and starting the healing process between the two of you.

Now look more closely at you. Look at the situation which is causing you to feel disharmony at the moment.

What do you need to address for you? What have they triggered in your emotions? What behaviour patterns have they triggered? What do you need to work on within you today?

Have they triggered off some unknown feelings? Is it frustration, sadness, anger, lack of boundaries? Is it work-related, relationships, lack of money, illness, disabilities, sense of satisfaction or purpose? What are you reacting to? How are you reacting? Or maybe, why are you over-reacting to this situation?

Often the way you are reacting, may not just be about what is actually happening in this moment. It could be a reaction to an accumulated list of memories, and things which have happened over time. Maybe you are over-reacting because of things which have happened in the past, and they have not been resolved or healed. Does this feeling come from a deeper feeling you have not acknowledged?

Quite often your reactions, or over-reactions have become a pattern of behaviour, or a way of life, and it can seem impossible to unravel the way you think or behave. Record your thoughts as they flow. Say it as it is. Do not try to filter through your thoughts, and make them gentler. You are looking to be honest with yourself, so you can turn around anything which no longer serves you.

Your life, your cleansing

Create your list for today, and work through it one step at a time. Record the date you acknowledge what is happening, and how you feel, and start to work on each issue. Work with one aspect at a time. Do not think too much about what you should write. Just write down any thoughts which pop into your mind, and then any other thoughts which follow.

You can keep adding to your list of things to resolve as your journey unfolds. The more you heal, the deeper the healing will be. More things coming to the surface, shows you are working through the process of recovery and beyond. This is a good indication of your mind, your body and your soul being ready to release and repair itself.

Observe what you are seeing

If you find that you continue to see only the negative within a person or a situation, you will continue to compound the problem. Your mind responds to this negative thinking, and keeps you within it. Taking time out, to look at the way you are thinking and feeling can help you get a different perspective on what is happening. Taking time to process what you are observing is necessary to allow the healing to happen.

Take some time to chill out

Take some time to do something you enjoy, something that makes you feel relaxed, or laugh. Anything which lifts up your spirits can enable you to get a wider and clearer perspective.

Talking to someone is a great way to process what you are experiencing too. Pick up the phone to chat to a friend, or go out for a walk with someone who you feel comfortable with. Sharing your problems really does help heal and lighten your load. When your mind is processing and relaxing, then you can start to see solutions, and how you can heal it for yourself. You may get a deeper insight into the other people concerned, and find a way to resolve how you feel about the situation, and how you feel about them.

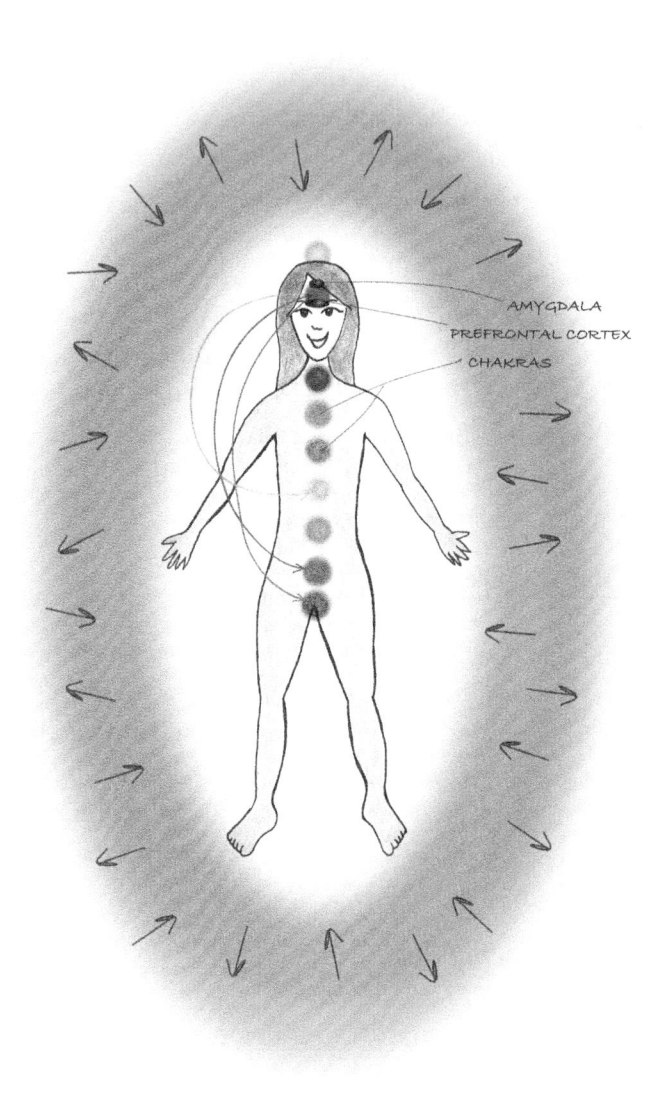

Acknowledge what you need to address. Love, respect and nurture yourself through it, and set about creating the changes. Have compassion for yourself for what you are experiencing and working through. You are creating healing and changes on many levels, for you, and for everyone concerned. As your mind starts to let go and heal, you are encouraging your amygdala to produce the wonderful feel-good chemicals so you soon start to feel more uplifted. As you heal yourself, you attract towards you people who are more uplifting and supportive.

Not every situation or relationship can be healed right now, but remember that you are starting to create a healing space within you, a space where you are experiencing peace and joy for yourself. In time, you will create a healing space for those around you too, and by looking at and addressing these issues you will achieve that in the most appropriate way.

A simple example would be: When you recognise there is a pattern of frustration and impatience between you and someone else, turn it around by sending out thoughts of forgiveness for both of you. Use an appropriate affirmation to help resolve the pattern, 'We are being more patient and compassionate towards each other. Everything is flowing more joyfully and smoothly now. Our hearts are filled with love'.

When you see the good within others, this too is a reflection of the good within you. Acknowledge what you see, and praise yourself for the wonderful qualities you see. When you can see the good within others and within yourself, your world becomes a better place to be. Keep working with the healing forgiveness meditation, and allow yourself to move gently through this new transformation. You are transforming your life, and that takes time.

Praise, and thank yourself for the valuable healing work you are doing. The healing will happen, and it will be so worth it. You will be able to move forward without remorse, regret or need for retribution. You will feel enabled to live with love and compassion, and find true happiness and peace of mind.

Remember to take some time out, to ground your energies down with your barefoot exercise, and your yawning exercise, (YSSiO).

CHAPTER 38

WHAT YOU BELIEVE IS TRUE FOR YOU

WHEN WE HAVE CHOICES WE can change things. We all have so many choices. You will achieve what you perceive in your mind to be true.

Being mindful of your thoughts throughout the day is powerful. This awareness is key to helping you start to make changes. Every moment of every day you have a choice, a chance to reset your triggers to what is causing your stress and distress. Be gentle on yourself. Acknowledge what you need to change, and start to adjust one thought pattern at a time.

Your new thoughts will start to create your new way of life, which will ultimately be the significant driver of your inner feelings of success and happiness.

One of the main driving forces behind making changes is firstly acknowledging you are not happy with yourself, or the situation you are in. Recognising how you feel, and how you have lost your way, helps you identify a good starting point for wanting to make changes.

It is this desire to make changes, which will keep driving you forward.

You attach to the emotions you feel, but know there is so much more to you

Often, knowing that the emotions you are experiencing are not really who you are, can cause inner confusion to arise. The more intense the emotions are, the deeper the hurt you feel. This deeper hurt can often manifest as a physical discomfort such as stomach cramps or headaches.

As you start to work with the Bach Flower Remedies, these physical ailments can subside. This is your mind, and your body starting to peel away the layers of tension and distress. If old patterns or physical pain reoccur, acknowledge them, and start to honour the pain your body is showing you. Acknowledging pain and discomfort helps you recognise what is shifting in your emotions.

When you have pain or discomfort, it may be natural to feel agitated or frustrated towards the pain, or even towards yourself. This pattern needs to change. From today, be grateful for the pains and for your emotions, because as they show themselves, they are ready to be released and transformed.

Nurture your pains

Let's take this concept of being kinder to yourself a stage further: to a greater understanding and deeper level of awareness. Every cell of your body has its own consciousness. If you continue to neglect or say harsh things about the painful parts of your body, the consciousness of those cells will respond accordingly. From this day forward, whenever you have a pain or discomfort in part of your body, acknowledge it, and speak kindly towards the part of your body where the pain is showing itself. Start to give the pain more attention, and start to treat it gently and with more respect.

As you become more gentle towards your illness or pain and discomfort, your brain will produce more healing chemicals to help ease your pains, and your heart will be filled with joy and love. Holding feelings of frustration towards your pain and distress, causes your brain to release unhelpful chemicals again, and this can accentuate the hurts and pain.

If you are kinder, and more loving towards yourself when you are feeling out of sorts, your body will respond accordingly, by producing the chemicals which help with your healing, and therefore speed the recovery process for you. Your body needs to be nurtured and encouraged, to allow it to go gently through a period of recovery. From this place, you are allowing the real healing to take place.

The emotional stress and imbalances may have been going on for a long time, maybe even a lifetime, so it is imperative you be gentle on yourself as your body returns to a more natural state. This needs to be a period of patience, nurturing and gentle adjustment for you and your body.

When you start to use the Remedies, they may start to trigger some of these deeper hurts, but this is natural. This is a major part of the healing process. Your body is letting go. Be kind to yourself as you go through these periods of growth, and the harmony will soon resume. Drink plenty of water to aid your healing.

Always remember that these feelings of more intense emotions are temporary, as your body is going through a time of transformation, and this healing process should not be rushed. This time will pass, and you will soon start to feel the benefits of these healing times of transformation. More clarity and peace of mind will follow.

Is your mind working with you now?

To sum up, your mind is an amazing piece of machinery. If you are in charge of your mind, it can manifest for you anything you desire.

So why do you get stuck in situations which are unsuitable for you, and cause you to feel in disharmony? Every moment of every day, you feed your mind with thoughts. If these thoughts are negative or condescending towards yourself, you will feel disharmony within yourself. Constantly trying to control these negative thoughts and feelings can wear you down. They can make you feel stressed and anxious. When you feel run down or out of sorts, the desire to understand yourself, and why you react the way you do, often seems out of your reach.

One of the initial starting points behind making changes, is recognising and acknowledging that how you feel when you are out of sorts, is not who you really are, closely followed by the recognition that you have lost your way.

Where can you start today?

Recognise how your current ways of thinking, are making you feel unhappy or discontented.

The first key is to be realistic, and recognise these feelings are having an impact on your feelings of well-being.

The second key to transforming your life, is to acknowledge that how you feel about yourself at this moment, is not who you really are, and that you realise you have lost your way.

The third key is making a decision that you are ready to change.

The main desire we all have is to find inner peace and a feeling of well-being, and this is often the greatest driving force of all. Make a decision today that you are ready to make the changes necessary, to help you find your inner happiness and your peace of mind.

Your fourth key to transformation, is making a decision to have the tenacity to keep following through on the new choices you make every day.

The inner peace, clarity and contentment you will achieve is priceless.

If every thought you have determines and creates your reality, what is going on in your life? Do you like what you are manifesting for yourself today?

Dr Bach's philosophy was simple: *'When there is a void between your thinking, and what is your true self, is where 'dis-ease' sets in.'* Many of us have been living for so long in a false sense of who we are, we have become disillusioned about the truth of who we truly are.

You have a choice today to change your life by changing your thinking. The more you respect yourself, the stronger and more empowered you will feel.

I believe the Bach Flower Remedies are the greatest gift we could have been given to support us through these changes. It is often not the situations around us which cause us grief, but the way we think about them, and the way we react to them. You can choose to change this today.

The Remedies will help you gently rectify your thoughts, by gently moving them from a negative state to a more uplifting positive way of being. They also bring you clarity, and the insight of a greater understanding of yourself.

Do you always feel in control of your emotional responses? If not, this is your opportunity to choose to change the way you react or respond to every situation in your life.

If you can change your thoughts, you can change your emotions. You can have more control over how you think and feel about situations.

You will start to feel better about yourself, and your life. You can then determine your own feelings, your outcomes, and your own destiny.

The Bach Flower Remedies will help you move gently through the changes. They can be used for anything you need to emotionally adjust to, to bring you the best possible quality of life. They will enable you to see the way forward. This will bring a feeling of well-being, and from this new perspective you will start to feel better about yourself, and the situations around you.

The Remedies will help you see the truth of who you really are. From this new awareness, you will be free to make more accurate choices.

Choose to find your inner happiness today. Your true happiness really does come from within.

Do you need some reassurance?

If, at any time you feel unsure of the choices you are making, stop and take a few moments to connect with your higher self. Tap into, and pay more attention to your higher self, your intuition.

Take a moment to stop and think of a number between 1 and 555. Now flick through *'Free to be Me'*, and find that page number. The number you have chosen is your angel number for today. What message are you being drawn to today? Read through your chosen page, and see if you can relate to the guidance on that page.

Your chosen angel number is a simple answer from your intuition, guiding you to reach in to help yourself, or to reach out? Whichever way you are guided to go, allow yourself to go with the flow. The more frequently you trust in your intuition, your higher self, and the more clarity you will get.

CHAPTER 39

THE BACH FLOWER REMEDIES

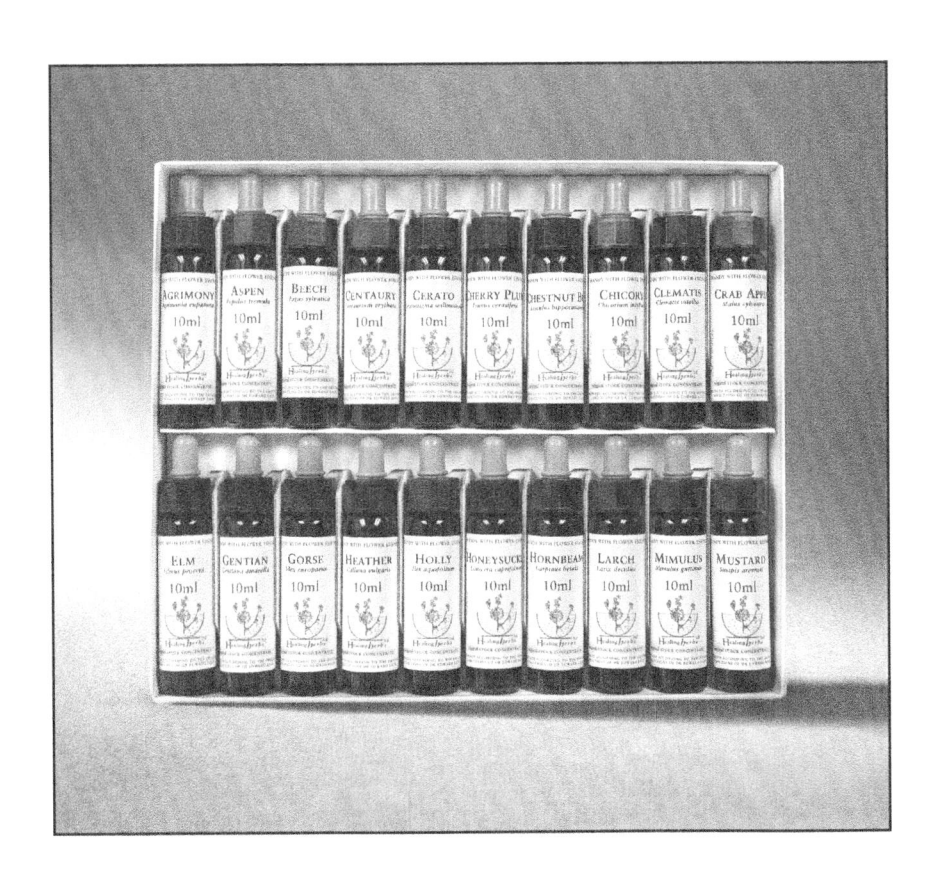

DAWN CHRYSTAL

DR.BACH'S NATURAL HEALING GIFT TO US ALL

Where to find your Bach Flower Remedies

Page 497	Agrimony
Page 440	Aspen
Page 482	Beech
Page 500	Centaury
Page 509	Cerato
Page 442	Cherry Plum
Page 454	Chestnut Bud
Page 485	Chicory
Page 457	Clematis
Page 418	Crab Apple
Page 421	Elm
Page 512	Gentian
Page 515	Gorse
Page 473	Heather
Page 503	Holly
Page 460	Honeysuckle
Page 518	Hornbeam
Page 476	Impatiens
Page 424	Larch
Page 445	Mimulus
Page 463	Mustard
Page 426	Oak
Page 466	Olive
Page 428	Pine
Page 448	Red Chestnut
Page 451	Rock Rose
Page 488	Rock Water
Page 521	Scleranthus
Page 431	Star of Bethlehem
Page 434	Sweet Chestnut
Page 491	Vervain

DAWN CHRYSTAL

Page 494   Vine
Page 506   Walnut
Page 479   Water Violet
Page 469   White Chestnut
Page 523   Wild Oat
Page 471   Wild Rose
Page 437   Willow

Disclaimer

DAWN CHRYSTAL DOES NOT GIVE medical advice, or prescribe any particular Bach Flower Remedy as a sole way to aid emotional ailments. Neither does she recommend the Bach Remedies as an alternative to any medical advice or medication you may need.

Dr Bach's wishes were that anyone should be able to use the Bach Flower Remedies as a form of self-healing, but it is important to take other support into consideration if that is appropriate. The Remedies can be used alongside most conventional medication you may be taking, and any medical advice you have been given.

You take responsibility for your own actions, and under no circumstances should you change your medications, or disregard medical advice, without first consulting your doctor or physician. If you choose to change your medication at any time, you should consult your doctor first.

If you are struggling with emotional issues, and would like more clarity about the use and benefits of the Bach Flower Remedies, please contact the author at dawnchrystal62@gmail.com, or seek the guidance of a Bach Flower Remedy practitioner near you.

The Remedies can also work well alongside other complementary therapies, but it is best to talk to the therapist(s) involved, to find out how the Bach Flower Remedies can be best used in that way.

The Bach Flower Remedies are a natural, gentle way to help you heal emotional imbalances. As with other therapies, your emotions may seem more intense for a while, before calm and balance return. If your emotions are extremely out of balance when you start on this healing journey, start with a single Remedy, and add additional Remedies when the calm starts to come.

Children and anyone who is extremely emotionally or mentally distressed should be supervised by a responsible adult when they start to explore working with the Bach Flower Remedies.

If you are working with anybody who is withdrawing from alcohol, do not use brandy. There are alcohol-free stock bottles available, and also sweets and chewing gum with the essences of Rescue Remedy.

If you are in any doubt, please contact Dawn Chrystal.

CHAPTER 40

YOU MAY NEED MEDICATION WITH YOUR NATURAL TECHNIQUES AND REMEDIES

IF YOU ARE TAKING MEDICATION, and choosing to work with the Bach Flower Remedies, and the other natural techniques Dawn shares with you, it is important to realise that the Bach Remedies and the healing techniques, are not an alternative to the medication or medical support you need. The natural Bach Flower Remedies and techniques are all a way to support you, alongside your medication. They can complement most medical advice or medication you are taking.

Working with the natural techniques and Remedies can bring you to a place where you do feel emotionally stronger and more confident, and from this place you will get a new perspective on everything in your life. One perspective which may radically change is your need for medication. As you feel emotionally stronger, and work with your emotional intelligence, you may feel tempted to change, or stop taking, some of your medication.

Please do not ever stop, or change your medication, without first consulting your doctor. Speak to your doctor about the changes you are choosing to make, and how you would like to re-assess your medication. When you let them know, the doctor can give you the best advice on how you can ease yourself off the medication, if it is appropriate to do so. Medication can work on many levels, soothing and suppressing your emotional and physical pains and feelings.

Quite often, the medication is a necessary part of your body's healing support. For some ailments and illnesses, it is essential that you take the prescribed medication. The medication is helping you to ease your distress, your discomfort and your pain on many levels.

If the medication is reduced or withdrawn, you may experience more emotional or physical pain for a while. This period needs to be supervised by a medical doctor. Any changes, or withdrawal from medication, need to be carefully monitored and guided by your doctor whilst your body is going through a period of adjusting.

Do not feel discouraged if your doctor recommends you stay on your medication. Your doctor will be able to give you a better insight into the medication you are taking, and the consequences of changing or stopping it.

Getting a better understanding of your medication, and the support it gives you, can help to alleviate any fears or misunderstandings you may have.

When the doctor advises you to carry on taking your medication, there are a lot of natural ways you can still help yourself. As we have said, the natural techniques are there to support you with all aspects of your life, on many levels, so they complement your medication needs. They should not be seen as an alternative, unless you have sought professional help and been advised that this is appropriate for you.

Medication and natural Remedies work alongside each other. Your doctor will know the best way for you to adjust your medicines. Many people will need to use medication to maintain a better quality of life.

Paying more attention to your breathing techniques, your thoughts, meditation, affirmations and self-care will all help support and sustain you through any adjustments your doctor recommends. When you choose to do things for yourself, your brain produces feel-good chemicals, which will help support and soothe you through your period of adjustment.

The Bach Flower Remedies, and all the natural techniques, are a complementary way to bring you emotional well-being and inner peace, and from that place most people experience less emotional and physical pain. But it is always important to recognise that, for some ailments and mental imbalances, it is essential to make any changes under the supervision of a qualified doctor or physician. Your doctor can help you integrate your natural techniques and Bach Flower Remedies into your medical support system. The more support you have, the smoother your progress will be.

Will you have an over-reaction to the Bach Flower Remedies?

Some people may be in a very highly stressed or emotional state when they start to use the Bach Flower Remedies. This can cause your emotions to over-react. The stress chemicals flowing through your body cause your emotions to surface quickly.

When you start using the Bach Flower Remedies, they may bring your emotions to the surface, and this can feel like your emotions are getting worse. This is a natural part of your healing process. The emotions are coming up to the surface, to allow your body to release them. This may feel like your emotions are becoming more intense. This is an essential, but temporary, part of the healing process, and this period will pass.

When you continue to take your Remedies you will start to feel some calmness come to you. As you become calmer, your brain will start to produce the gentle healing chemicals which will support your healing process. The Remedies help to heal your emotions in layers, and sometimes as the layers of old emotions surface, they can seem very painful and distressing.

Your initial reason for taking the Remedies may be soothed and corrected, and then the underlying reasons for your disharmony can become more apparent. This may be unsettling at first, but it is a natural part of the healing process. This unsettled time will pass as your mind starts to adjust and repair itself.

Are you feeling over-sensitive?

The Remedies cannot do you any harm, but if you are feeling particularly over-sensitive, vulnerable or angry at the moment, your emotions may seem more intense. Start by using single Remedies. This will help you to soothe and heal your emotions more slowly and gently.

You can take the single Remedies directly from your stock bottle, or put 2 drops into a glass of water, and keep sipping the water regularly for about 10 minutes. For deeper, more painful emotions you may need to take the Remedy regularly for a few hours, until you start to feel calmer again. Keep using your chosen Remedy until you feel at peace with yourself.

If you think of your years of accumulated emotions as 'layers of emotions', the Remedies are gently peeling away the layers of feelings which no longer serve you. When you start taking the Remedies they will gently ease you through the emotions you are feeling today, and then they will take you to a calmer place, where you are ready to get a deeper insight into what has caused your disharmony. Once you peel away the outer layers, you will get closer and closer to the truth of who you really are. This can take time and patience, but it will be the greatest gift you have ever given yourself.

When you first start taking the Remedies, they can make your emotions seem more intense for a short time. This is your body's way of bringing those emotions to the surface, to allow them to be healed. Each person will react, or respond differently, based on their circumstances, history and their personality.

Any intense feelings will subside, and calm will follow.

Dr Bach discovered there are 12 different personality types, and each personality may have a different healing experience when they are taking the Remedies. This is natural, so please do not compare your healing journey to anyone else. The Remedies will help you to heal in the most appropriate way for you.

Is this getting worse?

When I first used the Rescue Remedy, in some ways I felt much calmer, but in other ways I felt more angry and disagreeable. For me, I was suddenly very aware of how people had taken advantage of me, and how the way they had treated me had affected me, emotionally and mentally. This was a temporary state where I was 'waking up', and starting to see things more clearly. I felt angry, and a real sense of injustice.

When you start to peel away the superficial habits and patterns of behaviour you have accumulated, it can be alarming to be able to see how people and circumstances have had an impact on you, or what can be even more alarming, is how you may have allowed this to happen. Acknowledge and validate your feelings.

It can be quite a shock when you start to see things more clearly. STAR OF BETHLEHEM can help you to deal with any feelings of shock or trauma you may feel when you get a clearer perspective. STAR OF BETHLEHEM will help to soothe you through the time of healing and transition. AGRIMONY will help you to talk about how you feel, and will bring you a calmer and clearer mind.

Allow yourself to ease gently through this time of transformation. Drink plenty of water, rest when you need to, and be kind to yourself, to support the wonderful healing the Remedies are bringing you. This time of more intense emotions will pass and, with continued use of the Remedies, you will be brought to a place of calm and contentment. Be patient and very gentle on yourself as you work through this process. This is a natural way of supporting your mind and body to heal itself, by gently peeling away the layers of emotions and influences which no longer serve you. The Remedies are subtly working on your behalf.

Drink plenty of water to support the clearing your body is going through.

Acknowledge what you are going through

This is another natural part of your healing process. You may feel a sense of injustice, or a sadness, or even rage at what has happened in your past, or what you see happening now. This is you naturally peeling away the false illusions, and now being able to rebalance and heal your emotions.

You will start to get more clarity, and a deeper understanding into situations in your life, and how they have impacted on you. With this insight will come a feeling of being more empowered. This clarity will bring you renewed hope, and a stronger sense of who you are. Acknowledge the feelings you are experiencing, and take time to work through this. Reach out for help if you feel the need to. This is one of the reasons I encourage you to write down how you are feeling as you progress through your healing journey.

As you write things down, you are releasing some of the intense feelings you are having, and you will start to get a sense of relief. You will start to get a more objective view of your feelings. This will bring you a calmer and clearer mind, which will ultimately bring you more energy and peace of mind. You will soon start to see the amazing effects and healing the Remedies have brought to you. As your different emotions become more apparent, you can introduce new Remedies to help you peel away these old feelings and emotional pains.

Take the Remedies consistently, but less frequently, if your emotions do become very intense. Taking them less frequently can be more effective, and the results will be equally beneficial. It just takes a little bit more time. This is not a journey to be rushed. If you are gentle on your body, it will heal more naturally, and you will experience less distress or disruption. When you are feeling particularly sensitive, the more dilute the Remedies are, the more effective they can be for you.

Put 2 drops of your chosen Remedy into water, and sip the water throughout the day. This will give the Remedy time to slowly, and gently, bring you the fullness of what you are experiencing. It allows emotions to more subtly and gradually come to the surface, to allow you time to process what is happening, and allow your mind to gently heal itself on all levels.

This is a more soothing way of working through your emotional healing if your emotions feel extremely stressful, distressing or volatile. The more you use the Remedies, the stronger and more empowered you will feel.

After some time, you will start to be able to recognise why, and how, your confusion has manifested itself. The Remedies will keep gently working with you. They will bring you to a new plateau in your life, where you will be able to experience more uplifting feelings of well-being, and from this place you will start to discover who you truly are.

Always remember, this moment in time will pass, and you will get stronger.

CHAPTER 41

WHO DISCOVERED THE BACH FLOWER REMEDIES?

IN 1930, DR BACH WAS dissatisfied with medicine's focus on the disease, rather than the patient. He left a successful medical practice, to explore a more humane and natural way to treat emotional dis-ease.

Dr Bach was an extremely intuitive and caring man. He has left us all with a wonderful legacy, a way to heal ourselves emotionally, with the natural gentle vibration of Flower essences.

It constantly inspires me every day, when I observe the gentle, yet radical, healing process people go through with the Bach Flower Remedies.

Today, helping people understand themselves is still the first step towards their recovery and finding their true selves, and the Flower Remedies will help you with this amazing healing process.

Taking the Bach Flower Remedies consistently when you need them, will speed the process of recovery, and help you to maintain a positive state of mind.

The more you can understand yourself, the more effective and smoother the process becomes. When you can understand yourself, the world takes on a whole new meaning.

Be adventurous with the Bach Flower Remedies. An inappropriate Remedy will not harm you if you do not choose the right Remedies first time.

Enjoy the journey. Never be afraid to reach out and ask for help, and always be bold in your approach to the healing work you are doing.

The greatest healing will be your discovery of who you truly are. And through this journey of self-discovery, you will be able to recognise what has created blockages and negative thoughts about your life, and how the Bach Remedies can gently ease you away from those negative states of mind which no longer belong to you, or serve you.

In time you will find your true self. It will take persistence and patience, but it will happen. Be very gentle on yourself as you work through this healing process. Be proud of yourself, and of the steps you take. Embrace, and enjoy the beautiful person you become.

How do the Bach Flower Remedies work for you?

The Bach Remedies deal solely with negative states of mind. MIMULUS, for example, might have medicinal properties if used as a herb tea, or even perhaps as a homeopathic Remedy, but when it is taken as a Bach Remedy it deals with fear and anxiety. It has no direct influence on the body.

However, by transmuting fear and anxiety into their positive aspects of courage and understanding, healing on a physical level may indeed follow. Thus the Bach Remedies heal the body *indirectly*.

When we have been holding deep hurts for long periods of time, they can manifest as physical pain within your body. By healing your deeper emotional pains, your physical pains can be eased.

Where have your pains manifested from?

The Bach Flower Remedies may be seen as similar to homeopathy, in that both work on healing the vibrations of the mind and body when they have become out of balance.

Dr Bach discovered that there are thirty-eight states of mind. The Remedies help ease mental and emotional difficulties without harmful side-effects, regardless of how we have come to an emotional imbalance.

They can bring a way forward for us all, regardless of our past, our beliefs, the type of person we have become, or our circumstances. There is a Bach Flower Remedy, or a combination of Remedies, for every state of mind or emotion that is out of balance.

We often need to look deeper, and to begin by determining how, or why, any frequent condition of mind manifests. Feelings such as anger are often associated with hatred or envy, but can equally be caused by frustration, worry, resentment, or any other conditioned state of mind. So we need to ask ourselves, or the person for whom we are prescribing, what is the *cause* of this anger? In other words, it is by getting down to basics that the correct Remedy, or mixture of Remedies, will become apparent.

When you first start on your healing journey with the Remedies, you may not know the underlying cause of your feelings, so choose the Remedies you can relate to at this moment. Each mixture of Remedies will help you peel away layers of old emotions.

As your healing journey proceeds, the underlying cause of your disharmony will become more apparent. If you are unsure which Remedies you need first, use a pendulum if you are not sure where to start. Then read through the negative state of the Remedies you have chosen, to see if you can relate to them at the moment.

You can start with 1 or 2 Remedies you can relate to. Use a maximum of 7 Remedies mixed together. Then read through the positive state of each Remedy, to help you recognise where the Remedy can take you. Often you can recognise the positive potential within yourself. Keep focusing on the positive state of mind as you work through your process of change.

Keep it as simple as possible. No matter what you may be struggling with in your mind, there is a Bach Flower Remedy to suit each individual's personality and changing mood pattern.

If you would like some personal guidance, contact Dawn Chrystal at dawnchrystal62@gmail.com

Please do not sit in the confusion of not knowing where to start. Dawn will help get you started, and keep you on track if necessary, until you are ready to support yourself.

We all need a friend sometimes, to listen to us, and help us get started on the road to recovery.

Are you being sympathetic or empathic?

Sympathy means joining a person in their problem, and becoming a part of it, and so causing them to stay mentally and emotionally in the problem.

Empathy means being able to stay emotionally detached, and rise above the situation, whereby you can help lift someone up, and offer positive, constructive advice and guidance.

Empowering somebody

Turn the problem back to them by asking them, 'What do *you* think you should do?' This can help them to start to take some control of themselves, to think about their situation and challenges, and ultimately feel more empowered. They often know the answer to their problem, but have not looked beyond the problem to see a solution. They may have become so consumed by their confused thoughts and feelings, they have become fixed in their negative beliefs and expectations.

Asking them to think about solutions can kick-start a recovery process for them. They may not have all the answers, but can feel empowered because you are enabling them to start thinking of solutions.

Take some time to read about the Bach Flower Remedy RED CHESTNUT. Do you think it could help you to detach from other people's distress and dramas? Do you find yourself constantly thinking about other people, and you feel like you can't get them out of your head? Try WHITE CHESTNUT.

If you find yourself repeatedly being pulled into other people's situations or dramas, or are working as a therapist or in a caring capacity, a good combination of Remedies would be CHESTNUT BUD, CRAB APPLE, RED CHESTNUT, WALNUT. This combination can be used as a preventative, as well as a way to help you detach, if you find it hard to separate yourself from others' problems and situations. Add WHITE CHESTNUT if you keep constantly thinking about them.

Acknowledge what you are feeling

Whatever you are going through, acknowledge your distress, and do not rush to try to fix it. It is important to acknowledge how you are feeling first. What you are experiencing is important to you. Whether it seems very small, or something really traumatic, it has thrown your life off track. What may seem really trivial to one person, may seem life changing, or even soul-destroying for someone else. Validating your feelings, and what you are going through, creates a good foundation for working on you, and for the healing process to begin.

Everybody's pain is unique to them

Never compare two people's situation, or the way in which they may be suffering. Each person's suffering is unique to them, and needs to be acknowledged, before you move on to trying to sort it out with them.

If someone is in an emotionally distressed state, in a state of shock or trauma, and is struggling to express how they feel, AGRIMONY can help them speak about how they feel. STAR OF BETHLEHEM can help to release them from the traumatic feelings they are holding.

Place 2 drops of each Remedy in a glass of water, and allow them to drink it.

It will take some time to take effect. When they are in a calmer place, they will feel more enabled to talk about their thoughts and feelings, then you can see more clearly how to help them.

If they are unable to talk at the moment, add 2 drops of each of the Remedies to a 30ml bottle of water, and encourage them to use the mixture for a few days, to help gently release their trapped feelings.

Encourage them to write down how they feel when their emotions come to the surface. Let them know their emotions will sometimes become more intense, before they are soothed and start to heal, and this is a natural part of the healing process. Reassure them, that this temporary time of intense emotions will pass, and their emotions will become calmer again.

Do not be alarmed if someone becomes more emotional, as they start to open up to the Remedies and their healing powers. This is a natural part of the healing process, and allows them to start to come back to a place

FREE TO BE ME

of calm and composure. Be patient with the length of time this process can take.

By releasing their emotions, they are allowing the natural process of healing to happen.

Use a single Remedy, or a minimum amount of Remedies for a few days, until the calm starts to come. Then introduce more Remedies as necessary. It is better, and far more effective and soothing on the mind and the body, to release and heal gently and slowly.

Everybody's healing time and process will be unique, and will happen as it is meant to.

Encouraging them to write in a journal can be an effective way of processing what is happening, and the breathing techniques and meditation can help to bring back calm. When the person is being pro-active with their treatment, they can feel like they are taking back some control over their situation.

Observe each person individually, and know that each will heal and recover in their own way.

Keep a record of Remedies used, and how the person reacts and recovers. This will help you get a greater understanding of the person, and be helpful for future sessions.

CHAPTER 42

HOW TO MAKE, AND TAKE YOUR BACH FLOWER REMEDIES

THE ESSENCES OF THE REMEDIES come in glass dropper bottles. To make a combination bottle of Remedies you will need:

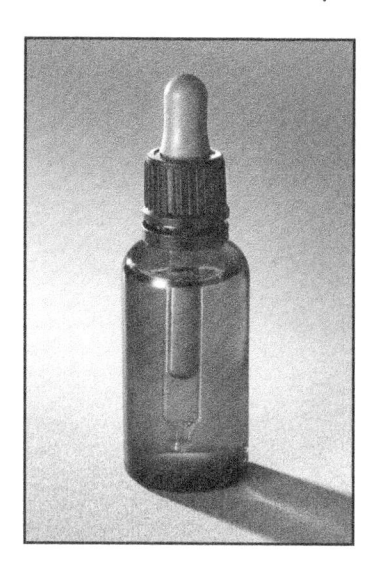

An empty 30 ml sterile glass dropper bottle, mineral water, brandy or glycerine oil to preserve the Remedy.

Making up your combination bottle:

Partly fill a sterile dropper bottle with mineral water
Add a teaspoon of brandy or glycerine oil, as appropriate (see note below).
Add 2 drops of each chosen Remedy to the bottle
you can use a combination of up to 7 Remedies together.
Put a label on the bottle, with your name and date on it.
Make a record of your Remedies for today.
When the combination is ready, take 2 drops on the tongue, or in a drink between 4 and 8 times a day

The exception is Rescue Remedy: add 4 drops of each of the 5 remedies, and take 4 drops, as frequently as needed on the tongue, in water, or on lips and pressure points if unconscious.

The essences of the Bach Flower Remedies come in individual glass dropper bottles, and are readily available in health-food shops, chemists, some supermarkets, and can be bought online.

They can be purchased as single Remedies, or you can order the complete set of 38 Remedies. The empty dropper bottles can be purchased online.

There are 38 bottles of remedies, and 2 Rescue Remedy bottles in a set.

Always put a label on your bottle, to remind you on which date you started taking the Remedy combination, how many drops to take, and how often to take them.

Also, make a note of which Remedy group your chosen Remedies come from. This will give you a greater understanding of what you are dealing with.

Do not add brandy if you are dependent on alcohol, or recovering from alcohol dependency.

Remember that you cannot wrongly diagnose any Remedy. If you don't need it, it will simply not have an effect. Keep trying the different Remedies you feel are appropriate, and you can add other Remedies to the bottle if other emotions become apparent, or if there does not seem to be a change in the way you feel after a couple of weeks.

If adding other Remedies produces no positive effect, you might need to change the mixture completely.

Try using just one of the catalyst Remedies, HOLLY or WILD OAT for a few days, to reveal the underlying thoughts and feelings which need to be addressed. Then add other Remedies as required.

CHAPTER 43

RESCUE REMEDY

DR BACH PUT TOGETHER A combination Remedy for any distressing or emergency situation. He called this powerful combination 'Rescue Remedy'. It may also be called 'emergency essence', or '5 Flower Remedy'. It can be used as a preventative to help deal with impending, past or on-going situations where you could be feeling fear or distress.

It can be used when you are feeling uptight and impatient, when your behaviour feels irrational, when you are ungrounded and find it hard to concentrate, when you have had a shock or distressing news, or when you feel fearful, anxious or panicky about a situation.

It has a calming effect, and can bring you the courage to deal with situations better. If you are anxious about something which is impending, the Rescue Remedy can help you maintain a calm disposition before the situation, during it and afterwards.

The combination Rescue Remedy is easily made up at home, but is also available through many chemists, supermarkets and health shops.

The 5 Remedies in the Rescue Remedy are:

CHERRY PLUM, CLEMATIS, IMPATIENS, ROCK ROSE, STAR OF BETHLEHEM.

Use Rescue Remedy as your first port of call for any situation, or if you are uncertain which Remedies to use.

It is a good Remedy to take for stress, for panic attacks, irrational moods, or a nervous disposition. Stay calm when with someone who is in a state of panic, and keep reassuring them, quietly but firmly. You could use Rescue Remedy for yourself, and for them.

If the client is not conscious, you can put the Rescue Remedy on to their lips and pressure points, as it can help to revive them from an unconscious state. You can then give it to them orally. It is wise to call a doctor or seek medical assistance.

Making your own Rescue Remedy

Partly fill a 30ml dropper bottle with mineral water, and add a teaspoon of brandy or vegetable glycerine (to preserve the Flower essences).

Take 4 drops of each of the 5 individual Remedies from their original stock bottles, and add to the prepared dropper bottle.

Cherry Plum, Clematis, Impatiens, Rock Rose, Star of Bethlehem.

To use Rescue Remedy, take 4 drops directly on the tongue, or add 4 drops to a drink and sip frequently until calm is restored.

If you do not have a dropper bottle to dilute the remedies, add 2 drops of each Remedy from the stock bottles straight into a drink, preferably water, and sip frequently.

If you do not like the taste of the brandy, add Remedies to a hot drink, which will burn off the taste of the brandy. Remedies can be put in any drink. If the person is unconscious the Rescue Remedy can be rubbed onto the lips and the pressure points.

Do not use Rescue Remedy with brandy in it if you have had an addiction or alcohol dependency in the past. You can buy bottles of Rescue Remedy with glycerine in instead. There are also Rescue Remedy pastilles and chewing gum available in shops and on line, which you can use as an alternative to the Rescue Remedy essences.

Simple combination Remedies

Use no more than 7 individual Bach Flower Remedies in any of the combinations.

Choose the individual Remedies whose negative aspects best reflect your needs at the moment.

The Remedies are more effective when you use fewer than 7 Remedies mixed together.

In any extreme emotional state, it is often more effective to use just a single Remedy, or a few Remedies together.

Any Remedies you use, can bring emotions to the surface, so using fewer Remedies is a lot gentler for the benefit of the healing process when someone is extremely distressed.

To make a combination bottle, add 2 drops of each Remedy into a 30ml bottle of mineral water, and a teaspoon of brandy or glycerine. Take 2 drops 4 to 8 times a day, in water, or on the tongue.

At the beginning, it is better to be adventurous and experiment with the Remedy combinations. You will get more clarity when you have shifted into the positive mind-set.

You will then be able to be more discerning about which Remedies would suit you best.

When you have a clearer perspective, try to choose a maximum of 7 Remedies at a time for the best results.

If 1 or 2 Remedies seem more appropriate, work with those Remedies first, then introduce more Remedies when you start to feel better.

Choose which Remedies seem most appropriate to you at the moment from each combination group. Remember taking less Bach Flower Remedies can be more effective.

Anger management - Agrimony, Centaury, Cherry Plum, Holly, Mustard, Pine, Vine, Willow.

Anxiety - Agrimony, Aspen, Centaury, Cherry Plum, Chestnut Bud, Larch, Mimulus, Rock Rose.

Assertiveness - Agrimony, Centaury, Cerato, Chicory, Elm, Larch, Walnut.

Being unable to talk about your feelings - Agrimony, Cherry Plum, Clematis, Impatiens, Mimulus, Rock Rose, Star of Bethlehem.

Being bullied - Agrimony, Aspen, Centaury, Cerato, Crab Apple, Larch, Mimulus.

If you are overwhelmed, or find it hard to choose to change the situation, use Centaury, Elm, Scleranthus, with Gorse, Sweet Chestnut or Wild Rose.

Confidence - Cerato, Chestnut Bud, Clematis, Elm, Gentian, Larch, Rock Rose, White Chestnut.

Feeling angry - If you are feeling particularly angry, start by using the HOLLY Remedy for a few days. Use it until the feelings of anger have subsided considerably, then introduce other Remedies, a few at a time.

Feeling disorientated - If you are feeling frustrated, confused, or uncertain on which path or course of action to take, start by using the WILD OAT Remedy for a few days, until the sense of frustration subsides, and then introduce other Remedies, a few at a time.

Low self-esteem - Cerato, Crab Apple, Gorse, Larch, Mustard, Rock Water, Walnut.

Moving forward - Centaury, Cerato, Chicory, Elm, Honeysuckle, Gentian, Scleranthus, Walnut, Wild Oat.

Premenstrual tension (PMT) - Cherry Plum, Clematis, Crab Apple, Impatiens, Mustard, Rock Water, Scleranthus, Water Violet.

Protection - Crab Apple, Chicory, Red Chestnut, Walnut.

Renewed energy - Agrimony, Elm, Gentian, Oak, Olive, Rock Water, Vervain, White Chestnut, Wild Rose.

Rescue Remedy - Cherry Plum, Clematis, Impatiens, Rock Rose, Star of Bethlehem. Take 4 drops on tongue, or in water frequently.

Restless nights - Agrimony, Aspen, Elm, Gentian, Olive, Rock Water, Vervain, White Chestnut.

Serenity; peace of mind - Agrimony, Aspen, Cerato, Elm, Mimulus, Walnut, Water Violet, White Chestnut.

Starting again - Centaury, Cerato, Chestnut Bud, Elm, Honeysuckle, Hornbeam, Larch, Rock Water, Star of Bethlehem, Walnut.

Trusting that others will be okay - Agrimony, Centaury, Chicory, Gentian, Impatiens, Red Chestnut, Star of Bethlehem, Walnut.

Winter blues - Agrimony, Clematis, Gentian, Gorse, Mustard, Scleranthus, Walnut, Water Violet, Wild Rose.

Catalyst Remedies - Both HOLLY and WILD OAT are catalyst Remedies.

If you think you need more than 7 Remedies, ask yourself, 'Are these feelings coming from being angry, or from feeling uncertainty?'

If the underlying feeling is anger, HOLLY is the Remedy you need.

If the underlying feeling is uncertainty, WILD OAT is the Remedy you need.

If you recognise the HOLLY or WILD OAT state of mind, take just HOLLY, or just WILD OAT for a few days, and when the intense negative feelings start to subside, gradually introduce some other Remedies.

Do not use Remedies with brandy in if you are addicted to alcohol, or have had an addiction or dependency on alcohol in the past.

Use just water, or add glycerine to preserve your combination bottle.

You can buy bottles of Remedies with glycerine in instead. There are also pastilles and chewing gum available in shops and on line, which you can use as an alternative to the Rescue Remedy essence.

CHAPTER 44

WHAT CAN YOU EXPECT WHEN TAKING THE REMEDIES?

THE REMEDIES WORK BY SOOTHING away negative feelings and emotions. Sometimes the emotions have been repressed, and they need to be cleansed from the system to allow you to flourish.

The Remedies work gently and subtly, but each person may have a different response, or reaction, to how their feelings are released, and also how slowly, or swiftly, the Remedies work for them.

Unexpected feelings may be stirred up. This is a good sign, and is part of the natural healing process. The feelings and emotions are coming to the surface to be released. You may feel more weary or tired for a while. Try to give yourself some time and space to accommodate this.

You may also experience an upset stomach, need to go to the toilet more often, or spots or blemishes may appear. These feelings and symptoms are all temporary, and a necessary part of your body releasing old emotions you have been holding on to.

Drink plenty of water to detox your body, and be gentle on yourself.

This process takes time. Be patient with yourself, and the process. The Remedies are gently working through layers of old emotions, to allow you to experience more contented and uplifting feelings.

It may take time

For some people the Remedies can work very quickly, and you will start to see an improvement in your feelings within a few days. For other people it can take more time.

Each person will have their own unique way of working through their emotions, and the time it takes to heal will also be unique to you.

Healing your emotions with the Bach Flower Remedies is a subtle and gentle form of healing. Each person heals in exactly the right way for them. Please do not compare your healing journey to anyone else.

Quite often people around you may start to notice the changes in you, before you notice them for yourself. As we said, the changes are very subtle, and this is why I encourage you to keep a healing journal to help you recognise the changes you are going through, and the progress you are making.

You may need several bottles of Remedies to achieve complete harmony. Be patient with yourself and the healing process, keep using your affirmations, and always focus on the positive outcome of each Remedy. Keep in touch with your healing journal.

Some individuals will start on a process of wanting to change, and then stop. If so, this is not a reflection on the Remedies. Rather, it is their choice, and could simply mean that they have reached an emotional level of well-being where they are comfortable.

This is a process of great patience, and every individual will change and grow at a different rate. So never compare yourself with others as you progress on your journey. Our paths, and our processes of recovery, are as varied as we are.

The Remedies will help get you back into a positive state, and bring things back into perspective. It is often easier to talk about situations once you are in a positive state. Never underestimate the power of finding someone you trust to support you through your healing. Someone who will listen to you, and genuinely encourage you.

If you are helping someone else on a healing journey with the Bach Flower Remedies, keep encouraging them to talk about their fears and problems. Give sincere encouragement and positive reassurance.

Finally, use deep-breathing exercises and affirmations, and drink more water to help with your healing process.

Contact Dawn Chrystal if you are not getting, or noticing, any changes in your emotions or you are uncertain of which Remedies to take. She can help you get a better understanding of which Remedies will help you to work through your personal circumstances.

The Bach Flower Remedies can help you bring your life back into a state of balance and harmony, so you can gain a greater understanding of yourself, and a new positive outlook on your life. From this place you will be able to find your inner strengths and achieve your real potential.

The Bach Flower Remedies are a natural way of healing your emotions. By healing your emotions, you can soothe and heal the confusion in your mind, which will bring you more clarity and peace of mind. With this renewed peace and calm will come a greater sense of who you really are, and how you can turn your life around.

Getting started

Each bottle of Bach Flower Remedy essence is a different state of mind or emotion. Start by reading through each section of the Remedies, to see if you can recognise how you are feeling right now.

Choose which Remedies you feel you need at the moment, and use them consistently for a few days, until you feel more calmness and clarity. You may need to take the Remedies you choose for a few weeks to get the most benefit from them.

The Remedies will help to shift your emotions to a place where you can get a positive new perspective on what is happening in your life, and how you can help yourself.

When you have more clarity, you may want to look at the Remedies again, to see which Remedies will help you in this new space you are in. The first bottle can peel away a layer of emotions to reveal some of the underlying feelings you are holding.

You can keep repeating this process until your emotions feel balanced, and you feel totally empowered.

You can always revisit the Remedies whenever you are going through new challenges in your life, and work through a similar process of healing with your Remedies.

The aim of this book is to help you recognise how you can turn any situation around, and gain an understanding of who you really are.

The Remedies will help you gain the potential to recognise the different emotions you are experiencing, and how you can turn them around.

Whatever you are going through right now, or if you have lost your way, you are about to embark on a beautiful new journey of self-discovery. Your potential is unlimited when you can understand yourself. The Bach Remedies will help you maintain this sense of knowing who you are, through any challenges life might present to you.

With this emotional intelligence, you will then be able to move ahead with positive expectations for yourself.

In time, as you start to feel emotionally stronger, and have a greater understanding of yourself, you will be more able to communicate to others about how you feel.

You will also gain the strength and composure to talk about how people have affected, or maybe even hurt you. This will bring a whole new healing on many levels for both of you. Feeling empowered, and gentle honesty, can help to heal many wounds and misunderstandings.

Getting it off your chest

If you feel anxious about speaking to someone, take some time beforehand to do your deep slow breaths. Think about, and rehearse what you would like to say in your mind, and write it down. And when the time is right to speak, take deep slow breaths again, and let the words calmly and assertively flow.

Remember, when you speak to them, you are not accusing them of anything. You are merely letting them know how they made you feel. Ask them to give you the time and space to finish what you have to say.

When you have finished speaking, thank them for listening, and do not expect an immediate response. It may take them time to process what you have said.

Be proud of yourself for what you have accomplished. They may over-react to what you have said. Do not take it personally. Nobody really wants to hear that they may have been in the wrong.

Stand your ground, and maintain your composure.

Do the Withinercise meditation for a few days beforehand. Imagine and create the scene, and visualise a good outcome. This will help your mind prepare you to expect the very best.

Always remember that things can get better, no matter where you are right now. And once you find your true self, and embrace the wonderful person you are, you will never lose sight of who you truly are. Never let anyone, or anything, take that away from you.

You are a truly unique and precious person on this earth, and your potential is unlimited when you are true to yourself.

In time you will be able to recognise the emotions and states of mind in other people around you. You will be able to help them look at their situations and challenges with optimism and faith, to enable them to move forward with a greater strength and courage.

It is a beautiful circle which begins with you understanding yourself, and why you act the way you do.

Where does your confusion come from?

Many of us walk around in a state of confusion, and wonder why we are so confused. Sometimes, it is hard to put your finger on what is the matter. It is often hard to describe how you really feel.

Dr Edward Bach was intrigued by the way different people react to different situations. He found the answer in nature's natural healing powers.

He spent the latter part of his life exploring the beautiful healing gifts of Mother Nature. Through his dedication, and his passion for helping people, we are now fortunate to be able to share and enjoy the amazing gifts he discovered for us. Specifically, he found that various plants and trees had different healing properties.

The Bach Flower Remedies Dr Bach created from trees, plants and flowing springs are a natural and gentle way of healing your emotional states.

Dr Bach recognised too, that there is often a connection between the way we feel emotionally, and the state of our health. To expand this concept for you, every thought you have becomes an emotion within you. If this emotion is negative, it can sit within a part of your body. If it is left unaddressed, it can become a state of dis-ease within your body.

This can then start to affect you on a deeper level. Every thought you have stimulates your brain to produce a chemical, to enable, or help you, to deal with the situation you are facing.

These chemicals are an essential part of your existence. They stimulate your neurological responses, and allow your body to function normally. But when these emotions are negative – stress and anxiety, for example – your body releases cortisol and adrenaline.

A constant flow of cortisol and adrenaline can be detrimental and harmful to your body, and can often result in a breakdown of your health and well-being.

Just imagine that each thought you have during the day adds to the multiple thoughts and feelings you are already experiencing.

How supportive are your words and thoughts?

Are you encouraging your body to produce the soothing chemicals to support you, or are you producing toxic chemicals with the thoughts and words you are using?

Dr Bach said, 'When there is a void between your thinking, and your spiritual self, that is often where dis-ease occurs within our physical body.' He recognised that if we can heal our emotional state of mind, we can often heal physical ailments as well.

When the calm returns, you can usually get a clearer perspective, enabling you to deal with the situation with greater strength, clarity and conviction.

Dr Bach believed that the Remedies he had discovered should be accessible to all. Rescue Remedy and other single Remedies are readily available in chemists, supermarkets, health food stores and online. If ever you find yourself in a confused state of mind, start by seeking out a bottle of Rescue Remedy, and allow it to ease some of your discomfort.

If you would like more guidance on which Remedies to use, please contact Dawn Chrystal, who can advise you, or prepare a mixture of Remedies for you.

The beauty of the Bach Flower Remedies is that they are gentle and natural. Even if you don't understand how they work, they can take effect on your behalf, gently shifting you into a calmer and more uplifted state. They work very subtly on your levels of tension and stress until you feel a sense of peace and clarity. With that peace and clarity comes renewed hope and faith.

The Remedies are not addictive, and you cannot overdose on them.

They can be taken by anyone, at any age. Whatever your circumstances are, and at whatever stage of life, the Bach Flower Remedies can bring you renewed hope and endurance, and a new perspective on your life.

They work well alongside most medications, but please be aware that they are not a replacement for any medication you may be taking. A doctor's advice should be taken before altering any medication.

Many therapists recommend the Bach Flower Remedies alongside their therapies, but there are times when they are sufficient on their own. Each therapy can bring up old emotions, so one treatment at a time is sometimes more beneficial.

Often, you might not recognise where the conflict within you comes from, and that, in itself can cause more stress and confusion. Sometimes the conflict within is so deep you cannot identify how you really feel, and the confusion you feel can make you tired and disorientated. you can lose your sense of self, your motivation, your energy and your sense of worth.

The Bach Flower Remedies help shift you through these heavy emotions, until you feel a sense of clarity and peace within you.

The negative emotions can take time to shift and release but, through persistent work with the Remedies, most states of mind can be altered and healed. Then, when you have healed your state of mind, you will be in a better place to understand how you feel. A course of Bach Flower Remedies can bring a feeling of well-being, renewed self-belief and inner conviction.

Dr Bach recognised that by taking the Flower essences he felt emotionally stronger, and had a clearer perspective on situations. It is through this insight, and his dedication to help others find that emotional strength, that the Bach Flower Remedies were created.

His legacy for us all is to be able to heal our emotions, and find the peace within, so we can move forward with renewed hope and faith.

Opening up

Do you find it hard to get in touch with your feelings?
Do you struggle to speak about how you are feeling?
Use AGRIMONY and STAR OF BETHLEHEM, to help you start to get in touch with your feelings, and to enable you to speak about how you feel.

CHAPTER 45

WHY USE THE BACH FLOWER REMEDIES?

THE HIDDEN GIFTS FOUND IN the Flower Remedies, were discovered by Dr Edward Bach (1886–1936). From the outset he kept the Remedies simple, so they could be understood, and used by anyone, to address the emotional problems they are experiencing. Dr Bach's philosophy was simple and profound, based on the innate perfection and spiritual nature of human beings. He wrote:

> *'Disease is often the result of a conflict between our spiritual and mortal selves.*
> *'Health and happiness result from being in harmony with our own nature, and doing the work for which we are individually suited.'*

'It means doing the housekeeping, painting, farming, acting or serving our fellow man in shops and houses. And this work, whatever it may be, if we love it above all else, is the work we are here to do in this world, and in which alone we can be our true selves.

'Disease is the reaction to interferences. This is temporary failure and unhappiness, and this occurs when we allow others to interfere with our purpose in life, and implant in our minds doubt, fear or indifference. 'Being so far from our true selves is what causes imbalances, distressed states and often resulting ailments and illnesses.

'If we follow our heart, and do not allow ourselves to be influenced by others, we would have no need for the Bach Flower Remedies. It is when your life starts to get out of balance, and you start to feel out of sorts, that the Flower Remedies can help get you back to your true self.'

The Bach Flower Remedies are unobtrusive and very subtle, and are a very gentle way of healing negative states of mind. They give you courage and strength to have a positive outlook on life, bringing you a feeling of well-being and better health.

These natural essences have been tried and tested around the world, with no side effects, fear of overdosing or addiction. They can be given to anyone, at any age. They can also be used for animals and plants.

They will complement any other complementary therapies being used, and can help to speed recovery.

Dr Edward Bach

In 1928 Dr Edward Bach began work on creating his own natural Remedies made from plants. In 1930, at the age of forty-three, he was so inspired by the natural healing powers he was discovering, he gave up his lucrative Harley Street practice and left London, to focus entirely on his passion to discover healing properties amongst nature's plants. He initially moved to Wales, where he discovered three more flowers with emotional healing properties, and perfected the Sun Method of potentisation to create the Remedy essences. In the spring and summer, he would gather plants and samples. Through the winter time, he would live in Cromer in Norfolk, England, where he would work more with his natural healing essences, helping people who needed emotional healing.

In 1930 he moved with his assistant, Nora Weeks, into a house called Mount Vernon in Brightwell-cum-Sotwell, in Oxfordshire. He found his final plants that he needed to complete his set of Remedies in the fields and lanes. By this time, his mind and body were so in tune with his holistic work, he would suffer the negative state that he needed to cure, and then search out the plant or flower that would help him to feel emotionally stronger. In this way, through much personal suffering and sacrifice, he was able to complete his life's work.

In 1934, he had completed his set of 38 healing Bach Flower Remedy essences we still use today. Dr Bach was convinced that his sense of purpose was what saved him. He had important work to do. He believed, that using the Flower Remedies to heal his emotions, helped his body to cope with the cancer for almost twenty years. A year after he announced that his search for Remedies was complete, Dr Bach passed away peacefully on the evening of 27th November, 1936. Though he was only fifty years old, he had outlived his doctor's prognosis by nearly twenty years. He left us with a legacy of several lifetimes' experience, and a natural healing system of medicine that is used all over the world.

Dr Bach had cancer when he died, but in fact he died of exhaustion, not of the disease itself. As he was only fifty when he died, people often ask why he wasn't able to cure himself. What many do not recognise, is that in 1917 he was first diagnosed with cancer and given just three months to live. From that time, until his death in 1936, he was working on healing his emotions, and so curing himself, every day for nineteen years. This enabled him to complete his work, the wonderful legacy of the Bach Flower Remedies.

The Bach Flower Remedies bring relief

You should start taking the Remedies, with the expectation that you will get some relief from your feelings and thought patterns which are out of balance. The Remedies may temporarily bring your old emotions to the surface, which can make your emotions seem more intense for a while. This is a natural part of the healing process, and is a positive sign that your body is releasing the negative emotions it has been holding: the Bach Flower

Remedies are working you through the healing process. As you release these emotions you are healing yourself. This 'clearing time' soon passes.

As you continue to take the Remedies, you will get a feeling of relief, and a sense of calmness. Balanced emotions and well-being will follow. Drinking plenty of water will help your body's clearing process. This healing process should be emphasised before treatment begins. The heightened emotions are a temporary state, and calm will follow.

If you are giving someone else some Remedies, it may be worth putting some after-care advice in writing, and giving it to them as they leave, so the person has something to remind them of what they need to do for themselves, and what they can expect from taking the Remedies.

For some people, the Bach Flower Remedies work quickly, but for others it can take more time. Be patient with the pace of your healing journey. Every person is unique, and has had a different journey with their own experiences. The more consistently you take your Remedies the more effective they will be. Be patient and work persistently with the Remedies, and you will achieve your ultimate peace and calm within. The Remedies normally work very quickly for children and animals.

Most states of mind can be altered and healed, but it is important never to claim to fix or cure someone with the Bach Flower Remedies. The body will take the healing from the Remedies if it is meant to. The 38 Bach Flower Remedies can help with every possible personality, attitude and negative state of mind. Negative states of mind which are left unhealed, can become physical ailments. The Remedies will work for those who are ready, and willing to make changes to improve their quality of well-being and their life.

It is often not the illness that is the problem, but the way we deal with it. Dr Bach found that different Personality Types reacted differently to situations, and it was being intrigued by this, that led him to search for answers among flowers and plants. His discoveries became the Flower Remedy essences we use today. It should be emphasised that if someone is not ready, or willing, to make changes in their thinking, their behaviour, or the way they have become, the Bach Flower Remedies will have little, or no impact on them and the way they are.

CHAPTER 46

DIFFERENT PERSONALITY TYPES

WHEN DR BACH WAS WORKING as a physician, he was intrigued by the way different Personality Types reacted to each type of drug they were prescribed. He recognised that people with differing personality traits were being given the same drugs, and yet the healing results were so varied.

For some people, the drugs were effective; for others, they resulted in varying degrees of healing and, for some Personality Types, they had no impact at all.

From his research, Dr Bach recognised twelve different types of people – or Personality Types – and discovered that there is a specific Remedy for each one.

These were the first twelve of the 38 Bach Flower Remedy essences.

The twelve Personality Types, or the '12 healers', are

AGRIMONY	*CENTAURY*	*CERATO*
CHICORY	*CLEMATIS*	*GENTIAN*
IMPATIENS	*MIMULUS*	*ROCK ROSE*
SCLERANTHUS	*VERVAIN*	*WATER VIOLET*

The 12 healers are fundamental states of being

As each personality type will react differently to situations, it is not possible to assume, or to generalise, how people will react to what is happening in their lives. So there can be no general guide to which Remedies need to be given.

Dr Bach realised that each personality needs to be treated appropriately for their personality type.

Having an understanding of your personality type, and an understanding of each personality type of the people around you, can help to build good strong foundations within any situation, without any detrimental reactions.

If you can recognise the different Personality Types of people in your life, it can help you to understand why they react the way they do. It can also help you to understand what would be the best way to deal with each person in situations that arise.

This can be particularly useful when dealing with your family, or work situations. What you think or feel, or the way you react, can be very different to the ways that others might deal with a situation.

The 12 healers

In the following panel is a brief description of some traits of each personality type. See if you can recognise the different personalities within your family.

AGRIMONY — *Do not like confrontation. Will shy away from loud people and arguments. Tend to be peacemakers.*

CENTAURY — *Like to help others. Put others' needs before their own. Don't like to say no. Can become doormats. Easily influenced. Lack of boundaries.*

CERATO — *Need others' approval. Don't trust their own intuition. May have lost their sense of identity. Always asking questions.*

CHICORY — *Possessive love. Can use emotional blackmail to get their way. Can demand constant attention. Can be very clingy to family and friends. Find it hard to let go of people.*

CLEMATIS — *Absent-minded, dreamy, find it hard it concentrate. May seem drowsy, can doze off at any time, listless. Think of unrealistic solutions to escape problems.*

GENTIAN — *Pessimistic. Easily discouraged. Depressed from a known cause. Persistent doubters. Very discouraging of others' ideas.*

IMPATIENS — *Impatient. Irritable. Can be tactless when with slower people. Always rushing. Nervous tension. Can suffer with headaches and heartburn.*

MIMULUS — *Shy, fearful, timid. Can have secret fears. Get tongue-tied. Often have a nervous giggle to cover their fears.*

ROCK ROSE — *Sensitive, delicate people. Nervous constitution. Can suffer with panic attacks or feelings of terror. Heart palpitations.*

SCLERANTHUS — *Indecisive, changeable. Can suffer with mood and energy swings. Often clumsy, so make mistakes.*

VERVAIN — *Overenthusiastic, try too hard. Hyperactivity. Can be highly strung. Can be fanatical and run a thing to death. Don't know when to pull back and when to push ahead.*

WATER VIOLET — *Proud, aloof. Often want to be alone, but can feel isolated. Very quiet. Speak gently. Very independent. Need space. Don't like interference.*

Every personality has its own way of reacting or responding

There is such variation in the way different Personality Types react to situations, it is no wonder there is often confusion within relationships, especially with those closest to us. We often expect those around us to respond to a situation in the same way we do.

Just assume for a moment, that you have three different Personality Types living within your home. There will be three different perspectives on every situation, and it might be very difficult to come to an amicable agreement over some things.

If you have an understanding of the types of personalities you are living with, and the way they can respond or react, it can make it a lot easier to maintain harmony within your home. When you come to an understanding of the people you are closest to, you can then start to work in the same way with others too.

It is amazing how much easier it is to flow through life, when you have a greater understanding of the people you are associating with. Later, we will talk more about the positive aspects of each personality trait but, for the time being, start to observe the people in your life.

If you are not sure which personality type you are, you could learn how to work with a pendulum to get the clarity you need.

Dr Bach thought that each person belongs to one main personality type, but it is often difficult to determine which one it is. When we are going through different situations we can react in ways that are influenced by other aspects of our lives, and by the emotions we are going through.

Quite often what we perceive as our personality, may have become altered by years of conditioning, or by negative experiences we have been through.

It may be hard to pinpoint what your true personality really is, but the more you work with the Bach Flower Remedies, the easier it will be to determine your personality type. Understanding this can help you understand why you react the way you do. This understanding can also help you to focus on what your positive personality traits are as well. It is important throughout your journey to look at your positive traits, so you can maintain the focus on your true potential.

The Remedies help to move you from the negative aspects of your personality, to the more positive ones. The more you use Bach Remedies, the easier it is to maintain those positive traits.

The Remedies help you maintain the positive characteristics which are true to you. When you are in a positive state, it is easier to deal with whatever comes your way. When you are working within your real personality, you feel more at peace with yourself, and all that is happening around you.

If you are new to the Bach Flower Remedies, start by working on yourself frequently. Having a greater understanding of yourself makes life a lot simpler, and brings a clearer perspective to what is happening around you.

Keep a journal of the emotions you go through, which Remedies you are using, and what you are observing about yourself. This is the easiest way to start understanding the benefits of the Remedies, and how they will work for you.

Then, take it a stage further, and make observations of those around you. This will help you to gain a greater understanding of other people, and how the Bach Remedies could help them, to make life more harmonious for you all.

It is a time of great transformation in your life.
Allow yourself to grow through these transformations.
It will bring you great rewards.
Keep focused on your growth.
Take time out, and remind yourself that challenges are opportunities to grow,
and those people who test you, are your best teachers.

'Working with Dawn and the Bach Flower Remedies
has helped to change my life for the better.
Dawn's knowledge of the Remedies and intuitive ability are outstanding,
as well as her gentle, grounded attitude, and infinite patience.
I highly recommend the Remedies for depression,
anxiety, and other emotional mood conditions.'

- Rachel Miller

CHAPTER 47

OTHER STATES OF MIND

DR BACH'S NEXT DISCOVERY WAS 26 other states of mind, which characterise the way we become, due to things that have been going on for a while.

Because of this, we may consciously, or unconsciously, have altered our true identity, possibly as a result of big changes, traumas, or challenges in our lives.

The 26 states of mind are made up of the '7 helpers', which are our first fundamental states of mind, and the '19 other helpers', which are our second fundamental states of mind.

Our second fundamental states of mind, often comes as a result of issues that have been long-standing, causing still deeper-rooted problems.

These states are often as a result of lots of bumps and knocks (many of them come into the despondency and despair group). These are states of mind which can be altered, but can take more time.

The 7 helpers

Gorse
Heather
Oak
Olive

Rock Water
Vine
Wild Oat

The 19 other helpers

Aspen
Beech
Cherry Plum
Chestnut Bud
Crab Apple
Elm
Holly
Honeysuckle
Hornbeam
Larch
Mustard
Pine
Red Chestnut
Star of Bethlehem
Sweet Chestnut
Walnut
White Chestnut
Wild Rose
Willow

THE 7 EMOTIONAL GROUPS OF FLOWER REMEDIES

Dr Bach divided the Remedies into seven emotional groups, which represent fundamental conflicts that prevent us from being true to ourselves:

Despondency and despair
Fear
Insufficient interest in present circumstances
Loneliness
Over-care for the welfare of others
Over-sensitive to ideas and influences
Uncertainty

Which Remedies are in the 7 emotional groups?

The Remedies marked with an asterisk (*) are the 12 healers, the Personality Types.

Despondency and despair
Crab Apple	Elm	Larch
Oak	Pine	Star of Bethlehem
Sweet Chestnut	Willow	

Fear
Aspen	Cherry Plum	Mimulus*
Red Chestnut	Rock Rose*	

Insufficient interest in present circumstances
Chestnut Bud	Clematis*	Honeysuckle
Mustard	Olive	White Chestnut
Wild Rose		

Loneliness
Heather	Impatiens*	Water Violet*

Over-care for the welfare of others
Beech	Chicory*	Rock Water
Vervain*	Vine	

Over-sensitive to ideas and influences
Agrimony*	Centaury*	Holly
Walnut		

Uncertainty
Cerato*	Gentian*	Gorse
Hornbeam	Scleranthus*	Wild Oat

CHAPTER 48

WORKING WITH A PENDULUM TO CHOOSE YOUR BACH FLOWER REMEDIES

AT THE BEGINNING OF YOUR journey, you may find it difficult to choose Remedies for yourself. You could use a pendulum to help you.

A pendulum is an object – e.g. a ring, or a crystal – on a chain or piece of cotton, which can be used to get clarity when you are learning to trust your intuition. You may need to experiment with different pendulums to find one which is right for you.

You may prefer to read through your book, and choose the most appropriate Remedies for today, or you could intuitively choose which Remedies you could work with at the moment. Your intuition is usually right, but it may take time to trust in your intuition.

Or you may prefer to work with a pendulum.

Working with a pendulum is often called dowsing, a technique that can give you visual confirmation of what your intuition is telling you. You can use the pendulum when you are unsure which Remedy to choose for yourself.

To find out which Remedies would help you, hold the pendulum over each Remedy in turn, and ask whether it will help you. Write down the names of the Remedies you choose.

If you are facing a particular challenge, you can focus on the situation, and ask which of the Remedies would help you with this situation. If you have something impending, such as a dentist appointment or an interview, you can ask which Remedies will help with this. You could also use your pendulum to get clarity around a situation, or for choosing Remedies within consultations. There are endless ways you can use your pendulum.

Working with a pendulum will help you to build trust in your intuition. Don't be discouraged if it does not work to begin with. Put the pendulum down, and return to it later. However, keep practising and it will get easier. The pendulum will support you with any work you are doing.

The Remedies you choose with your pendulum may be deeper emotions that you do not yet recognise.

If a Remedy description does not feel comfortable to you, or you cannot recognise the negative emotional state, do not use that Remedy at this present time.

You can come back to this Remedy at a later date when you are ready to address those issues and emotional states.

Using a pendulum

Relax your shoulders, bend your arm, and check you are comfortable, as you hold your pendulum up in front of you.

You can support your arm on a table, or the arm of a chair.

Hold the chain between the tip of your first finger and your thumb, so that the crystal can swing freely.

Relax your shoulders, and check your arm is comfortable.

If your arm is unsteady, you may want to support your elbow on a chair, or on a table.

Let the pendulum swing freely on the chain.

Ask your pendulum to show you a 'yes'. The pendulum will start to move in a certain direction.

It may swing from left to right, backwards and forwards, or it may turn in a circle. This is your 'yes'.

Ask your pendulum to show you a 'no'. The pendulum will start to move in a different direction.

It may swing from side to side, or turn in a circle. This is your 'no'.

The 'yes' direction, should be different from the 'no' direction.

Hold the pendulum, and ask it a direct question, that you know the answer to, such as 'Is my name Dawn?'

Watch which way the pendulum goes: this gives you clarity.

If your pendulum does not seem to be moving, it may be that your question is not specific enough. Try a different more specific question.

If you cannot get an answer, start again. Refocus yourself, by taking some slow deep breaths, until you feel calmer, then try working with your pendulum again.

This can be a very simple way of getting effective answers. The more you practise this method, the more clarity you will get.

If you don't have the essences of the Bach Flower Remedies:

Ask your pendulum, 'Are my Remedies in the Despondency group?' or, 'Are they in the Fear group?'

When the answer is 'yes', turn to the right emotional group section in your book.

Using your pendulum, work through each Remedy page in turn, asking, 'Will this Remedy help me at the moment?' or, 'Will this Remedy help me with (add your situation)?'

Read about the Remedies you have chosen. Can you recognise each negative description as the way you are feeling today?

Read about the positive potential of taking each Remedy – the potential you can receive from using that Remedy.

Then move on to the next Remedy, and repeat the procedure.

If you have less than 7 Remedies, you can look in the other Emotional Remedy sections for further Remedies to use.

If you have the bottles of Bach Remedy essences:

Hold your pendulum over each bottle in turn, and ask a direct question, such as 'Will this Remedy help me at the moment? Or, 'Will this Remedy help me with my patience?' Or 'Will this Remedy help me with my confidence (grief, exams, house move)?' Ask a direct question, and it will give you an appropriate answer. Then mix the Remedies you have chosen in a combination bottle.

How many Remedies should you take, and how much?

When you have chosen your 7 Remedies for today, you can use your pendulum to ask how many times a day you need to take the drops. The dosage is usually 2 drops, 4 to 8 times a day, but this may need to be adjusted, depending on your circumstances and state of mind today. The amount of Remedies you need may vary as well. You cannot overdose on them, and taking them less frequently is sometimes more effective.

The amount of Remedies you need may vary each time you use them.

When you are extremely emotional or stressed, using fewer Remedies can soothe your emotions more gently, and more effectively.

If you recognise 1 or 2 Remedies which are extremely out of balance, start with using just those Remedies, and then add other Remedies after a few days. You can also start with just 1 Remedy, if the negative state of that remedy matches the way you feel at the moment.

Add 2 drops of each chosen Remedy to your 30ml bottle, and take the combination of Remedies on your tongue or in water, 2 drops 4 to 8 times a day. The amount of times you take your combination Remedy may vary as well, depending on your circumstances and your state of mind.

If you are feeling extremely stressed or confused, take the Remedies less frequently throughout the day, maybe just 2 or 3 times a day, would be appropriate at the beginning, and then increase to 4 times a day when your emotions start to calm down.

Taking fewer Remedies, less frequently, can be gentler on your emotions, and more effective. When you take the Remedies, they will enable you to release your old feelings, empower you to shift gently through the changes, and help you maintain the new states of mind.

If you are taking medication, this can impact on the way the Remedies work for you. Their effectiveness may take longer. Speak to your doctor when you are introducing anything new. Your mental and emotional state needs to be addressed from all angles, and a doctor can advise you with this.

If you are unsure, please contact Dawn at dawnchrystal62@gmail.com so she can advise you, and help you get the best results.

If you would like some Remedies made up for you, Dawn can make a personal combination for you. These will be sent by post, and are normally with you within seven working days. The first 2 consultations will be half price, plus post and packing. Your consultations will include your own personal mixture of Remedies. Your combination bottle of Remedies will be with you within 7 days.

If you do not have the essences of the Remedies, it is still possible to help yourself, by reading your *Negative States of Mind* in this book, and starting to recognise when you are holding or using negative thoughts and feelings in your life.

Then, keep referring to the *Positive States of Mind* for your chosen Remedies, and set an intention to turn around your way of thinking. You can use the affirmations to help you work through the process of transformation.

This way may take longer, but can also be very effective. You can also use the Bach Flower Remedy healing cards. Keep a record of your Remedies, intentions and achievements. Your body will start to produce the uplifting chemicals which will lift up your spirits to work through the changes. The more consistently you use your Remedies or cards, the more effective they will be.

We now look at the 7 emotional groups of the Remedies, and a more in-depth look at each Remedy, to help you get a greater understanding of how the Remedy can help you.

CHAPTER 49

THE EMOTIONAL GROUPS OF THE BACH FLOWER REMEDIES

YOU MAY NOT RECOGNISE EVERY negative aspect of the Remedy you choose. If you can resonate with some of the negative emotions of your chosen remedy, this is the one for you today.

The following list of Remedies explains the state of mind, behaviour or emotions you will experience when you are in the negative state of mind, i.e. when you are emotionally out of balance or unhappy, and how the Remedy will help to lead you to a more positive state of mind. Most of us can generally identify how we feel – e.g. fearful or lonely – so the Remedies are grouped in their emotional categories:

Despondency and despair, Fear, Insufficient interest in present circumstances, Loneliness, Over-care for the welfare of others, Over-sensitive to ideas and influences, Uncertainty.

Within each category the Remedies are in alphabetical order, and the page for each Remedy includes the *negative* states of mind, the *positive* potential from taking the remedy, and some *affirmations*.

- **Negative.** *The emotions and States of Mind that are causing you to struggle or feel out of balance.*

+ **Positive.** *The benefits that can result from using the Remedy. The Remedies can help you to move on from the negative aspects of your personality to the* *more positive ones. These positive states of mind are your true potential way of being.*

Affirmation. *One or more simple statements to repeat to yourself, either with the Remedy essences, or when the essences are not available.*

So if you are feeling lonely, go to the 'Loneliness' section. Read the negative States of Mind for each Remedy, and choose which Remedy (or Remedies) most matches your emotions at this moment. Then read the positive States of Mind for your chosen Remedy, so you can focus on the outcome expected.

Although the Bach Flower Remedy essences can help you work gently through the healing process by themselves, using the appropriate affirmation alongside the Remedies will help you move more effectively through the healing process. Work with the first Remedies you choose.

If you feel no shift in your emotions after a few days, try another Remedy in that section. You can use up to 7 Remedies mixed together. You may also need Remedies from other groups to complement and support your initial feelings.

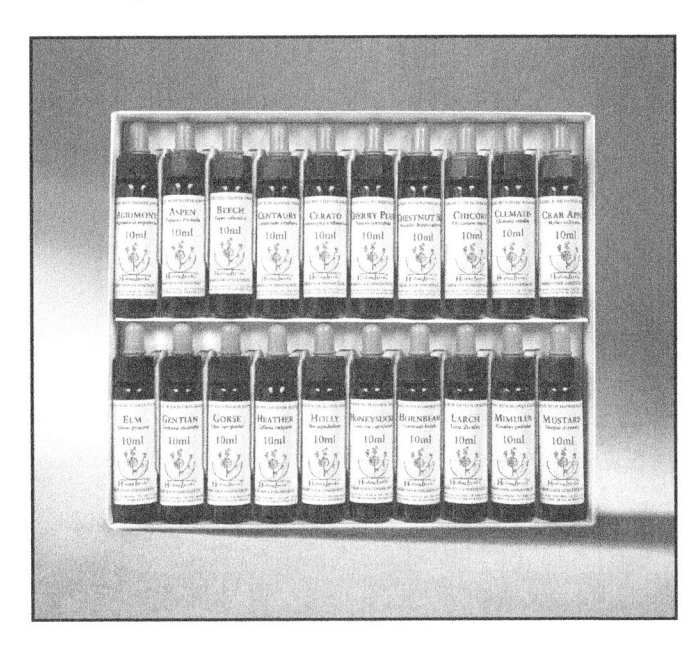

The Bach Flower Remedies
Dr. Bach's natural healing gift to us all

CRAB APPLE   *Despondency and despair*

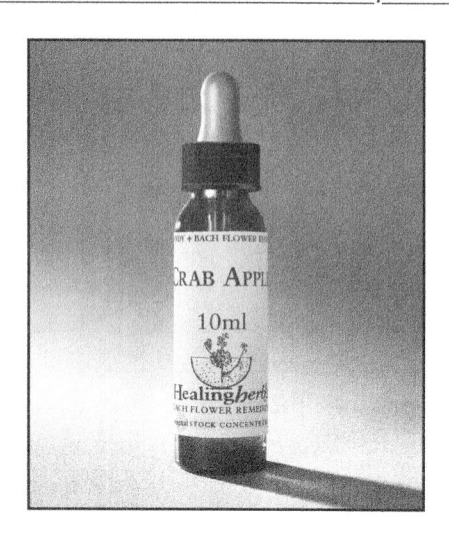

Negative

Self-dislike, even self-hatred. Not being good enough.
Can feel not to good, with comparison to others.
Feeling ashamed of physical condition and appearance, often focusing on one negative thing.
Can have bad breath or smelly feet, be prone to acne.
Can suffer with mastitis.
Being obsessed with skin complaints, and unable to be consoled.
Feeling unclean physically, emotionally or mentally.
Constant washing during menstrual periods.
Feeling compelled to clean your teeth.
Being unable to stand the mess when being sick.
Disliking yourself when ill, and despondent if treatment fails (try GENTIAN too).
Disliking the way you act, or have acted.
Obsessive behaviours, e.g. cleaning, spending, eating, dieting (add CHESTNUT BUD).
Being obsessed with small things; fussy, 'bee in bonnet' behaviour.
Can be obsessed with pornography.

Positive

CRAB APPLE helps dispel self-dislike or self- bringing self-acceptance and love.

It is the 'cleansing Remedy' for mind and body (for internal and external use), and assists against pollution and contamination.

It helps you control your thoughts, recognise difficulties, and see things in perspective.

CRAB APPLE can help you be less obsessed with housework, and be less compelled to overspend, eat, exercise or diet.

It can help with spots and acne, mastitis, mouth ulcers and bad breath, and makes you more accepting of yourself during menstrual periods.

CRAB APPLE helps with congestion. With Rescue Remedy it can help with constipation, and with CHESTNUT BUD and GENTIAN it can help with stopping smoking and other addictive habits.

Be aware that complaints can become worse before they improve, but bringing problems to the surface is an important part of the healing process. CRAB APPLE can help you be more accepting of yourself when illness is within your body.

With victims of any type of abuse, CRAB APPLE can help with the person's re-acceptance of themselves, and with intimate relationships.

Victims often suppress the problem, not realising how the abuse has affected them; adding STAR OF BETHLEHEM can help.

CRAB APPLE helps victims feel clean, acceptable and whole again and, together with PINE, it can help them realise the abuse was not their fault, and relieve them of feelings of guilt, shame and not feeling clean.

Affirmation

I have no need to compare myself to anyone else.
I am a loving, unique and special person.
I am enough.
I joyfully accept myself for who I am.

Advice

CRAB APPLE can be a good Remedy for people who have been abused, physically, mentally or emotionally, or raped. They can find physical relationships hard to form because of dislike of physical contact; disliking themselves and any form of intimacy, and they often put up invisible barriers to avoid contact. A combination of AGRIMONY, CRAB APPLE, MIMULUS, PINE, STAR OF BETHLEHEM will help.

ELM

Despondency and despair

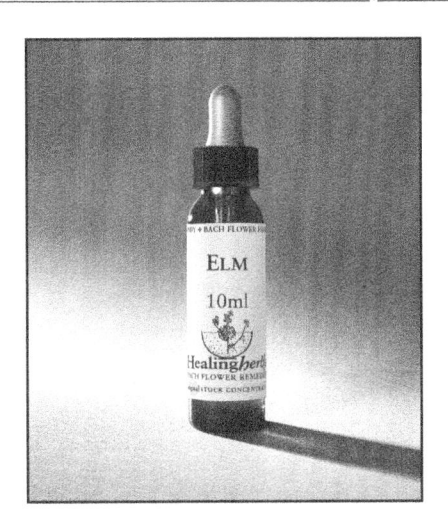

Negative

Often taking on too much.
Being temporarily overwhelmed by responsibility.
Occasional feelings of inadequacy, causing lack of confidence.
People in the negative ELM state of mind are usually very intuitive; they have important roles and are good at what they do.
They often hold positions of responsibility, where they feel they are indispensable.
But everything can become too much to deal with, bringing a feeling that things have got out of proportion and become like a mountain in front of you.
Feeling tired and unable to cope.
Seeing everything as a major challenge.
Consequential despondency and exhaustion with thoughts of being unequal to the job, and where even momentary doubting of abilities causes weakness and debility.
Key words: 'I can't cope', 'It's all too much'.
Can feel overwhelmed by your own emotions too.

Positive

ELM enables you to cope with responsibility.
It helps keep thoughts in perspective, giving the strength to perform, and renewed energy to deal with things, one piece at a time.
It can help you feel more capable, efficient and intuitive, and can bring greater awareness of responsibilities.
It brings confidence and self-assurance.
Emotions feel calmer and clarity comes back.
Able to keep their emotions in perspective.
When the emotions are calm, can deal with whatever comes along, one step at a time.

Affirmation

I am joyfully in total control of my life.
I happily keep things in perspective.
I calmly take on what I know I can handle.
I can deal with anything that comes my way.
I am confidently dealing with things one step at a time.
I can cope. I am happily dealing with one thing at a time.

Advice

ELM can often help people doing work which is their calling in life, and who hope to do something which is important – for the benefit of humanity, for example.
They sometimes hold key positions in society or industry: physicians, clergy, teachers etc.
They can be teachers, leaders, decision-makers and people of faith. Their abilities are usually directed towards the safety, welfare and betterment of others.
ELM can be used as a preventative: when you have a lot planned, it helps you to cope, one step at a time.

Also, write down everything you are trying to cope with. This can help keep things in perspective.

And remember: when you're out of balance, all feelings are only temporary, and balance will come to you when you take the ELM Remedy.

DAWN CHRYSTAL

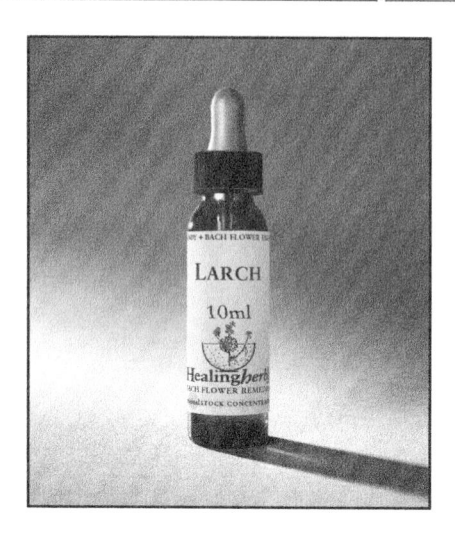

LARCH *Despondency and despair*

Negative

Lack of confidence.
Anticipation of failure.
Asking others to support you, and do things for you, instead of having a go yourself.
Having had a few knocks, being convinced you will fail.
Lacking determination.
Not trying, because of a belief that you will not succeed – better not to try than to risk failure, even when you know inside that you *are* capable.
Feeling inferior, while knowing deep down that you are not.
Thinking 'I can't,' yet secretly knowing you have the ability.
Not considering yourself as capable as others; believing others can do better than you.
Displaying false modesty.
Being deterred by negative setbacks.
Expecting failure.
Never feeling you can be a success. Adding GENTIAN can help.
Allowing lack of confidence to creep in at any time, causing you to stop what you have started.

Admiring the success of others, without envy or jealousy.
Stepping back, so that the possibility of failure is averted.
Using illness as an excuse – and quite often actually becoming ill – to avoid a situation you are uncomfortable with.

Positive

LARCH can bring an unshakable renewed self-confidence.
It can make you feel capable and unafraid.
It can give you determination and the tenacity to keep trying, again and again, never giving up despite the odds and the setbacks.
LARCH makes you willing to jump in and take risks.
It helps you never to be discouraged by negative results.
LARCH can bring an inner strength that means you no longer know the meaning of the word 'can't'.
It can bring you to a positive state in which you are a lot more confident.
LARCH is a good Remedy to take before exams and interviews.

Affirmation

I am confidently following through on anything I start.
I am learning from this setback (add CHESTNUT BUD and GENTIAN).
I am happily celebrating no setbacks are going to stop me.
I am confidently moving forward now.

Advice

GENTIAN can be helpful with LARCH to help you 'bounce back' with renewed optimism.
Remember too: the *desire* to want to do something can give you the confidence to do it without fear.

OAK *Despondency and despair*

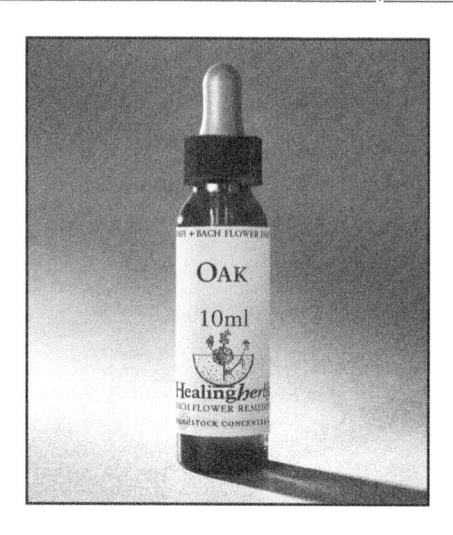

Negative

Overwhelming tiredness.
Being despondent, but struggling on, leading to despair.
Overworking, but hiding tiredness. Plodding on, never giving up hope.
Feeling and looking physically strong, regardless of extreme tiredness.
Saying, 'I must keep on going'; making relentless efforts, while feeling helpless and unable to succeed.
Being a tower of strength to others – very reliable, despite tiredness.
Often saying, 'It's no good complaining, it's got to be done!'
Getting exhausted, complaining of sore, tired legs.
Saying, 'I was brought to my knees.'
Not listening to your body's needs, which can wreck your health.
Displaying a strong constitution, and keeping going, which can lead to a nervous breakdown.
Nervous exhaustion.
Not had a holiday for years. Saying, 'I can't afford to take a holiday.'
Liking the image of being strong and reliable.
Not wanting to depend on others.
In some cases feeling deep tiredness when your soul is tired of the situation.

The negative OAK state may be a result of a long VERVAIN state.

Positive

OAK will help you recognise and admit your limitations.
It will give you strength and endurance.
It will bring courage and help you to be stable under all conditions.
OAK will enable you to like helping others, and to allow help to be given to you.
It will help you to be reliable, strong, patient, and full of common sense.
It will help you withstand great strain.
If you suffer from lack of sleep but have to work, take OAK.
If you have got a deadline to reach, take OAK to get you through it, but then you should stop when you have reached the deadline.
People in a positive OAK state are brave. They fight adversity, difficulties and illness without loss of hope. They persevere, and they are ceaseless in their effort to find a cure when unwell. This is a positive description, but it is when the inner strength begins to wane – when tiredness sets in and signs of losing the battle appear – that OAK is needed.
OAK can bring renewed strength and determination to your soul.

Affirmation

I am feeling stronger today. I have the strength to do whatever I need to do.
Every day in every way I am feeling strong. I am listening to my body's needs.
I joyfully choose to listen to what my body is telling me.
I gently choose to rest when my body needs to.

Advice

Take a break before you are forced to. You are not invincible.
If you spend a lot of time worrying, add VERVAIN, WHITE CHESTNUT and OLIVE.
Take OAK when you are tired but have something that needs to be finished.
    It will give you strength to keep going until a suitable time to stop.
Listen to what your body is telling you, and stop as soon as you can.

PINE — *Despondency and despair*

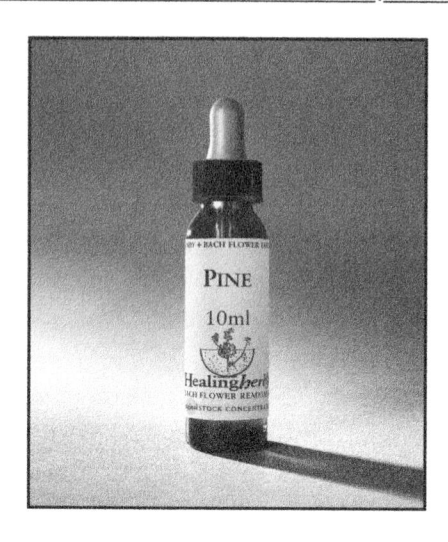

Negative

Having a guilt complex that takes away all joy; a heavy feeling that can overshadow other things you are doing.
Feeling guilty for anything and everything, and for the past situations too.
Blaming yourself for the mistakes of others, often taking all the blame.
Often saying, 'if only' and/or 'I'll never forgive myself'.
Always saying 'I'm sorry, even when it's not necessary.
A 'PINE child' or parent often accepts blame, even when not guilty.
Often takes the blame for others, to save them getting into trouble. (Add Red Chestnut).
A lack of self-worth, often feel unworthy of love.
Not honouring yourself, because you would feel guilty doing so.
Always putting yourself last, because someone else is doing without.
Being over-conscientious, but never content with your achievements, and often overworking.
Self-reproach. Even when successful, think you should have done better.
Not resting easily, because you feel guilty for doing so.

Looking to your limits, rather than your potential.
Setting high standards for yourself, but let others get away with murder.
Can feel responsible for others' dilemmas and unhappiness.

Positive

PINE relieves feelings of guilt.
It allows genuine regret, and brings forgiveness of yourself.
When you are able to forgive yourself, you can start to forgive others.
Remember that sometimes we need to make mistakes in order to learn.
To recognise your mistakes, learn from them, and take action, add CHESTNUT BUD.
PINE will help you recognise what part of the responsibility is yours.
It will enable you to take responsibility with a fair and balanced attitude.

Affirmation

I happily recognise what I am responsible for.
I genuinely regret what I have done, and what I have done.
I genuinely regret what has happened, and for the actions I have taken.
I am acknowledging who is responsible for what has happened.

Advice

Often your mistakes are your greatest teachers. It's okay to make mistakes, but not beneficial to keep repeating them. Combining PINE with CHESTNUT BUD will help you recognise your mistakes, learn from them and create new patterns. PINE will empower you to show great perseverance, humility and sound judgement.
Victims of mental, physical or emotional abuse will often take the blame for the abuse they have endured. PINE will help them let go of this and recognise who is responsible. STAR OF BETHLEHEM, CRAB APPLE and PINE can support victims and help clear their feelings of self-loathing and guilt.

The healing process can sometimes bring up a lot of emotions and flashbacks to unpleasant memories. This is a part of the natural healing process. Be patient with the recovery process as the pain is often very deep, and may not even be recognised for what it is. The emotions at this time can be as extreme as when the abuse took place, however long ago it was. Add STAR OF BETHLEHEM for the shock. Do not rush through this process. It takes as long as it takes.

AGRIMONY can help you to express how you feel, but it can take time to start working, so be patient. If the person starts to experience extremes emotions or feels panicky, add Rescue Remedy.

STAR OF BETHLEHEM *Despondency and despair*

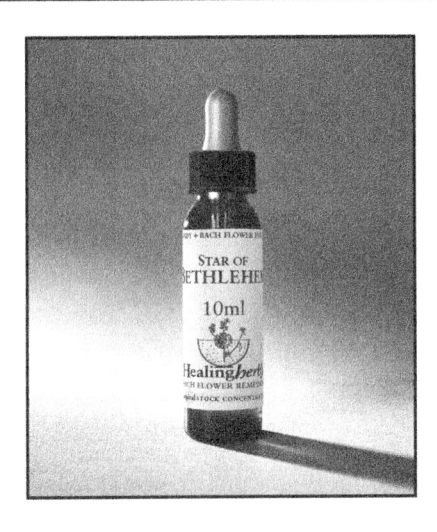

STAR OF BETHLEHEM is one of the five Remedies in Rescue Remedy

Negative

Experiencing shocks and trauma, or delayed reaction from shock.
Often cannot get in touch with how they are feeling.
Can be something which happened yesterday or back in childhood.
Sometimes the shock of being born can leave a baby in shock which appears later in life.
Shock or trauma caused by a recent or past incident, distressing argument, medical diagnosis, accident, loss or death of a loved one.
Can still be feeling as emotionally traumatised as if they had just received the bad news, or the incident had just happened.
Any distressing situation that causes great unhappiness.
Feeling pain too much to bear; like a shock to your whole system.
Feeling that your body (and/or mind) has switched off.
Having no feelings, or feeling totally devoid of emotions and feelings.
Receiving sudden bad news.
Had a bad fright or a grievous disappointment.
If you have suppressed your emotions, you can feel like you have got a lump in your throat. When shock dissolves, the lump clears.

Randomly starting to cry for no apparent reason. May be cold and shivering.
Can find it hard to get in touch with your feelings, add AGRIMONY.

Positive

STAR OF BETHLEHEM helps to release the feelings of shock from your body. It softens traumas and helps with reorientation.
It helps you to feel like you are ready to start again.
It neutralises, and softens the effect of shock (immediate or delayed).
STAR OF BETHLEHEM gives a feeling of reawakening after shock.
It is the comforter and soother of pains and sorrows.
It can help through childbirth, benefiting mother and baby.
It can help with the impact of a difficult birth, for both the child, and the mother.
It can be used for impending shock or bad news, including impending death for both the person suffering or dying, and for the relatives.

Affirmation

I calmly prepare to move forward. I am ready to move on now.
I am joyfully embracing being in a stronger place.

Advice: dealing with someone in shock

If someone in a state of shock cannot express how they feel, add AGRIMONY and STAR OF BETHLEHEM, and wait a while. They may seem detached, and be slow to react (not to be confused with a CLEMATIS state). They may have an empty look in their eyes. You could ask them if they have suffered a shock or trauma. They may show delayed reactions when answering.
If they are in a state of delayed shock, other Remedies may not show up. Give them some STAR OF BETHLEHEM, wait a while, then start again. Acknowledge their distress, and do not rush to try to fix it.

- They may become extremely emotional when they start to open up, or recognise why they have been feeling the way they have been.
- Go carefully and gently when dealing with someone in this state – they may be feeling very fragile, and may need to talk things through before you begin any other treatment.
- If someone has been through a traumatic experience, they may have a delayed reaction of emotions some time after starting to take the Remedies. Being in a state of shock can produce feelings of life being on hold. Taking STAR OF BETHLEHEM will help clear and heal the shock. After the shock has cleared, things will seem clearer and less traumatic, allowing the person to move on beyond the incident that has caused the shock. Be patient with someone in this state.

SWEET CHESTNUT — *Despondency and despair*

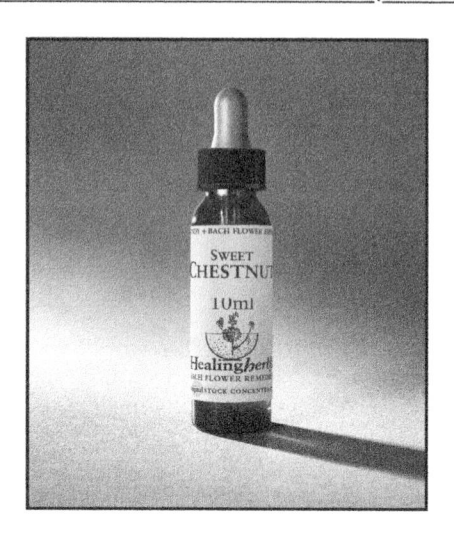

Negative

Extreme mental anguish, often to do with emotions.
Being unable to go on (but no thought of suicide).
A lot going on: often emotional things.
Feeling like you are trapped in a situation.
Feels it is all too much – a great weight on your shoulders.
Saying 'I can't take any more'.
Having a 'sick in the tummy' feeling.
Feeling the future is complete darkness; there is no light at the end of the tunnel. Feeling all ways forward are cut off.
Being unable to see any hope or peace in the future.
Wanting to hide away, go to bed and pull the quilt over your head. The feeling may not shift until your circumstances change.
Wanting to be left alone.
Feeling very tired and unable to do anything.
Feeling complete exhaustion and loneliness, and finding it hard to push beyond this feeling.
Having a lost, empty feeling inside.
Having abandoned hope; reached the limit of their endurance.

FREE TO BE ME

Feeling very distressed and distraught; lonely, with no hope.
Extreme tears and sobbing.
May be described as the 'dark night of the soul'.
If you talk to someone in a negative SWEET CHESTNUT state, they are in control of their emotions, and can talk about the way they feel.
Calling out for help, but not believing there is a solution.
Resisting change, but something within can suddenly help you find strength to make changes.
Often hitting rock bottom before you make changes.

Positive

SWEET CHESTNUT brings light at the end of the tunnel, and reveals more clarity.
Ask God, and your cry for help will be heard, and miracles can happen. Despite unbearable anguish, you can call on God for help and still put your trust in Him.
It can often be the beginning of a transformation into a new and better way of life.
SWEET CHESTNUT can bring a time of letting go of old beliefs and patterns, to make room for new levels of consciousness, even making a new connection to God and their divine spirituality.
It can help you recognise that a new inner journey has started, and to welcome the ability to believe again.
SWEET CHESTNUT can help you feel that a weight has been lifted.
It brings strong character and full control of emotions.
It enables you to keep your troubles to yourself, and to feel comfortable with that and be able to reach out if necessary.

Affirmation

I am joyfully seeing things clearly now.
My prayers have been answered.
I am happily feeling back in control of my emotions.

Advice

When dealing with someone in a negative SWEET CHESTNUT state, encourage them to talk about what the problem is.
Talking can help them start to feel a sense of relief, and an insight into what is causing their distress.
It's important to look for the cause, and maintain your resolve to move on, or it will reoccur. AGRIMONY can help you choose to confront the situation, and talk more freely about it. Quite often, when the situation is addressed and changed, the anguish is diminished.

WILLOW

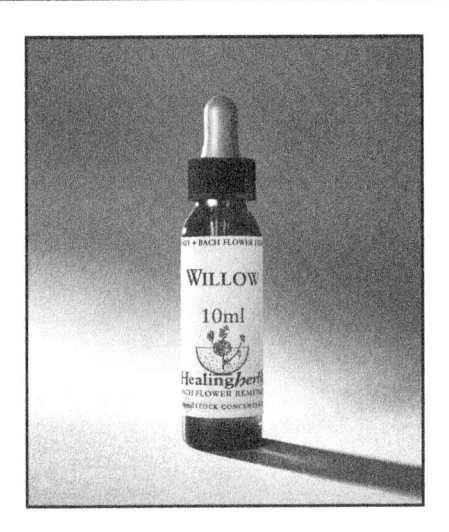

Despondency and despair

Negative

Resentment and bitterness. Feeling sorry for yourself, full of self-pity.
Blaming everyone but yourself – 'I don't deserve this misfortune'.
Often saying things like 'Why is it happening to me?', 'What have I done to deserve this?', 'Others sail through, why can't I?'
Always grumbling, mumbling and complaining.
Not being pleased or satisfied with anything.
Cannot see how they are compounding their situation, and that they could turn their situation around.
Not wanting to feel well when ill, and being a difficult patient.
Slamming doors when aggrieved.
Being an irritable, sulky, wet blanket who enjoys spreading gloom and despair – 'What are you so happy about?'
Being unable to snap out of it.
Having inner anger, like a volcano simmering inside.
Overreacting to incidents because old hurts haven't been dealt with, and just one more irritation can cause an explosion of emotions.
Having no interest in the affairs of others, except to decry and speak with unkindness.

Wanting to make others feel as bad as you do.
Taking without giving; accepting help as a right.
Being ungrateful, alienating, and reluctant to admit improvement.
Constantly bringing old hurts into the conversation.

Positive

WILLOW renews optimism and faith.
It will help you recognise the power to attract good or bad, according to the nature of your thoughts.
You get what you expect in life! WILLOW helps you recognise negative thoughts, and to realise what you are attracting to yourself.
It will enable you to have more constructive thoughts, to be uncomplaining and to be accepting of life and situations.
Most of us can suffer the negative feeling of WILLOW at times – this Remedy will neutralise these feelings, help you regain a sense of humour and see things in their true perspective.
WILLOW can help you take responsibility for yourself and recognise that you are responsible for your demeanour.

Affirmation

I am joyfully taking control of myself, and my circumstances.
I am happily taking responsibility for myself.
I am taking responsibility for my happiness and well-being.
I am joyfully choosing to be happy today. I am loving.

Advice

AGRIMONY can help you to talk about old hurts. The problem could be caused by long-standing suppressed hurts and grievances bubbling up inside, which can be destructive when the passive anger comes out.
CENTAURY in a negative state often go into a WILLOW state of mind. The difference between HOLLY and WILLOW is that HOLLY helps with anger being displayed outwardly, and WILLOW helps with

underlying passive anger and resentments which are not always so obvious.

WHITE CHESTNUT helps with thoughts racing around in your mind.

GORSE helps when you are feeling helpless to change the situation.

SWEET CHESTNUT helps when it has become extreme emotional anguish.

WILD ROSE helps when you have resigned yourself to the situation, and you either can't be bothered to change it, or think 'what's the point?'

ASPEN *Fear*

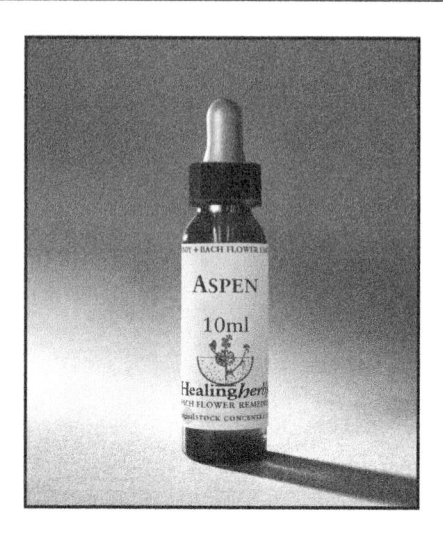

Negative

Vague fears of the unknown.
Talking about feelings of fearfulness, but not knowing why.
Fears, by day and night, for no known reason.
Apprehension, foreboding.
Terror on waking, as if from a bad dream, though you may have forgotten the dream.
Fear of going to sleep again.
Being afraid to tell others your fears and troubles.
In exams, feelings of anxiety and apprehension due to not knowing what questions to expect.
Fears often accompanied by trembling, sweating, flutters in tummy, sweaty palms.
Children often needing to have a light on at night.
Fears can include darkness, death, thoughts of disaster, inexplicable fear when alone (or suddenly, among friends),
Fear of fear, not knowing what to expect or what's involved at interviews, meetings, new places;

Fear of lack of money, which brings up the feelings of not knowing what to expect, or how to change the situation. 'I have no idea what will happen to me.' Add MIMULUS too.

When fears become extreme, they can become panic or terror – in this case use ROCK ROSE with ASPEN.

Positive

ASPEN brings courage and calm, which helps to calm fear.

It helps you to trust in the unknown – to trust that all shall be well.

It brings fearlessness, with the understanding that the power of love stands behind and overcomes all things.

Once we realise this, we are beyond pain, suffering, care, worry and fear – we become participants of true joy. Such faith causes a desire for adventure, for experiences with disregard for difficulty or danger.

Remember that you cannot display the negative if you didn't already have the positive within you – keep looking positively ahead. Get excited, raise your beliefs and expectations.

Affirmation

I am joyfully trusting everything will be all right.

I am confidently embracing I have the courage to do anything.

I am thankfully feeling safe.

I am confidently moving forward.

CHERRY PLUM *Fear*

CHERRY PLUM is one of the five Remedies in Rescue Remedy

Negative

Irrational thinking or behaviour.
Fear of losing control, of your mind giving way.
Desperation.
Feeling on the verge of nervous breakdown.
Feeling close to hysteria, silently screaming for help in your mind, and not voicing your despair.
Verbally, often erratically and in a volatile manner, calling out to others for help.
In the extreme state, experiencing suicidal thoughts.
Fear of losing control and reason; fear of insanity.
Feel as though your head is going to explode.
Feeling trapped in a situation, and unable to see a way out.
Can make irrational decisions in this state.
Wanting to be the one in control.
Temper tantrums; having a volatile temper.

Fear of hurting someone, or doing dreadful things – even though you know they are wrong, still there is the thought and impulse to do them.

Keeping inner conflicts in, and feeling afraid of letting go inside.

Trying to stop feelings coming out (your body is saying it is time to sort them out).

Irrational mood swings or lashing out.

Sudden murderous and violent impulses.

Saying horrible things, as though you have a split personality.

Premenstrual mood change (often known as PMT).

Random outbursts of tearfulness or temper.

Positive

CHERRY PLUM brings calm, balance and control.

It instils mental calm, and gives stability, composure and quiet courage.

It helps you to trust in your own abilities.

CHERRY PLUM helps strengthen inner resolve and the ability to cope.

It gives calmness and endurance, in spite of stress, obstacles and challenges, and helps you feel you have your sanity back. It helps people who have suffered mental and physical torture (e.g. victims of abuse, victims of war, prisoners of war) to hold onto their sanity.

It drives away false ideas, and so gives the sufferer mental strength and confidence.

Affirmation

I am gratefully feeling calm, poised and balanced.

I am feeling calm and confident.

I am embracing I have the courage to do anything calmly at the right time.

Advice

Parents are sometimes afraid of losing control. If they can stay in control – that is, respond to the situation, and not react with temper – calm will return faster. CHERRY PLUM will help if both parent and child use the Remedy.

Quick tip: if a child, or anyone, erupts, shouts and has a temper tantrum, wait until they have finished, then calmly lower your voice to a whisper to talk to them.

This is far more effective than shouting, and the situation can be resolved more calmly and amicably. It may take time to adjust to this way of dealing with things, but patience and persistence will bring you better results in challenging situations. You are setting an example.

MIMULUS — *Fear*

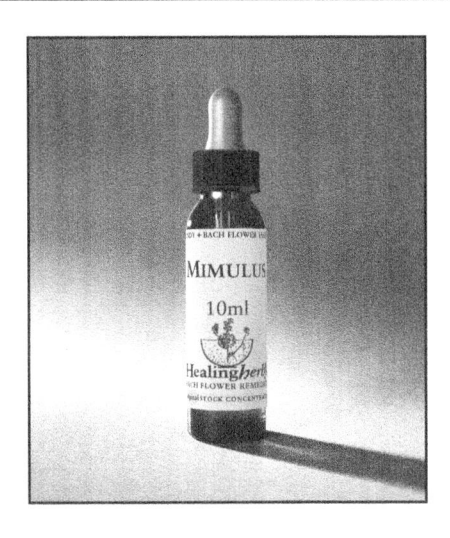

MIMULUS is one of the 12 healers

Negative

Fear of known things: of illness and of consequences; of accidents and of pain; of dark, or damp and cold, or of poverty.
Fear of people; of animals; of speaking in public; of losing friends, illness or of death.
Having secret fears, trying to hide fears and anxieties.
Not talking directly about the fear in question, but about other fears.
Becoming tongue-tied, having stage fright, maybe stammering.
Having many phobias.
Being shy, yet talking non-stop. Shyness hidden by incessant chat.
Being easily embarrassed. Blushing easily, giggling nervously.
Not liking being alone, but getting muddled in company.
Not knowing how to react around people.
Becoming ill as a way to cope with fear or pressure.
Extreme fear ('I feel sick with fear').
Struggling to find a way to deal with fears.
Taking longer to recover from illness – being over-cautious and feeling fearful it will return.

Disliking noise, bright lights or the cold.

When asked, 'As a child, did you blush easily, or were you easily embarrassed?' a person's reaction or emotion will reveal whether this is the right Remedy. For example, they may start to blush just because you mention it. Don't always go by the words they use – also listen to their voice tone, and watch their reaction.

When a person is in a negative mimulus state, their body language may even appear introverted, like they are going in on themselves. They often have rounded shoulders, and seem to be stooping, rather than standing up tall and proud.

Positive

MIMULUS brings the ability to recognise fears.
It helps you regain your courage.
It gives quiet courage to face trials and difficulties with equanimity and humour.
It brings understanding, bravery and confidence.
MIMULUS helps bring emotions completely under control, restoring the ability to enjoy life without irrational fears.
It helps you recognise that fears have no hold over you.
It brings boldness in your approach to people and situations.
Mimulus brings you the courage to speak up for yourself, add AGRIMONY.
It helps you have more trust in yourself when faced with illness or disabilities.

Affirmation

I am joyfully knowing I have the courage to do anything.
I am confidently dealing with this.
I am feeling in control of my emotions.
I am happily taking control of my emotions.
I am feeling brave and trusting it is going to be all right.

Advice

A person in a negative MIMULUS state may have limiting beliefs about themselves. Look at your beliefs and recognise their impact on you. Self-praise and positive recognition will help build your trust in yourself, and so help to alleviate your fears.

Add CERATO and LARCH to help with self-belief and renewed confidence.

Add CENTAURY to help you if you need to reset your boundaries, and AGRIMONY if you need to speak up for yourself.

RED CHESTNUT *Fear*

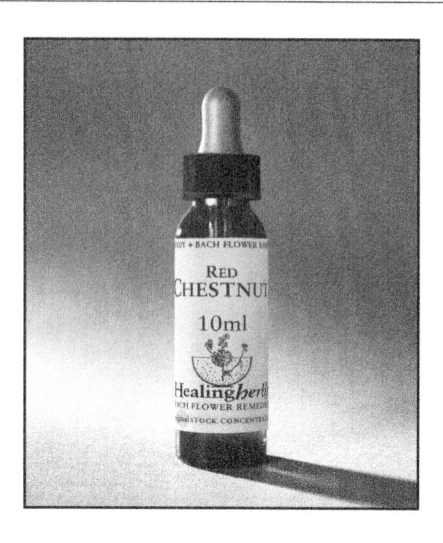

Negative

Having fear and anxiety for others.
Excessive concern and worry for those near and dear.
Fear of calamity befalling others.
Fearing the worst.
Find it hard to not worry about others.
Experiencing extreme fears of danger, when a child or partner is elsewhere, or comes in late.
Over-fussing when someone is ill.
Fear that a minor complaint in someone will become a serious one.
Getting caught up in others' problems, and not being able to detach from them.
Become sympathetic instead of empathic. So get caught up in others' problems and situations.
Such fearful, negative thoughts harm us and those around us, as we can impose our negative fears onto others. For example, a nervous mother's negative thinking and expectations can create a nervous child.

Positive

RED CHESTNUT helps you have trust for others' lives, and that they will be looked after. Trusting they will be safe and can can get through their situation.
It enables you to radiate positive thoughts and expectations to others – thoughts of good health, security, courage and well-being.
It gives an ability to remain calm, mentally and physically, in any situation or emergency.
Able to lift someone above the problem – through empathy – and showing them a way forward, gives back their positive expectations, and helps them take control of situations, thereby giving them back their own personal power.

Affirmation

I am happily trusting they will be all right.
I am joyfully trusting they will be safe.
I am calmly trusting they are safe.

Advice

When someone faces challenges, remember that you don't have to have all the answers. Remember, too, the difference between sympathy and empathy. Are you being sympathetic or empathic?
RED CHESTNUT is a good preventative Remedy for parents, carers, doctors, nurses, therapists, teachers, etc. to take – people who may be prone to picking up on others' emotions, or who find it hard to detach from other people's problems.
Adding WALNUT helps with over-sensitivity to others, or being influenced by their fears.
Add CRAB APPLE to cleanse yourself of any emotions you may have picked up. You can use CRAB APPLE to strengthen your immunity to picking up others' emotions.

If you work or live with people who are unhappy, unwell or negative, use it regularly to help you be around them. Using it regularly will keep you feeling emotionally protected.

You cannot over-use the Remedies. CHESTNUT BUD, CRAB APPLE, RED CHESTNUT and WALNUT will help you feel less over-sensitive, and help you offer empathic support, instead of getting too involved.

ROCK ROSE *Fear*

ROCK ROSE is one of the five Remedies in Rescue Remedy
ROCK ROSE is one of the 12 healers

Negative

Terror, panic.
Being oversensitive or extremely delicate.
Having a nervous constitution – using a lot of nervous energy, resulting in feeling exhausted.
Experiencing stage fright; losing words or other faculties.
Hating to speak to someone you can't see – on the phone, for example.
Feeling as though you have been punched in the stomach.
Having heart palpitations.
Suffering from panic attacks – wobbly legs, nervous stomach, palpitations, tightening of chest muscles, shortness of breath or dizziness, for example, all rising from feelings of panic.
Either 'freezing' or running around in a crazy state when in state of panic, and thus imparting fear to others.
Can feel distressed by the thought, or the siting of an accident, or someone in distress.

Even watching something distressing on the TV can trigger off extreme fears.

Positive

ROCK ROSE brings calm, peace and tranquillity to those caught up in an emergency.
It restores rationality and brings bravery and steadfastness, which will help you feel more in control of the situation, and of your feelings.
It helps you to forget the self.
ROCK ROSE gives strength of will and character.
It brings the courage needed to win through despite the odds, even to make a person willing to risk their life for others.
ROCK ROSE helps people such as firefighters and doctors to maintain their own calm and courage, and to communicate a sense of calm and bravery to others, regardless of what is going on around them.
It helps people suffering from panic attacks, and can be used not only as a calmer during a panic attack, but also as a preventative (see also Rescue Remedy).

Affirmation

I am happily embracing I have the courage to do anything.
I am rejoicing being in a calm space, I am calmly being courageous today.
I am calmly and confidently embracing this opportunity.
I am feeling calm and confident I can do this.

Advice

Whenever there's terror or panic in the air – resulting from an accident, a narrow escape or even the sighting of an accident – both the panicking person and those around are affected. ROCK ROSE is the Remedy for rescuing from terror or panic. Or use Rescue Remedy.

For a child feeling terror as a result of a nightmare, a few drops of ROCK ROSE in a drink, sipped frequently, will help with the immediate feelings, and with the fear of going back to sleep.

If a person is in a state of panic, the ROCK ROSE Remedy can be applied to the lips. It can also be massaged into the pressure points to help relieve the feeling of panic. Or use Rescue Remedy.

A firefighter, a doctor, or anyone who does a job requiring courage in crisis situations, can often cope with the situation, and then go into a state of negative ROCK ROSE state afterwards.

ROCK ROSE can also be used to prevent panic within an impending situation. Add CHESTNUT BUD and RED CHESTNUT for several days beforehand, to help prepare you for what is impending.

Gentle deep-breathing techniques will help calm anyone in a state of panic.

CHESTNUT BUD — *Insufficient interest in present circumstances*

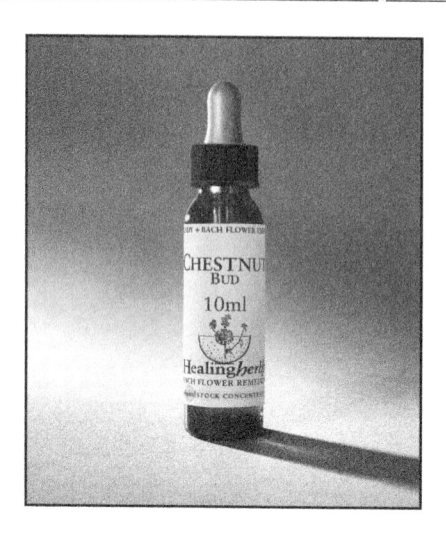

Negative

Failure to learn from past mistakes, so keep repeating the same mistakes over and over again.
Create the same errors and keep experiencing the same difficulties.
Jumping from one stressful experience into another one.
Not observing mistakes, or finding it hard to see them.
Needing to look at the experience, understand it, learn from it, and realise what no longer serves you.
Trying to forget the past, but with no alternative insight to help yourself, now or in the future.
Feeling stuck in a pitiful situation, until mistakes are recognised and corrected, or adjusted.
Children not learning easily; struggling to learn.
Constantly forgetting things – e.g. where things are.
Forget spellings, timetables – and having to keep repeating them.
Short attention span, including ADHD.
Suffering from migraines, tension; being stressed, argumentative. There's usually something you are not learning that causes this stress.
Seeming to be indifferent to mistakes and experiences – 'who cares?'

FREE TO BE ME

Attempting to forget experience immediately, but not learning from it, and staying stuck in old patterns (different from GENTIAN).

Being a slow learner.

Referring to the situation as a 'mental block' or saying, 'Oh, it's just the way I am', or 'I feel stuck'.

Positive

CHESTNUT BUD helps you to be keenly observant of mistakes, and to recognise what is no longer suitable for you.

It gives the ability to learn by mistakes and experiences, and to gain knowledge and wisdom from them.

It enables you to learn from other people's mistakes and recognising you don't have to learn by going down that road.

CHESTNUT BUD helps you take in and retain information, and CLEMATIS helps keep your attention in the present.

It helps to bring concentration to ADHD sufferers.

It helps you retain new skills when learning.

It is useful when learning a new job or attending lectures.

It can support you when giving up a long-standing habit such as smoking, bad eating habits, alcohol or drugs.

It helps you create new patterns and retain them.

CHESTNUT BUD can help you maintain a new diet, a new physical exercise routine, or a new way of life.

Affirmation

I am joyfully learning from my mistakes.
I happily recognise where I need to make changes.
I am embracing I can remember new things I learn.
I am joyfully creating new, uplifting patterns for myself.

Advice

When you ignore the lessons, your intuition goes – if you switch off negative, you switch off positive. You can't ignore the problem. CHESTNUT BUD helps you learn from it, and enables you to move on.

ADHD note: CHESTNUT BUD and CLEMATIS will help with concentration.

GENTIAN will help you with setbacks and maintain positive expectations.

WALNUT will help with adjusting to any changes created by new patterns.

GORSE will help if you have lost hope or feel helpless to change the situation.

Dr Bach wrote, 'This Remedy is to help us take full advantage of our daily experiences, and to see ourselves as others do.'

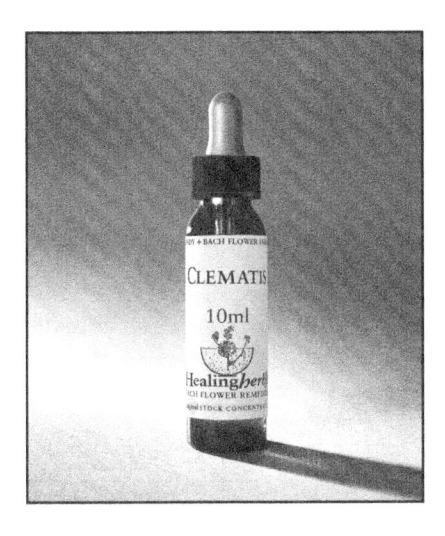

CLEMATIS *Insufficient interest in present circumstances*

CLEMATIS is one of the five Remedies in Rescue Remedy
CLEMATIS is one of the 12 healers

Negative

Being a daydreamer, absent-minded, not hearing what others say.
Light-headedness. Living more in thoughts, than in actions.
Often needing lots of sleep, and having a marked paleness of complexion. May be having inner problems or worries.
Having a dazed, glazed look; not seeing people as they pass by.
Being impractical, bemused, indifferent. Thinking of unrealistic solutions to escape problems.
Seeming drowsy, able to doze off at any time – being listless, a heavy sleeper.
Unhappy children can go into a daydream world, often with an imaginary friend, if their circumstances are not happy.
Lacking interest in the present – being preoccupied, inattentive.
Living in your own thoughts or daydreams, can be to escape reality.
Can have thoughts, and talk about wanting to run away.
Clumsiness or carelessness, which might cause a fall or car accident.
Stressful (and joyful) events can result in a bemused CLEMATIS state.

Saying, 'Really, you don't say', while being totally indifferent to what is being said.

This state of mind can affect the eyes and the hearing. May even need to wear a hearing aid.

Seeming detached and forgetful when falling in love, then coming down to earth with a bump.

Being forgetful when starting things, and then forgetting what you started.

Needing 'grounding' – to do something hands-on, or to go out into nature.

Escaping into a CLEMATIS state through loss of a friendship or job, or a complete change of present or impending circumstances.

Can go into this extreme state when they have lost a loved one, through death or a change of circumstances.

Positive

CLEMATIS brings a lively interest in all things.

It helps you to be down-to-earth, centred, grounded.

It gives you the ability to be the master of all your own thoughts.

It can make you sensitive to inspiration.

CLEMATIS can help you to use your creative potential as, for example, a writer, artist, painter or gardener.

It helps you to be purposeful and realistic – 'down-to-earth'.

It can help you be in the present moment, and to face up to, and deal with, your situation. Other Remedies would be needed for support, e.g. CENTAURY, CERATO, ELM, GENTIAN, LARCH.

It helps keep spiritual workers connected with reality.

CLEMATIS can be given to someone in an unconscious state, hence its presence in the Rescue Remedy – it will help to bring them round. Rub the Remedy on the person's lips if they cannot take it orally.

Affirmation

I am feeling centred and grounded.
I am joyfully living in the present.
I am happily using my true creative potential.
I am happily being realistic about my life.

Advice

Shock can take someone into a CLEMATIS state. In this case add STAR OF BETHLEHEM or Rescue Remedy.
When working with the spiritual world, you can very often drift off into a CLEMATIS state. CLEMATIS will help you re-ground yourself, and be fully present in the moment.

HONEYSUCKLE *Insufficient interest in present circumstances*

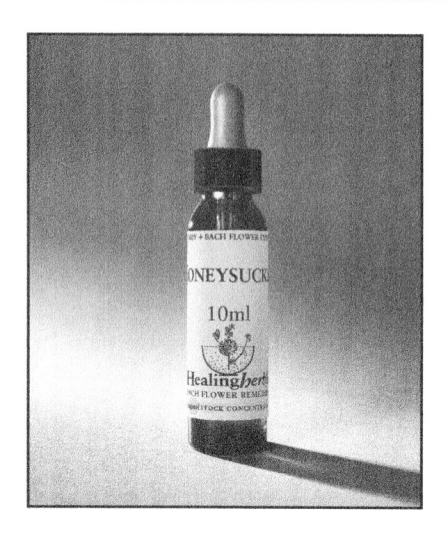

Negative

Living in the past in your mind.
Being nostalgic and/or melancholic. Mind stuck in the past.
Keep focusing on things and memories in the past.
Cannot let past experiences go.
Having regrets for missed opportunities or missed dreams.
Slowing down of vital forces.
Losing interest in the present; constantly referring to the past.
Often talking about a deceased person, possibly with regrets.
Recollecting war stories, times gone by – had better times, and more self-worth then.
Often saying, 'I used to...' or 'Things were always happier back then.' focusing on the past – past friends, past experiences – and hardly ever talking about the present.
When looking back, and often fearing what lies ahead: a state of 'this is my life', a 'torn in half' condition that keeps you in a state of melancholy.
For children: finding it hard to settle at school, or away from home. When at school, their mind is really with home and mum, feeling they would

be happier there. Yet when at home, their mind is at school or with friends. They feel they would be happier somewhere else, and are never content.

Homesick when on holidays.

Seeming unhappy in present time, situation, job or relationship; finding it hard to let go of a situation, of old jobs or old homes, old relationships or friendships.

Bring old patterns into new relationships and spoiling them – finding it hard to dissociate an old partner's ways from a new partner's.

Positive

HONEYSUCKLE can help you retain wisdom from the past, to enable you to build the future. It is okay to go back to the past and find memories, as long as you don't stay there.

It brings a capacity for change; an ability to establish new links.

HONEYSUCKLE enables you to be involved in the present.

It helps you lay the past to rest, and let go of it without forgetting.

It will enable you to move forward.

Overpowering the past is now seen as an essential experience. Laying the past to rest allows one to progress mentally, emotionally and spiritually.

HONEYSUCKLE is the Remedy for memories – it is a great help to widows, orphans, people adjusting to a deterioration in health or who have failed in business, and to older folk who live alone.

It helps with settling into a new relationship, home, school or career.

It helps with holiday homesickness; use as a pre-holiday preventative.

Affirmation

I happily lay the past to rest now. I am feeling able to move forward.
I am joyfully living in the present.

Advice

With a new partner, new job, new situation, you need to remember this is a new beginning and a new person, so a completely new way of being. This situation is not the old one – this is completely new. HONEYSUCKLE helps with this shift in perspective.

Plus WALNUT would help with adjusting to changes.

Add PINE for genuine regret.

Add WHITE CHESTNUT for continual thoughts going round and round in the mind.

WILD ROSE can help restore inner motivation for the present.

MUSTARD   *Insufficient interest in present circumstances*

Negative

Deep gloom for no apparent reason.
Black depression, which descends all of a sudden, and which can lift just as quickly.
Having no control over the gloom/depression.
Being able to say you feel depressed, but not why you do.
Hopelessness, despair.
Depressive melancholy.
Feeling very stuck in the gloom.
Feeling helpless – unable to try ways to escape it.
The gloom, like a cold, dark cloud, can be very severe, depriving the sufferer of normal cheerfulness and thoughts.
Feeling completely depleted of energy and motivation.
Suffering bad headaches.
Sudden closing down of the person. This depression is so severe it takes away all your interest in the daily routine of your life.
All of your thoughts are turned inward.
It is more distressing because it seems impossible to be free of this feeling until it lifts of its own accord.

Nothing seems worthwhile, or can make you feel cheerful when you are in this state of mind.

This gloom can often come as a result of deep frustration, or things which have made you feel angry, but you have not acknowledged as causing you disharmony.

Continually pushing your feelings and needs down, or not expressing your thoughts and needs can cause this state of mind. Add AGRIMONY and CENTAURY.

Positive

MUSTARD helps lift the dark cloud.
It brings back happiness, and lifts up your spirits.
It helps achieve stability and clarity.
It brings cheerfulness and inner serenity.
It enables joy and peace that nothing can shake or destroy.

Affirmation

I am calmly recognising what is causing this anger (or frustration or gloominess).
I am happily turning it around so I can see the positive in this situation – this is becoming my strength now.
I am feeling cheerful and happy.

Advice

It might be caused by unrecognised anger and frustration – if the sufferer can recognise where the anger comes from, they may recover quicker. Writing down how you feel can help you recognise where the anger or frustration comes from.

The gloom or frustration can also be part of pre-menstrual syndrome – add WALNUT, CRAB APPLE and SCLERANTHUS. Maybe this is a time when you need to take more care of yourself, and be gentle on yourself.

The heaviness and gloom can also come as a result of winter blues – CLEMATIS, MUSTARD and WALNUT can help with this.

Ideally, when you are in the negative state of MUSTARD you need to get outside more in nature, take deep, gentle breaths in, and take some gentle exercise. This can help to lift the gloominess, and can bring you more clarity and insight into what is creating your negative state of mind.

The dark cloud can lift as quickly as it came in, but you do need to take time to address what is causing your discontent and frustration, or the heavy feelings will keep reoccurring.

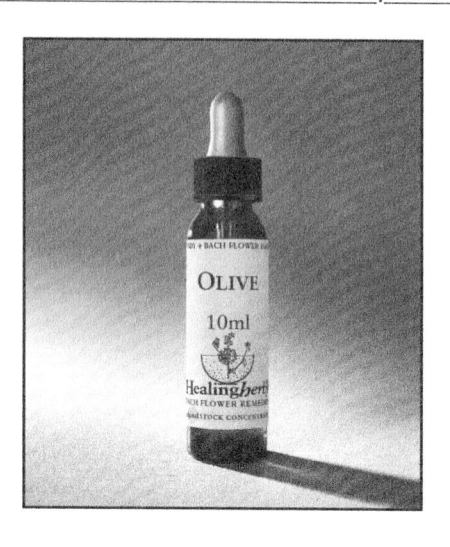

OLIVE *Insufficient interest in present circumstances*

Negative

Complete exhaustion – total fatigue of mind and body, which is often caused by a very busy, overactive mind.
'I am so tired I could cry.'
'I don't want to hear, see or do anything. I just want to sleep.'
Having no reserves of strength.
Finding everything an effort, even just the thought of the daily necessities.
Feeling washed out.
Having little time for relaxation and enjoyment.
Being unable to enjoy work or things that used to give pleasure.
Giving up things you used to enjoy, because you're so tired.
Tiring easily. Often finding it hard to sleep, even though mentally exhausted.
Lacking zest. Waking up as tired as when you went to sleep. Feeling unrevitalised by sleep.
Having suffered long under adverse conditions, or having your vitality sapped by a long illness, possibly M.E. (chronic fatigue syndrome).

Positive

OLIVE is a Remedy for convalescence.
It is a Remedy of faith and trust that things will work themselves out.
It brings an ability to recognise when excessive or intense thinking has created exhaustion.
It restores peace of mind, vitality, strength and interest.
It brings strength and vitality to sustain and guide others in need.
OLIVE enables you to maintain peace, harmony and interest, even while you may be forced to remain inactive.
Helps bring you more peace in your mind, which enables more clarity.
It gives renewed energy and regeneration.
It helps you feel rested and supported.

Affirmation

I am feeling rested and supported.
I happily choose to write down the things I am worrying about.
I am joyfully choosing to let go of all these thoughts.
I am rejoicing I have peace of mind.

Advice

If you are in this state of exhaustion, you really need more rest, and maybe you need to stop and address some things in your life. Ask yourself:
What am I willing to put up with?
What am I not willing to put up with?
Do I know what is causing the problem?
What do I need to change?
How can I make adjustments?
Put these thoughts in writing to help you get clarity.
Doing gentle, deep breathing exercises can help to calm a busy or worried mind.
When finding it hard to sleep, even though mentally exhausted, add WHITE CHESTNUT, VERVAIN.

- Use the exercise where you cover your eyes with your hands to calm your mind.
- A calmer mind can help to alleviate the tension which comes from an over-active mind.

WHITE CHESTNUT

Insufficient interest in present circumstances

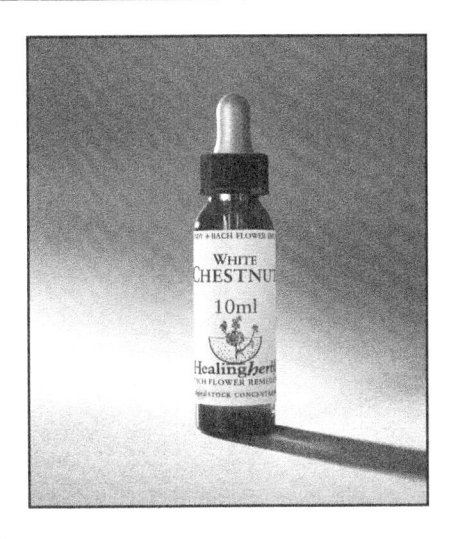

Negative

Unwanted thoughts.
Mental arguments (may need AGRIMONY too).
Worrying or distressing occurrences preying on the mind.
Disagreements keep spinning round in your mind.
Thoughts going round and round, like a hamster on a wheel.
A tune going around in your head.
Anything you don't desire playing on your mind.
Being helpless to stop the thoughts.
Being unable to sleep – feeling tired, have tension headaches, or depressed, with thoughts still spinning.
Not switching off during sleep.
Grinding your teeth (taking the WHITE CHESTNUT Remedy should stop this within a week).
Tension in the jaw.
Being preoccupied, lacking concentration, and often not hearing when someone speaks to you – a state of mind that could lead to accidents.
Often suffering from frontal headaches.

Positive

WHITE CHESTNUT brings a quiet, calm mind.
It helps you to be at peace with yourself and others, which enables you to control your thoughts.
Helps you put your calm thoughts to constructive use, enabling you to solve your problems.
It gives your mind the ability to discriminate – 'This is unnecessary' – and let it go.
It gives clarity of thinking.
WHITE CHESTNUT works quickly and is long-lasting.
It helps you to sleep.

Affirmation

My mind is happily clearing, and at peace.
I am joyfully choosing to let go of unnecessary thoughts.
I am seeing things more clearly now, and my mind is calm.

Advice

Another aid to clearing your mind is putting your thoughts down on paper, which can help you to stop worrying about them, and helps keep things in perspective.
Remember: half the things that happen we can't change, and the other half might never happen anyway.
Keeping journals and 'to do' lists will help keep your mind and thinking calmer and clearer.
For sleeping problems, use the WHITE CHESTNUT Remedy throughout the day, not just at bedtime.
AGRIMONY, ASPEN, OLIVE and VERVAIN can also help with sleeplessness.
Deep-breathing exercises or meditation will help you relax and clear your mind.
Practise covering your eyes to calm your mind down.
Doing a grounding meditation, or taking a walk in nature can clear your mind and re-energise you.

WILD ROSE *Insufficient interest in present circumstances*

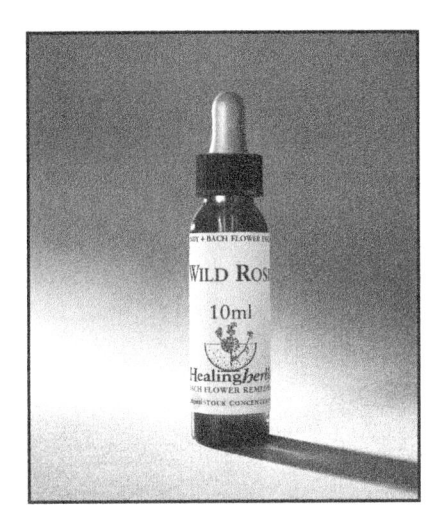

Negative

Being in a very extreme apathetic state – lower than SWEET CHESTNUT.
Have little, or no energy or enthusiasm.
Being resigned to illness, too apathetic to get well.
Not complaining.
Having tried to get better, then given up, accepting your lot.
Resignation, surrender – 'I must learn to live with it, it's in the family.'
Believing a condition or situation is incurable.
Not wanting to get out of the chair or bed – extreme depression.
Being chronically bored, washed out.
Accepting that 'this is my life'.
Being resigned to monotonous work, and feeling too apathetic to change.
Lacking ambition.
Giving up on making change, because it's just the way it is!
Being too apathetic to enjoy simple pleasures.
Being a drifter.
Always being weary, and lacking vitality.
Speaking in a voice that's dull, monotonous, slow and/ or expressionless.
Being a dull companion.

Failing to realise that you have actually created these conditions, nourished and maintained them.
Being unable to see the possibility of change, or any way out of their situation.
The negative state is very common in elderly people, and in people who become severely ill or disabled.
In the extreme, people can become ill and die. They lose the will to live.

Positive

WILD ROSE brings renewed enthusiasm.
It gives a lively interest in all happenings.
It produces a spirit of joy and adventure.
WILD ROSE brings devotion and inner motivation.
It helps make you feel ambitious and purposeful.
It strengthens interest and vitality which, in turn, produces happiness, the enrichment and enjoyment of life, relationships, family, friends, and good health.
WILD ROSE can help you turn around what was once a very apathetic state.

Affirmation

I have inner drive and motivation.
I am embracing I can do anything I choose to do.
I am feeling passionate about my life.

HEATHER *Loneliness*

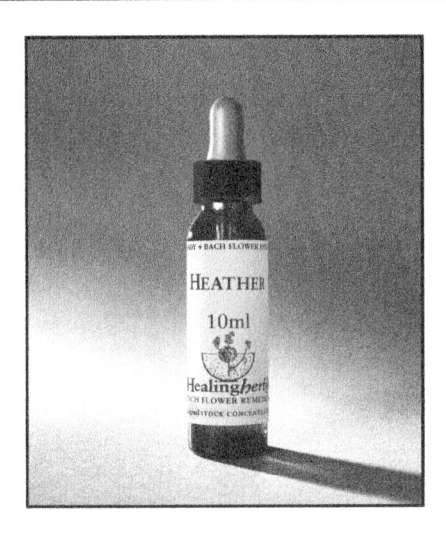

Negative

Feeling lonely, isolated or alone.
Being self-centred, full of self-concern.
Often feel like nobody cares about them. Add WILLOW.
Always wanting to talk about yourself and your problems; turning conversation back to yourself.
Repeating the same conversation over and over.
Talking incessantly, and sapping the vitality of others, often causing people to avoid you.
Being a poor listener, and having little interest in others' problems, except where those problems affect you.
Are facing problems that seem insurmountable.
Constantly needing to talk and express how you are feeling, but being unable to let go of your woes.
Being obsessed with ailments, problems and trivia.
Coming (too) close and speaking close to others' faces: 'buttonholing'.
Often knowing you are boring others, but needing to offload.
Making mountains out of molehills.

Sometimes being very weepy.
Needing others' undivided attention.
Disliking being alone, so often seeking someone to talk to.
Looking for sympathy and constant acknowledgement of your situation.
Finding it hard to see beyond your own problems.

Positive

HEATHER helps you learn to enjoy your own company, and develop a lively interest in others.

It can help you become a good listener – a selfless, understanding person, and not (often) feeling sorry for yourself.

It can enable you to see beyond your own problems and situations, to become a good empathiser (especially as you know what it is like to have suffered), to be absorbed in others' problems, and unsparing in your efforts to help.

HEATHER brings compassion and understanding, helping you to be a good listener, ready to help others.

Affirmation

I am joyfully being a good listener.
I am happily enjoying my own company.
I happily love to help others.

Advice

With STAR OF BETHLEHEM, HEATHER brings rebirth or reawakening, lifting the haze.

With GENTIAN, it helps you when you feel disappointed, discouraged or stuck. It brings renewed optimism.

With CERATO, it helps self-doubters to trust in their own ability to help themselves.

With LARCH, it brings renewed confidence and courage to those who fear failure – courage to try again.

With HONEYSUCKLE it helps to lay the past to rest, enabling you to move beyond what has happened.

IMPATIENS   *Loneliness*

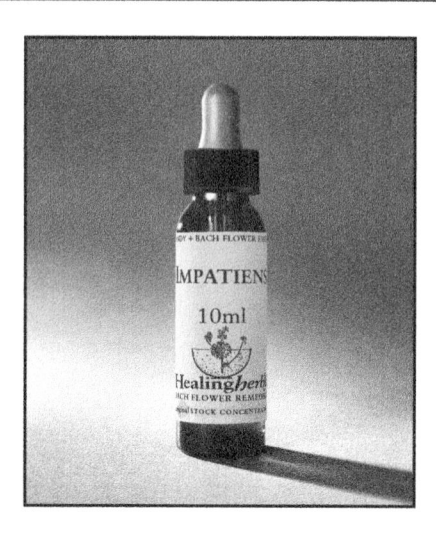

IMPATIENS is one of the five Remedies in Rescue Remedy
IMPATIENS is one of the 12 healers

Negative

Being a perfectionist.
Impatience and irritability, with themselves, and with others.
Doing everything quickly, and often far too quickly.
Nervous tension, and mental tension through frustration.
Having itchy skin (adding CRAB APPLE can help).
Speaking quickly, often too quickly for others to understand.
Finishing other people's sentences, interrupting conversations.
Preferring to work alone, and lacking tact with slower people.
Thinking you can do things faster, and better and making no allowances for slower people.
Being irritated by slow workers, patients or family members.
Snatching things from people's hands.
Being accident-prone through impetuosity.
Making mistakes because you are trying to rush too far ahead, your mind often ahead of the task in hand.

Not being able to suffer fools gladly.
Having a very quick and active mind, but your mind is preoccupied with too much intense thinking, so you feel stressed and you can't find peace within.
Worrying about what others think of you, and wanting to set an example.
Always rushing around, and trying to rush the process, so can miss important details.
Experiencing mental tension through frustration and other pressures.
Suffering headaches and neck tension through stress. Appearing quite rigid in your demeanour.
Suffering from heartburn and stomach disorders due to eating too quickly.
When sitting, tapping fingers and fidgety legs, and often sitting on the edge of your seat instead of relaxing in it. Often looking as though you are getting ready to get up and run.
Disliking queues. Road rage.

Positive

IMPATIENS brings patience and gentleness.
It enables tolerance and sympathy for slower people.
It makes it easier to go with the flow.
It helps you recognise the need for synchronicity – i.e. have patience, and knowing things will happen at the right time.
IMPATIENS brings more tolerance of situations and conditions, regardless of what is going on around you.
It can make you very focused and reliable.
It helps you to be less hasty in action and thought.
It brings restfulness.
It relieves tensions and pains.
IMPATIENS can bring relief from mental tension caused by frustration and impatience.

Affirmation

I am peacefully being patient and tolerant.
I am joyfully staying focused and do not try to rush.
I am happily recognising the need for synchronicity.
I calmly know everything will happen at the right time.

WATER VIOLET *Loneliness*

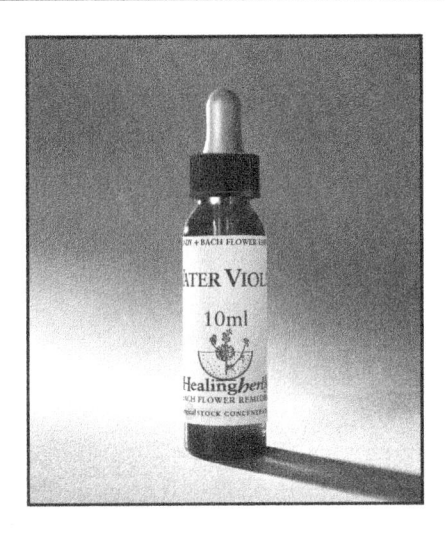

WATER VIOLET is one of the 12 healers

Negative

Being proud, aloof. Appearing snobbish, but are not. Being a stiff, upright person.

Appearing, because of your knowledge and capability, to be proud, aloof, disdainful and condescending. Experiencing physical stiffness and tension as a result of such mental rigidity.

Disliking interference. Appearing withdrawn.

Needing your own space.

Isolate yourself at social events. Wanting to get away, preferring to stay away from parties and gatherings, especially when they are noisy.

Often feeling you don't fit in, feeling like an outsider, or you don't belong.

Find it hard to mix, feel uncomfortable or awkward around people.

Being very quiet; speaking very little and gently.

Getting angry when laughed at.

Disliking confrontations and disharmony.

Avoiding emotional disputes until it feels safe.

Being unable to abide people who are unpleasant to others.

Being very sensitive to others' energies and the way they feel.

In a negative state, finding it hard to share or socialise.

Wanting to be alone, but in the extreme negative state, can have feelings of loneliness and isolation.

Not permitting others to interfere, and not interfering with others.

Often turning inwards to gain space or deal with your own problems. You can become very shut off when you have a problem, which creates a feeling of isolation. You may find it hard to come out from this place of withdrawal.

Being too proud to ask for help, because you believe that nobody understands how you feel, or they may judge you.

Possessing your own inner reserve, but possibly being too independent and ignoring, or avoiding, the need to ask for help.

Liking net curtains indoors and fences all around; preferring a secluded garden.

Finding loud people and places too much to deal with. Preferring quiet, like-minded people. Feeling uncomfortable with people who have prickly energies, or who are loud and abrasive.

Positive

In a positive state, you like to be alone – you enjoy your own company.

WATER VIOLET releases tension, and brings inner serenity.

It gives independence and self-reliance, but enables you to reach out if necessary.

It can help bring you out from the place of feeling withdrawn and alone.

It helps you to be quiet, gentle, tranquil.

It helps you to be able to mix and socialise when necessary, and be more discerning about whether you need to, or choose to socialise, or not.

It enables you to be sympathetic and wise, with poise and dignity, and to use your capabilities in the service of others.

WATER VIOLET brings a positive state of mind that enables you to offer advice and empathy, without becoming personally involved in the affairs of others.

WATER VIOLET brings humanity and compassion.

It frees you to share your wisdom and knowledge.

It helps you to be peaceful and calm in service of others.
It gives the strength to bear grief and sorrows in silence.
WATER VIOLET enables you to reach out for help if necessary.

Affirmation

I have inner serenity.
I am feeling inner serenity. I am at peace.
I am enjoying my own company, and feel able to socialise when I choose to.

BEECH   *Over-care for the welfare of others*

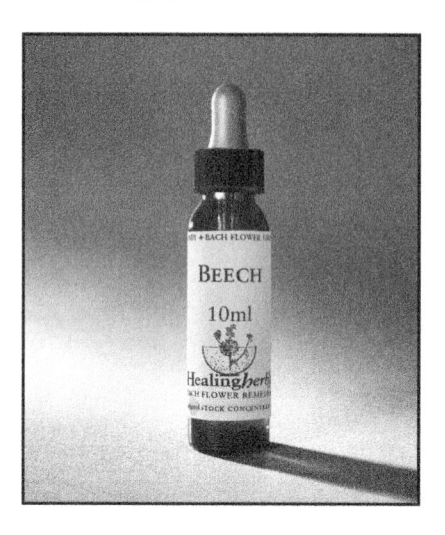

Negative

Intolerance, criticism, always passing judgement on others.
Not trying to understand others, or make allowances for them.
Lacking in humility and sympathy.
focusing on the bad aspects of things.
Needing exactness, order, discipline.
Being annoyed by others' habits and mannerisms.
Impatience (sometimes characterised by a shaky leg); inwardly saying, 'Hurry up!'
Always criticising and complaining about others, regardless of any help you are receiving – it is never enough.
Not realising that you are compounding your own problems, or that the complaining and criticism keeps people away.
Being a taskmaster, complaining about others, even when they have helped you; never being satisfied.
Always complaining and putting others down.
Narrow-mindedness.
Always looking on the negative side.

Having a chip on your shoulder. Always feeling wronged against, and feeling you have had a bad deal.

Isolating yourself, sometimes feeling lonely.

Often acting according to this old habit: I'll get at you before you get at me!

Needing to loosen up a lot, and find more joy in life.

Self-defence: verbal abuse, wanting to bring others lower than you are. Becoming very critical and judgemental as a way of life. Being unable to help yourself from being that way.

Suffering digestion and stomach problems (an inward sign).

Positive

BEECH brings tolerance, sympathy and empathy.

It enables you to put yourself in others' shoes, to see the others' point of view.

It helps you to see good in others.

It enables you to be more lenient and understanding.

BEECH brings high ideals and strong convictions.

It enables you to see good growing within, although much appears to be wrong.

It helps you to see where the problem is, to see things in perspective.

It helps you recognise that even though you have been wronged, you don't have to lash out verbally at others to gain the upper hand.

BEECH helps you recognise when you are being verbally abusive, intolerant or overly critical. It brings the realisation of when to be quiet and to withdraw.

It enables you to offer advice, guidance and criticism that is constructive.

It makes you more pleasant to be around.

Affirmation

I am choosing to have tolerance and understanding.
I am kinder to myself and everyone I meet.

Advice

If you are refusing, or struggling to see the effect of your actions on others, add CHESTNUT BUD.

If you are nicer and kinder to yourself, ROCK WATER will help you feel kinder and more lenient towards others.

Adding ROCK WATER will enable you to be kinder and gentler on yourself, so you will feel kinder and more lenient towards others.

CHICORY *Over-care for the welfare of others*

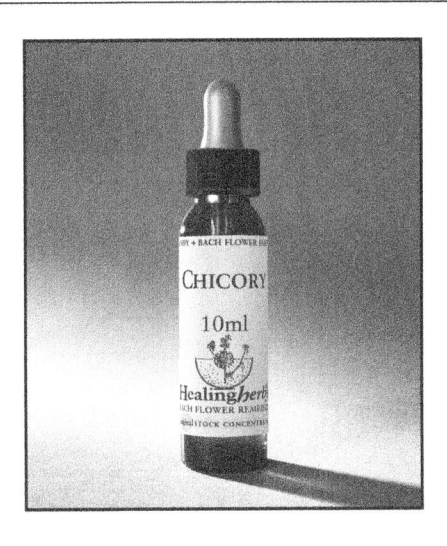

CHICORY is one of the 12 healers

Negative

Possessive love, selfishness, self-absorbed, self-pity.
Looking on people as possessions.
Very needy and clingy, but actually appear demanding.
Tears and temper tantrums when you don't gain control.
Feeling tearful, neglected and dejected. Impose guilt on you.
Requiring others, especially those near and dear, to conform to your 'high sense of values'.
Interfering, and find it hard to forgive or forget old hurts.
Being distressed and consumed by such emotions.
Needing constant attention; dislike being alone.
A child may intentionally fall, hurt themselves, or say they are unwell to get attention.
May become naughty to get attention, even if it is negative attention.
When feeling needy, they may also find other ways to get the attention of others. May not always be consciously doing so, but it is a way of getting other's attention.
Caring for others very, very much, but not knowing the correct way to care.

Finding it hard to let go of children, friends, ex-partners.
Find it hard to accept that others have their own lives to lead.
Find it hard to realise and accept that they do not need you as much.
Use emotional blackmail and manipulation to get others' attention (e.g. 'I love you, on condition that...').
Talking or thinking of 'duty owed' to you (e.g. saying, 'After all I've done for you').
Holding on to the 'strings' of family members and friends, and continuing to try to manipulate or control them, even though they have moved away. In this circumstance people will feel manipulated, and will visit through a sense of duty, not willingly.
Constantly expects more from other people, regardless of how much they have already been given.
Becoming, or feeling ill to get attention when you can't get what you want.
Being selfish, deceitful, strong-willed, talkative and/or irritable, and enjoying arguments.

Positive

CHICORY brings unconditional love.
It enables you to give without thought of return.
It helps you to show selfless care and concern for others.
It helps you recognise you have everything you need within you.
It helps you to become a down-to-earth, caring person.
CHICORY enables you to give others the freedom to live their own lives, without you feeling dejected, or experiencing a need to hold on to them.

Affirmation

I am joyfully choosing to let go when the time is right.
I am allowing others to live as freely as they choose.
I am embracing loving everyone unconditionally.
I have all that I need within me. I am feeling strong.

Advice

May feel bound to someone who does not treat them well, because they feel they need them. They may stay longer in a harmful relationship because they feel they need the other person. Other remedies, and outside support may be needed to help them become stronger, to enable them to walk away from the situation or seek help.

CHICORY is a good Remedy to give to help break the bond when a friendship or relationship has finished.

Or when the circumstances and expectations within, and around the relationship have changed.

Add CENTAURY, CHESTNUT BUD, CLEMATIS, HONEYSUCKLE, GENTIAN, LARCH, WALNUT.

ROCK WATER   *Over-care for the welfare of others*

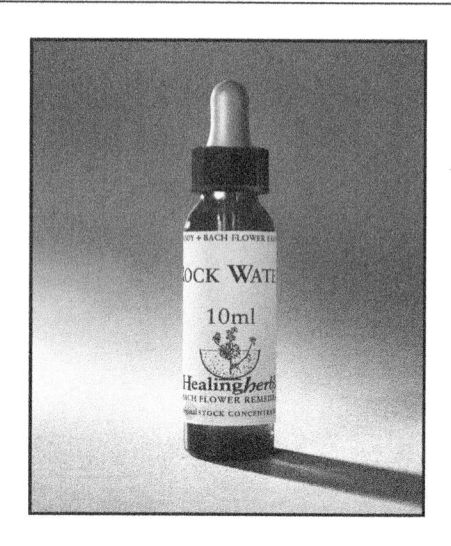

Negative

Setting unrealistically high standards for yourself, then getting agitated with yourself when things don't work out.
Being a hard taskmaster on yourself. Self-repression.
Whatever you do is not good enough.
Needing to be kinder and gentler on yourself.
Allowing yourself to be ruled by theories, and being inflexible in your thoughts and actions.
Always saying, 'It's got to be done', so denying yourself simple pleasures like relaxing or time out.
Self-denial. Being too strict with yourself – setting rigid, high standards.
Deny yourself small pleasures, or any flexibility.
Being strong-willed, holding strong opinions.
Putting yourself on a pedestal.
Wanting to be so perfect, always thinking you should have done better, however well you have done.
Living as if the world is watching, but you are the only one setting the standards.

Being strict and rigid with yourself often causes a stiff neck and tension, and headaches at the back of the head.

Saying things like 'I'm going to lose weight, even if it kills me.' Self-martyrdom.

Giving up things you like. Having strict diets, exercise, routines, with no flexibility.

Wanting to be on top form, but to an extreme – being a 'saint'.

Suppressing emotional needs.

Someone in a negative ROCK WATER state needs to learn to forgive themselves, and honour their inner needs.

They usually don't interfere in the lives of others, because they are too concerned with their own perfection, and with setting an example for all to behold, but when you do, their way is the only way.

Not being open to discussion. Convinced they are right, and things should be done their way.

Positive

ROCK WATER brings adaptability, flexibility and open-mindedness.

It allows you to be kinder on yourself.

It helps you honour your own needs.

It enables someone with high ideals to have a flexible mind, and to be willing to forsake an original theory if a greater truth is revealed.

ROCK WATER brings sufficient conviction to not be easily influenced by others.

It helps you to not interfere in the lives of others, or to impose your opinions on them, but instead to give constructive advice.

It gives inner freedom, and helps you to be kinder to yourself.

It makes you less rigid in stature and posture.

Eases tension in neck and shoulders.

ROCK WATER brings such joy and peace, that others will be encouraged to follow.

Affirmation

I am being more flexible and adapting more easily.
I am easily keeping an open mind.
I am being gentler on myself and honouring my own needs.
I happily allow others to make their own choices.

Advice

Some drops added to a bath can help with stress and tension.

VERVAIN — *Over-care for the welfare of others*

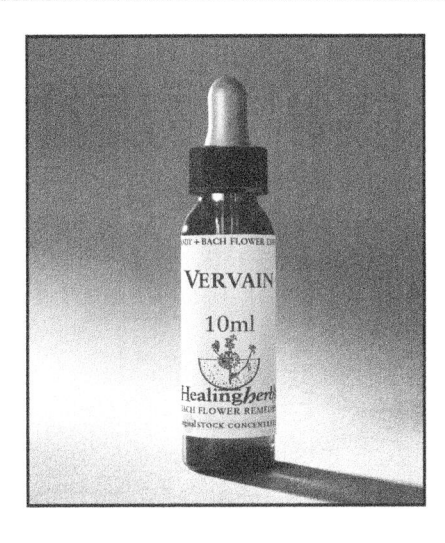

VERVAIN is one of the 12 healers

Negative

Being over-the-top. Cannot calm down, or find balance.
Showing over-enthusiasm, excessive effort, over-care.
Stressed, hyper-anxiety, living on your nerves.
Extremes of emotions and energy levels.
Perfectionism. Rigidity.
Extremes of effort when they see injustice, or others in need.
Won't let go of something until it is sorted.
Hyperactivity. Push to, and beyond extremes of mental and physical capabilities. Won't stop, even when unwell or injured.
Carry on regardless, beyond the reasonable.
Mind and body can feel like they are on over-drive, and no will, or belief that they can change this if necessary.
Forcing actions beyond your physical strength.
Wanting to convert others to your way of thinking.
Saying or believing that 'It's for the good of everybody.'
Experiencing tension that causes an inability to relax, and sleeplessness.

Feeling a strain on your energies, being highly-strung, uptight, tense or irritable.

Becoming fanatical about situations, and not being able to let go.

'Running a thing to death' and always believing you are right.

Finding it hard to let go of an idea or situation, whether negative or positive, right or wrong, and keeps going over and over it in their mind, and in conversations.

Cannot be persuaded, or encouraged to see others' points of view.

Being incensed by injustice. Convinced it is the way they see it, and it has to be sorted.

Having big ideals and being ambitious for the good of humanity, and making sacrifices to achieve related goals.

Being very strong-willed, often to your own detriment in health and well-being.

Not listening to what your body is saying, which often causes tension in neck and shoulders, and can cause digestion problems.

Positive

VERVAIN gives the ability to realise – and to set an example – that great accomplishments are achieved by being, rather than doing.

It brings quiet, calm, wisdom and tolerance.

It enables you to relax.

It helps you to be always ready to listen.

VERVAIN enables you to keep things in perspective.

It helps you recognise when things are getting too much,

when to stop, and that doing nothing can be equally productive.

It brings self-discipline and restraint.

It helps you function better, as you lose the 'over'-element of things.

VERVAIN enables you to think more clearly.

It brings great courage, with a calmness to see things through to fruition.

It enables you to face danger willingly to defend a cause, while knowing when to be inactive.

It gives you the flexibility to change strongly-held opinions.

It enhances your understanding of when to push ahead, and when to be still.

Affirmation

I am embracing I easily know when to stop and relax.
I am joyfully quiet, calm and tolerant.

Advice

VERVAIN types' minds are always ahead. They are inclined to tackle too many jobs at once. They are often caught speeding when driving.
They take on too much. They are convinced their thinking is right, and are very hard to treat – they feel 'It has to be done.' Adding CHESTNUT BUD and IMPATIENS can help.
It's okay to be busy and enthusiastic – it's being *over*-busy and *over*-enthusiastic that causes the problems.
The VERVAIN personalities are here on earth to make changes, and make a difference, but it is the extremes they push themselves to which causes them to be out of balance.
You cannot reason with someone in this state of mind. Allow the remedies to start having an impact and then ask them to look at the situation more closely.
VERVAIN and CHERRY PLUM can help when their thinking or behaviour becomes irrational, and they feel trapped in their situation.

VINE — *Over-care for the welfare of others*

Negative

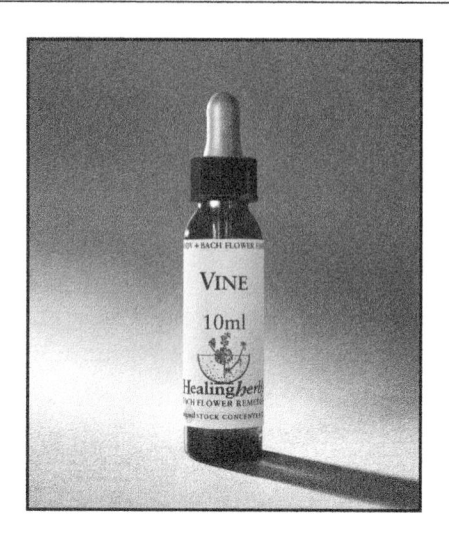

Being domineering, inflexible and arrogant.
Controlling. Riding roughshod over others' opinions.
Behave like a dictator. Are demanding, expect obedience.
Knowing better than anyone: 'I refuse to discuss this.'
Never being pleased or satisfied.
Being hard, cruel and without compassion; often using under-lying threats. Using punishments 'for their own good'.
Liking to be in control, and in authority. Aggressive pride.
Often a workaholic. Like to see themselves as important.
Craving power, being greedy for, and empowered by authority.
Are ambitious, but can be ruthless when dealing with others.
Convinced others are in the wrong, and not open to suggestions.
Dislike being disagreed with, which can lead to a ruthless attitude, belittling others, and to anger and aggression to gain, or maintain control. Convinced others are wrong.
Being bossy; ruling by fear. Being military in approach and posture.
Being stubborn and strong-willed; forcing your will upon others.

Using your 'gifts' to gain power, but not knowing either how to use them, or the most appropriate way to inspire others to get their co-operation.

Caring for, and admiring, the hierarchy, but not for 'under people'.

Being dismissive and condescending to those you think are lower than you, e.g. colleagues, family members, or friends.

In the case of a parent, dominating the home with iron discipline, ('You will do what I say!'), and underlying threat.

Fear loss of control. Will use a loud voice, ultimatums or upright body language to maintain, or appear in control. Will try to convince others they are in the wrong, often successfully.

Appearing intimidating, so others back down, and are reluctant to ask for their needs to be met.

Not wanting to admit weaknesses, or to let others see them.

At school, at home or at work, being a bully.

Not knowing how to care appropriately, believing your actions are for the others' own good. Can have narcissistic tendencies.

Positive

VINE helps you bring out your true teaching and leadership qualities.

It enables you to lead others without needing to dominate or dictate.

It enables you to inspire and guide others to follow you.

It brings natural authority and confidence.

VINE brings to you the potential to be a wise, loving, understanding ruler, leader or teacher.

It can help you be a better parent, carer, companion or employer.

It helps you to feel capable and flexible, without the need to dictate.

It helps people to know themselves and find their path in life.

VINE enables leaders to inspire others through their unshakeable confidence and certainty.

It helps you to work for a common goal for the good of others.

It enables you to be relied upon to get things done, and to lead others to do the same.

VINE helps you to be very good in a crisis, and lead others through a crisis.

Affirmation

I am joyfully setting the right example and lead by inspiring others.
I am lovingly inspiring others to make changes.
I love mentoring and nurturing others to reach their true potential.

Advice

A negative CENTAURY personality type who has lost control can become a VINE state of mind. Where the underlying personality is weak-willed (negative CENTAURY), they can become bossy or aggressive, and use volatile behaviour to gain control. This is a way of trying to cover their own weaknesses and insecurities caused by lack of personal boundaries. They probably cannot see, nor acknowledge the way they are, or the effect they have on others. They cannot see there is a problem with the way they are acting.

If they feel wronged against, add WILLOW. If there is a lot of anger, add HOLLY, or you could use just HOLLY, and then add other Remedies when the anger subsides.

If their behaviour has become irrational, and they cannot find balance, add CHERRY PLUM and VERVAIN.

AGRIMONY *Over-sensitive to ideas and influences*

AGRIMONY is one of the 12 healers

Negative

Putting on a brave face when you have inner torment.
Appearing cheerful and carefree, and making light of difficulties.
Enjoying company to get away from worries and problems.
Often being the life and soul at gatherings.
Not discussing problems. Saying, 'I'm fine', when asked how you are, whether it's true or not. Playing down illness, problems, discomfort.
Expecting people to be mind-readers: being quietly hopeful others will notice they are not happy, but not expressing their unhappiness.
Resorting to alcohol when under stress, in order to calm your mind.
Using drugs (prescribed or otherwise) to dull mental torment.
Resort to alcohol or drugs to numb feelings, or to keep up a facade.
Can be holding deep torment held from childhood.
Being a peacemaker. Avoiding arguments and confrontations.
Fear of upsetting people, and of the possible repercussions.
Believing that if you are kind to others, others will be kind back, and not understanding when they are not.

Liking harmony and quiet people. Avoiding loud people.
Wearing a false smile, and hiding the turmoil beneath.
Bottling things up for so long, then exploding and feeling worse.
Hating conflict within the family – just wanting a peaceful life.
Being restless at night due to churning thoughts. This restlessness can cause upset tummies.
Over-reacting when in a negative state – an active mind causes an active disposition, which sometimes creates an explosive temper.

Positive

AGRIMONY helps you to talk about your feelings.
It helps you open up about things you have held on to, however far in the past the incident was.
It enables you to communicate your emotions.
Enables you to speak from the heart, and not from frustration or anger.
It enables you to confront others with confidence when necessary.
AGRIMONY helps you to be honest with yourself.
It makes you less oversensitive, able to laugh at your own worries.
It helps you to be cheerful and carefree, and to have a fine sense of humour, without pretence.
It makes you a good companion.
It helps you make light of discomfort, and even pain, during illness.
AGRIMONY enables you to deal with quarrels and arguments, and still feel at peace.
It enables you to be a peacemaker, and a genuine optimist.

Affirmation

I joyously verbalise everything I need to say, in a calm way.
I lovingly speak from my heart, and am calmly confronting them.

Advice

AGRIMONY is a good Remedy to use when you first start working with the Bach Flower Remedies.

Take out the thought that you are confronting someone, and replace it with the thought that you are speaking from the heart, and that this needs to be said for the good of all concerned.

This could be the perfect timing to speak your truth, and you may be the only person who has the opportunity to tell them what they need to hear. You need to talk about how you feel to enable the situation to be healed or sorted out.

An AGRIMONY child, (you will be seen and not heard) can become an AGRIMONY adult: who is afraid to speak about their feelings, or cannot, or will not speak about their emotions, and are quiet and withdrawn.

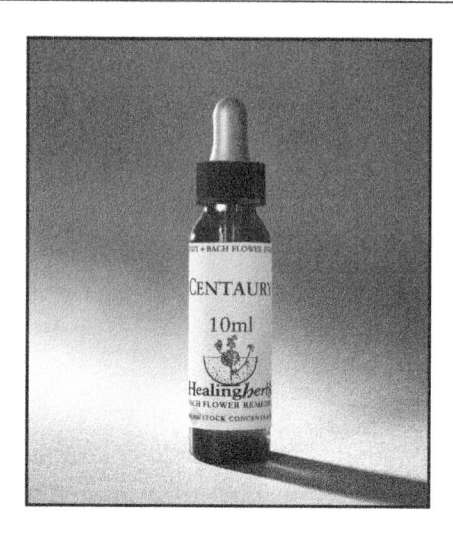

CENTAURY — Over-sensitive to ideas and influences

CENTAURY is one of the 12 healers

Negative

Can be too kind and gentle, just wanting to help and please others.
Being too easily influenced. Having difficulty saying 'no'.
Timidity. Not arguing or standing up for yourself.
Being too good-natured, not wanting to upset others, so not getting your requests or needs met.
Being subservient, and especially so to someone more dominant.
Having weaker will than a stronger person, which can lead to being a 'doormat'. Too keen to help others, sometimes to keep the peace.
Being a Cinderella, letting others take advantage of your good nature. Starting off keen to help, then running out of energy, but not stopping because they are not respecting their own needs, and are putting others' needs above their own.
Becoming subservient rather than being a willing helper.
Feeling unable to say 'no', then asking, 'Why did I say yes?', causing them inner agitation.

Withdrawing into yourself. Appearing mousy and timid, and can become afraid to speak up, or stand up, for themselves, or afraid of the consequences of doing so.

Caring genuinely for others, and enjoying having the chance to help them, but often putting others' needs above your own.

Exhausting yourself by trying to maintain, reset or reclaim your own boundaries.

Wanting recognition and, in striving for it, ignoring your own needs.

Having an alert mind, but often a weary body.

Often allowing your thoughts and actions to be coloured by stronger personalities, and the ideas and needs of others.

Feeling 'bound' to family, or a parent or child.

Positive

CENTAURY enables you to say 'no', to stand up for yourself.

It helps you to look for and see recognition within yourself.

It brings self-realisation and positive self-determination.

It helps you fulfil your own needs and recognise them as a priority.

CENTAURY helps you to serve wisely and quietly, to know when to give and when to withhold, to have strong individuality, and to mix well and support your own opinions.

It helps you to become an active, positive worker.

It enables you to help others, but not to the detriment of yourself.

It can help you move away from unsuitable or abusive situations or people, add LARCH and WALNUT.

Affirmation

I am confidently knowing when to give and when to say 'no'.

I am assertively recognising and maintaining my boundaries. I am important. My needs are a priority.

Advice

A person in a negative CENTAURY state needs to ask, 'Do I really want to do this?' If the answer is no, do not do it. Keeping quiet can be draining, as you don't feel heard or valued. They also need to ask, 'What am I willing to put up with?' 'Are my needs being met or honoured in this situation?' In both cases, doing things against their wishes can lead to feeling agitated and resentful (need WILLOW). If needs are left unfulfilled, they can become withdrawn and exhausted (need OLIVE and OAK).

AGRIMONY, CENTAURY, CHESTNUT BUD, LARCH and ROCK WATER would be a good combination to help you change patterns of subservience.

Use CENTAURY and WILLOW if you have got into a bitter, resentful state.

Use CENTAURY and PINE if you feel guilty about saying 'no'.

Add RED CHESTNUT if you are more concerned about others' needs than your own.

Add CHESTNUT BUD and ROCK WATER if you are beating yourself up for wanting, and needing, to make changes.

Use CENTAURY and AGRIMONY if you want to confront someone.

Pre-plan in writing, or in a visualisation, what you need to say.

You are allowed to say, 'No, I do not want to do that', or 'I want to do something for me.' Others will change when they realise you mean it, and the harmony will start to return, or you may need to walk away.

HOLLY *Over-sensitive to ideas and influences*

Negative

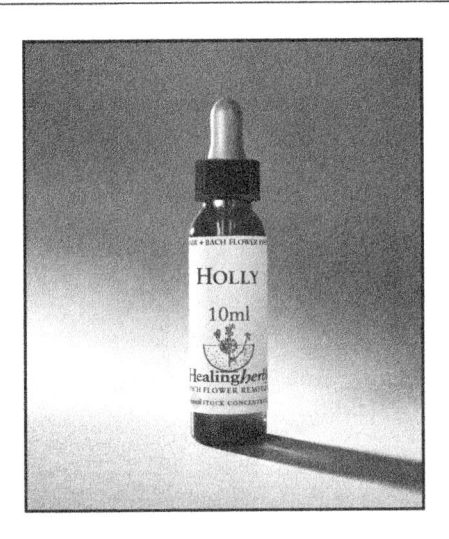

Hatred, envy, jealousy, suspicion, hurt, anger, aggressiveness, greed. Absence of love. Misunderstanding. Experiencing instant, spontaneous anger. Anger towards others.
Various forms of vexation; being easily annoyed.
Bad temper, verging on outburst of volatility about the smallest of things. Expressing anger, but not being able to see the real reason for it.
Find it hard to let go of anger towards others, or situations they feel have hurt them, even if it was years ago. Suffering much, often with no cause.
Having trusted and been let down by somebody, and are feeling deep hurt, which often manifests as anger.
Hardly ever grateful, or say thank you for things or help offered. Can say that they are an angry person.
Cannot see the impact their anger is having on others, or on their own life.
Can often not see any good within anything in their lives, only how angry they feel about things, and about people.
Can bring old hurts through with you when you are beginning a new relationship or a new direction. Being defensive before you get hurt,

then lashing out. Not understanding why. Blocked off 'love' emotions, and hardens your heart. Fear of being deceived. Add MIMULUS.

In an extreme case, wanting to retaliate against someone (or the property of someone) who has caused you damage – wanting them to feel how you feel.

Belittling others, which can happen when your heart is hardened.

Feeling angry and knowing why, but not willing to let go of anger.

May be angry about one thing, but that spills over into other things, so can get angry at the wrong people, or at inappropriate times. Being super-sensitive to people's comments, and not knowing why.

Being agitated towards the smallest of things, but taking frustration out on someone or something else, because they cannot see the underlying cause of their own frustration and anger.

Not being able to explain why they feel the way they do. Overly quick to react with volatile behaviour or words. Physically lashing out, or if verbally lashing out, add BEECH. They cannot be reasoned with when they are stuck in this angry state of mind.

Positive

HOLLY brings all-encompassing love.

It brings unconditional love and helps you to be more loving and to be tolerant.

HOLLY protects from hatred, and from anything that is not of love.

It brings understanding: of you, of others and of your frustrations.

It enables you to rejoice in the success of others, and brings you a willingness to share.

It brings you the ability to release your anger gently and appropriately.

HOLLY helps you not to be angry, greedy or possessive despite vexations and personal loss or pain.

It enables you to see and feel good in people and situations, where once you could not see the good.

Helps you to see the good within situations, and within people.

When you are beyond anger you can start to see solutions where once you could see none.

It makes you happy to give without thought of return.

Affirmation

I am happily embracing the success of others. I am feeling loving and tolerant.

I am happily holding only loving thoughts in my heart.

HOLLY is one of the two catalyst Remedies. If you are feeling extremely angry take just HOLLY frequently for a few days, until the anger subsides. Then slowly introduce other Remedies as you start to feel the calm resume. When anger, if the underlying cause of your distress, and lots of emotions seem out of proportion, HOLLY will help you to come back to a place where you can think more clearly as you release the anger.

Remember, being angry is not a natural state to be in. Anger comes as a result of lots of accumulated emotions being knocked off balance by your life experiences and traumas.

The only true emotion you should be carrying in your body is love, and HOLLY helps to bring you back to this natural state of unconditional love.

When someone seems to have no control over their outbursts of anger, and can have no wish to change the way they are acting, add CHERRY PLUM.

When the heart is hardened by anger it seems hard to recognise the help or support being offered. Can seem ungrateful, and cannot see the joy within anything. If resentful too, add WILLOW.

Remember, anger can be constructive when used to make changes.

DAWN CHRYSTAL

WALNUT *Over-sensitive to ideas and influences*

Negative

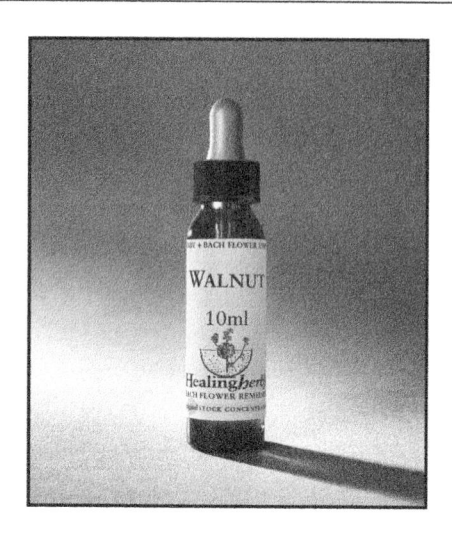

Needing protection from change and from outside influences.
Being overly sensitive to influences, ideas.
Can be affected by other people's moods and atmospheres.
Being drawn into, and affected by other people's moods.
Finding it hard to move from one situation to another.
Being physically separated, but still having emotional ties.
Having difficulty adjusting to change following serious illness, e.g. a stroke or disability.
Feeling unable to get rid of old patterns.
Having difficulty with change or perhaps wanting to resist change, e.g. starting new school or job.
Finding it difficult to resist powerful influences.
Knowing what you want to change, but not how to make that step, and are finding it hard to cross that bridge.
Being affected by a dominating personality, a forceful circumstance, a link with the past, a family tie or a binding habit. Any of these can hinder and frustrate your plans, or even the course of your life.

Can be overly affected and over-sensitive to lunar cycles, cosmic energies and different seasons or weather.

Distress caused by anything to do with change. The connection with change could be biological (e.g. growing pains, puberty, menstrual, pregnancy, new baby, teenage years, menopause, growing older, or the death of a loved one).

Can feel over-sensitive to lifestyle-oriented changes (e.g. starting school, becoming a parent, a job, a vocation or a new relationship).

Can find it hard to adapt to recent decisions and choices you have made.

May become overly sensitive when embarking upon, or evolving through your healing or spiritual journey.

Positive

WALNUT brings constancy and determination to realise and achieve your intentions and ambitions, despite adverse circumstances, dependency, others' opinions and ridicule.

It gives protection against the adverse effects of over-sensitivity to certain ideas, atmospheres and influences.

It is the Remedy for the transition stages in life – teething, puberty, menopause, and definitely the link-breaking, spell-breaking and bond-freeing Remedy.

WALNUT is of much value when making big decisions, such as changing religion, occupation, relationships, or when moving house.

It is valuable, too, when taking 'great steps forward', breaking away from old conventions, restrictions, relationships, etc., and when starting a new way of life.

It helps with letting go, and cutting ties with past associates and relationships.

It gently helps assist you with change, and it helps with over-sensitivity and perseverance through change.

It helps adapt to a new beginning, enabling you to be unaffected by it, enabling you to embrace the new.

WALNUT is a link-breaker. Nothing to do with logic – right brain operating.

It helps mothers and children adjust to starting school.

Taking WALNUT can help protect you from the experience of being over-sensitive to atmospheres, and the feelings from other people.

WALNUT helps when you are finding it hard to determine which are your own feelings, and which are not.

WALNUT helps with over-sensitivity to weather conditions, seasons of the year, winter blues, and cosmic energies.

Affirmation

I am happily choosing to let go, and move forward now.
I am easily recognising when I am being affected by outside influences.
I gently adapt to changes, and stay strong.
I am gently accepting, and embracing changes in my life. I go with the flow.

CERATO _Uncertainty_

Negative

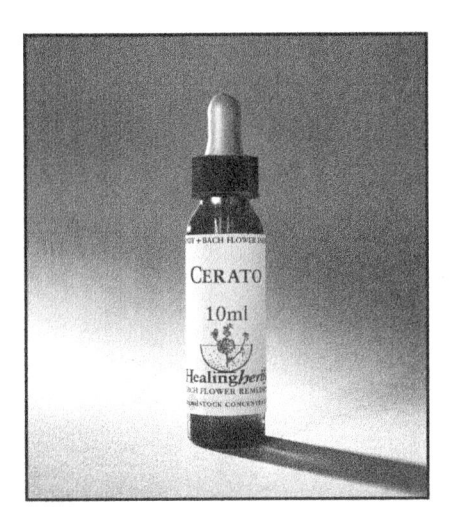

Wanting to move forward, but being confused by uncertainty.
Self-distrust. Doubting your own abilities. Not using your intuition.
Not listening to, or acting on, your inner voice and your higher self.
Thinking, or saying, 'I knew I should have done that.'
Having heard advice or knowledge, but not used it.
Going to others for advice, listening to it, then realising it's wrong.
Knowing what you want to do, but going to others for confirmation, then feeling agitated when things don't work out for you.
Constantly questioning things.
Concentrating too much on details in life.
Being unable to discriminate between right and wrong, between important and superficial.
Needing others' approval. Worrying what other people think of you.
Constantly seeking advice, approval, and confirmation from others.
Repeatedly asking questions about what you should do, say or wear.
Feeling guilty when you don't conform to others' ideas (add PINE).
Not trusting in your own 'gut' feeling, or the choices you need to make.
Going against your own gut instinct.

Feeling like you have been kicked in the stomach when things don't work out after you've gone with others' opinions.

Being swayed by others, and so possibly losing your sense of identity, trust in your own judgements, and ultimately yourself and your own needs.

Can be led astray, or drawn into the wrong advice, or company because you seek the approval of those you are associating with, and not listening to your intuition, your gut feeling.

Having a constant thirst for knowledge. Quoting others.

Being a conformist.

Admiring others who know the answers, and who are quick thinkers.

Appearing foolish, even though you are not.

Positive

CERATO helps you to find, and trust your own individuality, your personality, freed from outside influences.

It helps you use your inner wisdom, your intuition.

It helps you to be true to yourself, and trust in yourself and your own choices.

It helps you to identify who you are, and believe in you.

It enables you to be intuitive, to use your gut instinct, and trust in your instincts.

It brings inner certainty, no matter what.

CERATO helps you not to be swayed by others.

It frees you from needing others' approval.

It brings self-assurance. Trust in your own potential.

It brings quiet approval of yourself, and the choices you make.

It helps you to feel quietly confident and happy with yourself.

It helps you to trust in yourself, and in the validity of your opinions and needs. Adding CENTAURY will help with boundaries, staying strong-willed, and standing your ground.

Helps you move beyond needing others' approval.

Takes away the need to worry what others think of you.

CERATO helps you to know who you are, and to be happy with who you are, on all levels.

Affirmation

Yes, I know I can do it. I know who I am. I approve of myself, and the choices I make.
I am embracing I am my own best judge. I am making the right decisions.
I am embracing knowing what is best for me! I am trusting myself.
I happily trust my intuition. I am loving being me.
I am happily approving of myself, and my choices.

Advice

CERATO is a great Remedy to use when starting to work with your spiritual path: it helps you trust what you are receiving, rather than constantly trying to analyse things.

Trusting your own instincts, and following through is the quickest and best way of moving forward. It is also the best way of learning to approve of yourself, be true to yourself, and recognising the truth of who you are.

When you are listening to, and trusting your intuition, you are more in touch with your higher self, and your sense of purpose. From this place you can have more strength of character and unshakeable trust in the choices you make.

GENTIAN — *Uncertainty*

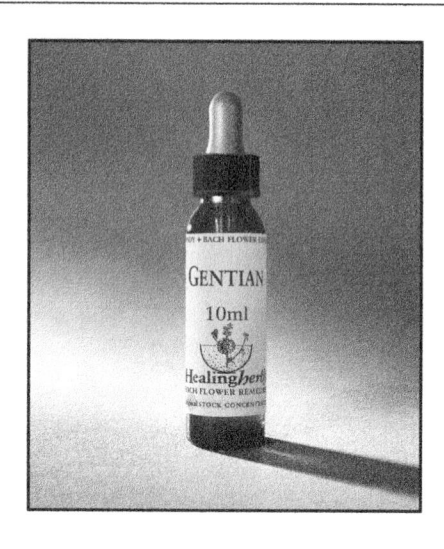

GENTIAN is one of the 12 healers

Negative

Discouragement. Depression from a known cause. Disappointed. You are able to tell others why you feel depressed or disappointed.

Being a 'Doubting Thomas', needing proof, feeling that 'seeing is believing'. They do not expect things to get better. Cannot see how things can work out.

Being despondent when difficulties arise.

Having little faith. Being an eternal pessimist, a persistent doubter.

Always looking at the negative in any situation.

Relapsing into illness. Going back to the doctor for another diagnosis, convinced something is wrong.

Say they are taking three steps forward, two steps back.

Convinced things will not work out, or will get worse.

Constant feelings of disappointment, and expecting the worst. Saying, 'You get what you expect,' and staying in a negative-thinking state.

Wanting things to go your own way, but making little effort to make changes. Speak with a dull, monotonous, almost sad tone of voice.

FREE TO BE ME

Being very discouraging towards others' ideas. Bring negativity into any situation.

Finding it hard to rise above the negative, or say anything positive.

Becoming depressed and discouraged by setbacks, often getting stuck in the setbacks, and finding it hard to get started again, or to move beyond them, (LARCH can help).

Even if they were given a prime opportunity, they would find some negative within the situation. Push people away from themselves because of their pessimistic outlook on life. Cannot see, nor change the way they perceive things.

It can be very hard to be around people in this state, and maintain your optimism or upbeat state of mind. They really believe they cannot change the way they see things, and what they believe is true. They can expect the worst, and may feel helpless to see things any other way. GORSE will help someone in this state of mind. They genuinely cannot see the good within any situation, often saying, 'I'm just being realistic,' followed by their negative or discouraging opinion. Sometimes we need to walk away from these people and situations.

Positive

GENTIAN brings thoughts of encouragement and unshakeable faith.

It brings optimism, positive expectations, and total confidence to push forward. It enables you to see the good in situations, past, present or future.

GENTIAN helps you to be very encouraging to others, and of yourself.

It enables you to see the reasons for setbacks and to start again, as soon as possible, and to maintain momentum.

It helps you not to be discouraged by setbacks, and brings perseverance, regardless of difficulties. Taking GENTIAN can help you stop your emotions spiralling down. Taking it as soon as possible will lead to a speedier positive outlook.

It can help children with setbacks in school, or adults when learning.

It helps you see the positive in any situation, such as a challenging relationship or failed business. It brings you the tenacity to bounce back and start again. GENTIAN helps with positive expectations in exams, interviews, a new career, relationships. Take GENTIAN for 2 weeks beforehand, or as soon as you have negative thoughts about something impending.

Affirmation

This was just a setback, I am happily learning from this experience, and I am moving swiftly forward.
Everything is working out great for me. Nothing can stop me.
I am joyfully optimistic. I am seeing the good within this situation, and expecting the best.

Advice

It is very difficult to maintain a positive attitude when around people in a negative GENTIAN state – it can drain your positivity! They can be hard to live and work around, as they drain others' energy with negative expectations and opinions. Increase your protection and keep your mind-set as upbeat as possible to maintain your own sense of well-being.

When around someone in a negative GENTIAN state, it can be better to keep your positive expectations and opinions to yourself, or you may be discouraged by their negative opinions. They always have a negative insight into anything you share with them.

They are the spreaders of doom and gloom, and can quickly make you feel like you have lost your enthusiasm, or even that you may be wrong. Take CENTAURY, CERATO and WALNUT, to help you not be affected by them, and to maintain trust in your own choices and decisions.

GORSE *Uncertainty*

Negative

Hopelessness, despair.
Feeling helpless, and cannot see a way out of a situation.
Saying, 'I feel helpless' or, 'I feel hopeless'.
Having lost heart, and almost given up.
Having almost, but not quite, given up.
Asking 'What's the use?' or 'What's the point?'
May try once again, often to please others.
Feeling deep inner stagnation. Feeling empty.
Having suffered much, your courage fails.
Having pale, waxy skin, with dark circles under the eyes, or have sunken eyes. Looking very drawn and pale.
A GORSE state often follows a long-running GENTIAN state.
Often a fear Remedy will help, and AGRIMONY.
May be beyond feelings of fear, terror or torment, only have a feeling of hopelessness, often with a feeling of feeling helpless.
There is often a void between your thoughts, and your true identity.
Not listening to higher self, and so not recognising that you have the ability to get better, or change the situation. Often stuck in a karmic pattern.

Feeling like you are stuck in a hopeless situation – maybe in a relationship, within illness, at work, or in a crisis.

Could feel helpless about anything, from a money situation to a negative way of thinking.

Finding it hard to deal with, or rise above a situation, illness or disability, which may have brought on the feeling of hopelessness in the first place.

Feeling no hope during a long illness or disability, especially when they have endured a lot of pain or suffering.

Positive

GORSE renews your feelings of hope.
It brings positive faith, and helps you see a way forward.
It brings you the will to try again, or start again.
It strengthens the will to survive, and the will to live.
GORSE provides a good first step for convalescence or recovery.
It can help keep expectations positive during serious illnesses or disability, and any difficult or challenging situation.
It helps you to see potential and understanding where previously you could not.
Helps you see new possibilities, where once there was uncertainty and loss of hope.
GORSE can help you to start seeing the potential to help yourself, and see renewed potential within your situation.

Affirmation

I am happily trusting everything will work out.
I am loving staying optimistic and positive.
I am calmly feeling hopeful.
I am embracing I have renewed hope and faith
I am feeling more optimistic now. I can see a way forward.

Advice

When you start to feel more hopeful, your body starts to produce the appropriate healing chemicals, which will bring you an improved feeling of well-being, regardless of the circumstances around you. This can lift up your spirits, through and above your current situation. This then, enables you to have a greater insight, and an understanding of how to deal with what you are experiencing.

HORNBEAM — *Uncertainty*

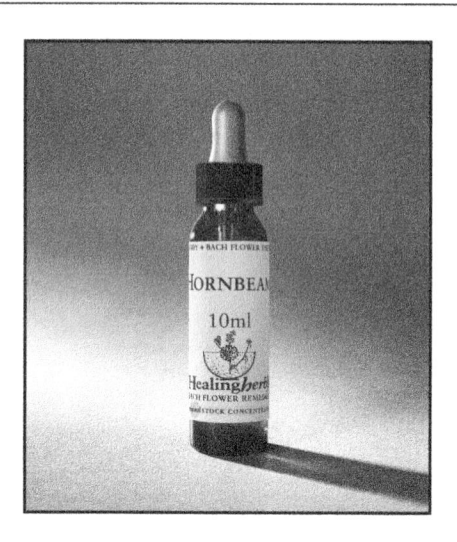

Negative

Procrastinating – putting off something you don't want to do.

Experiencing a 'Monday morning feeling', every day, and throughout the day.

Being more tired in the morning than when you went to bed. Feel like you have a 'heavy head'.

The thought of doing something, like going to work, just feels really hard work.

The constant feeling of putting off doing something is more draining than actually doing the necessary task.

It can be mundane things which we are putting off, or if could be something important like a phone call or going back to work.

Often eventually get round to doing the necessary task, but without enthusiasm or motivation.

Feeling tired, and mentally and physically exhausted.

Often feeling stuck in a boring, or repetitive job or situation.

When you are in this state of mind, it can rob you of joy in other things you are doing.

Feeling weary with life, but when there's something nice to do, you suddenly feel full of energy and motivation.

Putting off returning to school or work after illness.

When you keep procrastinating, putting off doing things that you need to do, it can drain you of energy, and make you feel weary in your mind and your body. The more you put off doing what is necessary, the more weary you feel. It is not that you are actually tired, it is the fact that your mind is avoiding what you need to do, that makes you feel weary.

A lack of willingness to do things can be covered up by making what seem like genuine excuses, like, 'I am too tired', or 'I have too much to do'.

Positive

HORNBEAM brings inner vitality, and freshness of mind.

It strengthens and supports you.

It helps stop procrastination. If you get the thing you don't enjoy out of the way first, your vitality will come back, and you will have a better quality day. Ask yourself, 'what am I avoiding doing?'

Whatever you are avoiding, (usually something you don't enjoy) is draining your energy.

HORNBEAM is an effective treatment for individuals stuck in dull routines that result in intellectual weariness and exhaustion.

HORNBEAM can help anyone stuck in a dull, repetitive or boring job.

Ask yourself, 'What do I need to change?' If you cannot change, HORNBEAM can bring renewed energy to help you deal with a repetitive job or routine.

HORNBEAM can help you feel revitalised enough to make those necessary changes.

Affirmation

I am joyfully choosing to do things I have been putting off.

I am feeling revitalised and supported.

I am feeling motivated and enthusiastic.

I take action at the right time.

We often have a natural tendency to put off doing something, or to start to change something, even when we know we really need to.

Wanting to change does not give you the motivation to change.

Add 4 drops of HORNBEAM to a drink, and drink it. Then add 4 more drops to another drink, and keep drinking it whilst you complete the necessary task. HORNBEAM helps to move you from this feeling of stagnation.

There is often a fear behind our reason for procrastinating. Ask yourself, 'What am I afraid of?'

Read through the fear Remedies, and recognise which ones you connect with. They will help you to move beyond this need to procrastinate.

HORNBEAM will often work by itself, and give you the energy and renewed enthusiasm to move on, but if you do feel some resistance, take some fear Remedies with the HORNBEAM. You can take them both in a drink, or make up a combination bottle. Keep taking the combination until you feel like you have completed the necessary task, or tasks you have been putting off.

SCLERANTHUS *Uncertainty*

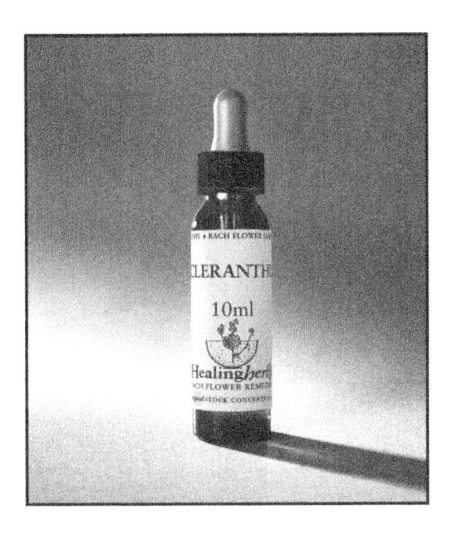

SCLERANTHUS is one of the 12 healers

Negative

Uncertainty, indecision, hesitancy.
Constantly thinking, 'Should I? Or shouldn't I?'
Imbalance. Sometimes feeling physically unbalanced too.
Being clumsy and making mistakes.
Have extreme mood swings and fluctuating energy levels.
Losing a lot of energy coming to decisions and being unable to make your mind up.
Missing opportunities because of indecision.
During illness, having symptoms that move around and disappear.
Being erratic in conversation, making conversations very confusing to follow.
Mind all over the place – 'butterfly mind'.
Being fidgety, even when trying to sit still.
Suffering with sinus trouble.
Finding it hard to complete a project, always flitting from one thing to another.
Seeming very restless and all over the place.

Having extreme body temperatures – cold hands and feet.
Suffer with travel sickness.
Find it hard to concentrate, with too much going on in your head (add AGRIMONY, CHESTNUT BUD, CLEMATIS and WHITE CHESTNUT).
Negative SCLERANTHUS can be more prominent in women around PMT and menopausal times.

Positive

+ SCLERANTHUS brings real decisiveness.
+ It gives poise and balance.
+ It helps give calmness and determination.
+ It brings assertiveness and sense of purpose.
+ SCLERANTHUS helps calm mood swings.
+ It helps with travel sickness.

Affirmation

I am happily knowing what is right for me.
I am thinking clearly and happily making the right decisions.
I am confidently acting on my decisions.
I am enjoying being clear and consistent. I feel balanced.
I am celebrating I always make the right decisions.
I am embracing always making the right choices.

Advice

If you are in an indecisive mood, use SCLERANTHUS, but also write down the things you are indecisive about. It really does help to see things more clearly, and get them sorted.
Make a decision to work with one task at a time, and finish it before moving on to the next task.

WILD OAT *Uncertainty*

Negative

Feeling depressed. Feeling restless and disillusioned about your life.
Having a feeling that there should be more to life. Often wondering what life is all about.
Being unable to find satisfaction in what you are doing.
Feel bored and cannot see the purpose in what you are doing.
Needing to try many things, but finding that none brings happiness.
Being good at whatever you try, yet remaining unsatisfied.
Feeling you should have a sense of purpose, but have no idea which path to take.
Having aspirations to experience life and achieve great things, but having no strong calling or sense of direction.
Uncertainty, regarding which path to take in life, which causes you despondency and dissatisfaction.
Being unable to find direction, often when private or professional life is not right.
Indecision about which courses to take, or which career to follow.
Being talented and ambitious, with lots of ideas, but becoming frustrated and bored.

Wanting to do something important in life, always searching.
Feeling as though you don't fit in.
Frustration, and sometimes a feeling of not belonging, which may come from a need to be doing something more worthwhile and rewarding.
Although feeling dissatisfied, have no strong conviction to make any necessary changes.
Often get a feeling of dissatisfaction and uncertainty just before needing to make big changes, or just before moving onto your spiritual path.

Positive

WILD OAT helps define character, talents and ambitions.
It helps you to be at peace, with whatever you are doing, and wherever you are in your life. From this place you can feel calmer and more content, and get more inspiration and clarity.
Brings the acceptance that whatever you are doing is what you are meant to be doing, and has a greater purpose.
It enables you to find your vocation and purposefulness.
It gives clear direction, and brings clarity of thought.
WILD OAT helps in selecting a career, or new direction.
It helps in making ambitions feel fulfilled.
It helps in finding a true path in life (often meaningful and spiritual).
Helps you feel motivated and stay focused.

Affirmation

I am feeling contented in all that I do.
I am joyously creating the opportunities I need.
I have a strong sense of purpose.
I have definite ambitions to fulfil.
I am calmly following my life direction.

FREE TO BE ME

Advice

Don't forget, that being a mum or a dad, a husband, a wife, or partner, or carer is an ideal vocation, as long as you feel content.

It is not the job which makes you feel content, it is feeling content within the job, or your chosen situation, which brings a feeling of contentment and well-being.

When you feel content in whatever you are doing, you have more peace within you, and are more prepared for the next step in your life, when you are ready to move on.

If you are feeling dissatisfied in your life, take WILD OAT four times a day for one week. WILD OAT helps you be more settled, content, and accepting of the situation you are in.

You are then in a more appropriate and calmer, more viable place to be open, prepared and receptive to the next step forward on your journey.

WILD OAT helps bring peace, clarity, and a new sense of purpose or direction.

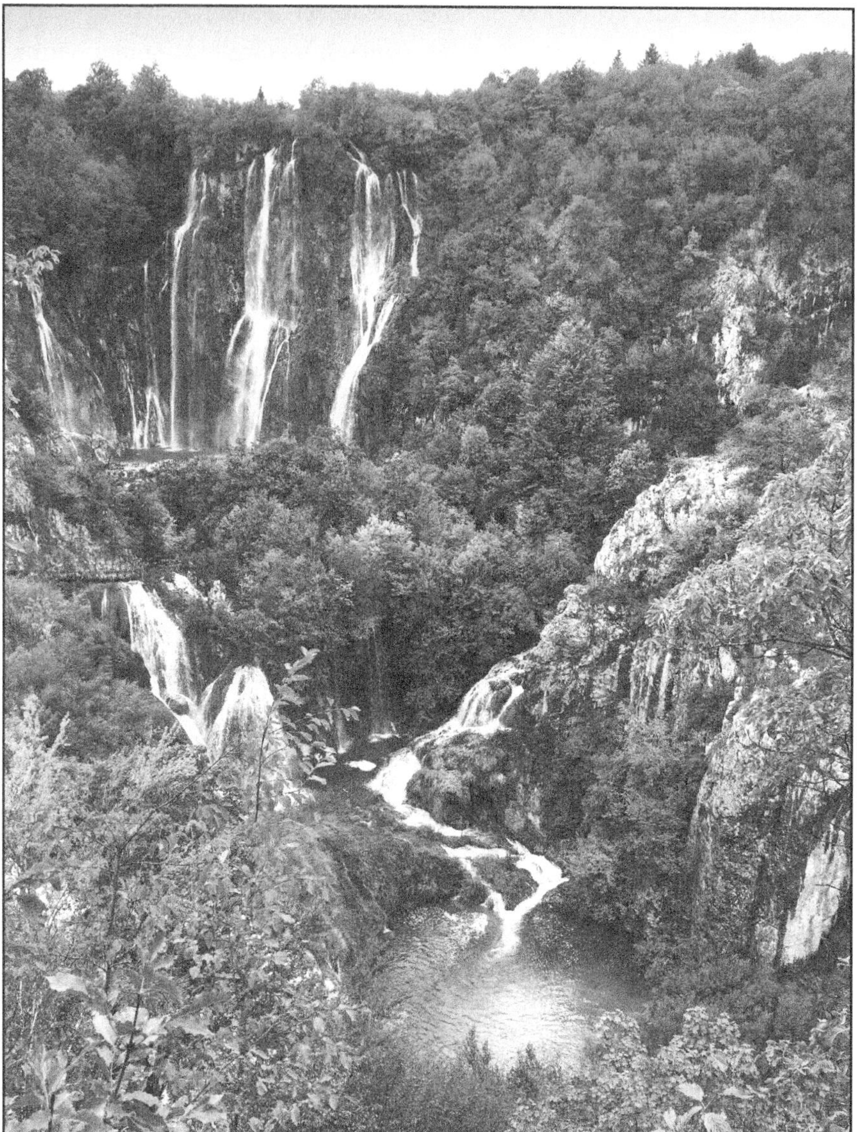

CHAPTER 50

WHY THIS BOOK?

THE SUBJECT I WANT TO cover in this section of the book may seem controversial. There are many people who walk around in a daze, with a dark cloud over their heads. They may not understand why they feel so confused, or why they feel so low in spirit.

Their enthusiasm is low and their motivation is minimal. They are, in their own way, trying to do the best that they can do.

Why the confusion?

My mind was constantly consumed by what had gone wrong, or more to the point, what I felt I had done wrong, or what was wrong with me?

There are many ways in which we can learn. Each person is born with their own unique personality, and their own unique way of learning and understanding.

Much of the educational system, and expectations of the children, is designed for students who are academic and left-brained. If you are left-brained, and can retain vast amounts of detail and information, you will thrive easily. But for students who are right-brained, and are not so able to retain the information they are given, this can lead them into a state of confusion, of believing they are not clever enough. In these conditions, it is so easy for the children to start to compare themselves to those who can learn more easily.

We are fortunate, that nowadays, many teachers do now work more with their own intuitive teaching, but many schools do not have the option to allow this to happen. With fewer options to explore hands-on practical and creative subjects in schools, many more children are struggling to feel good about themselves.

These children need to be taught with more right-brained learning, with pictures, and with subjects being physically demonstrated, to help them retain the information and skills they need. Their talents are usually more practical, and people-orientated, but these skills can be overlooked or disregarded as being a priority. These more practical skills are made to seem less important within the academic learning system. In many schools they have even been cut from the curriculum.

When a teacher is right-brained, they are often more able to adapt their teaching to the students who need more intuitive learning. For students who have a similar personality, and way of learning to their teacher, they will get the message, and they will learn.

But for others, of different Personality Types, and those who need different learning methods, left-brained academic learning can be very confusing.

How is this affecting our children today?

Unfortunately, the education system has also become results-oriented, instead of people-oriented. The government encourages the schools to push the children for academic results, and those who do not achieve can become disillusioned about their abilities.

When they do not get the academic results expected of them, they can start to judge themselves based on the results, or lack of results, they get. Even if they do know this is unjustified, it can be hard not to feel disappointed or disillusioned, when others are doing what appears to be better than you. And sadly, these students are often judged for the future, by the results they get in school. This can all lead to those children struggling with their self-worth.

The results system, of comparing what is a real achievement, starts when the child is very young and can influence the way each see themselves, not only in school results, but also in the way they start to think and feel. It can seem hard to feel really good about yourself, when others always appear to be doing better than you, or you are constantly being compared to others.

Academic test results can seem out of reach to students who are not academically minded, and unfortunately the results, or lack of results, can be the bench-mark for how they, and others, start to categorise them. And, to add to the confusion, teachers are often judged and paid on the results of their students. This can cause disharmony with the teachers too, because they are doing their best under the guidelines they must stick to, but are not being adequately rewarded for the care and work they put in. They are often judged and paid, based on their students' results, regardless of the students' learning capabilities.

The modern teaching system does not take into consideration the different personalities sitting before them, or the different way each student needs to learn and retain information. Or does it take into account, any of the underlying emotional or social reasons why a child might not achieve better grades. This causes frustration, confusion, and quite often a feeling of inferiority within those who do not have the way of left-brain learning through which they are being taught.

Teachers are inspired to teach, based on their desire to help others, but they are restricted in the way they can teach because of the strict curriculum. They are not given the freedom or opportunity to teach the children more intuitively.

Many of us are right-brained, and we need to learn in a way that relates to us; in a way that is appropriate, and that we can understand. Right-brained people need to be taught in a way that is demonstrated with pictures, with visual descriptions, with touch, with colours and shapes, with experiences they can visualise and relate to. Their way of learning and retaining information is to associate details like names, facts and stories with pictures and emotions. If this is the way they are taught, this is the way they can remember. This will give them confidence, belief in themselves, and ultimately a way they can teach others.

If each child has a unique way of learning, why is this not being brought into the system in which our children learn?

The teaching system in my schooldays, was often based on knowledge which has been learnt by our superiors, and the majority of the teaching was aimed towards children who were academic, and left-brained, with a high level of facts and details, but no visual aids for those children who were right-brained.

In the present times, there is more scope for children to learn in other ways, and many schools are even introducing meditation, mindfulness and holistic ways to help the students. But, for the majority of the time, the school system is still not geared towards children who are not so academic or left-brained, and there are more and more children struggling within the school system.

These children often become confused and disheartened, because they cannot comprehend the way the information is being given to them. They are often labelled with learning problems or, worse still, behavioural problems, which they adapt to live to. Often, when living with these labels, they become disillusioned about themselves and who they are. They can come away from school with a completely false opinion of who they really are.

Because of the way the system now sees them, they may live to that expectation, that label. This affects how they feel, and react, to not only school work, but also other areas of their life.

They can become withdrawn, have low self-esteem, and even become apathetic about learning, and about themselves. Or, they can go the other way, and rebel and become angry or disruptive. They become the label that has been put on them, with all its restrictions, limitations and expectations. It is not long before they lose their way, and their sense of identity. The deeper they go into this confusing state of self-belief, the lower their self-worth will be.

They may not display the outward signs of how they are feeling, but the longer they live in a state of confusion their body may show signs of weariness and extreme tiredness.

If you recognise someone is in this state, OAK is the Bach Flower Remedy for when you have pushed your body too hard against its natural way of being. OAK brings strength to the strong in their moments of weakness. When the tiredness lifts, you are more able to see the underlying cause of what you are experiencing.

Nobody has given the children a different insight into who they really are, and so they choose to take on what the school system and society say about them. Much of their confusion and their re-active behaviour come about because their true self is not being listened to and what they really need, and how they are feeling is not being addressed.

Learning can be a truly rewarding and uplifting experience when you feel you are being understood, and taught in a way which relates to you.

Having a diagnosis of what you are experiencing, can be highly beneficial. It will give you a foundation to work from. But it is often not the way you are which causes you problems. It is the way you feel about yourself, your abilities, and your situation, which can cause you to feel discouraged, and so go into a state of disharmony, or even anxiety or depression. The longer this state of mind sets in, the more disillusioned you can feel.

Within many mainstream schools there are not the facilities or time to give children with different levels of learning the help and support they need.

It is sad, but true, in this 'results-oriented world', many children will leave school believing that they are not as bright, or as able, as those who are more academically minded.

Instead of recognising it is because of their different way of learning that they are struggling, they will assume that they are not good enough, or clever enough, to learn what they are being taught. And their lack of academic results will confirm what they believe about themselves and their abilities.

Is it any wonder there is such a high rate of children who are going through school believing they are not good enough? They can undervalue themselves because they do not think they are good enough. This can lead to all sorts of other confusion and inappropriate patterns being created in their lives.

If you do not believe you are good enough to be respected, and treated as such, you will accept and rationalise all kinds of mistreatment. Your low self-esteem will allow you to accept inappropriate behaviour from others.

When someone has low self-confidence, and low self-esteem that cannot command respect, they often allow themselves to be treated inappropriately because, on some level, they believe it is the way it is meant to be. The way people treat them, is often a reflection of the value they put on themselves. The lower their self-worth, the more they allow things to happen. They have lost their inner drive and belief in themselves to be able to change the circumstances.

If we can encourage these children to recognise their self-worth, they can turn their lives around by creating more healthy patterns of self-belief, with an inner strength and awareness of how they improve their life.

A downward spiral

Pushing children to achieve results, and constantly comparing them to their peers, based on the results they achieve, or do not achieve, can lead many children into a downward spiral of despondency and despair. If this is not acknowledged, or addressed with the appropriate support, it can lead to even deeper emotional and mental problems, such as depression and even self-harming.

Unfortunately, there is now an increasing number of children being diagnosed with depression and anxiety. And, even worse, there are an increasing number of children who are self-harming, or even taking their own lives, because they have become so unhappy they cannot stand their inner torment.

Things are starting to turn around in many schools. It is good that the children's feelings are starting to be acknowledged, but are we looking close enough at the underlying reasons why they are experiencing such extremes of mental and emotional pain? There are still far too many children who are not being heard.

More confusion

To add to the confusion, when potentially good teachers are being judged and paid on the results of their students, and the results are not up to the criteria being set, this can cause disharmony with the teachers too, because they are doing their best under the guidelines they must stick to, but are not being acknowledged for the contributions they do make. Many good teachers are drifting away from the education system because of these increasing pressures.

As I said earlier, the system does not take into account many of the underlying emotional, physical, learning or social reasons why a child may not achieve better grades. This causes frustration, confusion, and quite often a feeling of inferiority within those who would love to teach, but are being judged on things which are out of their control.

I have a lot of respect for teachers, because I know there are a lot of wonderful teachers doing a great job. But the modern teaching system, and the curriculum, often does not allow teachers either to make their own choices, or to make allowances for different ways of learning. What is taught in many schools is often based on facts and figures, which may not seem relevant to those who are not logically minded and left-brained. Some students may flourish with this way of learning, but for many, it creates a multitude of confusing thoughts and feelings about themselves.

Let the children play

Our children are being taught to read, write and retain information before they have learnt to play and got an understanding of the importance of fun in their lives. This can have a serious impact on their understanding of themselves and their social well-being as children. Later in life, they may be unable to socialise, or to see playing, fun and laughter as important parts of their lives. Consequently they may become too serious and uptight from an early age, which can ultimately lead to tension and stress.

The experiences we have in our first few years often influence the way we become as adults. Playing expands the possibility to imagine, and to be able to create. It brings the potential to learn, to share, to laugh and to be sociable.

Is it any wonder we have generations of people who are misunderstood because they do not understand who they really are?

All children are unique

From a young age, people who are right-brained can visualise, articulate and describe exactly what they are trying to say. They find it hard to understand or explain why they cannot retain information, and this can cause them deep frustration, despondency, and often self-condemnation, lack of confidence, and low self-esteem.

A lot of these children are very wise young souls, who need their true selves, their true personality, to be acknowledged and encouraged in a way that helps them to flourish. These children are normally very artistic, creative and empathic people. They can be super-sensitive to what is going on around them, and within people they meet.

They can be overly sensitive to others' criticism and opinions. When supported and encouraged to learn in an empathic right-brained, creative way, they can thrive and accomplish so much more. These children are often very wise old souls who just need to be acknowledged for who they are. They have come to this earth with a sense of purpose, and just need to be acknowledged and encouraged to be true to who they really are. If these children are acknowledged for who they are, they can blossom into the future leaders of our world.

I recognise every day there are more and more people, and especially children, who have become disillusioned with themselves, how they see themselves, and their way of life.

I felt inspired to write this book, to reach people I may never get the chance to meet. To reach out to anyone who needs some gentle, natural ways to get a greater understanding of themselves, and what may be holding them in a place of discontent and disharmony.

My mission is to help everyone recognise, that if they feel some discontent within their mind, and within their soul, from today they can turn their life around, with some simple, natural solutions and gentle healing Remedies.

If you are the parent, carer, guardian or teacher of a child, they mainly need someone to listen to them, respect them for who they are, give them encouragement, love, and the understanding that they are a beautiful and unique person.

They need to know that they can change their lives, by rising above any labels, problems, comparisons, negative situations or peer pressure they may be experiencing.

Hopefully, together, we can help those children who have lost themselves, and lost their way.

Letting them know that you believe in them, and that they are each unique and they are beautiful, can be a turning point in their lives. They need to be constantly reassured that their uniqueness is their special gift to the world, and is what makes them so special.

They need to recognise that being different, and being able to maintain that uniqueness, will give them inner strength, and it will bring them the best rewards possible.

Being different is okay. You are who you are meant to be here on this earth.

Things are changing

As these right-brained children grow up, and drift into the teaching system, we are getting more intuitive teachers who understand each child's individual needs, and can lead those children into a life where they feel that their way of learning, and who they are, is a blessing. These teachers can help the children recognise they are special, and that they have a unique way of learning.

They can teach, and encourage them, in a way which is appropriate for them to flourish. This will boost their confidence and their self-esteem. They will not question whether or not they are good enough, just because they are not academically strong.

We are fortunate now, that there are many more teachers and schools that do understand children have different ways of learning. They are encouraging children to learn in the way that suits them best. They are teaching from a place of greater understanding and compassion for their students.

Feeling inspired

One of my inspirations for making a difference came initially through acknowledging how my schooldays had impacted on me. My short term memory, and what would nowadays be called ADHD, kept me in a state of constant confusion and disillusionment about myself and my abilities. I felt out of my depth and completely lost. My schooldays felt like a constant struggle.

My passion to want to make changes for our children who have lost their way became stronger through observing my own son. He was struggling in school, so I chose to move him to another school where the headmistress, Mrs Delamere, and one of the teachers, Mrs Rounce, acknowledged why my son was struggling, and went out of their way to encourage and support him in a way that helped him to flourish.

Through their help and encouragement, my son was able to be himself, and learn in a way that made sense to him. Those two ladies really helped him to turn his life around. My own realisation and inspiration came from watching him grow within. I wanted to be like those teachers, and help other children to find themselves.

Sometimes you need to go through the struggles to get a real understanding of them, and of yourself. It is often through your most vulnerable moments that you will get a greater insight into who you really are, and you will find your own inner strengths. It is through your own personal struggles and challenges that you will become stronger.

You have the inner wisdom and power, the strength, and everything you need within you, to make changes and to overcome those challenges.

It is often not until you go through the biggest struggles in life, that you find out who you really are.

Start today by working on yourself, and you will be more prepared for any new challenges which come your way. Instead of just surviving the challenges, you will thrive. You will become stronger with every step you take.

When your inner strength, your higher self, kicks in, you will find the strength, courage and conviction within you to make radical changes.

Start by making a radical change in your life, and the solutions will begin to come to you. Dare to step out and make the changes you need to make. Every small step you take will make a difference, and will help you to feel more empowered.

My natural instincts kicked in whilst helping others

When I decided to start working with the Bach Flower Remedies, initially for myself and for my family and friends, I started to feel a real passion, and an inner knowing, that I could help people in a way I had never helped before. I seemed to have a natural instinct for knowing when people were not happy, and had discovered a natural way I could help them. I realised I had a natural intuition where I could see beyond what they were showing on the surface.

I have since learnt that this natural ability is called clairsentience and empathy. Many people have this ability to sense how others feel, and to be able to help them, but when we are stressed, and stuck in a pattern of thinking too much, we can become out of touch with these natural gifts.

When your mind is more relaxed and at peace, you can get back in touch with these natural abilities.

Many children and adults were constantly being sent to me who had lost their way, and had become disillusioned about themselves and their lives. It seemed like almost every child, friend or client was reflecting how I had been feeling.

The more people I helped, the more I realised how many people had lost their way. I started to wonder, 'What if I could encourage each child, each person, to take responsibility for their own feelings and well-being when they have gone off track. What if each person could choose to heal their life as naturally as possible?' It seemed like a big mission, but I found a real passion growing inside me to want to make a difference.

The more people I worked with, the more I realised how unhappy and disoriented people became when their minds had become confused.

Initially, this book was to be aimed at children to help them understand how they can help themselves. I was on a mission to go to every school to share my knowledge about the Remedies. That was my initial plan and, for a while, it worked. I was able to help many young people recognise how they could help themselves when they were struggling, stressed or confused. But there are not enough hours in the day to reach every child.

My mission was still the same, but I needed a different approach. I realised that each and every person who had lost their way needed to have a choice to be able to turn their lives around, with some natural Remedies, and a few simple guidelines and techniques, and a book could reach people I would never be able to reach.

I discovered that almost each and every person I met had the ability to turn their lives around, with just a few natural techniques and Remedies. They just needed some simple guidelines on how to heal their inner-child, so they, too, could discover who they were meant to be.

Each day I set the intention to help people turn their lives around, and every week more parents and teachers are being sent my way for help and insight for themselves. And through the healing work we do together, and the insight we can share, it inspires me to know that these wonderful teachers and parents are now using their more intuitive abilities, to inspire and lead our children to believe in themselves.

The wonderful children and clients I have met along my journey have been the inspiration to keep going to bring this book together.

Together we can make a difference

Through the work we have done together, we can all contribute to encouraging children to be proud of themselves, instead of struggling. We can help them recognise it's okay to be different, and to be able to learn in more creative ways.

I believe we are all, at this moment in time, a result of what has happened to us as a child. If you recognise you have become unhappy with yourself, you can start to heal your inner-child, with some natural techniques and gentle Remedies.

Regardless of how your life has been, you can turn your life around.

Things are changing for our children

I feel totally inspired, when my 6-year-old grandson comes round and tells me how the teacher has taught him ways to retain information through rhymes and pictures, and how encouraging his teachers are to get the children involved in more creative activities. He is really blossoming in school.

My heart rejoices when he shares what is happening in his school, and how supportive the teachers are. Last week they did an assembly on forgiveness, and he was able to resolve a friendship situation which had been troubling him. Things are turning around for our children. This week he said he is learning mindfulness and yoga, which helps him to chill out, concentrate and to sleep.

The education system is changing, but in some places, not fast enough to stop many more children starting off with a foundation which leads them to believe they are not good enough, or clever enough.

My passion would be to be able to help each and every child who is struggling, or has lost their way, to recognise that they can turn their lives around with a few simple techniques and some natural Flower Remedies. I may not be able to reach every child, or every person, but hopefully I can help those who are ready to make changes.

My purpose and my mission is to help each person, however young or old they are, to recognise they have a choice to turn their life around, if they feel unhappy with who they have become.

It's never too late to turn things around

You all have choices. You can choose to make new choices from today.

Life shouldn't be about holding onto the past, or struggling with every possible thing that happens, or could happen, for you. It isn't about living by the labels, opinions and comments others have made to you, about you.

Dwelling on the past, and what has gone wrong, is a waste of valuable energy you could be putting into something more productive, like creating a new you.

Your life is about living in this moment, and finding contentment and peace within every moment, within every experience, in your day.

Your mission, and your life purpose in this lifetime, is to find true peace and contentment within your precious body, and that can start every day with discovering who you were born to be.

When you can truly accept yourself, and every aspect of who you are, you will find your inner happiness, and recognise who you were born to be.

There is so much pressure from the outside world to be something other than what you were born to be. This is the ideal moment in time to let go of any peer pressure or influences which may be holding you back, to enable you to find the person you are destined to be.

Life is about validating, respecting and loving yourself, and enjoying the beautiful essence of who you truly are. It is about flowing through the waves of transformation and allowing yourself to blossom, regardless of the circumstances around you.

If you find yourself feeling sad, down, angry, stressed, disillusioned, argumentative, or agitated, take a few moments to stop and re-evaluate what is really happening for you right now.

Is your argument or frustration really with others, or with your higher self who is trying to show you the best in you.

Food for thought

What if any disharmony being shown to you today is to help you recognise what you can, and need, to adjust, to get you back to your true spirit, your real self?

Nourish yourself and your soul every day and you will create the life you desire, and you deserve.

When you find your inner contentment and peace within your mind, and within your soul, you can live the life you are destined to live.

Everything you have been through in your life has prepared you for this moment. Use the wisdom, and the experiences you have been given, to turn your life around, and you will make your world a better place. Sharing your wisdom will bring you the greatest joy and knowledge of who you truly are.

When you find this place of inner contentment and peace within yourself, then you will be ready, and can take on the world. You can choose to share your wisdom with others, and the whole world becomes a wonderful place to be.

Be at peace with all that is happening in your life and you will find the harmony you seek. Peace and happiness are not something you find outside of yourself. They are something you have deep within you that is waiting to be ignited.

CHAPTER 51

EVERY CLOUD HAS A SILVER LINING

I HAVE BEEN TRULY BLESSED in the last twenty-five years to work with the wonderful Bach Flower Remedies, which have given me a whole new perspective on my life. They have helped not only me, but those around me and anyone who comes my way.

And through this journey with the Remedies I have also met some inspirational teachers, who have helped, inspired and supported me through my journey. They have given me support and valuable input through other simple yet profound methods of self-help.

My inspiration for this book was to touch anyone who had become confused, or disillusioned with themselves and their way of life.

Hopefully this book will reach people I may never get the chance to meet. To reach out to anyone who may have lost their way and needs some gentle, natural ways to get a greater understanding of themselves, and what may be holding them in a place of discontent.

My mission, through this book, is to help everyone recognise that they can turn their life around with simple, natural Remedies today. I sincerely hope 'Free to be Me' can find its way into every classroom and place of learning or healing.

Get me out of here

Throughout my school days, all I remember is a feeling of wanting to be away from this place, of needing to escape, of not belonging. I could see neither the need for, or the sense of, the stuff I was being taught. And on top of all that, I could not, however much I tried, remember the information I was being taught.

My mind did not seem to be able to retain the information I was given, and then I would condemn myself for not being able to retain the things I was supposed to be learning. I was always being told to pay more attention and stop daydreaming. Or, as my school reports constantly said, 'Dawn could do better if she was to stop daydreaming and tried harder.' So frustrating: I was doing my best.

It was not until I was in my forties, that I started to recognise that some of the traits I had would nowadays be described as ADHD. This understanding opened my eyes to help me recognise that there was nothing wrong with me, it was just that I need to learn in a different way.

I am right-brained, and need to learn in a way that is different to how some other people learn, and that is okay. It was a revelation: I was normal and I just had a different way of learning. I felt a massive sense of relief as I recognised that there was nothing wrong with me.

If, back then in my schooldays, there had been different labels to the ones I was given, I would have been labelled as ADHD, with a short-term memory loss and sequential learning difficulties; which meant I could only retain so much information in one go, with the majority of the information being disregarded by my brain.

I emphasise that there is nothing wrong with my mind, there is nothing wrong with me – I just have a different way of learning. If only I had understood this when I was a child, I would not have spent so many years thinking that I was inferior or inadequate. I would not have spent so much of my life beating myself up for not being good enough. I probably would not have got myself into such an emotional state where I was constantly struggling with anxiety, illness and debilitating panic attacks.

If I could have understood that I had a different way of learning, and that was the way in which I needed to learn, I probably would not have become so withdrawn and confused, and ended up with constant feelings of anxiety and despondency. I feel sure if I had had a greater understanding of myself, maybe I could have had a much more uplifting opinion of myself, and even a more contented way of life.

There is nothing wrong with me

I believe my journey has seemed long, painful, and often arduous because of the way I did not learn, and the barriers I put up to protect myself.

Until I woke up, and recognised all was okay. There was nothing wrong with me. I was just reacting to the way I felt about myself.

On a more positive and constructive note and with a greater insight, without the crazy journey I have been through, I would not be who I am today. Without all of my life experiences, challenges and obstacles, without all those people who have influenced, tested and confused me, I would not have found the wonderful Bach Flower Remedies and the amazing spiritual healing journey I have been given.

I believe, it is truly through our most vulnerable moments and experiences that we can discover our inner strengths. These strengths will keep showing themselves, but often we do not recognise them.

When you start to acknowledge your own inner strengths and qualities, you can build on these, and you can turn your life around.

As you work through your healing journey, you will find the answers you need to create the life you desire, and you will feel the love for yourself, in your heart and in your soul.

I may not have all the answers you need, but I know that when you start listening to your higher self, your inner voice, you have all the answers you need within you.

Regularly take some time out to reflect on what has happened, and how your journey is progressing. Within the silence you will find the answers you seek. You have all that you need within you.

If ever you feel guilty about taking some time out, take PINE and ROCK WATER to help you release those feelings of being too hard on yourself. Some of your old patterns may randomly emerge later in your journey, and that is natural.

Take some time out to acknowledge what you are feeling, and work gently through your healing. This is just another layer of old feelings coming up to be cleared, and you can clear these old patterns by revisiting and doing your self-help techniques. The more you look after you, the sooner you can come back to a place of inner peace and contentment.

You will never go back to the old place where you started, but there may be residue of old patterns to work through. Be gentle on yourself and work through the basics, and these old feelings will soon dissolve.

Looking after you, and treating yourself as someone important, will raise up your self-worth, and your whole life will take on a new perspective.

Remember to take time out for you whenever you need the space to get a new perspective.

How has this lead me to where I am now, and what I would like to accomplish?

I recognise within the children I work with, the students, my own children, family and friends, that each and every person is different.

Through my journey, and working with the understanding Dr Bach has brought me, I have learnt that each person has their own unique way of learning, and each person is a unique personality who needs to be nurtured, in their own appropriate way. I needed to adapt my teaching to encompass this, so that each person will walk away from me with a feeling that they have learnt something. They will feel understood, and they have learnt what they need for this day, in their own way.

What is wrong with me?

I spent the majority of my younger life asking, 'What is wrong with me?', 'Why don't I fit in?' and, 'Why can't I be like everyone else?'

I spent the majority of my life feeling inadequate, feeling I was useless, feeling I didn't belong, feeling disheartened and confused, because I didn't understand what was wrong with me. I really believed there was something wrong with me.

Some of the labels we are given in our lives, some of the ways we are taught to be, are appropriate for the journey we have chosen to take, and they can be helpful in giving us some understanding. But it is the way we think about ourselves, with or without those labels, which can cause the biggest problems.

Finding the blessings within the past

If my childhood was not so traumatic for me, and my way of learning had not taken me down a road which resulted in me not understanding myself, and feeling inferior, I would not have so much compassion and patience for others who are struggling. I would not have gained the knowledge and wisdom I needed to help others.

I would not have gained a greater understanding of those children and adults who had been brought to me for help and support, with their challenges of low self-esteem and lack of confidence, with their lack of understanding about themselves and their way of learning.

And, ultimately, if I had not had this roller-coaster of a journey, I would not have been led to Dr Bach's wonderful Flower Remedies.

Now every day I am being sent people who need help and support, and these people are mirroring my passion to help others too. As I became stronger I attracted to me people who reflected my inner strength, and together we can all work on changing this world for our children, and for all those who have lost their way.

Sometimes the labels we are given, the way our superiors have moulded or chastised us, or pushed us into a realm of comparing ourselves to others, can ultimately lead us to a feeling of inferiority. I want to say that, maybe, this is just a way of them saying, 'I do not understand you, or know how to deal with this'.

I have spent many years observing, and recognising a great need for our children, and indeed adults, to know that there is nothing wrong with them. Each person is unique; they have different personalities, and may have a different way of learning. They need to be taught to respect themselves, and all that they are. They need nurturing, and they need encouragement to be true to who they were born to be.

We need to help them correct the false beliefs they have gathered, and encourage children and adults alike to be able to see the good within themselves. We are then encouraging a whole generation of people who can feel good about themselves, and recognise that it is okay to be different. These students can then go on to accomplish whatever they choose to do. These people could be the ones who will help to change our world.

Being me is okay

It's okay to daydream and spend hours in my own company. I now know that escaping out into the countryside is my way of bringing me back to me. I am not running away from situations, I am simply helping me to find myself.

It is okay for me to be right-brained, and a dreamer. It is okay to forget things I don't need to retain.

I have learnt through experience during my adult years, that if I write things down, it helps me to retain information. If I record things, I can listen back when I have finished the lecture. If I draw pictures or doodle, it helps me to retain information I may have missed.

I recognise that I need pictures to help me retain information, and if I attach emotionally to the information, I have a better understanding of what I am learning. Being told a story around facts and figures will also help me retain the information. I acknowledge now, that I need to be holding something in my hand to help stimulate my mind. This is called kinaesthetic learning. Holding something in the hand or fingertips helps to stimulate parts of the brain that would not have been stimulated. And this is natural for me.

There may have been people in your life who have given you guidance, teachings or wisdom, and some of this will sit well with you. You will be comfortable with this, and it will help you to grow, and that is good. It will have encouraged you to grow and blossom. But there may be many, many more people out there, who do not know who they are, based on the opinions and influences, and maybe even labels, that have been given to them.

And along this journey of discovery, I have filtered out what is not right or true about me. I have taken from each experience, and each teacher, what feels right to me, what could help me to grow. I have turned around my challenges. I have turned them into the gift, which brings me the wisdom, to help others understand how they have lost their way. I can share ways to help people recognise how they can turn their lives around if they have been wandering in confusion.

My journey has given me more compassion and patience I need to work with those who have lost themselves. I don't think I would have the understanding, patience and compassion I have today without having walked that path.

I never would have believed that I could turn my life around, or that I would be helping thousands of people to help themselves. Anything is possible when you take the time to heal yourself.

CHAPTER 52

I BRING YOU THIS MESSAGE TODAY. THERE IS SO MUCH MORE TO YOU

STOP, AND TAKE SOME TIME to read through the pages of this book, and ask yourself 'Have I lost my way, who am I, what do I really want, and what feels right to me?'

Do not settle for what does not feel comfortable. Do not allow yourself to be pushed into a corner to please others. Do not compromise your needs because others say it is right for you. Do not limit your dreams and aspirations to appease another.

Each and every person on this earth is here for a reason. They have been given vast quantities of gifts, experiences and wisdom which will help them to grow. One of the secrets of learning and growing is to listen to the inner voice within you. Listen to your heart, your intuition, your higher self. And then trust, and follow through on the inspirations from your inner voice. Your higher self, your soul, knows what is right for you, and is waiting to guide you.

You can make a difference?

If you are one of the fortunate people who have learnt and been treated in the way that is appropriate for you, I am truly grateful and happy for you. Maybe someone around you needs to address some issues they are uncomfortable with. Help them to unravel the confusion in their mind to find their contentment and inner peace.

If you are one of those people who can recognise that, somewhere along the road, you have started to have a feeling of discontent within your mind, and within your soul, please take a little time to stop and read. To stop, and assess where you are right now, in your mind, in your soul and in your life. Stop to process what has happened, and why you are not feeling contentment and joy within you.

My healing journey has been long, and frequently I felt discouraged, anxious and depressed, but fortunately someone recognised my distress and offered me some natural Remedies to help me correct the path that I was taking. They helped me recognise and correct the way I felt about myself and my life, and guided me onto a new path, to help me find out who I really was.

Over twenty-five years ago, I was introduced to the wonderful Bach Flower Remedies, and I have worked with them ever since. They have helped me discover a whole new me, a person I never dreamt I could be. Our learned friend Dr Bach discovered that there are twelve Personality Types, and each of these Personality Types needs a different way of understanding and learning. This understanding helped me to get a greater understanding of myself, and has given me greater insight into how each person needs to be nurtured to learn in their own way.

Through my journey, I have found other wonderful teachers, who have shown me different ways that I can help myself. All of them are natural and uplifting. These techniques are simple, and can be used alongside the Bach Flower Remedies. I have included some of these techniques, to help you to find your way back to your natural self.

When you want to change direction you need to stay flexible, and open to suggestions

When I started to write this book, it was going to be just about the wonderful Bach Flower Remedies, and how grateful I am that they have come into my life. But, as the book has evolved and progressed, I started to recognise that often we overlook all of the other natural gifts we have within us, to help ourselves, so I have incorporated some of this help in the book you are holding today.

Each of you are born with the ability to help yourself, and to recognise when you have gone off track. But sometimes, you can lose your sense of what is right for you. You doubt your ability to make changes, because you have lost your confidence and belief in you.

This lack of self-belief often comes when you have stopped listening to your gut feeling, of what is right for you and your life. You may have lost sight of who you really are. You may have been taught, or conditioned, to be something that you do not feel comfortable with today and, through this state of mind, you lose touch with your 'inner voice' that wants to help you.

Within this space, it is natural to stop listening to your 'inner voice', your higher guidance, your gut feeling. It is when you stop listening, and acknowledging ways you can help yourself, that you can come to a feeling of hopelessness and despair.

You may have been floundering around, trying to make the best of your life, and the situations you find yourself in. But somewhere deep within you, there is still a yearning for something different, to be something, or someone different. You may have had a strong sense of knowing that something is wrong, or out of order, but you cannot put a finger on what it is.

Start to listen more closely to the little voice within you. It will guide you, nurture you, and help you become the person you were born to be.

Your book, *'Free to be me'*, is my way of saying 'thank you', not only to Dr Bach and his natural Remedies, but to all of those inspirational teachers and students I have been sent along my journey. And a massive thank you to you too, for choosing to pick up this book. Helping you has been my inspiration, and my strength. Thank you.

This is your time

This is a book directly written for you. To help you recognise how you may have lost yourself, and why you may feel disoriented. Ultimately, as you work through your healing journey, you can discover the truth of who you are.

Take the time to be different, to step back from whatever you think is a priority right now, and step up and take back your own personal power. I know for many of you, the past has had a serious impact on how you see yourself. Please know, that whatever has become out of balance, you can change it. You can turn it around.

Recognise, and acknowledge that whatever is behind you, is behind you. Do not let your past hold you back. You cannot change it, but you can heal the past, and move beyond it. Let your past experiences become your strengths which define you, and the wonderful person you have become.

There will be people who may judge you, or try to hold you in the place within which they are comfortable with you. Do not let that sway you from making new choices for yourself, and for your life. You are a unique and special person, with a destiny only you can design. If there is something you would like to accomplish, or someone you would like to be, you are the person who can make a difference. You have everything you need within you.

Make a choice to start again today

Whatever you have been through, you still have the potential to create a new way of seeing yourself and your potential. Make a decision to start to take a few deep breaths in, make some new choices, and you can create your new future.

The difference between where you are right now, and where you can be, starts now, with a few simple changes and some natural Remedies. This is the day when you can step up and say, 'This is who I am, and I am happy with who I have become. I am enough.'

Giving to yourself first

I hope you have enjoyed creating your new journey through this book of natural healing, and bringing the understanding, the natural techniques and Bach Flower Remedies into your life.

One of the greatest gifts on earth is helping to lift others up. It was the driving motivation for me to want to share this book with you. Helping others find themselves, gave me the tenacity to keep going when I felt distracted and challenged. When you are feeling uplifted, it will be very tempting to throw yourself into wanting to help sort out others' lives, and that is quite natural when you know what a difference you can make. But, too often, we can throw ourselves into sorting out other people's problems, whilst our body is still healing, and needing to be healed.

Often helping others can be a distraction from looking at your own situations you need to address.

You are the greatest gift of all. When you heal your emotions, everyone around you will benefit. Keep doing random acts of kindness for yourself, and for others throughout your day. Keep encouraging yourself with lots of praise, gratitude and compassion, and you will soon find yourself in a place where you feel more able to help others.

We are moving into a massive time of transformation, and needing to put down new stronger foundations. It is a time when we all need to be more pro-active in working for the 'good of all', but always remember, when you have good, strong foundations you will have so much more to give. From this place you will feel able to accomplish everything you set out to do, and that includes helping others.

Pace yourself. Rectify, heal, and enjoy your new way of life and, when the time is right, you will have all the wisdom, skills, energy and motivation to help change the world of those who are ready to move on. As much as I do believe helping others is a wonderful gift, and is one of the main reasons we are all here, the best gift you can give to the world is to lift up yourself and heal your life first. The stronger you feel, the more you will have to share.

Synchronicity

There is always a perfect time to help others, just as there is a perfect time to help yourself. Enjoy your new way of life, and embrace being your own priority. Everything happens at the time it is meant to be. Build up you, and then you will know how you can make a difference. Be patient with your own healing process, and have the strength and tenacity to keep moving forward.

At the perfect time, you will be sent the people who you can support and, at that time, you will be in the best place possible to be able to share your wisdom.

Forever growing

As your journey unfolds you will be sent the people and opportunities you need, at the perfect time for you and your journey. When those opportunities are presented, you will be adequately prepared, and wise enough to embrace all the challenges they bring to you.

During my journey I realised that my workload was increasingly getting bigger and bigger, and I needed to adjust this. I didn't want to stop helping people, or taking on more clients, but I did need to be realistic. It was during a meditation, that I got an insight to be a part of a group of therapists, and within two weeks I was introduced to a wonderful healing centre in Gorleston, which is just fifteen minutes from where I live. As I have said many times, when you are prepared for the next step the opportunities will be presented to you. Now, each day, I am supported by many wonderful therapists at Divine Time, and we have many more therapies to offer anyone who needs help and support on their journey. If you are interested in other types of therapies and workshops which could support you, check out www.divinetime.me.uk

Last year, when I started to wonder which way my journey would take me, I was given the opportunity to do a radio chat show. I was excited, but quietly apprehensive about my ability to follow this through, so I went right back to the basics with my own natural techniques, and the support of the wonderful Bach Flower Remedies. I even learnt to embrace technology.

As this book is coming to a close, I have been invited to help create a new Speakers Club in Gt. Yarmouth. This has been on my wish list for a long time. It never ceases to amaze me when the right opportunities are presented at the perfect time.

I wonder what the universe has in store for you? When you become passionate about something, believe me, the right opportunities will be presented to you. They will bring you more growth, more inspiration, and a deeper insight and understanding of who you truly are, and what you can achieve. You will always be growing. Always be prepared for the next step. It will come to you at the perfect time. Be prepared for what is being sent your way, by working on you every day.

This is a wonderful journey, which will be filled with growth, joy and amazing opportunities for you to discover who you are, and what you can achieve. The right opportunities will always come along when you are prepared and willing to take the next step. It is always at the perfect time for you, and you will be ready. Keep taking baby steps every day, and you will reach your true potential. The universe provides all that you ask for and knows you can achieve. Make sure you are sending out the right requests for you.

There is also a shorter version of this book called You can Transform your Life available, and an e-book of Free to be Me.

Go to www.dawnchrystal.com *for more details, and I look forward to hearing from you, for your discounted consultations, and finding out more about you.*

CHAPTER 53

TRAINING IN BACH FLOWER REMEDY THERAPIES

AS YOU EMBRACE THE AMAZING healing gifts of the Bach Flower Remedies, you may be ready to share them with others. You can share them with people close to you, and give them the chance to enhance and change their lives. There are people out there, waiting for you to recognise they need help, and you may be the only one who will have a chance to help them. You too can help others find natural healing and the true happiness which comes with the peace of mind of knowing who you are.

Dr Bach intended this healing treatment to be a simple self-help measure, available to people from all walks of life, so the books and leaflets available were considered sufficient in themselves. The Bach Remedies are rarely advertised (although talks and seminars are given by individuals intent on spreading the word), and Dr Bach initially said that there does not need be a professional qualification in Bach Flower therapy. Most practitioners are qualified in some other form of therapy, and employ the Bach Remedies as an additional support to their healing work.

However, we live in a world where there is so much uncertainty, and guidelines are forever changing, so nowadays there is a need for qualifications in Bach Flower Remedies, and a need for insurance for public liability, to enable you to share the Remedies with other people. If you choose to offer the Bach Flower Remedies to others as a therapist, it would be wise to gain a practitioner certificate in the Bach Flower Remedies, and this will enable you to get public liability insurance.

Moving to a more spiritual understanding

If you would like to explore your journey on a more spiritual level, I have written a book called Divine Intervention. Divine Intervention is a step-by-step guide to help you make your connection with the spiritual realm. This is available through my website dawnchrystal.com

To order a box of the Bach Flower Remedy cards, the e-book version of *'Free to be Me'*, or any of the meditations mentioned within *'Free to be Me'*, they are also available through my website.

Meditations to help you on your journey.

The meditations mentioned in, *'Free to be Me'*, plus many more, are available through my website.

ACKNOWLEDGEMENTS

A massive thank you to Dr Bach for creating the wonderful Bach Flower Remedies, and leaving us all with a legacy which has enabled me to find myself, and my sense of purpose.

Thank you to Carol Richardson, the inspirational lady who recognised my distress, and introduced me to the Bach Flower Remedies. Thank you for your love, friendship, support and compassion, through my journey to well-being. What you have given me is priceless, and I shall be eternally grateful.

Thank you to Dawn White of Vibrational Essences for her patience and teaching.

Thank you to my wonderful children, Gemma and Jamie, who gave me greater strength, and the incentive to stay strong, and who helped me realise how valuable the Bach Flower Remedies are in helping our children through every day, and through life-changing situations. I am so very proud of you both. You are beautiful people.

Thank you to my family for their input through the years, and to Mum and Dad for the constant love and support you have given me. A particularly big thank you to April for being there for me and my children for all her support over the years, and for giving a loving hand to help us along. It is so wonderful to have a sister who is also my best friend.

And thank you to April Stowers, Jaz Richards, Carole Reeve, Mabel Regis, Maggie Stickney, Justine Palmer, Linda Smith, Keith Bird, Reno Fanucci and Shirley Archibald, for your valuable input, editing and support in bringing this book together, and to Oli Archibald, Clare Corey and April for allowing me to use their photographs. I really appreciate your help. And to those wonderful people who have enhanced my book by providing testimonials. Your testimonial will inspire others to help themselves.

A massive thank you to Gemma Bringloe, who stepped in at the final moment to do the wonderful photographs, and also to Gemma and Emma Lilly Thomas for your beautiful pictures and diagrams.

Thank you to all my spiritual friends, Reiki teachers and fellow companions who have always been there for loyal support and inspirational guidance. Thank you to all my wonderful clients and students over the years. It is you, who have given me great inspiration, and the tenacity to keep moving forward. Without you all, this journey would not have given me such insights, joy and meaning. Each and every one of you has made a difference.

Thank you to all the wonderful friends around me, and to those I have lost touch with for the moment. You are the amazing people who have become my new family. You have always made me feel welcome and that I truly belong. Massive hugs full of love to you all.

Thank you to Ruth Bennett, who came back into my life, and reignited my passion to work with children and young people when you invited me into the college to help inspire your students. And a thank you to all the children and more mature students I have worked with over the years. Your experiences and insights were invaluable as I put my new project together.

Thank you to Paul's dad, Bernard, and to Susanne Lakin, without whom this project would not be possible. I am truly grateful. And thank you to Paul, who was sent into my life six years ago. You were the missing piece in my jigsaw puzzle. Without your love and support I would not have had the time to bring this book to fruition. And for all the other gifts you bring me, I am truly grateful.

Thank you to the team at Balboa, for creating my book, and sending it out to the world. Thank you to Healing Herbs, and to the Bach Centre for supplying photographs which appear in this book.

Finally a massive thank you, to you for choosing to read this book, and taking a leap of faith into discovering who you truly are. Reaching, and helping you has been my inspiration. Enjoy your new journey and the person you choose to create.

Love and blessings to you,
Dawn

Author's details: Dawn Chrystal www.dawnchrystal.com
email: dawnchrystal62@gmail.com

Photographs by Gemma Bringloe www.gemmabringloe.co.uk
email: gemmab.photo@gmail.com
www.gemmabringloe.co.uk instagram: gemmabphoto

Pictures by Emma Lilly Thomas www.emmalillythomas.wordpress.com

Book cover
Designed by Andrew Baker www.aj-baker.com
Photograph by Gemma Bringloe

Some recommended books to read

Divine Intervention by Dawn Chrystal
Salsa & We Hear You Angels by Jennifer Lynch
Monsters Live Amongst Us by Jason Edwards
Brain Unchained by Kay Reeve
The Sticky Book of Stuckness by Cindy Hurn
The Untethered Soul by Michael A. Singer
Grandad's Glasses by Daniel Adams
You Can Heal Your Life by Louise Hay
Angel Numbers by Doreen Virtue

**Everyone of you reading *'Free to be Me'* has the potential for a book within you.
What would your book say to the world?**

DAWN'S HEALING JOURNEY

My healing journey started with the Bach Flower Remedies when I was thirty one years old. I had spent the earlier years of my life tormented by anxiety, depression, feeling fearful and struggling with constant health problems. From an early age, I learnt to be withdrawn, and always felt like I didn't belong. Through a really troubled time in my life, a kind lady offered me a bottle of Rescue Remedy, but it took me two more years of torment, to reach out for help.

I was introduced to the wonderful Bach flower remedies, and from that moment in time, my life was about to turn around. The remedies are natural, and gentle, and they helped me to gradually make sense of myself, and my life. Over a few sessions, I learnt about my true self, and started to let go of many of my inhibitions and fears. I noticed a change in my attitude, towards myself, and the things that were happening around me. I felt more assertive and peaceful within myself. I felt enabled to deal with situations that I had avoided in the past. I felt more clarity, and was able to get a clearer perspective on how I could make changes in my life.

The impact the remedies had on me, was priceless, and I felt a real need to share the Bach Flower Remedies with others, so I became a practitioner. Later on, I experienced some Reiki healing, and was so impressed with the impact it had I was attuned to Reiki. Reiki is a gentle way of healing emotional and physical aches and pains. It wasn't long before I was noticing a big change in my physical energies, and my aches and pains seemed to be easing too.

During my healing journey I was introduced to the Spiritual world. I soon I realised I had been using this special guidance throughout most of my life. I learnt to work as a medium, and found I had a natural ability to read people, and work on behalf of the spiritual world. I love to share this knowledge, and special way of working with our angels and spiritual friends.

As well as Reiki, Angelic Reiki, Bach Flower Remedy consultations, mentoring & Angel and Spiritual readings, I also run spiritual development groups, meditation and holistic life coaching and workshops, to help you rebalance and realign your life.

Everything I work with is natural, and as simple as can be. My aim is to help you recognise how you can transform your life in the most natural way.

Printed and bound by CPI Group (UK) Ltd, Croydon, CR0 4YY